ILLEGAL DRUGS

AMERICA'S ANGUISH

ISSN 1536-5220

ILLEGAL DRUGS

AMERICA'S ANGUISH

Robert Jacobson

INFORMATION PLUS® REFERENCE SERIES
Formerly Published by Information Plus, Wylie, Texas

THOMSON

GALE

Detroit • New York • San Francisco • San Diego • New Haven, Conn. • Waterville, Maine • London • Munich

Illegal Drugs: America's Anguish
Robert Jacobson
Paula Kepos, Series Editor

Project Editor
John McCoy

Permissions
Margaret Abendroth, Edna Hedblad,
Emma Hull

Composition and Electronic Prepress
Evi Seoud

Manufacturing
Drew Kalasky

ISBN 0-7876-5103-6 (set)
ISBN 1-4144-0419-0
ISSN 1536-5220

This title is also available as an e-book.
ISBN 1-4144-0477-8 (set)
Contact your Thomson Gale sales representative for ordering information.

Printed in the United States of America
10 9 8 7 6 5 4 3 2 1

TABLE OF CONTENTS

PREFACE

Illegal Drugs: America's Anguish is part of the *Information Plus Reference Series*. The purpose of each volume of the series is to present the latest facts on a topic of pressing concern in modern American life. These topics include today's most controversial and most studied social issues: abortion, capital punishment, care for the elderly, crime, the environment, health care, immigration, minorities, national security, social welfare, women, youth, and many more. Although written especially for the high school and undergraduate student, this series is an excellent resource for anyone in need of factual information on current affairs.

By presenting the facts, it is Thomson Gale's intention to provide its readers with everything they need to reach an informed opinion on current issues. To that end, there is a particular emphasis in this series on the presentation of scientific studies, surveys, and statistics. These data are generally presented in the form of tables, charts, and other graphics placed within the text of each book. Every graphic is directly referred to and carefully explained in the text. The source of each graphic is presented within the graphic itself. The data used in these graphics are drawn from the most reputable and reliable sources, in particular from the various branches of the U.S. government and from major independent polling organizations. Every effort has been made to secure the most recent information available. The reader should bear in mind that many major studies take years to conduct, and that additional years often pass before the data from these studies are made available to the public. Therefore, in many cases the most recent information available in 2005 dated from 2002 or 2003. Older statistics are sometimes presented as well if they are of particular interest and no more recent information exists.

Although statistics are a major focus of the *Information Plus Reference Series*, they are by no means its only content. Each book also presents the widely held positions and important ideas that shape how the book's subject is discussed in the United States. These positions are explained in detail and, where possible, in the words of their proponents. Some of the other material to be found in these books includes: historical background; descriptions of major events related to the subject; relevant laws and court cases; and examples of how these issues play out in American life. Some books also feature primary documents or have pro and con debate sections giving the words and opinions of prominent Americans on both sides of a controversial topic. All material is presented in an even-handed and unbiased manner; the reader will never be encouraged to accept one view of an issue over another.

HOW TO USE THIS BOOK

Prescription and over-the-counter drugs can cure people of illnesses or relieve their pain, but there are other drugs that serve no medical purpose but are used by individuals for their effects on perceptions, emotions, and levels of energy. These substances, although illegal, are prevalent in modern-day America and can pose major health risks to individuals, not least psychological and/or physical dependence. The U.S. government has attempted to control the spread of illegal drugs using a strategy combining prevention through education, treatment of abusers, law enforcement, interdiction of drugs at the border, and control of drugs in their countries of origin. Since the 1970s, this effort has been known as the "war on drugs." This book provides an overview of illegal drugs, including their history, health impacts, addictive nature, and potential for abuse. Also discussed are the political and economic ramifications of illegal drugs, their use by youth and other groupings of the population, treatment programs for drug abuse, drug production and distribution, the relationship between drugs and criminal behavior, and public views on the legalization of drug use.

Illegal Drugs: America's Anguish consists of eleven chapters and three appendices. Each of the chapters is devoted to a particular aspect of illegal drug use in the United States. For a summary of the information covered in each chapter, please see the synopses provided in the Table of Contents at the front of the book. Chapters generally begin with an overview of the basic facts and background information on the chapter's topic, then proceed to examine subtopics of particular interest. For example, Chapter 9, AIDS and Intravenous Drug Use, provides a background for the AIDS epidemic, describes the linkage between illegal drug use and AIDS through the sharing of needles and syringes in intravenous drug use, and covers issues related to legalization of syringe exchange programs. Readers can find their way through a chapter by looking for the section and subsection headings, which are clearly set off from the text. They can also refer to the book's extensive index if they already know what they are looking for.

Statistical Information

The tables and figures featured throughout *Illegal Drugs: America's Anguish* will be of particular use to the reader in learning about this issue. These tables and figures represent an extensive collection of the most recent and important statistics on illegal drugs and related issues—for example, graphics in the book cover the number of people thought to be currently using illegal drugs, expenditures on controlling the traffic in drugs, the number of people seeking treatment, the results of drug treatment, and many other topics. Thomson Gale believes that making this information available to the reader is the most important way in which we fulfill the goal of this book: to help readers to understand the issues and controversies surrounding illegal drug use in the United States and to reach their own conclusions.

Each table or figure has a unique identifier appearing above it for ease of identification and reference. Titles for the tables and figures explain their purpose. At the end of each table or figure, the original source of the data is provided.

In order to help readers understand these often complicated statistics, all tables and figures are explained in the text. References in the text direct the reader to the relevant statistics. Furthermore, the contents of all tables and figures are fully indexed. Please see the opening section of the index at the back of this volume for a description of how to find tables and figures within it.

Appendices

In addition to the main body text and images, *Illegal Drugs: America's Anguish* has three appendices. The first is the Important Names and Addresses directory. Here the reader will find contact information for a number of government and private organizations that can provide further information on drug use, treatment, and prevention. The second appendix is the Resources section, which can also assist the reader in conducting his or her own research. In this section, the author and editors of *Illegal Drugs: America's Anguish* describe some of the sources that were most useful during the compilation of this book. The final appendix is the detailed Index, which facilitates reader access to specific topics in this book.

ADVISORY BOARD CONTRIBUTIONS

The staff of Information Plus would like to extend their heartfelt appreciation to the Information Plus Advisory Board. This dedicated group of media professionals provides feedback on the series on an ongoing basis. Their comments allow the editorial staff who work on the project to make the series better and more user-friendly. Our top priorities are to produce the highest-quality and most useful books possible, and the Advisory Board's contributions to this process are invaluable.

The members of the Information Plus Advisory Board are:

- Kathleen R. Bonn, Librarian, Newbury Park High School, Newbury Park, California

- Madelyn Garner, Librarian, San Jacinto College— North Campus, Houston, Texas

- Anne Oxenrider, Media Specialist, Dundee High School, Dundee, Michigan

- Charles R. Rodgers, Director of Libraries, Pasco-Hernando Community College, Dade City, Florida

- James N. Zitzelsberger, Library Media Department Chairman, Oshkosh West High School, Oshkosh, Wisconsin

COMMENTS AND SUGGESTIONS

The editors of the *Information Plus Reference Series* welcome your feedback on *Illegal Drugs: America's Anguish*. Please direct all correspondence to:

Editors
Information Plus Reference Series
27500 Drake Rd.
Farmington Hills, MI 48331-3535

CHAPTER 1
DRUGS—A LONG AND VARIED HISTORY

Humans have experimented with narcotic and hallucinogenic plants since before recorded history, discovering their properties as they tested plants for edibility or were attracted by the odors of some leaves when these were burned. Ancient cultures used narcotic plants to relieve pain or to heighten pleasure; they used hallucinogenic plants to induce trance-like states during religious ceremonies. Natural substances, used directly or in refined extracts, have also served simply to increase or to dull alertness, to invigorate the body, or to change the mood.

TYPES OF NARCOTICS
Opium

In medicine, and as defined by the Drug Enforcement Administration (DEA), the term "narcotic" refers to opium, opium derivatives, and semi-synthetic substitutes. The word itself comes from the Greek word "torpor," a synonym for lethargy, which in this context means indifference to pain, hardship, and suffering. A plant named *Papaver somniferum* is the main source of natural narcotics. Records from Mesopotamia (5000–4000 B.C.E.) refer to this plant, the poppy flower. The ancient Greek and Egyptian societies used extracts from the opium poppy to quiet children, among other things. The Greek physician Galen prescribed opium for headaches, deafness, epilepsy, asthma, coughs, fevers, "women's problems," and for melancholy moods. Hippocrates (c. 400 B.C.E.), widely considered the father of modern medicine, used medicinal herbs, including opium. In those days, opium cakes and candles were sold in the streets. The Romans undoubtedly learned of opium during their eastern Mediterranean conquests.

The Islamic civilization preserved the medical arts after the decline of the Roman Empire and by the tenth century had established trade and an interchange of medical knowledge between Persia, China, and India.

Laudanum—an alcoholic solution ("tincture") of opium—was introduced by Paracelsus in the sixteenth century and came to be widely used in Europe during the next two hundred years. In the early 1700s a professor of chemistry at the University of Leiden in the Netherlands discovered that a combination of camphor and tincture of opium, called paregoric, was an excellent pain reliever.

In the eighteenth century the British Society of Arts awarded prizes and gold medals for growing the most attractive *Papaver somniferum*. By the nineteenth century many babies in the United Kingdom were being soothed to sleep with a sleeping preparation containing laudanum. British Prime Minister William Gladstone (1809–98) put laudanum in his coffee so that he could speak better in front of Parliament. British writers Samuel Taylor Coleridge and Elizabeth Barrett Browning were addicted to opiates like laudanum, while author Charles Dickens calmed himself with opium.

The famed British trader William Jardine considered the sale of opium "the safest and most gentleman-like speculation I am aware of." At the height of the opium trade, the "noble house" of Jardine and his partner had eighteen well-fitted opium clipper ships and fourteen receiving ships along the Chinese coast to help unload opium shipments.

Perhaps because so few other painkillers and therapeutics were available until the nineteenth century, there appears to have been little real concern about excessive use of opium in many parts of the world. An exception was China: in 1729 the Manchu dynasty (1644–1912), in an attempt to discourage the importation and use of opium in that country, passed laws directing that opium dealers be strangled.

Since Great Britain then held a monopoly on the importation of opium into China, the British fought to keep their highly profitable trade. The British defeated the Chinese in the Opium War (1839–42) to guarantee their right to continue to sell opium to the Chinese people. The illegal opium trade that developed in China to avoid tariffs (extra costs imposed by the government) led to gangsterism—not unlike the growth of the crime underworld in the United States when the sale of alcohol was banned during Prohibition (1920–1933).

In 1803 Friedrich Wilhelm Sertürner, a German pharmacist, discovered how to isolate the alkaloid morphine, the primary active agent in opium. Morphine is ten times more potent than opium. The name comes from Morpheus, the Greek god of sleep. In 1832 Pierre-Jean Robiquet, a French chemist, was the first to isolate codeine from opium, another alkaloid but milder than morphine; it came to be used in cough remedies. The development of the hypodermic needle in the early 1850s made it easier to use morphine. It became a common medicine for treating severe pain, such as battlefield injuries. During the American Civil War, so many soldiers became addicted to morphine that the addiction was later called "soldier's disease."

The most potent narcotic hidden within opium, and thus within the poppy, was heroin, first synthesized in 1874 by C. R. Alder Wright at St. Mary's Hospital in London. The medical potential of the drug was not fully realized for another twenty-four years. In 1898 Heinrich Dreser published his findings in Germany on the physiological consequences of what was then still known as diacetylmorphine. The Bayer Company in Eberfeld, Germany, began to market the drug as a cough remedy and painkiller under the brand name Heroin, the word derived from the German word for "heroic," intended to convey the drug's power and potency ("History of Heroin", Office on Drugs and Crime, United Nations, http://www.unodc.org/unodc/bulletin/bulletin_1953-01-01_2_page004.html). The drug was an instant success and was soon exported to twenty-three countries.

Coca

Coca, formally *Erythroxylum coca*, is a small tree native to tropical mountain regions in Peru and Bolivia; its leaves hold the alkaloid cocaine. The ancient South American rite of burying coca with the dead dates back to about 3000 B.C.E. In ancient times the deceased were buried in a sitting position, wrapped in cloths and surrounded by pottery containing artifacts, maize, and bags of coca to sustain them on their way to the afterlife. Even then, the Incas knew that cocaine, extracted from coca leaves, was capable of producing euphoria, hyperactivity, and hallucinations. After the Spanish conquest, coca was grown on plantations and used as wages to pay workers. The drug seemed to negate the effects of exhaustion and malnutrition, especially at high altitudes. Many South

Americans still chew coca leaves to alleviate the effects of high altitudes.

In the 1850s Paolo Mantegazza, an Italian doctor, came to value the restorative powers of coca while living in Lima, Peru. In the late 1850s he published a book praising the drug, which led to interest in coca in the United States and Europe. At that time in Europe the chemist Angelo Mariani extracted cocaine from coca leaves; cough syrup and tonics holding drops of cocaine in solution became very popular ("Mariani's Coca Wine" and "Dr. Mariani's French Tonic"). Pope Leo XIII awarded Mariani a medal for his invention. Thomas Edison, President William McKinley, Jules Verne, and H. G. Wells were among those praising the product (Arthur C. Gibson, *Freud's Magical Drug*, Los Angeles: University of California, http://www.botgard.ucla.edu/html/botanytextbooks/economicbotany/Erythroxylum/index.html). William Hammond, U.S. surgeon general under President Abraham Lincoln, was impressed with the drug, but most doctors were unsure. Popular response, on the other hand, was very favorable, as extracts from coca leaves appeared in wine, chewing gum, tea, and throat lozenges.

A developing temperance movement helped fuel the public's fondness for nonalcoholic products containing coca. In the mid-1880s Atlanta, Georgia, became one of the first major American cities to forbid the sale of alcohol. It was there that pharmacist John Pemberton first marketed Coca-Cola, a syrup that then contained extracts of both coca and the kola nut, as a "temperance drink."

Most doctors of the time generally felt uncomfortable with cocaine. They were not alone. In 1914, when Congress outlawed the sale of narcotics (with the Harrison Narcotic Act), cocaine, although a stimulant rather than a narcotic, was bundled in legislatively with opium and its derivatives. The government considered cocaine a social danger—particularly among southern African-Americans—rather than a physically dangerous drug.

Hallucinogens

Hallucinogens are drugs that have the ability to alter people's perceptions, sensations, and emotions. Naturally occurring hallucinogens derived from plants have been used by various cultures for magical, religious, recreational, and health-related purposes for thousands of years. For more than two thousand years Native American societies often used such hallucinogens as the psilocybin mushroom of Mexico and the peyote cactus of the Southwest in religious ceremonies. The religious use of peyote has been a matter of legal controversy. Federal law made its use illegal but granted states the right to make exceptions. Several states, including Arizona, Texas, and New Mexico, have allowed its use in certain circumstances, such as when it was used by Native Americans in "bona fide religious rites" or by those who were members of the

Native American Church. In 1990 the Supreme Court decided the First Amendment did not guarantee this right, only permitted it. Three years later Congress reinstated the right by overturning portions of the court's decision with the Religious Freedom Restoration Act of 1993 (RFRA). In 1997 the Supreme Court ruled that the RFRA was unconstitutional. Later, a number of states began to allow peyote use under limited conditions.

Although scientists were slow to discover the medicinal possibilities of hallucinogens, by 1919 they had isolated mescaline from the peyote cactus and recognized its resemblance to the adrenal hormone epinephrine (or adrenaline). Research was also done on hallucinogens, particularly the synthetic hallucinogen lysergic acid diethylamide (LSD), for possible use in psychotherapy and treating alcoholism during the 1950s and 1960s, with debatable results.

Cannabis

Cannabis is the term generally applied to the Indian hemp plant *Cannabis sativa* from which marijuana, bhang, ganja, and hashish are derived. Bhang is equivalent to the U.S.-style marijuana, consisting of the leaves, fruits, and stems of the plant. Ganja is prepared by crushing the flowering tips of cannabis and collecting a resinous paste; ganja and hashish are the same thing, and more potent than marijuana and bhang (Arthur C. Gibson, "The Weed of Controversy" Los Angeles: University of California, http://www.botgard.ucla.edu/html/botanytextbooks/economicbotany/Cannabis/index.html). Cannabis dates back more than five thousand years to central Asia and China; from there it spread to India and the Near East.

Cannabis was highly regarded as a medicinal plant used in folk medicines. It was long valued as an analgesic, topical anesthetic, antispasmodic, antidepressant, appetite stimulant, antiasthmatic, and antibiotic. But by the mid-twentieth century its use as a "recreational drug" had spread, eclipsing its traditional medicinal uses. According to the Almanac of Policy Issues ("Drug Trafficking in the United States," http://www.policyalmanac.org/crime/archive/drug_trafficking.shtml, May 2004), smoking marijuana is by far the most common illicit drug-using activity in the United States. Its medical uses are not forgotten, however, and one argument for the legalization of marijuana is to ease the suffering of patients with cancer, glaucoma, and a number of other conditions.

AVAILABILITY OF DRUGS

In late nineteenth century America it was possible to buy, in a store or by mail order, many medicines (or alleged medicines) containing morphine, cocaine, and even heroin. Until 1903 the soft drink Coca-Cola contained cocaine. The cocaine was later removed and more caffeine (already present in the old drink from the kola nut) was added. Pharmacies sold cocaine in pure form, as well as many drugs made from opium, such as morphine and heroin.

Beginning in 1898 heroin became widely available when the Bayer Company marketed it as a powerful cough suppressant. According to the U.S. Government Office of Technology Assessment ("Technologies for Understanding and Preventing Substance Abuse and Addiction: Appendix A, Drug Control Policy in the United States—Historical Perspectives," http://www.drugtext.org/library/reports/ota/appa.htm), physician prescriptions of these drugs increased from 1% of all prescriptions in 1874 to 20–25% in 1902. These drugs were not only available but also widely used, with little concern for negative health consequences.

Cocaine, heroin, and other drugs were taken off the market for a number of reasons. A growing awareness of the dangers of drug use and food contamination led to the passage of such laws as the Pure Food and Drug Act of 1906 (PL 59-384). Among other things, the act required the removal of false claims from patent medicines. Medical labels also had to state the amount of any narcotic ingredient the medicine contained and whether that medicine was habit-forming. A growing temperance movement, the development of safe, alternative painkillers (such as aspirin), and more alternative medical treatments contributed to the passage of laws limiting drug use, although these laws did not completely outlaw the drugs.

In addition to health-related worries, by the mid- to late 1800s drug use had come to be associated with "undesirables." The term usually included poor Americans, often African-Americans and immigrants, especially from southern Europe and Asia, who were arriving in ever greater numbers in the United States.

In the United States especially, narcotic use was thought to be confined to the poor and disadvantaged, while evidence of use among the wealthier classes was overlooked. When drug users were thought to live only in the slums, drug use was considered solely a criminal problem; but when it was finally recognized in middle-class neighborhoods, it came to be seen as a mental health problem.

By the turn of the century, the use of narcotics was considered an international problem. In 1909 the International Opium Commission met to discuss drugs. This meeting led to the signing of a treaty two years later in the Netherlands, requiring all signatories to pass laws limiting the use of narcotics for medicinal purposes. After nearly three years of debate, Congress in 1914 passed the Harrison Narcotic Act (PL 63-223), which called for the strict control of opium and coca.

REGULATING DRUGS

The passage of the Harrison Narcotic Act reflected, in part, a growing belief that opium and cocaine were medicines to be taken only when a person was sick (and then only when prescribed by a doctor). In addition, many people were beginning to believe that these drugs caused insanity or led to crime, particularly among foreigners and minorities. For example, opium use was strongly associated with Chinese immigrants. Many Americans also believed that cocaine affected African-Americans more powerfully than it did whites, surmising the drug frequently incited the minority group to violence.

"The Cocaine Habit," an article published in 1900 in the *Journal of the American Medical Association* (vol. 34), claimed that southern African-Americans were the major purchasers of an inexpensive form of cocaine known as the "5-cent sniff." Because temperance laws had led to an increase in the price of alcohol, it was thought that many poor Americans, especially African-Americans, were turning to less expensive drugs. In addition, many observers claimed that the "drug-habit menace" had led to increased crime, particularly among African-Americans.

During the 1920s the federal government regulated drugs through the U.S. Treasury Department. In 1930 President Herbert Hoover created the Federal Bureau of Narcotics, headed by Commissioner of Narcotics Harry J. Anslinger. For the next thirty-two years, Anslinger, believing all drug users were deviant criminals, vigorously enforced the law. Marijuana, for example, was presented as a "killer weed" that threatened the very fabric of American society.

Marijuana was believed to have been brought into the country and promoted by Mexican immigrants and then picked up by African-American jazz musicians. These beliefs played a part in the passage of the 1937 Marijuana Tax Act (PL 75-238), which tried to control the use of marijuana. The act made the use or sale of marijuana without a tax stamp a federal offense. Since by this time the sale of marijuana was illegal in most states, buying a federal tax stamp would alert the police in a particular state to who was selling drugs. Naturally, no marijuana dealer wanted to buy a stamp and expose his or her identity to the police. (The federal tax stamp for gambling serves the same purpose.)

From the 1940s through the 1960s, the Food and Drug Administration (FDA), based on the authority granted by the 1938 Food, Drug, and Cosmetic Act (52 Stat. 1040), began to police the sale of certain drugs. The act had required the FDA to stipulate if specific drugs, such as amphetamines, barbiturates, and sulfa drugs, were safe for self-medication.

After studying most amphetamines and barbiturates, the agency concluded that it simply could not declare them safe for self-medication. Therefore, it ruled that these drugs could only be used under medical supervision—that is, with a physician's prescription. For all pharmaceutical products other than narcotics, this marked the beginning of the distinction between prescription and over-the-counter drugs.

For twenty-five years, undercover FDA inspectors tracked down pharmacists who sold amphetamines and barbiturates without a prescription and doctors who wrote illegal prescriptions. In the 1950s, with the growing sale of amphetamines, barbiturates, and, eventually, LSD and other hallucinogens at cafés, truck stops, flophouses, and weight-reduction salons, and by street-corner pushers, FDA authorities went after these other illegal dealers. In 1968 the drug-enforcement responsibilities of the FDA were transferred to the U.S. Department of Justice.

WAR IS DECLARED

From the mid-1960s to the late 1970s, the demographic profile of drug users changed. Previously, drug use had generally been associated with minorities, lower classes, or young "hippies" and "beatniks." During this period, drug use among middle-class whites became widespread and more generally accepted. Cocaine, an expensive drug, began to be used by middle- and upper-class whites, many of whom looked upon it as a nonaddictive recreational drug and status symbol. Drugs also become much more prevalent in the military, as they were cheap and plentiful in Vietnam.

While drug use gained wider acceptance in some circles, other sectors of the public came to see drugs as a threat to their communities—much as, forty years earlier, alcohol had acquired a negative image, leading to Prohibition. Drugs not only symbolized poverty but were associated with protest movements against the Vietnam War and the "establishment." Many parents began to perceive the widespread availability of drugs as a threat to their children. By the end of the 1960s such views began to acquire a political expression.

When he ran for president in 1968, Richard Nixon included a strong antidrug plank in his law-and-order platform, calling for a "War on Drugs." As president, Nixon created the President's National Commission on Marihuana and Drug Abuse—but ignored its findings, which called for the legalization of marijuana (*Marihuana: A Signal of Misunderstanding*, Report of the National Commission on Marihuana and Drug Abuse, March 1972, http://www.cognitiveliberty.org/news/schafer.htm). (Marihuana is a variant spelling of marijuana.) Since that time the U.S. government has been waging a war on drugs in some form or another. In 1973 Congress authorized formation of the Drug Enforcement Administration to reduce the supply of drugs. A year later the National Institute on Drug Abuse (NIDA) was created to lead the effort to reduce the demand for drugs and to direct research and federal prevention and treatment services.

Under the Nixon, Ford, and Carter administrations, federal spending tended to emphasize the treatment of drug abusers. Meanwhile, a growing number of parents, fearing that their children were being exposed to drugs, began to pressure elected officials and government agencies to do more about the growing use of drugs. In response, NIDA began widely publicizing the dangers of marijuana and other drugs once thought not to be particularly harmful.

The Reagan administration favored a strict approach to drug use and increased enforcement efforts. The budget to fight drugs rose from $1.5 billion in 1981 to $4.2 billion in 1989. By the end of the Reagan administration, two-thirds of all drug-control funding went for law enforcement and one-third went for treatment and prevention. First Lady Nancy Reagan vigorously campaigned against drug use, urging children to "just say no!" The Crime Control Act of 1984 (PL 98-473) dramatically increased the penalties for drug use and drug trafficking.

CRACK COCAINE

Cocaine use increased dramatically in the 1960s and 1970s, but the drug's high cost restricted its use to the more affluent. In the early 1980s cocaine dealers discovered a way to prepare the cocaine so that it could be smoked in small and inexpensive but very powerful and highly addictive amounts. The creation of this so-called crack cocaine meant that poor people could now afford to use the drug, and a whole new market was opened up. In addition, the AIDS epidemic caused some intravenous (IV) drug users to switch to smoking crack to avoid HIV exposure from sharing needles.

Battles for control of the distribution and sale of the drug led to a violent black market. The easy availability of sophisticated firearms and the huge amounts of money to be made selling crack and other drugs transformed many areas of the nation—but particularly the inner cities—into dangerous places.

The widespread fear of crack cocaine led to increasingly harsh laws and penalties. Authorities warned that crack was instantly addictive and spreading rapidly, and they predicted a subsequent generation of "crack babies," or babies born addicted to crack because their mothers were using it.

HEROIN GETS CHEAPER, PURER

The dangers associated with crack cocaine caused changes in the use of heroin in the 1990s. Many reported deaths from heroin overdosing had lessened the drug's attraction in the 1980s. In addition, heroin had to be injected by syringe, and concerns regarding HIV infection contributed to the dangers of using the drug. In the 1990s an oversupply of heroin, innovations that produced a smokable variety of the drug, and the appearance of purer forms of the drug restored its attractiveness to the relatively small number of people addicted to "hard" drugs. It was no longer necessary to take the drug intravenously—it could be sniffed like cocaine—although many users continued to use needles.

THE WAR GOES ON

The Anti-Drug Abuse Act of 1988 (PL 100-690) created the Office of National Drug Control Policy (ONDCP), to be headed by a director—popularly referred to as the "drug czar"—who would coordinate the nation's drug policy. Federal budget documents indicate that spending for drug control rose from $4.2 billion under President Ronald Reagan to $12.2 billion in the last year of the elder President George Bush's term. As was the case during the Reagan administration, the monetary split was roughly two-thirds for law enforcement and one-third for treatment and prevention. By 1990 every state that had once decriminalized the use of marijuana had repealed those laws.

When he took office in 1993, President Bill Clinton cut the ONDCP staff from 146 to twenty-five, while at the same time raising the director of the ONDCP to cabinet status. Clinton called for one hundred thousand more police officers on the streets and advocated drug treatment on demand. White House budget documents indicate that in 1998 drug-control spending totaled $16.1 billion, with the split remaining at about two-thirds for law enforcement and one-third for treatment and prevention.

Taking office in 2001, President George W. Bush promised to continue national efforts to eradicate illegal drugs in the United States and abroad. On May 10, 2001, Bush appointed John Walters the new drug czar. Together they pledged to continue "an all-out effort to reduce illegal drug use in America," according to the White House news release announcing the appointment. Their proposed goals included increased spending on treatment, intensified work with foreign nations, and an adamant opposition to the legalization of any currently illegal drugs. The Bush administration also wove its anti-drug message into its arguments for invading Afghanistan. While Bush's case was built primarily on the notion that Afghanistan's Taliban leaders had harbored terrorist Osama bin Laden, he regularly referred to Afghanistan's role as the world's biggest producer of the opium poppies from which heroin is made.

Over the course of Bush's first term, White House budget documents indicate that federal spending on drug control grew from $9.8 billion to $12.1 billion (it is important to note that in the mid-1990s, changes were made in the list of expenditures included in this tally, making it difficult to analyze historical drug control spending trends), with treatment still accounting for just under one-third of the total.

Questioning the War on Drugs

By 2005 there was considerable controversy surrounding the necessity and effectiveness of the war on drugs. Decades of effort have led to large numbers of people serving prison sentences for manufacturing, sell-ing, or using drugs. And yet the illegal drug trade continued to thrive. Many liberal critics have argued that a different approach is necessary. Even some prominent conservatives and Bush allies, including commentator William F. Buckley and former Secretary of State George Schultz, had begun to question whether illicit drugs were an enemy worth waging war against, especially such a costly war during a time of rapidly rising federal budget deficits.

CHAPTER 2
DRUGS OF ABUSE—ORIGINS, USES, AND EFFECTS

SCHEDULING OF DRUGS

The federal strategy to reduce illicit drug use is based on the Comprehensive Drug Abuse Prevention and Control Act of 1970, Title II (PL 91-513)—commonly called the Controlled Substances Act. This act establishes the criteria for "scheduling," or categorizing, all substances regulated under existing federal law. (See Table 2.1.)

- Schedule I—These drugs have a high potential for abuse and have no currently accepted medical use in treatment in the United States. Included in this class are heroin; most hallucinogens, such as LSD and MDMA (Ecstasy); and the members of the cannabis family, including marijuana and hashish.

- Schedule II—These drugs also have a high potential for abuse but have been accepted for medical use in the United States, with severe restrictions. Abuse of these drugs may lead to severe psychological or physical dependence. Opium, morphine, PCP, methamphetamine, methadone, certain barbiturates, and cocaine are some of the drugs in this schedule. A number of painkillers that were once Schedule III substances, including oxycodone and hydrocodone, were reclassified as Schedule II in 2004.

- Schedule III—The drugs in this class have less potential for abuse than those in the first two schedules. They are currently accepted for medical use in the United States, but abuse may lead to moderate or low physical dependence or high psychological dependence. Included in this category are anabolic steroids and some barbiturates.

- Schedule IV—These drugs have even less potential for abuse than those in Schedule III and are currently accepted for medical use in the United States. Abuse may lead to limited physical and psychological dependence. Darvon, Equanil, Valium, and Xanax are included here.

- Schedule V—These drugs have a lower potential for abuse than those in Schedule IV. They are accepted for medical use, but abuse may lead to limited physical or psychological dependence. Some narcotics used for antidiarrheal or antitussive (cough suppressing) purposes are included here.

While less addictive than Schedule I and II drugs, Schedule III, IV, and V drugs can be very dangerous to an abuser's health. A significant black market has developed for these drugs. Drug abusers visit their doctors complaining of a problem they know will likely be treated by a drug they desire. If the physician is fooled, he or she writes a prescription, which the drug abuser has filled at a pharmacy. The abuser then either uses the drugs personally or sells them to another addict.

Considerations in Determining the Schedule

According to the Drug Enforcement Administration (DEA) (http://www.usdoj.gov/dea/pubs/csa/811.htm#c], in structuring the regulatory requirements shown in Table 2.2, federal agencies must first consider eight specific factors:

- The drug's actual or relative potential for abuse.

- Scientific evidence of its pharmacological effect, if known.

- The state of current scientific knowledge about the drug.

- Its history and current pattern of abuse.

- The scope, duration, and significance of abuse.

- The risk, if any, to public health.

- The drug's psychological or physiological "dependence liability" (the chance that the user may become addicted to it).

- The substance's potential to be a source for a drug already regulated under federal law.

TABLE 2.1

Uses and abuses of controlled substances

Drugs	CSA schedules	Trade or other names	Medical uses	Dependence Physical	Dependence Psychological	Tolerance	Duration (hours)	Usual method	Possible effects	Effects of overdose	Withdrawal syndrome
Narcotics											
Heroin	Substance I	Diamorphine, horse, smack, black tar, *chiva, negra* (black tar)	None in U.S., analgesic, antitussive	High	High	Yes	3–4	Injected, snorted, smoked	Euphoria, drowsiness, respiratory depression, constricted pupils, nausea	Slow and shallow breathing, clammy skin, convulsions, coma, possible death	Watery eyes, runny nose, yawning, loss of appetite, irritability, tremors, panic, cramps, nausea, chills and sweating
Morphine	Substance II	MS-contin, Roxanol, Oramorph SR, MSIR	Analgesic	High	High	Yes	3–12	Oral, injected			
Hydrocodone	Substance II, product III, V	Hydrocodone w/ Acetaminophen, Vicodin, Vicoprofen, Tussionex, Lortab	Analgesic, antitussive	High	High	Yes	3–6	Oral			
Hydromorphone	Substance II	Dilaudid	Analgesic	High	High	Yes	3–4	Oral, injected			
Oxycodone	Substance II	Roxicet, Oxycodone w/ Acetaminophen, OxyContin, Endocet, Percocet, Percodan	Analgesic	High	High	Yes	3–12	Oral			
Codeine	Substance II, products III, V	Acetaminophen, Guaifenesin or Promethazine w/Codeine, Fiorinal, Fioricet or Tylenol w/Codeine	Analgesic, antitussive	Moderate	Moderate	Yes	3–4	Oral, injected			
Other narcotics	Substance II, III, IV	Fentanyl, Demerol, Methadone, Darvon, Stadol, Talwin, Paregoric, Buprenex	Analgesic, antidiarrheal, antitussive	High-low	High-low	Yes	Variable	Oral, injected snorted, smoked			
Depressants											
Gamma hydroxybutyric acid	Sub I, product III	GHB, Liquid Ecstasy, Liquid X, Sodium Oxybate, Xyrem®	None in U.S., anesthetic	Moderate	Moderate	Yes	3–6	Oral	Slurred speech, disorientation, drunken behavior without odor of alcohol, impaired memory of events, interacts with alcohol	Shallow respiration, clammy skin, dilated pupils, weak and rapid pulse, coma, possible death	Anxiety, insomnia, tremors, delirium, convulsions, possible death
Benzodiazepines	Substance IV	Valium, Xanax, Halcion, Ativan, Restoril, Rohypnol (Roofies, R-2), Klonopin	Antianxiety, sedative, anticonvulsant, hypnotic, muscle relaxant	Moderate	Moderate	Yes	1–8	Oral, injected			
Other depressants	Substance I, II, III, IV	Ambien, Sonata, Meprobamate, Chloral Hydrate, Barbiturates, Methaqualone (quaalude)	Antianxiety, sedative, hypnotic	Moderate	Modeat	Yes	2–6	Oral			

TABLE 2.1

Uses and abuses of controlled substances (continued)

Drugs	CSA schedules	Trade or other names	Medical uses	Dependence Physical	Dependence Psychological	Tolerance	Duration (hours)	Usual method	Possible effects	Effects of overdose	Withdrawal syndrome
Stimulants											
Cocaine	Substance II	Coke, flake, snow, crack, coca, blanca, perico, nieve, soda	Local anesthetic	Possible	High	Yes	1–2	Snorted, smoked, injected	Increased alertness, excitation, euphoria, increased pulse rate & blood pressure, insomnia, loss of appetite	Agitation, increased body temperature, hallucinations, convulsions, possible death	Apathy, long periods of sleep, irritability, depression, disorientation
Amphetamine/methamphetamine	Sub II	Crank, ice, cristal, krystal meth, speed, Adderall, Dexedrine, Desoxyn	Attention deficit/hyperactivity disorder, narcolepsy, weight control	Possible	High	Yes	2–4	Oral, injected, smoked			
Methylphenidate	Substance II	Ritalin (Illy's), Concerta, Focalin, Metadate	Attention deficit/hyperactivity disorder, narcolepsy, weight control	Possible	High	Yes	2–4	Oral, injected, snorted, smoked			
Other stimulants	Substance III, IV	Adipex P, Lonamin, Prelu-2, Didrex, Provigil	Vasoconstriction	Possible	Moderate	Yes	2–4	Oral			
Hallucinogens											
MDMA and analogs	Substance I	(Ecstasy, XTC, Adam), MDA (love drug), MDEA (eve), MBDB	None	None	Moderate	Yes	4–6	Oral, snorted, smoked	Heightened senses, teeth grinding and dehydration	Increased body temperature, electrolyte imbalance, cardiac arrest	Muscle aches, drowsiness, depression, acne
LSD	Substance I	Acid, microdot, sunshine, boomers	None	None	Unknown	Yes	8–12	Oral	Illusions and hallucinations, altered perception of time and distance	(LSD) Longer, more intense "trip" episodes	None
Phencyclidine and analogs	Sub I, II, III	PCP, angel dust, hog, loveboat, Ketamine (special K), PCE, PCPy, TCP	Anesthetic (Ketamine)	Possible	High	Yes	1–12	Smoked, oral, injected, snorted			
Other hallucinogens	Substance I	Psilocybe mushrooms, mescaline, peyote cactus, Ayahausca, DMT, Dextromethorphan* (DXM)	None	None	None	Possible	4–8	Oral		Unable to direct movement, feel pain, or remember	Drug seeking behavior *Not regulated
Cannabis											
Marijuana	Substance I	Pot, grass, sinsemilla, blunts, mota, yerba, grifa	None	Unknown	Moderate	Yes	2–4	Smoked, oral	Euphoria, relaxed inhibitions, increased appetite, disorientation	Fatigue, paranoia, possible psychosis	Occasional reports of insomnia, hyperactivity, decreased appetite
Tetrahydrocannabinol	Sub I, product III	THC, Marinol	Antinauseant, appetite stimulant	Yes	Moderate	Yes	2–4	Smoked, oral			
Hashish and hashish oil	Substance I	Hash, hash oil	None	Unknown	Moderate	Yes	2–4	Smoked, oral			
Anabolic steroids											
Testosterone	Substance III	Depo Testosterone, Sustanon, Sten, Cypt	Hypogonadism	Unknown	Unknown	Unknown	14–28 days	Injected	Virilization, edema, testicular atrophy, gynecomastia, acne, aggressive behavior	Unknown	Possible depression
Other anabolic steroids	Substance III	Parabolan, Winstrol, Equipose, Anadrol, Dianabol, Primabolin-Depo, D-Ball	Anemia, breast cancer	Unknown	Yes	Unknown	Variable	Oral, injected			

TABLE 2.1

Uses and abuses of controlled substances [CONTINUED]

Drugs	CSA schedules	Trade or other names	Medical uses	Dependence Physical	Dependence Psychological	Tolerance	Duration (hours)	Usual method	Possible effects	Effects of overdose	Withdrawal syndrome
Inhalants											
Amyl and butyl nitrates		Pearls, poppers, rush, lockerroom	Angina (Amyl)	Unknown	Unknown	No	1	Inhaled	Flushing, hypotension, headache	Methemoglobinemia	Agitation
Nitrous oxide		Laughing gas, baloons, whippets	Anesthetic	Unknown	Low	No	0.5	Inhaled	Impaired memory, slurred speech, drunken behavior, slow onset vitamin deficiency, organ damage	Vomiting, respiratory depression, loss of consciousness, possible death	Trembling, anxiety, insomnia, vitamin deficiency, confusion, hallucinations, convulsions
Other inhalants		Adhesives, spray paint, hair spray, dry cleaning fluid, spot remover, lighter fluid	None	Unknown	High	No	0.5–2	Inhaled			
Alcohol		Beer, wine, liquor	None	High	High	Yes	1–3	Oral			

SOURCE: Donald E. Joseph, ed., "Drugs of Abuse/Uses and Effects," in *Drugs of Abuse, 2005 Edition*, U.S. Department of Justice, Drug Enforcement Administration, 2005, http://www.usdoj.gov/dea/pubs/abuse/index.htm (accessed February 11, 2005)

TABLE 2.2

Regulatory requirements for controlled substances

	Schedule I	Schedule II	Schedule III	Schedule IV	Schedule V
Registration	Required	Required	Required	Required	Required
Recordkeeping	Separate	Separate	Readily retrievable	Readily retrievable	Readily retrievable
Distribution restrictions	Order forms	Order forms	Records required	Records required	Records required
Dispensing limits	Research use only	Rx: written; no refills	Rx: written or oral; refills note 1	Rx: written or oral; refills note 1	OTC (Rx drugs limited to M.D.'s order)
Manufacturing Security	Vault/safe	Vault/safe	Secure storage area	Secure storage area	Secure storage area
Manufacturing Quotas	Yes	Yes	No, but some drugs limited by schedule II	No, but some drugs limited by schedule II	No, but some drugs limited by schedule II
Import/export Narcotic	Permit	Permit	Permit	Permit	Permit to import; declaration to export
Import/export Non-narcotic	Permit	Permit	Note 2	Declaration	Declaration
Reports to DEA by manufacturer/ distributor Narcotic	Yes	Yes	Yes	Manufacturer only	Manufacturer only
Reports to DEA by manufacturer/ distributor Non-narcotic	Yes	Yes	Note 3	Note 3	No

SOURCE: Donald E. Joseph, ed., "Regulatory Requirements: Controlled Substances," in *Drugs of Abuse, 2005 Edition*, U.S. Department of Justice, Drug Enforcement Administration, 2005, http://www.usdoj.gov/dea/pubs/abuse/index.htm (accessed February 11, 2005)

NATURAL NARCOTICS

Narcotics are opium, opium derivatives, or synthetic substitutes used medically to relieve intense pain. (See Table 2.1.) The main source of nonsynthetic narcotics is resin from the poppy *Papaver somniferum*. (See Figure 2.1.) Opium gum is produced from the resin, which is scraped by hand from cut, unripe seedpods and air-dried.

A more modern method of harvesting, known as the industrial poppy straw process, involves extracting alkaloids (organic compounds found in living organisms) from the mature dried plant. The extract may be in a number of forms. Most poppy straw concentrate made available commercially is a fine brownish powder with a distinct odor.

Opium

Opium can come in several forms, but it usually appears as dark brown chunks or powder that can be either smoked or eaten. The DEA claims that there is little opium abuse in this country because of laws governing the production and distribution of narcotic substances. Numerous drugs derived from or chemically similar to opium, however, are popular in the United States.

At least twenty-five alkaloids, divided into two general categories, can be extracted from opium (Dzulkfli Abdul Razak, "Narcotic Abuse: Effects and Treatment," http://www.prn2.usm.my/mainsite/bulletin/sun/1996/sun30.html). Drugs of the first type, represented by morphine and codeine, are used as analgesics (pain relievers) and cough suppressants, and are known as phenanthrene alkaloids. Those in the second group, isoquinoline alkaloids, are used as intestinal relaxants and also as cough suppressants.

Isoquinoline alkaloids have no significant influence on the central nervous system and are not regulated under the Controlled Substances Act. Virtually all of the opium imported into this country is broken down into alkaloid constituents—principally morphine and codeine.

FIGURE 2.1

Opium poppies. (© *Galen Rowell/CORBIS.*)

Morphine

Morphine is one of the most effective drugs known for pain relief. It is marketed in the form of oral solutions, sustained-release tablets, and injectable preparations. It is odorless, bitter, and darkens with age. Morphine can be administered orally, subcutaneously, intramuscularly, or intravenously, the latter method being the one most frequently used by drug addicts. Tolerance and dependence develop rapidly in the user.

Morphine is used legally only in hospitals or hospices, usually to control the severe pain resulting from such illnesses as cancer. Only a small portion of the morphine obtained from opium is used medicinally; most is converted to codeine and, secondarily, to hydromorphone, a powerful pain killer.

Codeine

Codeine is found in raw opium. Although it occurs naturally, most is produced from morphine. Compared with morphine, codeine produces less pain relief but also produces less sedation and respiratory depression. It is used for moderate pain relief by itself or combined with other products, such as aspirin or acetaminophen (Tylenol). Robitussin AC and Cheracol are examples of liquid codeine preparations. According to the DEA,

codeine is the most widely used naturally occurring narcotic in medical treatment.

SEMISYNTHETIC NARCOTICS

Semisynthetic narcotics are derived by altering chemicals contained in opium. The two most commonly produced are heroin and hydromorphone.

Heroin

Heroin was first synthesized from morphine in 1874 but was not used extensively until the Bayer Company of Germany first began commercial production in 1898. It was widely accepted as a painkiller for years, with the medical profession largely unaware of its potential for addiction. The Harrison Narcotic Act of 1914 established control of heroin in the United States.

Pure heroin, a bitter white powder, is usually dissolved and injected. Heroin found "on the street" may vary in color from white to dark brown depending on the amount of impurities left from the manufacturing process or the presence of additives, such as food coloring, cocoa, or brown sugar.

For many years, the typical "bag" (single dose) of street heroin weighed about 100 milligrams and frequently contained less than 10% actual heroin, with the remainder made up of sugar, starch, powdered milk, or quinine. By the 1990s, however, the national average of heroin purity ranged between 35 and 40%, according to the DEA. In 1997 the highest-purity heroin was reported in cities in the Northeast, such as Philadelphia (79.5%) and New York City (62.5%).

"Black tar" heroin is popular in the western United States. A crudely processed form of heroin, black tar is manufactured illegally in Mexico and derives its name from its sticky, dark brown or black appearance. According to USNoDrugs.com, black tar is often sold on the street in its tar-like state and can have purities ranging from 20 to 80%. It can be diluted with substances such as burnt cornstarch or converted into a powder. It is most commonly injected.

Until recently, heroin was usually injected—intravenously (the preferred method), subcutaneously ("skin popping"), or intramuscularly. The increased availability of high-purity heroin, however, meant that users could snort or smoke the drug, which contributed to an increase in heroin use. Snorting or smoking is more appealing to those users who fear contracting diseases like human immunodeficiency virus and acquired immunodeficiency syndrome (HIV/AIDS) and hepatitis through shared syringes; users who smoke or snort heroin also avoid the historical stigma attached to heroin use—the marks of the needle left on one's skin. Once hooked, however, many abusers who started by snorting or smoking the drug shift to intravenous use.

Because of the increased availability of heroin, the price of the drug dropped—in the 1990s street-level prices were generally $10 to $20 a bag, or even less, according to the National Institute on Drug Abuse (NIDA). The National Drug Intelligence Center, in its *National Drug Threat Assessment 2005: Threat Matrix*, put the 2005 street price of heroin at $10 per dose. Heroin use has increased in recent years, and officials believe the increase is primarily due to lower prices, greater availability, and higher purity.

SYMPTOMS AND RELATED PROBLEMS. Symptoms and signs of heroin use include euphoria, drowsiness, respiratory depression, constricted pupils, and nausea. Withdrawal symptoms include watery eyes, runny nose, yawning, loss of appetite, tremors, panic, chills, sweating, nausea, diarrhea, muscle cramps, and insomnia. Elevations in blood pressure, pulse, respiratory rate, and temperature occur as withdrawal progresses. Because heroin abusers are often unaware of the actual strength of the drug and its true contents, they are at risk of overdose. Symptoms of overdose, which may result in death, include shallow breathing, clammy skin, convulsions, and coma. According to the Substance Abuse and Mental Health Services Administration, which is part of the U.S. Department of Health and Human Services, heroin is one of the most frequently reported drugs in drug-abuse deaths, either singly or in combination with cocaine and/or alcohol.

Sharing unsterilized needles with other addicts increases the risk of exposure to HIV, the virus that causes AIDS. The use of heroin, as well as the self-abusing lifestyle that often accompanies its use, may compromise the body's ability to withstand infection, compounding the devastating effects of HIV. As a result, drug abusers have become one of the fastest-growing groups of HIV sufferers in the United States.

Pregnant women addicted to heroin often give birth to addicted babies. These babies must go through painful withdrawal and may not develop normally. Some women give birth to children carrying HIV, some of whom will eventually develop AIDS. In addition, children born to addicted mothers are at greater risk of sudden infant death syndrome (SIDS), a disorder in which infants suddenly and inexplicably stop breathing and die.

Hydromorphone

Commonly called by the trade name Dilaudid, hydromorphone is the second-oldest semisynthetic narcotic painkiller. It is shorter-acting, more sedating, and two to eight times more intense than morphine. Easily abused, it is sought after by addicts—usually through theft or fraudulent prescriptions. Hydromorphone tablets, which are stronger than liquid forms of the drug, may be dissolved and injected.

SYNTHETIC NARCOTICS

Unlike products derived directly or indirectly from narcotics of natural origin, synthetic narcotics are produced entirely in the laboratory. The primary objective of laboratory production is to produce a drug that will have the analgesic properties of morphine while minimizing the potential for addiction. The products most widely available—hydrocodone, oxycodone, meperidine, and methadone—are still addictive however.

Hydrocodone and Oxycodone

Hydrocodone and oxycodone are two of the most commonly prescribed narcotic painkillers in the United States. Although they are designed to have less euphoric effect than morphine, they are still highly sought after by recreational users and addicts. Like morphine, these drugs have enough potential for abuse that they are classified as Schedule II substances. (See Table 2.1.)

In 2001 the drug OxyContin, produced by Purdue Pharma L.P., received an enormous amount of media attention. Although the active ingredient, oxycodone, has been around for a long time in drugs such as Percocet and Percodan, media and law enforcement noted a new wave of use. OxyContin, which is sold in high-dosage time-release pills, can be easily swallowed, chewed, or even crushed and injected, for a heroin-like high. The manufacturer, after DEA pressure, agreed to try to produce its product in ways that had less potential for abuse. As of 2003, however, abuse of OxyContin was still on the rise, according to the National Drug Intelligence Center.

Meperidine (Pethidine)

First introduced in the 1930s, meperidine parallels morphine's pain-relieving strength. It is the most widely used drug for relief of moderate to severe pain and is frequently used during childbirth and after operations. Tolerance and dependence develop with chronic use, and large doses can result in convulsions. Demerol and Pethadal are meperidine products.

Methadone and Related Drugs

Methadone was first synthesized by German scientists during World War II because of a shortage of morphine. Although its chemical makeup is unlike that of morphine or heroin, it produces many of the same effects as those drugs. It was introduced to the United States in 1947 and became widely used in the 1960s to help treat narcotic addicts.

The effects of methadone last up to twenty-four hours, and the drug is almost as effective when administered orally as by injection. Tolerance and dependence can develop, and in some metropolitan areas, methadone has become just another illegal drug. It has also emerged as an important cause of overdose deaths.

Levo-alpha-acetylmethadol (LAAM) is a closely related synthetic compound with an even longer duration of action (forty-eight to seventy-two hours), allowing for fewer clinic visits and eliminating take-home medication. In 1994 it was approved for use in the treatment of narcotic addiction. Another close relative of methadone is dextropropoxyphene, first marketed in 1957 under the trade name Darvon for the relief of mild to moderate pain. There is less chance of dependence, but also less pain relief. It has one-half to one-third the potency of codeine but is about ten times stronger than aspirin. Because of misuse, bulk dextropropoxyphene was placed in Schedule II, while preparations containing it are in Schedule IV. (See Table 2.1.)

DEPRESSANTS

The Controlled Substances Act regulates depressants because they have a high potential for abuse and are associated with both physical and psychological dependence. Taken as prescribed by a physician, depressants may be beneficial for the relief of anxiety, irritability, and tension, as well as for the symptomatic relief of insomnia. When taken in excessive amounts, however, they produce a state of intoxication very similar to that of alcohol. Unlike most other illegal drugs, depressants (except for methaqualone) are rarely produced in secret laboratories. Instead, they are generally obtained through theft and fraudulent prescriptions and sold illegally on the black market.

Chloral Hydrate

The oldest of the hypnotic (sleep-inducing) drugs, chloral hydrate was first synthesized in 1832 and soon replaced alcohol, opium, and cannabis for bringing about sedation and sleep. Its effects are similar to those of alcohol, and withdrawal symptoms resemble delirium tremens (the "DTs"). Cases of poisoning have occurred from mixing chloral hydrate with alcohol. Older adults are the most common abusers of this drug; it is not a street drug of choice.

Barbiturates

According to Charles E. Ophardt in *Virtual Chembook* (http://www.elmhurst.edu/~chm/vchembook/6673barbit.html), about twenty-five hundred derivatives of barbituric acid have been synthesized, but only fifteen are used medically. Small therapeutic doses calm nervous conditions; larger doses cause sleep within a short period of time. A feeling of excitement precedes the sedation. Too large a dose can bring a person through stages of sedation, sleep, and coma and ultimately cause death via respiratory failure and cardiovascular complications.

Barbiturates are classified as ultrashort-, short-, intermediate-, and long-acting. Ultrashort-acting barbiturates produce anesthesia within one minute of intravenous delivery into the system. Pentathol, Brevital, and Surital are among those currently in medical use. Because of the rapid onset and brief duration of effect, drug abusers find these drugs unattractive.

Short-acting and intermediate-acting barbiturates, including Nembutal, Seconal, and Amytal, with durations of up to six hours, are much more in demand by thrill-seekers. Long-acting barbiturates, such as Veronal, Luminal, and Mebaral, have onset times of up to one hour and durations of up to sixteen hours. These are used medicinally as sedatives, hypnotics, and anticonvulsants.

Glutethimide and Methaqualone

Glutethimide (Doriden) was introduced in 1954 and methaqualone (Quaalude, Sopor) in 1965 as safe substitutes for barbiturates. Usually prescribed for pain and sleep disturbance, in medically approved doses they cause feelings of calm, drowsiness, and euphoria. They are administered orally; in large doses they can cause tremors and altered sleep patterns. In 1991 glutethimide was transferred to Schedule II because of its potential for abuse.

Not long after its introduction, methaqualone became a drug of choice among drug users who thought it was both nonaddictive and an aphrodisiac. Extensive use and abuse of methaqualone can cause hallucinations, anxiety, numbness, tingling, and even serious poisoning. In 1984 the United States stopped production and distribution of methaqualone pharmaceutical products because of growing abuse, and the drug was transferred to Schedule I of the Controlled Substances Act. Counterfeit copies containing diazepam (Valium), flurazepan, and phenobarbital are prevalent on the U.S. illicit drug market.

Benzodiazepines

Benzodiazepines are depressants that relieve anxiety, tension, and muscle spasms; produce sedation; and prevent convulsions. They have a relatively slow onset but long duration of action. They also have a greater margin of safety than other depressants. According to the DEA, benzodiazepines are among the most widely prescribed medications in the United States. Xanax (alprazolam), Librium (zepoxide), and Valium (diazepam) are in this group.

Prolonged use of excessive doses may result in physical and psychological dependence. Because benzodiazepines are eliminated from the body slowly, withdrawal symptoms generally develop slowly, usually seven to ten days after continued high doses are stopped. When these drugs are used illicitly, they are often taken with alcohol or marijuana to achieve a euphoric "high." Since benzodiazepines are legal, they are usually obtained by getting prescriptions from doctors or forging prescriptions. They are also bought illegally on the black market.

Rohypnol (flunitrazepam), another benzodiazepine, has become increasingly popular among young people. The drug, manufactured as a short-term treatment for severe sleeping disorders, is not marketed legally in the United States and must be smuggled in. It is widely known as a "date-rape drug," because would-be rapists have been known to drop it secretly into a woman's drink to facilitate sexual assault. Several states—including Florida, Idaho, Minnesota, New Mexico, North Dakota, Oklahoma, and Pennsylvania—placed the drug under Schedule I control, and the United States has banned its importation and imposed stiff federal penalties for its sale. Responding to pressure from the American government, the Mexican producer of Rohypnol, Roche, began putting a blue dye in the pill so that it could be seen when dissolved in a drink.

STIMULANTS

Potent stimulants make users feel stronger, more decisive, and self-possessed. Because of the buildup effect, chronic users often develop a pattern of using "uppers" in the morning and "downers," such as alcohol or sleeping pills, at night. Such manipulation interferes with normal body processes and can lead to mental and physical illness.

Large doses can produce paranoia and auditory and visual hallucinations. Overdoses can also produce dizziness, tremors, agitation, hostility, panic, headaches, flushed skin, chest pain with palpitations, excessive sweating, vomiting, and abdominal cramps. Chronic high-dose users exhibit profound depression, apathy, fatigue, and disturbed sleep for up to twenty hours when going through withdrawal, which may last for several days.

Cocaine

Cocaine, the most potent stimulant of natural origin, is extracted from the leaves of the coca plant (*Erythroxylon coca*), which has been cultivated in the Andean highlands of South America since prehistoric times. The coca leaves are frequently chewed for refreshment and relief from fatigue—in much the same way some North Americans chew tobacco.

According to the Office of National Drug Control Policy (http://www.whitehousedrugpolicy.gov/drugfact/cocaine/), pure cocaine was first isolated in the 1880s and used as a local anesthetic in eye surgery. In the late nineteenth and early twentieth centuries it became popular in this country as an anesthetic for nose and throat surgery. Since then, other drugs, such as lidocaine and novocaine, have replaced it as an anesthetic.

FIGURE 2.2

Refined cocaine. (© *Francoise de Mulder/CORBIS.*)

Illicit cocaine is distributed as a white crystalline powder, often contaminated, or "cut," with sugars or local anesthetics. (See Figure 2.2.) The drug is commonly sniffed, or "snorted," through the nasal passages. Less commonly, it is mixed with water and injected, which brings a more intense high because the drug reaches the brain more rapidly.

For some time, people thought cocaine was relatively safe from undesirable side effects—not true for those who become heavy users. Cocaine produces a very short but extremely powerful rush of energy and confidence. Because the pleasurable effects are so intense, cocaine can lead to severe mental dependency, destroying a person's life as the need for the drug supersedes any other considerations. Physically, cocaine users risk permanent damage to their noses by exposing the cartilage and dissolving the nasal septum (membrane), resulting in a collapsed nose. Cocaine significantly increases the risk of heart attack in the first hour after use. Heavy use (two grams or more a week) impairs memory, decision making, and manual dexterity.

In the 1970s cocaine was popularly accepted as a recreational drug—particularly by the wealthy, who were among the few who could afford to use it. The coming years, however, would see a development that would bring cocaine to the masses: "crack."

Freebasing is a process in which dissolved cocaine is mixed with ether or rum and sodium hydroxide, or baking powder. The salt base dissolves, leaving granules of pure cocaine. These are next heated in a pipe until they vaporize. The vapor is inhaled directly into the lungs, causing an immediate high that lasts about ten minutes.

There is a danger of being badly burned if the open flame gets too close to the ether or the rum, causing them to flare up as they burn. When actor-comedian Richard Pryor set himself on fire while freebasing in 1980, many users started to search for a safer way to achieve the same high. The dangers inherent in freebasing may have been the catalyst for the development of crack cocaine.

Crack

Cocaine hydrochloride, the powdered form of cocaine, is soluble in water, can be injected, and is fairly insensitive to heat. When cocaine hydrochloride is converted to cocaine base, it yields a substance that becomes volatile when heated. "Crack" (as described by several government Web sites, including that of NIDA [http://www.nida.nih.gov/Infofacts/cocaine.html]) is processed by mixing cocaine with baking soda and heating it to remove the hydrochloride rather than by the more volatile method of using ether. The resultant chips, or "rocks," of pure cocaine are usually smoked in a pipe or added to a cigarette or marijuana joint. (See Figure 2.3 and Figure 2.4.) The name comes from the crackling sound made when the mixture is smoked.

Inhaling the cocaine fumes produces a rapid, intense, and short-lived effect. This incredible intensity is followed within minutes by an abnormally disconcerting and anxious "crash," which leads almost inevitably to the need for more of the drug—and a great likelihood of addiction.

MARKETING CRACK. The mass marketing of crack began in the mid-1980s. A glut of powdered cocaine had saturated the market, driving down prices and cutting into dealers' profits. This coincided with the discovery of crack, which could "hook" users after just a few tries.

Experimenters in the Caribbean developed the first prototypes of crack by mixing cocaine with baking soda, water, and rum. At that time, most cocaine was being shipped to the United States through the extensive islands and bays of the Bahamas, and a sizable portion of it was being diverted to the local population.

When dealers saw the attraction that this new product had for Bahamian users, they were quick to realize the potential profits that could be made by

FIGURE 2.3

Crack pipe. *(Corbis Corporation [Bellevue].)*

FIGURE 2.4

Crack granules. *(© Roger Ressmeyer/CORBIS.)*

introducing it on the streets of the United States—first in Miami, Los Angeles, and New York. Pushers in those cities began to offer crack at low prices, knowing that users would quickly become addicted and come back for more.

Once introduced in the mid-1980s, crack spread rapidly. The most convenient distribution method was to use inner-city street gangs; they were located in areas with the heaviest concentration of drug users. Crack sold for only $5 to $10 a hit and could more easily be sold to poor people living in these areas. Expanding from Miami, Los Angeles, and New York, crack spread across the nation through interstate and intrastate transport.

Although crack spread rapidly in the mid-1980s and received a lot of attention from the media and government, it faded from view somewhat in the 1990s. Crack use dropped throughout the 1990s as its devastating effects on users became widely known; users switched to other drugs, and new users were difficult for pushers to attract—they had been scared away. News stories stopped appearing, and the government began to focus its attention on other drugs, such as methamphetamine and Ecstasy.

Amphetamines

Amphetamines are synthetic drugs similar to the hormone adrenaline and the stimulant ephedrine. The history of the illicit use of amphetamines is very much like that of cocaine. As documented by the DEA, amphetamines were first marketed in the 1930s, under the name Benzedrine, in an over-the-counter inhaler to treat nasal congestion. Abuse of these inhalers soon became popular among teenagers and prisoners. In 1937 Benzedrine became available in pill form, and the number of abusers quickly increased.

Medically, amphetamines are used mainly to treat depression, narcolepsy (a rare disorder that causes people to fall asleep involuntarily), hyperactive disorders in children (now called attention deficit hyperactivity disorder, or ADHD), and certain cases of obesity. During World War II pilots took Benzedrine to stay awake.

"Speed freaks," who injected amphetamines, became famous in the drug culture for their strange and often violent behavior. In 1965 federal food and drug laws were amended to curb the growing black market in amphetamines. Many legal drugs using amphetamines were removed from the market, and doctors began prescribing them less frequently. As a result, clandestine laboratories increased their production to meet the growing black market demand. Today, most amphetamines are produced in these clandestine laboratories.

Extended amphetamine use can lead to a number of health problems. Short-term effects include sleeplessness, which can lead to and compound psychotic episodes brought on by heavy use. Long-term effects are unknown, although some research has suggested that chronic amphetamine use may contribute to neurological damage, such as the development of Parkinson's disease.

Methamphetamines

Methamphetamines are synthetic stimulants similar to amphetamines. As documented by NIDA, they were first developed by a Japanese pharmacologist in 1919. They came to market during the 1930s as a treatment for narcolepsy, attention deficit disorder, and obesity. A form of the drug often referred to as "speed" became popular during the 1960s and led to government control over the manufacture of the drug. Methamphetamine abuse fell off in the 1970s as cocaine became increasingly available. In the 1990s, however, its use increased dramatically, though use began to taper off somewhat again around the turn of the millennium.

Methamphetamines have traditionally been distributed by outlaw motorcycle gangs and other independent producers. While these groups still play a role in the drug's sale, traffickers operating out of Mexico have taken over major distribution. Using money raised from the sale of other drugs, they have built sophisticated new laboratories that produce large quantities of the drug. At first, these traffickers limited distribution to the western United States, but they have since expanded their distribution channels well into the Midwest.

Methamphetamines can be either injected or inhaled. To make the drug more attractive, Mexican traffickers have increased its purity. This has made it easier to inhale and, therefore, more attractive to potential users who might be concerned about the dangers of using syringes.

The effects of methamphetamines are similar to those of cocaine, but their onset is slower and they last longer. Methamphetamines cause increased activity, decreased appetite, and a sense of euphoria in the user. Abusers frequently become paranoid, pick at their skin, and suffer from auditory and/or visual hallucinations. Chronic abusers may exhibit violent and erratic behavior. Methamphetamines are associated with such health conditions as memory loss and heart and brain damage. Crystallized methamphetamine hydrochloride, or "ice," is a smokable form of methamphetamine.

One of the key ingredients often used in the manufacture of methamphetamones is pseudoephedrine, a drug found in many common nasal decongestants, such as Sudafed. In 2005 this led some government officials to consider outlawing sale of these decongestants, which are currently available over the counter under many brand names.

Methcathinone—"Cat"

"Cat," or methcathinone, a more recent drug of abuse in the United States, was placed into Schedule I of the Controlled Substances Act in 1993. "Cat" is produced in clandestine laboratories and is usually snorted, although it can be mixed in a beverage and taken orally or diluted in water and injected intravenously.

Methcathinone has about the same abuse potential as methamphetamines and produces similar results: excessive energy, hyperactivity, extended wakefulness, and loss of appetite. The user feels both euphoric and invincible. At the same time, use of "cat" can lead to anxiety, tremors, insomnia, weight loss, sweating, stomach pains, a pounding heart, nose bleeds, and body aches. Excessive use can lead to convulsions, paranoia, hallucinations, and depression.

Phenmetrazine (Preludin) and Methylphenidate (Ritalin)

Abuse patterns of these drugs are similar to those of other stimulants. Preludin is used medically as an appetite suppressant, and Ritalin, frequently prescribed by physicians, is used mainly to treat children with attention deficit disorders. These drugs are most subject to abuse in countries where they are easily available, such as in the United States.

Debates have arisen regarding the overprescription of Ritalin. The American Medical Association has estimated that as of 2003, four to eight million children in the United States were being treated with Ritalin for attention deficit disorders. Opponents of Ritalin prescription argue that the diagnosis of attention deficit hyperactivity disorder (ADHD) is simply a way of labeling children who make classroom management difficult and medicating them so they will stop acting out. Proponents argue that ADHD is a very serious medical condition and that stimulant drugs are necessary in helping children with the condition develop correctly. Experts on both sides agree that the ADHD diagnosis is sometimes applied—and medication prescribed—in cases where it is unnecessary.

Anorectic Drugs

These drugs are relatively recent attempts to replace amphetamines as appetite suppressants. They produce many of the same effects but are generally less potent. Abuse patterns have not been determined, but all drugs in this group are classified as controlled substances because of their similarity to amphetamines. They include Didrex, Pre-Sate, Tenuate, Tepanil, Pondimin, Mazanor, Ionamin, Adipex-P, and Sanorex.

Khat

Khat is a natural substance derived from the fresh young leaves of the *Catha edulis* shrub, native to East Africa and the Arabian peninsula. People in these areas have been chewing khat for centuries, often in communal social situations—the same way Americans drink coffee or tea. Chewed in moderation, khat alleviates fatigue and reduces appetite. Excessive use may result in paranoia and hallucinations. Khat contains many chemicals that are controlled substances, including cathinone (Schedule I) and cathine (Schedule IV).

HALLUCINOGENS

Hallucinogenic drugs, or psychedelics, are natural or synthetic substances that distort the perceptions of reality. They cause excitation, which can vary from a sense of well-being to severe depression. Time may appear to stand still, and forms and colors seem to change and take on new meaning. The heart rate may increase, blood pressure rise, and pupils dilate. The experience may be pleasurable or extremely frightening. The effects of hallucinogens vary from use to use and cannot be predicted.

The most common danger of using hallucinogens is impaired judgment, which can lead to rash decisions and accidents. Long after hallucinogens have been eliminated from the body, users may experience "flashbacks," in the form of perceived intensity of color, the apparent motion of fixed objects, or illusions that present one object when another one is present. Some hallucinogens are present in plants (e.g. mescaline in the peyote cactus); others, such as LSD, are synthetic. The abuse of hallucinogens in the United States peaked in the late 1960s, but the 1990s and early 2000s saw a resurgence in the use of these drugs.

Peyote and Mescaline

Mescaline is a psychoactive chemical found naturally in the peyote cactus, *Lophophor williamsii*, a small, spineless plant native to Mexico and the southwestern United States. The top of the cactus, often called the crown, is made up of disk-shaped buttons that can be cut off and dried. These buttons are generally chewed or soaked in water to produce an intoxicating liquid. A dose of 350 to 500 milligrams produces hallucinations lasting from five to twelve hours. Mescaline can be extracted from peyote or produced synthetically.

Peyote and mescaline have long been used by American Indians in religious ceremonies. Recently, however, this use has come into serious question. In 1990 the U.S. Supreme Court, in *Employment Division, Department of Human Resources v. Smith* (494 US 872), ruled that the state of Oregon could bar the Native American Church from using peyote in its religious ceremonies. The passage of the Religious Freedom Restoration Act of 1993 (PL 103-141) allowed the church to use peyote in those ceremonies; but in 1997 the Supreme Court, in *Boerne v. Flores* (65 LW 4612), declared the Religious Freedom Restoration Act unconstitutional. This left the use of peyote back in the jurisdiction of the states, and states may decide individually on its use.

Arizona law allows the use of peyote in connection with the practice of a religious belief if it is an integral part of a religious exercise and if it is used in a manner not dangerous to public health. Several other states, mainly in the Southwest, continue to allow the use of peyote in religious ceremonies if certain conditions are met, such as Native American origin or proof of religious affiliation. In general, in most states that allow peyote use, the Native American Church is the only recognized organization with a bona fide claim that peyote is a sacrament in its rituals.

DOM, DOB, MDA, MDMA, and "Designer Drugs"

DOM (4-methyl-2,5-mimethoxyamphetamine), DOB (4-bromo-2,5-dimethoxyamphetamine), MDA (3,4-methylenedioxyamphetamine), MDMA (3,4 methylenedioxymethamphetamine), and "designer drugs" are chemical variations of mescaline and amphetamines that have been synthesized in the laboratory. They differ from one another in speed of onset, duration of action, and potency. They are usually taken orally, are sometimes snorted, but they are rarely injected intravenously.

Because they are produced illegally, these drugs are seldom pure. Dosage quantity and quality vary considerably. These drugs are often used at "raves"—large, all-night dance parties once held in unusual places such as warehouses or railroad yards. Although many raves became mainstream events, professionally organized and held at public venues, the underground style and culture of raves remains an alluring draw to many teenagers. Part of the allure is drug use.

The most noted designer drug, MDMA (also called ADAM, Ecstasy, or X) was first banned by the DEA in 1985. Widespread abuse placed it in Schedule I of the Controlled Substances Act. Some doctors suggest that the pure form of the drug is not as harmful as one might think and may even have potential uses as an antidepressant or antipsychotic drug. However, the form of the drug found on the street is rarely a pure form. According to an October 2002 article in *Pediatrics* (Eric Sigel, "Club Drugs: Nothing to Rave About," vol. 19, no. 10), tablets of MDMA that have been tested have contained from zero to 140 milligrams of MDMA, as well as additional drugs such as ephedrine, dextromethorphan, or amphetamine.

Users of MDMA have been known to suffer serious psychological effects—including confusion, depression, sleep problems, drug craving, severe anxiety, and paranoia—both during, and sometimes weeks after, taking the drug. Physical symptoms include muscle tension, involuntary teeth clenching, nausea, blurred vision, rapid eye movement, faintness, and chills or sweating. Severe dehydration, particularly among users who dance for hours while under the drug's influence, is also a serious hazard.

MDA, the parent drug of MDMA, has been found to destroy serotonin-producing neurons, which play a direct role in regulating aggression, mood, sexual activity, sleep, and pain sensitivity. This may explain the sense of heightened sexual experience, tranquility, and conviviality said to accompany MDA use. The Anti-Drug Abuse Act of 1986 (PL 99-570) made all designer drugs illegal. By 2004, as reported by the University of Michigan News Service (http://www.umich.edu/news/?BG/ecstasy_cocaine), use of Ecstasy was on the decline, along with the novelty of the rave culture that helped give rise to its spread.

LSD (LSD-25, Lysergide)

LSD, an abbreviation of the German term for lysergic acid diethylamide, is one of the most potent mood-changing chemicals in existence. It is often called "acid." Odorless, colorless, and tasteless, it is produced from a substance derived from ergot fungus

or from a chemical found in morning glory seeds. Both chemicals are found in Schedule III of the Controlled Substances Act while LSD itself is a Schedule I substance.

LSD is usually sold in tablets ("microdots"), thin squares of gelatin ("window panes"), or impregnated paper ("blotter acid"). Effects of doses higher than thirty to fifty micrograms can persist for ten to twelve hours, severely impairing judgment and decision-making. Tolerance develops rapidly, and more of the drug is needed to achieve the desired effect.

Dr. Albert Hoffman originally synthesized LSD in 1938, but it was not until 1943 that he accidentally took the drug and recorded his "trip." He was aware of vertigo and an intensification of light. During the two-hour experience, he also saw a stream of fantastically vivid images, coupled with an unusual play of colors.

Because of its structural similarity to a chemical present in the brain, LSD was originally used as a research tool to study the mechanism of mental illness. It was later adopted by the drug culture of the 1960s. During the 1960s LSD use was seen by users and nonusers alike as central to full participation in the emerging counterculture movement. Such major icons as author Ken Kesey and Harvard professor Timothy Leary began to promote a culture in which certain political values and drug use were almost synonymous.

LSD use dropped in the 1980s but showed a resurgence in the 1990s. It is inexpensive (according to the DEA, $1 to $10 per dosage unit—usually twenty to eighty micrograms), nonaddictive, and one hit can last for eight to twelve hours. Many young people have rediscovered the drug, taking it in a liquid form dropped on the tongue or in the eyes with an eye dropper, or by placing impregnated blotter paper on their tongues.

Phencyclidine (PCP) and Related Drugs

Many drug-treatment professionals believe that phencyclidine (PCP) poses greater risks to the user than any other drug. PCP was originally investigated in the 1950s as an anesthetic but was discontinued for human use because of its side effects, which included confusion and delirium. The drug is still occasionally used on animals, but even many veterinarians are now turning away from it.

In the United States virtually all PCP is manufactured in clandestine laboratories and sold on the black market. This drug is sold under at least fifty different names, many of which reflect its bizarre and volatile effects: Angel Dust, Crystal, Supergrass, Killer Weed, Embalming Fluid, Rocket Fuel, and others. It is often sold to users who think they are buying mescaline or LSD.

In its pure form, PCP is a white crystalline powder that readily dissolves in water. It can also be taken in tablet or capsule form. It can be swallowed, sniffed, smoked, or injected. It is commonly applied to a leafy material, such as parsley, mint, oregano, or marijuana, and smoked.

Because PCP is an anesthetic, it produces an inability to feel pain, which can lead to serious bodily injury. Unlike other hallucinogens, PCP produces depression in some individuals. Regular use often impairs memory, perception, concentration, motor movement, and judgment. PCP can also produce a psychotic state in many ways indistinguishable from schizophrenia, or it can lead to hallucinations, mood swings, paranoia, and amnesia.

Because of the extreme psychic disorders associated with repeated use, or even one dose, of PCP and related drugs, Congress passed the Psychotropic Substances Act of 1978 (PL 95-633). The penalties imposed for the manufacture or possession of these chemicals are the stiffest of any nonnarcotic violation under the Controlled Substances Act.

CANNABIS

Cannabis sativa, the hemp plant from which marijuana is made, grows wild throughout most of the world's tropic and temperate regions, including Mexico, the Middle East, Africa, and India. (See Figure 2.5.) For centuries, its therapeutic potential has been explored, including uses as an analgesic and anticonvulsant. But with the advent of new, synthetic drugs and the passage of the Marijuana Tax Act of 1937, interest in marijuana—even for medicinal purposes—faded. In 1970 the Controlled Substances Act classified marijuana as a Schedule I drug, having "no currently accepted medical use in treatment in the United States," though this classification is debated by those in favor of using it for medical and recreational purposes.

Cannabis plants are usually smoked in the form of loosely rolled cigarettes ("joints") or in various kinds of pipes. The effects are felt within minutes, usually peaking in ten to thirty minutes and lingering for two to three hours. Low doses induce restlessness and an increasing sense of well-being, followed by a dreamy state of relaxation and, frequently, hunger. Changes in sensory perception—a more vivid sense of sight, smell, touch, taste, and hearing—may occur, with subtle alterations in thought formation and expression. Drugs made from the cannabis plant are widely distributed on the U.S. black market.

Marijuana

Marijuana is a tobacco-like substance produced by drying the leaves and flowery top of the cannabis plant. (See Figure 2.5.) Its potency varies considerably, depending on how much of the chemical THC (delta-9-tetrahydrocannabinol) is present. The National Drug Intelligence Center estimates that wild U.S.

FIGURE 2.5

Budding cannabis plant. (© *Bill Lisenby/CORBIS.*)

cannabis has a THC content of less than 0.5%; it is considered inferior to Jamaican, Colombian, and Mexican varieties, whose THC content ranges between 0.5 and 0.7%.

The most potent form of marijuana is *sinsemilla* (Spanish for "without seed"), which comes from the unpollinated female cannabis plant and can contain up to 17% THC. Another potent form, Southeast Asian "Thai stick" (marijuana buds bound into short sections of bamboo), is not often found in the United States.

Marijuana is grown illegally throughout the United States, both indoors and out. Growers generally try to achieve the highest possible THC content in order to produce the greatest possible effect. It is thought that most marijuana smoked in the United States is grown in the United States, much of it in the Midwest using sophisticated hydroponic techniques (growing the plants in water instead of soil). Street names for marijuana include "pot," "grass," "weed," "Mary Jane," and "reefer."

USE AND EFFECTS. Every survey the federal government conducts on drug use indicates that marijuana is by far the most extensively used illicit drug in the United States. During the 1960s and 1970s it was as common at many parties as beer and wine. In 2003 an estimated 96.6 million Americans—more than a third of the population age twelve and over—had tried marijuana at some point in their life, according to results from the *National Survey on Drug Use and Health*, conducted annually by the Substance Abuse and Mental Health Services Administration.

Extensive research by NIDA uncovered the effect that THC has on the hippocampus, a part of the brain that is crucial for learning, memory, and the integration of sensory experiences with emotions and motivation. Many feel that these studies, when taken together, may explain the euphoria and memory loss induced by marijuana, as well as provide definitive proof of the drug's toxic effect on brain cells.

Scientists at UCLA's Jonsson Comprehensive Cancer Center found in 1997 that smoking one to three marijuana cigarettes produces the same lung damage and potential cancer risk as smoking five times as many cigarettes. And NIDA, as shown on their Web site (http://www.nida.nih.gov/pdf/mono graphs/download44.html), reported as far back as 1984 that marijuana adversely affects reproductive function in both males and females.

The immediate physical effects of marijuana include a faster heartbeat (by as much as 50%), bloodshot eyes, and a dry mouth and throat. It can reduce short-term memory, alter one's sense of time, and reduce concentration and coordination. Some users experience light-headedness and giddiness, while others feel depressed and sad. Many users have also reported experiencing severe anxiety attacks.

Although symptoms usually disappear in about four to six hours, it takes about three days for 50% of the drug to be broken down and eliminated from the body. It takes three weeks to completely excrete the THC from one marijuana cigarette. If a user smokes two joints a week, it takes months for all traces of the THC to disappear from the body.

SUPPORT FOR PATIENT USE. In the past marijuana has been used to treat glaucoma and several neurological disorders. However, an Institute of Medicine (IOM) report concluded that the drug was not useful in glaucoma treatment because its effects were short-lived (Janet E. Joy, Stanley J. Watson, Jr., and John A. Benson, Jr., *Marijuana and Medicine: Assessing the Science Base*, National Academies Press, 1999). The report also indicated that marijuana was ineffective in treating patients suffering from Parkinson's or Huntington's diseases. According to one of the principal investigators for the IOM, John Benson, Jr., the medical effects of marijuana are generally modest, and only patients who do not respond well to other medications should use it. Marijuana appears to be useful in treating conditions such as chemotherapy-induced nausea or the wasting caused by AIDS. It may also help relieve muscle spasms associated with multiple sclerosis.

In May 1991 nearly half of all cancer specialists who responded to an unofficial Harvard University survey said that they would prescribe marijuana for some of their patients if the drug were legal. A somewhat smaller percentage said that despite the drug's illegal status, they had already recommended it to patients as a means of enhancing appetite and relieving chemotherapy-related nausea.

As noted at the beginning of this chapter, one of the criteria used by the DEA in classifying drugs is whether there is a "currently accepted medical use in treatment in the United States." In 1988 Francis Young, the adminis-trative judge of the DEA, noted that marijuana "in its natural form, is one of the safest therapeutically active substances known to man" and recommended that physicians be authorized to use it. The DEA refused to relax the restrictions.

In 1991 the Massachusetts Supreme Court, in *Massachusetts v. Hutchins* (49 CRL 1442), ruled that society's interest in preventing illegal drug use outweighed a patient's "medical necessity" to use marijuana. The defendant, who began growing his own marijuana when he was unable to get government approval to use the drug to relieve the pain of his chronic illness, had been charged with possession and cultivation of the cannabis plant.

THE COURTS UPHOLD THE DEA ON MARIJUANA RESCHEDULING. Over the past two decades a number of legal attempts have been made to get marijuana rescheduled from Schedule I, the most restrictive classification, to a less restrictive schedule. The first petition was filed in 1972 and reached the Court of Appeals of the District of Columbia four times: *National Organization for the Reform of Marijuana Laws v. Ingersoll* (497 F.2d 654, 1974), *National Organization for the Reform of Marijuana Laws v. Drug Enforcement Administration* (559 F.2d 735, 1977), *National Organization for the Reform of Marijuana Laws v. Drug Enforcement Administration & Department of Health, Education and Welfare* (No. 79-1660, 1980), and *Alliance for Cannabis Therapeutics and The National Organization for the Reform of Marijuana Laws v. Drug Enforcement Administration* (930 F.2d 936, 1991). All of these petitions failed.

In another attempt, *Alliance for Cannabis Therapeutics and Drug Policy Foundation v. Drug Enforcement Administration* (15 F.3d 1131, 1994), the petitioners claimed that the DEA had failed to recognize that "marijuana is misclassified because it has been shown to serve various medicinal purposes . . . marijuana alleviates some side effects of chemotherapy in cancer patients, aids in the treatment of glaucoma and eye diseases, and reduces muscle spasticity in patients suffering from multiple sclerosis and other maladies of the central nervous system" (Schaffer Library of Drug Policy, http://www.drug library.org/schaffer/hemp/medical/court_ruling.htm).

In support of their case, the petitioners submitted affidavits and testimonials from a number of patients and doctors who said marijuana had been helpful in treatment. The Food and Drug Administration (FDA) claimed that the testimonials were not scientific proof and that no scientific study had shown that marijuana was useful in medical treatment.

The FDA claimed that, when questioned under oath, each witness supporting the rescheduling of marijuana "admitted he was basing his opinion on anecdotal evidence, on stories he heard from patients, and on his impressions about the drug." The appeals court agreed with the FDA that "only rigorous scientific proof can satisfy" the requirements needed to change marijuana's rating and let the FDA's position stand.

THE MEDICAL USE OF MARIJUANA—A POLITICAL ISSUE OR A SCIENTIFIC ISSUE? In 1997 the White House Office of National Drug Control Policy (ONDCP) made an effort to take the issue out of the political arena and place it in the scientific arena. The ONDCP asked the Institute of Medicine (IOM), a private, nonprofit organization that provides health-policy advice to Congress, to review the scientific evidence on the potential health benefits and risks of marijuana. Following an eighteen-month study, the investigators concluded that "the future of cannabinoid drugs lies not in smoked marijuana, but in chemically defined drugs that act on . . . human physiology" (Institute of Medicine, "Marijuana and Medicine: Assessing the Science Base," Washington, DC: National Academy Press, 1999). Rigorous clinical trials, along with the development of new delivery mechanisms for the drug, were among the recommendations of the IOM's report.

Yet the debate continued in the political arena. By the late 1990s voters in nine states—Alaska, Arizona, California, Colorado, Hawaii, Maine, Nevada, Oregon, and Washington—had approved initiatives intended to make marijuana legal for medical purposes. However, the initiatives were ineffective. The federal government threatened to prosecute doctors who wrote prescriptions for marijuana. In 1997 a group of doctors sued to prevent the federal government from revoking doctors' registrations, and a federal judge permanently enjoined the federal government from doing so in September 2000.

Patients, though, found it increasingly difficult to obtain the drug, especially since the federal government started closing down "buyers' clubs," or organizations that distribute medical marijuana to seriously ill patients who wouldn't be able to obtain it otherwise. Debate continued as federal prosecutors went up against the Oakland Cannabis Buyers Cooperative, a nonprofit organization that provides marijuana to doctor-approved patients. Though its operations were legal under California law, the federal government ordered an injunction against its operation. A new defense, that of "medical necessity," came out of the legal wrangling, and the Ninth Circuit Court of Appeals upheld the defense. But in 2001 the Supreme Court ruled that there is no "medical necessity" exception to drug laws since Schedule I states there is "no currently accepted medical use in treatment in the United States" for marijuana. This ruling, though it did not overrule state laws, did allow federal prosecutors to continue enforcing federal drug laws.

Hashish

Hashish is made from the THC-rich resinous material of the cannabis plant. This resin is collected, dried, and compressed into a variety of forms, including balls, cakes, and sticks. Pieces are then broken off and smoked. Most hashish comes from the Middle East, North Africa, Pakistan, and Afghanistan. According to the DEA, the THC content of hashish in the United States hovered around 6% during the 1990s. Demand in this country is limited.

Hash Oil

Despite the name, hash oil is not directly related to hashish. It is produced by extracting the cannabinoids from the cannabis plant with a solvent. The color and odor of hash oil depend on the solvent used. Most recently, seized hash oil has ranged from amber to dark brown with about 15% THC. In terms of effect, a drop or two of hash oil on a cigarette is equal to a single joint of marijuana.

ANABOLIC STEROIDS

Anabolic steroids are drugs derived from the male sex hormone testosterone. They are used illegally by some athletes, including weight lifters, bodybuilders, long-distance runners, cyclists, and others who believe that these drugs can give them a competitive advantage or improve their physical appearance. When used in combination with exercise training and a high-protein diet, anabolic steroids can lead to increased size and strength of muscles, improved endurance, and shorter recovery time between workouts.

Steroids are taken orally or by intramuscular injection. Most are smuggled into the United States and sold at gyms and competitions or by mail-order companies. The most commonly used steroids include boldenone (Equipoise), ethylestrenol (Maxibolin), fluoxymesterone (Halotestin), methandriol, methandrostenolone (Dianabol), methyltestosterone, nandrolone (Durabolin, Deca-Durabolin), oxandrolone (Anavar), oxymetholone (Anadrol), stanozolol (Winstrol), testosterone, and trenbolone (Finajet).

Steroid use was once considered a problem limited to professional athletes, but the Centers for Disease Control and Prevention reported in 2004 that 5 to 12% of male high school students and 1% of female students use steroids by the time they are seniors. Concerns about the drug led Congress, in 1991, to place anabolic steroids into Schedule III of the Controlled Substances Act.

Because concern about anabolic steroids is relatively recent, the adverse effects of large doses are not well established. Nonetheless, there is growing evidence of serious health problems, including cardiovascular damage, liver damage, and harm to reproductive organs. The Department of Justice and the DEA's Diversion Control Program lists the effects of steroids on its Web site (http://www.deadiversion.usdoj.gov/pubs/brochures/steroids/hidden/). Physical side effects include elevated blood pressure and cholesterol levels, severe acne, premature balding, reduced sexual desire, and atrophying of the testicles. Males may develop breasts, while females may experience a deepening of the voice, increased body-hair growth, fewer menstrual cycles, and diminished breast size. Some of these effects can be irreversible. In adolescents, bone development may stop, causing stunted growth. Some users become violently aggressive.

By the early 2000s, some professional sports agencies had begun to acknowledge that widespread steroid use was taking place in their ranks. In 2005 Major League Baseball initiated regular testing of players for steroid use.

CHAPTER 3
TRENDS IN DRUG USE

TRENDS IN INCIDENCE

Before people begin to use a drug more or less regularly, they have to use it for the first time. The government's drug experts call first use of a drug its "incidence" of use or the event of "initiation." The government's chief drug survey, the *National Survey on Drug Use and Health* (formerly called the *National Household Survey on Drug Abuse*, conducted annually by the Substance Abuse and Mental Health Services Administration (SAMHSA) of the U.S. Department of Health and Human Services, tracks both first use of important drugs and their prevalence. Prevalence, discussed in the next section, is the extent of current and lifetime use of drugs by the population. Increases in *incidence* have been found to foreshadow increases in *prevalence*; similarly, when the number of initial uses of a drug drop, after a lag of years so will the number of people who regularly take the drug.

The survey began in 1971 and has increased from a survey of about three thousand respondents every two to three years to almost seventy thousand people in the fifty states and Washington, D.C., every year. The latest survey available, *2003 National Survey on Drug Use and Health (NSDUH)*, was published in September of 2004 (http://www.oas. samhsa.gov/nhsda/2k3nsduh/2k3ResultsW.pdf). The population surveyed by SAMHSA consists of noninstitutionalized civilians over the age of twelve living in households, dormitories, homeless shelters, rooming houses, and military institutions. This excludes homeless people not in shelters, active-duty military personnel, and persons in jails and prisons, but the survey is still considered to be the most comprehensive analysis of drug use in America. The results are statistically projected to the entire population to produce an estimate of drug use prevalence nationwide. Survey methods were changed in 1999 when SAMHSA switched from a paper-and-pencil survey to a computer-assisted survey. Therefore, the results for the years from 1999 forward are not strictly comparable to earlier years. The changes were

introduced so that more accurate state-level results could be obtained and over- or under-sampling of regions (urban versus rural, for instance) or populations (African-Americans versus whites) could be corrected.

SAMHSA tracks initial use by asking those who participate in the *National Survey* when they first used a drug. Respondents also report how old they are. SAMHSA can thus calculate the number of people first using a drug in any given year—and also how old they were at that time. People who use drugs have a higher rate of mortality than nonusers; current samples cannot, of course, include the dead. Reporting on the "harder" drugs is also less reliable because of what SAMHSA calls "underreporting due to desire for social acceptability or fear of disclosure" ("Chapter 5. Trends in Initiation of Substance Use," *2003 National Survey on Drug Use and Health [NSDUH]*, Rockville, MD: SAMHSA, 2004).

Initial use shows different cycles for different drugs over the last four decades. The peaks and troughs of different drugs do not always coincide. The patterns suggest a demographic underpinning, since initial drug use is generally a youth phenomenon, and different drugs are used more by some age groups than others. As the number of people in each age category shifts, so do the incidents of drug usage in each category.

Marijuana

By far the most frequently tried illegal substance is marijuana. In the thirty-seven-year period shown in Figure 3.1, initial use of marijuana shows several peaks, with two of the highest in 1973 and 2000. In 1973, 3.5 million people tried marijuana for the first time. Initial tries dropped to about one and a half million by 1990. New tries then climbed to a new peak of 2.9 million first-time users in 2000, before tapering off slightly to 2.6 million in 2002, about two-thirds of whom were under age eighteen.

FIGURE 3.1

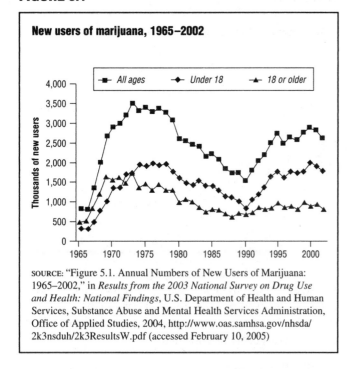

New users of marijuana, 1965–2002

SOURCE: "Figure 5.1. Annual Numbers of New Users of Marijuana: 1965–2002," in *Results from the 2003 National Survey on Drug Use and Health: National Findings*, U.S. Department of Health and Human Services, Substance Abuse and Mental Health Services Administration, Office of Applied Studies, 2004, http://www.oas.samhsa.gov/nhsda/2k3nsduh/2k3ResultsW.pdf (accessed February 10, 2005)

TABLE 3.1

Number of new users of cocaine, 1965–2002

[In thousands]

	Number of initiate (1,000s)				Age specific rates[a]	
Year	All ages	Under 18	18 or older	Mean age	12–17	18–25
1965	62	*	49	*	*	*
1966	35	*	27	*	*	*
1967	98	*	98	*	*	*
1968	185	67	118	19.2	2.9	5.0
1969	210	50	160	21.6	2.0	5.0
1970	288	85	204	18.9	3.7	8.0
1971	424	81	343	20.7	3.3	11.0
1972	433	111	322	19.5	4.5	10.8
1973	592	174	418	20.3	7.2	13.5
1974	885	202	683	21.7	8.3	18.1
1975	876	197	679	20.9	8.1	19.6
1976	1,026	212	813	21.2	8.9	24.3
1977	1,102	264	838	21.2	11.3	23.4
1978	1,329	237	1,092	21.3	10.4	31.7
1979	1,360	277	1,083	21.0	12.4	32.9
1980	1,562	296	1,266	22.4	13.6	33.0
1981	1,543	284	1,259	21.5	13.5	36.3
1982	1,502	299	1,203	22.0	14.3	32.7
1983	1,450	235	1,215	22.1	11.4	35.5
1984	1,363	267	1,097	22.1	13.1	30.8
1985	1,371	289	1,082	22.2	14.4	29.6
1986	1,264	231	1,033	23.2	11.7	28.3
1987	1,173	247	926	22.5	12.6	26.8
1988	1,147	166	982	23.1	8.6	28.3
1989	981	163	818	23.1	8.5	22.8
1990	942	195	748	23.5	10.4	19.7
1991	706	115	591	23.1	6.0	16.6
1992	781	166	615	24.5	8.3	14.3
1993	634	150	484	22.1	7.5	14.3
1994	662	151	511	22.6	6.9	14.4
1995	776	222	554	21.1	10.3	17.2
1996	880	272	608	21.9	12.3	18.4
1997	886	252	634	20.8	11.1	21.3
1998	926	278	648	20.8	12.0	20.9
1999	959	283	677	20.8	12.0	21.5
2000	1,019	309	709	20.9	12.8	22.4
2001	1,167	372	795	20.8	15.3	24.1
2002[b]	1,059	323	736	20.3	13.1	22.6

*Low precision; no estimate reported.
Note: Comparisons between years, particularly between recent estimates and those from 10 or more years prior, should be made with caution due to potential reporting and other biases.
[a]The numerator of each rate is the number of persons in the age group who first used the drug in the year, while the denominator is the person-time exposure of persons in the age group measured in thousands of years.
[b]Estimated using 2003 data only.

SOURCE: "Table G.32. Numbers (in Thousands) of Persons Who First Used Cocaine in the United States, Their Mean Age at First Use, and Rates of First Use (Per 1,000 Person-Years of Exposure): 1965–2002, Based on 2002 and 2003 NSDUHs," in *Results from the 2003 National Survey on Drug Use and Health: National Findings*, U.S. Department of Health and Human Services, Substance Abuse and Mental Health Services Administration, Office of Applied Studies, September 2004, http://www.oas.samhsa.gov/nhsda/2k3nsduh/2k3ResultsW.pdf (accessed February 10, 2005)

The demographic underpinning is suggested by the age of members of the baby boom generation at the 1973 peak of marijuana experimentation and the age of the so-called "baby boom echo" (children of the baby boom) in 2000. A large percentage of the boomers (born between 1945 and 1960) were between sixteen and twenty-five years of age in the mid-1970s; at around forty million strong, this was the largest single group of this age ever in America ("Live Births by Age of Mother and Race: United States, 1933–98," Washington, DC: National Center for Health Statistics, http://www.cdc.gov/nchs/data/natality/mage33tr.pdf).

The second peak in this series (in 2000) suggests that the children of those who experimented in the 1970s were now doing the same thing. In 2000 the youngest boomers were forty and the oldest fifty-five, and all were of an age to have teenagers in the house or away in college.

With the passage of time during this thirty-seven-year period, the younger age group also became more important. Experimentation is driven by the under-eighteen age group. (See Figure 3.1.) SAMHSA also calculates the average age of the initial users. The general trend over time has been that those trying marijuana are younger and younger on average. The average age in the late 1960s was about nineteen; the average age in 2002 was 17.2.

Cocaine

Data on the incidence of cocaine use produce a different pattern in the 1965–2002 period. (See Table 3.1.) The number of initial users reached its peak in 1980 (1.56 million), seven years after the first marijuana peak.

Cocaine is used by an older age group. The average age of cocaine initiates was around twenty-two years in the early 1980s, rose to about twenty-three in the late 1980s, then declined to about twenty-one by the late 1990s. The average age of initiates in 2002 was 20.3 years.

Until the mid-1980s cocaine was a relatively expensive powdered drug snorted by well-off users at parties. The much cheaper crack cocaine, which could be smoked, appeared early in the 1980s but did not reach mass distribution until some years later.

Hallucinogens, Inhalants, and Prescription Drugs

Demographics underlie but do not entirely explain the incidence of drug use. The availability of drugs, their cost, the emergence of new varieties, the dangers associated with the drug (and the spread of information about such dangers) all have a bearing. Hallucinogens, inhalants, and psychotropic medications used in nonmedical settings have similar usage patterns.

HALLUCINOGENS. Drugs that produce hallucinations reached their first-use peak in 2001. (See Figure 3.2.) The best known and most commonly used of these drugs is LSD (as measured in prevalence). The two other hallucinogens tracked by SAMHSA are PCP and Ecstasy (MDMA). In 2001, according to SAMHSA's 2003 report, 1.6 million people first took a hallucinogenic drug. The earlier peak in usage came in 1972, around the same time marijuana reached its highest incidence.

INHALANTS. Substances intended for other purposes but inhaled for an effect include glue, gasoline, paint, and turpentine. Inhalant first use increased during the 1990s, with teenagers generally fueling the trend. Though a fairly steady group of eighteen- to twenty-year-olds has continued to join the inhalers over the past four decades, the growth in incidents has been driven mainly by the younger grouping of those twelve to seventeen. More than half (52%) of those who sniffed such items in 1978 were twelve to seventeen. According to the SAMHSA's 2003 report, in 2002 about one million people tried inhalants for the first time. As in the past, this group was dominated by those under eighteen, representing 78% of new users.

PRESCRIPTION DRUGS. SAMHSA data show that use of prescription-type pain relievers as recreational drugs rather than for medical purposes has slowly risen from 1965 to 1995, after which it dramatically rose. Similar trends are seen for other prescription drugs, such as tranquilizers, stimulants, and sedatives. Incidence of these drugs reached early peaks in the mid- to late 1970s. All but the sedatives reached new highs since 2000, with pain relievers leading the way. The average age of those using pain relievers was twenty-two in 2002, according to SAMHSA's 2003 report. About 2.5 million new people tried prescription pain relievers each year from 2000 to 2002.

Incidence of Heroin Use

People who try heroin for the first time are, on average, the oldest "drug experimenters." According to a previous SAMHSA report, in the 1965–2000 period the average age of initial heroin users was 22.8 years. In the 1980–2000 period the average was 24.8, and in the 1990–2000 period it was 25.4. The users also represent the

FIGURE 3.2

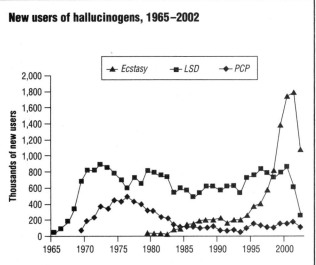

New users of hallucinogens, 1965–2002

SOURCE: "Figure 5.2. Annual Numbers of New Users of Ecstasy, LSD, and PCP: 1965–2002," in *Results from the 2003 National Survey on Drug Use and Health: National Findings*, U.S. Department of Health and Human Services, Substance Abuse and Mental Health Services Administration, Office of Applied Studies, 2004, http://www.oas.samhsa.gov/nhsda/2k3nsduh/2k3ResultsW.pdf (accessed February 10, 2005)

smallest number of people who try a drug. The 2003 SAMHSA study reports that from 1995 to 2002 the annual number of new heroin users ranged from 121,000 to 164,000. Incidence reporting on heroin may be the least reliable because of social bias associated with heroin addicts and because many addicts die and thus do not participate in SAMHSA's household surveys that look back on the 1960s and 1970s.

TRENDS IN PREVALENCE

The prevalence of drug use is tracked by SAMHSA in its *National Survey* and by the Drug Abuse Warning Network (DAWN), also sponsored by SAMHSA, which collects data from the emergency departments of the nation's hospitals. DAWN also collects drug-related mortality data, as does the National Center for Health Statistics, another element of the U.S. Department of Health and Human Services. Data from these sources are presented here. A discussion of different groupings of drug users (pregnant women, youths, the working population, military people, and persons arrested) is presented in Chapter 4.

The findings of SAMHSA's *National Survey* will be explored in this section, and the other surveys will be discussed separately below. The *National Survey* divides illicit drug use responses into three categories: lifetime use, past year use, and current use. Current use is defined as use of a drug within the last month. Data for the 1979 to 2001 period, by age groups, are shown in Table 3.2. Comparing 1979 with 1998 data (the period before the sampling redesign took effect) shows that for all ages and

TABLE 3.2

Illicit drug use, 1979–2001

Age of respondent and recency of drug use	1979	1985	1988	1990	1993	1996	1998	Change 1993 to 1998	1999*	2000*	2001*	Change 1999 to 2001
12–17												
Ever	31.8%	27.4%	22.8%	20.9%	16.4%	22.1%	21.3%		27.6%	26.9%	28.4%	
Past year	24.3	20.7	14.9	14.1	11.9	16.7	16.4		19.8	18.6	20.8	
Past 30 days	16.3	13.2	8.1	7.1	5.7	9.0	9.9	4.2	9.8	9.7	10.8	1.0
18–25												
Ever	69.0%	62.9%	58.1%	54.9%	50.2%	48.0%	48.1%		52.6%	51.2%	55.6%	
Past year	45.5	37.4	29.1	26.1	24.2	26.8	27.4		29.1	27.9	31.9	
Past 30 days	38.0	25.3	17.9	15.0	13.6	15.6	16.1	2.5	16.4	15.9	18.8	2.4
26–34												
Ever	49.0%	59.5%	61.2%	59.8%	58.2%	53.1%	50.6%		53.2%	50.9%	53.3%	
Past year	23.0	26.2	19.1	18.4	14.6	14.6	12.7		13.5	13.4	16.1	
Past 30 days	20.8	23.1	14.7	10.9	9.5	8.4	7.0	−2.5	6.8	7.8	8.8	2.0
35 and older												
Ever	11.8%	18.1%	20.0%	22.5%	26.1%	29.0%	31.8%		35.7%	35.5%	38.4%	
Past year	3.9	5.5	5.1	5.2	5.5	5.3	5.5		5.9	5.5	6.3	
Past 30 days	2.8	3.9	2.3	3.1	3.0	2.9	3.3	0.3	3.4	3.3	3.5	0.1
All ages 12 and older												
Ever	31.3%	34.4%	34.0%	34.2%	34.2%	34.8%	35.8%		39.7%	38.9%	41.7%	
Past year	17.5	16.3	12.4	11.7	10.3	10.8	10.6		11.5	11.0	12.6	
Past 30 days	14.1	12.1	7.7	6.7	5.9	6.1	6.2	0.3	6.2	6.3	7.1	0.8

Note: Any illicit drug use includes use of marijuana, cocaine, hallucinogens, inhalants, heroin, or nonmedical use of sedatives, tranquilizers, stimulants, or analgesics. Prior to 1979, data were not totaled for overall drug use and instead were published by specific drug type only.
*Changes made to the design and execution of National Household Survey of Drug Abuse (NHSDA) in 1999 make the 1999, 2000, and 2001 data incomparable to previous years. However, 1999, 2000, and 2001 data are comparable to each other.

SOURCE: Adapted from "Table 1. Trends on the Percentage of Persons Reporting Any Illicit Drug Use: 1979–2001," in *Drug Use Trends*, Fact Sheet, Office of National Drug Control Policy, Executive Office of the President, October 2002

for any illicit drug, lifetime use of drugs increased from 31.3% of the population in 1979 to nearly 36% in 1998. Past year use dropped from 17.5 to 10.6% of the population, and current use (in the past month) dropped from 14.1% to 6.2% in this period. Results between 1999 and 2001 indicate a change in this pattern: drug prevalence showed an increase in the more recent period—most likely because incidence of drug use went up in the early 1990s and was now beginning to be mirrored in prevalence after a lag in time.

Looking at results for the 1999–2001 period, the biggest increases in current use were among those aged eighteen to twenty-five, up 2.4%, and the next highest increase was among those aged twenty-six to thirty-four, up two percentage points. Respondents aged twelve to seventeen had an increase of 1% between 1999 and 2001, and those aged thirty-five and older the lowest increase, at 0.1%. Looking back at the previous five years (1993 to 1998), the age group leading growth was the youngest, increasing in current use from 5.7 to 9.9%, up 4.2%; next were those aged eighteen to twenty-five, up 2.5% from 13.6% in 1993 to 16.1% in 1998. Those aged twenty-six to thirty-four saw a decline of 2.5 points from 9.5% to 7%. Those in the oldest group registered a small increase of 0.3%.

Figure 3.3 shows current drug use by age group for 2003. Those aged eighteen to twenty reported the highest current illicit drug use, at 23.3%, followed by those in the sixteen to seventeen age range, at 19.2%, and those in the twenty-one to twenty-five range, at 18.3%. Table 3.3 and Table 3.4 show that illicit drug use among persons aged twelve and over continued to increase in 2002 and 2003, both in terms of total number and percentage. In 2003, 46.4% of respondents reported that they had used some illicit drug in their lifetime.

Current use prevalence patterns for "any illicit drug" and for marijuana, cocaine, and heroin are shown in Figure 3.4, with more recent data in percentage terms shown in Figure 3.5. While current use of all drugs generally decreased from 1979 forward, cocaine's prevalence rose after 1979 and reached a peak in 1985, two years after it had reached its "first use" peak. SAMHSA does not claim hard-and-fast correlations between incidence and prevalence, but the agency points out that peaks in prevalence tend to follow peaks in incidence by some two or three years.

In 1979, 25.4 million people aged twelve years and older were using drugs. (See Figure 3.4.) The lowest point was reached in 1992, when current users dropped to twelve million individuals. By 2003, current users had increased substantially again to about 19.5 million. (See Table 3.3.) Expressed as percentages of the total population, these numbers were 14.1% in 1979, 5.8% in 1992, and

FIGURE 3.3

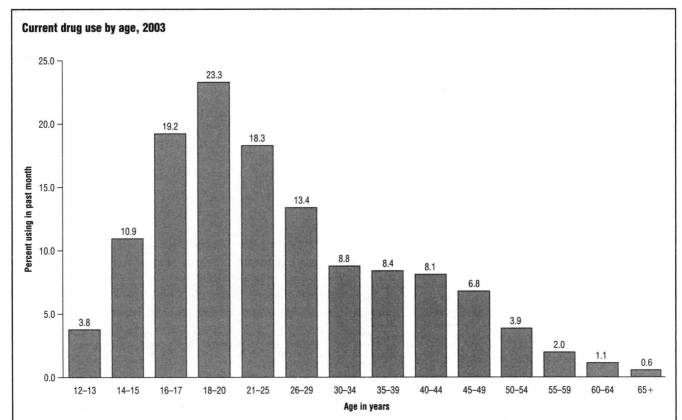

Current drug use by age, 2003

SOURCE: "Figure 2.5. Past Month Illicit Drug Use, by Age: 2003," in *Results from the 2003 National Survey on Drug Use and Health: National Findings*, U.S. Department of Health and Human Services, Substance Abuse and Mental Health Services Administration, Office of Applied Studies, 2004, http://www.oas.samhsa.gov/nhsda/2k3nsduh/2k3ResultsW.pdf (accessed February 10, 2005)

8.2% in 2003, according to SAMHSA. Current use rises and falls as a percentage of population, but lifetime usage has simply increased over the years. SAMHSA reports that in 1979, 70.2 million people had used drugs in their lifetime (31.3% of the 1979 population). In 2003, more than 110 million people had used a drug sometime in their lives (46.4% of the 2003 population).

Any Illicit Drug

By age group in 2003, eighteen- to twenty-five-year-olds used drugs more than any other age group—in their lifetime, in the past year, and in the past month. (See Table 3.5.) Next came those aged twelve to seventeen in all categories except lifetime. The twenty-six and older age group had the second-highest proportion of lifetime use and the lowest past year and current usage. Males consistently outnumber females among drug users. In lifetime usage, the difference is 9.3 points: 51.2% of males but only 41.9% of females had used drugs in their lifetimes in 2003. Among racial categories, the largest user group was American Indians or Alaska Natives: 62.4% of this group had used drugs in their lifetimes. Those reporting being of more than one race were second (60.1% lifetime use). More whites (49.2%) than African-Americans (44.6%) reported ever having used drugs. For use within the last

year, that pattern has now reversed: 14.9% of whites and 15.4% of African-Americans reported use. For current use (within the last month), slightly more African-Americans (8.7%) had used drugs than whites (8.3%). Nearly all of these percentages are higher than they were reported two years earlier by SAMHSA.

Drug-by-Drug

The SAMHSA definition of "any illicit drug" covers quite a variety of substances. In terms of prevalence of current use, the most used drug category in 2003 was marijuana and hashish, which 14.6 million people had used in the previous month. (See Table 3.3.) Nearly 4.7 million people took prescription-type pain relievers in nonmedical applications in the previous month. In 2003 another 1.8 million abused tranquilizers in the past month. (Figure 3.6 outlines the number of lifetime nonmedical users taking various brands of pain relievers in 2002 and 2003.) Current cocaine users numbered nearly 2.3 million in 2003; of those, 604,000 smoked crack cocaine. In both cases, cocaine use was up well over the 2000 levels reported by SAMHSA. Hallucinogens represented the next most frequently used illegal drug, listed as currently used by just over one million people in 2003. Ecstasy accounted for nearly half of those users.

TABLE 3.3

Use of illicit drugs among persons aged 12 or older, by type of drug, 2002 and 2003

[Numbers in thousands]

	Time period					
	Lifetime		Past year		Past month	
Drug	2002	2003	2002	2003	2002	2003
Any illicit drug[a]	108,255	110,205	35,132	34,993	19,522	19,470
Marijuana and hashish	94,946	96,611	25,755	25,231	14,584	14,638
Cocaine	33,910	34,891	5,902	5,908	2,020	2,281
Crack	8,402	7,949	1,554	1,406	567	604
Heroin	3,668	3,744	404	314	166	119
Hallucinogens	34,314	34,363	4,749[d]	3,936	1,196	1,042
LSD	24,516	24,424	999[d]	558	112	133
PCP	7,418	7,107	235	219	58	56
Ecstasy	10,150	10,904	3,167[d]	2,119	676[c]	470
Inhalants	22,870	22,995	2,084	2,075	635	570
Nonmedical use of any psychotherapeutic[b]	46,558	47,882	14,680	14,986	6,210	6,336
Pain relievers	29,611[c]	31,207	10,992	11,671	4,377	4,693
Tranquilizers	19,267	20,220	4,849	5,051	1,804	1,830
Stimulants	21,072	20,798	3,181[c]	2,751	1,218	1,191
Methamphetamine	12,383	12,303	1,541	1,315	597	607
Sedatives	9,960	9,510	981	831	436	294
Any illicit drug other than marijuana[a]	70,300	71,128	20,423	20,305	8,777	8,849

[a]Any illicit drug includes marijuana/hashish, cocaine (including crack), heroin, hallucinogens, inhalants, or any prescription-type psychotherapeutic used nonmedically. Any illicit drug other than marijuana includes cocaine (including crack), heroin, hallucinogens, inhalants, or any prescription-type psychotherapeutic used nonmedically.
[b]Nonmedical use of any prescription-type pain reliever, tranquilizer, stimulant, or sedative; does not include over-the-counter drugs.
[c]Difference between estimate and 2003 estimate is statistically significant at the 0.05 level.
[d]Difference between estimate and 2003 estimate is statistically significant at the 0.01 level.

SOURCE: "Table G.1. Illicit Drug Use in Lifetime, Past Year, and Past Month among Persons Aged 12 or Older: Numbers in Thousands, 2002 and 2003," in *Results from the 2003 National Survey on Drug Use and Health: National Findings*, U.S. Department of Health and Human Services, Substance Abuse and Mental Health Services Administration, Office of Applied Studies, 2004, http://www.oas.samhsa.gov/nhsda/2k3nsduh/2k3ResultsW.pdf (accessed February 10, 2005)

TABLE 3.4

Percentage of illicit drug use among persons aged 12 or older, by type of drug, 2002 and 2003

[Numbers are percentages]

	Time period					
	Lifetime		Past year		Past month	
Drug	2002	2003	2002	2003	2002	2003
Any illicit drug[a]	46.0	46.4	14.9	14.7	8.3	8.2
Marijuana and hashish	40.4	40.6	11.0	10.6	6.2	6.2
Cocaine	14.4	14.7	2.5	2.5	0.9	1.0
Crack	3.6	3.3	0.7	0.6	0.2	0.3
Heroin	1.6	1.6	0.2	0.1	0.1	0.1
Hallucinogens	14.6	14.5	2.0[d]	1.7	0.5	0.4
LSD	10.4	10.3	0.4[d]	0.2	0.0	0.1
PCP	3.2	3.0	0.1	0.1	0.0	0.0
Ecstasy	4.3	4.6	1.3[d]	0.9	0.3[c]	0.2
Inhalants	9.7	9.7	0.9	0.9	0.3	0.2
Nonmedical use of any psychotherapeutic[b]	19.8	20.1	6.2	6.3	2.6	2.7
Pain relievers	12.6	13.1	4.7	4.9	1.9	2.0
Tranquilizers	8.2	8.5	2.1	2.1	0.8	0.8
Stimulants	9.0	8.8	1.4[c]	1.2	0.5	0.5
Methamphetamine	5.3	5.2	0.7	0.6	0.3	0.3
Sedatives	4.2	4.0	0.4	0.3	0.2	0.1
Any illicit drug other than marijuana[a]	29.9	29.9	8.7	8.5	3.7	3.7

[a]Any illicit drug includes marijuana/hashish, cocaine (including crack), heroin, hallucinogens, inhalants, or any prescription-type psychotherapeutic used nonmedically. Any illicit drug other than marijuana includes cocaine (including crack), heroin, hallucinogens, inhalants, or any prescription-type psychotherapeutic used nonmedically.
[b]Nonmedical use of any prescription-type pain reliever, tranquilizer, stimulant, or sedative; does not include over-the-counter drugs.
[c]Difference between estimate and 2003 estimate is statistically significant at the 0.05 level.
[d]Difference between estimate and 2003 estimate is statistically significant at the 0.01 level.

SOURCE: "Table G.2. Illicit Drug Use in Lifetime, Past Year, and Past Month among Persons Aged 12 or Older: Percentages, 2002 and 2003," in *Results from the 2003 National Survey on Drug Use and Health: National Findings*, U.S. Department of Health and Human Services, Substance Abuse and Mental Health Services Administration, Office of Applied Studies, 2004, http://www.oas.samhsa.gov/nhsda/2k3nsduh/2k3ResultsW.pdf (accessed February 10, 2005)

FIGURE 3.4

Estimated number of current users of selected illegal drugs, 1979–2001

[In thousands]

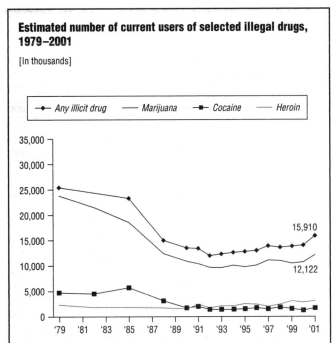

Note: "Any illicit drug use" includes use of marijuana, cocaine, hallucinogens, inhalants (except in 1982), heroin, or nonmedical use of sedatives, tranquilizers, stimulants, or analgesics. The exclusion of inhalants in 1982 is believed to have resulted in underestimates of any illicit use for that year, especially for adolescents. Data for heroin are lifetime users of the drug. In 1999, the survey methodology changed from a paper-and-pencil interview to a computer-assisted interview. Estimates based on the new methodology are not directly comparable to previous years.

SOURCE: Adapted from National Institute on Drug Abuse (1979–1991) and Substance Abuse and Mental Health Services Administration (1992–2001), *National Household Survey on Drug Abuse*, as reported by the Office of National Drug Control Policy, The White House, http://www.whitehousedrugpolicy.gov/publications/policy/ndcs03/table1.html, and population data from U.S. Census Bureau

Also within that category, 133,000 people used LSD in 2003—up slightly from the previous year—and PCP users remained stable at about 56,000 users. Heroin was currently used by the smallest number of people, 119,000 in 2003, declining from 166,000 users in 2002. In both years, users represented 0.1% of the population, or one in a thousand. (See Table 3.4.)

Marijuana

Marijuana remains the most commonly used illicit substance in the United States. It was used by slightly more than 75% of current illicit drug users—either alone or with another illicit drug in 2003. (See Figure 3.7.) Marijuana is almost always smoked in the form of hand-rolled cigarettes or in pipes. Occasionally it is ingested.

Well over a third of the population twelve or older has used marijuana at least once. (See Table 3.4.) In 2003, 40.6%, or 96.6 million people, had used it at least once in their lifetime. The statistics on marijuana mirror those for "any illicit drug" because marijuana is the most commonly used illegal drug and dominates the survey numbers. Use of the plant has been increasing again. Among current users of any illicit drug, more than 1.6 million more people told SAMHSA in 2003 that they had used marijuana in their lifetime than had done so the year before. (See Table 3.3.) SAMHSA reports that African-Americans and whites used marijuana in similar percentages in the last month, but more whites had smoked pot in their lifetimes than African-Americans. Marijuana was least used by Asians and those of Hispanic origin.

FIGURE 3.5

Current use of selected drugs by persons aged 12 or older, 2002 and 2003

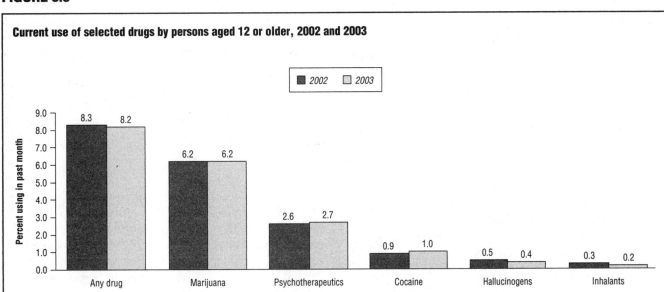

SOURCE: "Figure 2.2. Past Month Use of Selected Illicit Drugs among Persons Aged 12 or Older: 2002 and 2003," in *Results from the 2003 National Survey on Drug Use and Health: National Findings*, U.S. Department of Health and Human Services, Substance Abuse and Mental Health Services Administration, Office of Applied Studies, 2004, http://www.oas.samhsa.gov/nhsda/2k3nsduh/2k3ResultsW.pdf (accessed February 10, 2005)

TABLE 3.5

Use of illicit drugs among persons aged 12 and older, by demographic characteristics, 2002 and 2003

[Numbers are percentages]

Demographic characteristic	Lifetime		Past year		Past month	
	Time period					
	2002	2003	2002	2003	2002	2003
Total	**46.0**	**46.4**	**14.9**	**14.7**	**8.3**	**8.2**
Age						
12–17	30.9	30.5	22.2	21.8	11.6	11.2
18–25	59.8	60.5	35.5	34.6	20.2	20.3
26 or older	45.7	46.1	10.4	10.3	5.8	5.6
Gender						
Male	50.7	51.2	17.6	17.2	10.3	10.0
Female	41.7	41.9	12.5	12.4	6.4	6.5
Hispanic origin and race						
Not Hispanic or Latino	47.0	47.7	14.9	14.7	8.5	8.2
White	48.5	49.2	14.9	14.9	8.5	8.3
Black or African American	43.8	44.6	16.8	15.4	9.7	8.7
American Indian or Alaska Native	58.4	62.4	19.4	18.9	10.1	12.1
Native Hawaiian or other						
Pacific Islander	*	51.0	17.0	18.5	7.9	11.1
Asian	25.6	25.6	7.6	7.1	3.5	3.8
Two or more races	54.0	60.1	20.9	20.1	11.4	12.0
Hispanic or Latino	38.9	37.0	15.0	14.7	7.2	8.0

*Low precision; no estimate reported.
Note: Any illicit drug includes marijuana/hashish, cocaine (including crack), heroin, hallucinogens, inhalants, or any prescription-type psychotherapeutic used nonmedically.

SOURCE: "Table G.7. Any Illicit Drug Use in Lifetime, Past Year, and Past Month among Persons Aged 12 or Older, by Demographic Characteristics: Percentages, 2002 and 2003," in *Results from the 2003 National Survey on Drug Use and Health: National Findings*, U.S. Department of Health and Human Services, Substance Abuse and Mental Health Services Administration, Office of Applied Studies, 2004, http://www.oas.samhsa.gov/nhsda/2k3nsduh/2k3ResultsW.pdf (accessed February 10, 2005).

Cocaine

Cocaine is usually sniffed or "snorted." The drug enters the body through the mucous membranes of the nose. It can also be injected or smoked, and it is sometimes used in conjunction with other drugs. The most popular and notorious combination of cocaine and another illegal drug is the "speedball," a dangerous mixture of heroin and cocaine. Crack is a purified, smokable form of cocaine obtained by chemical processing. Its low prices (generally about $5 to $10 per dose) have made this form of cocaine available to all segments of the American population. According to SAMHSA, about a fifth of all consumers of cocaine in 2003 smoked crack.

The costs of powdered cocaine and the dangers associated with crack have restricted lifetime use of the drug to 14.7% of the population (34.9 million people in 2003). (See Table 3.3 and Table 3.4.) Current users, some 2.3 million individuals, were two-thirds male according to SAMHSA's 2003 survey. Overall, 1% of those surveyed had used cocaine in the previous month. Those eighteen to twenty-five had the highest current usage rate for cocaine.

Heroin

As shown in Table 3.3, in 2003, 119,000 individuals were current users and 3.7 million reported having used heroin at least once in their lifetime. SAMHSA has not provided additional data on heroin users comparable to those shown for other drugs since 1998—in part because data on such users became less reliable using the new sampling techniques. Even before the methodological change, heroin use was underreported, according to SAMHSA, because users, especially current users, are disinclined to talk to surveyors. Data for 1998 indicate (*NHSDA 1998*, Rockville, MD: SAMHSA, 2000) that a higher percentage of African-Americans had used heroin in their lifetime (1.9%) than whites (1%). Data for use of heroin in the past year was 0.1% of whites and 0.2% of African-Americans. In nearly all other drug categories, a higher percentage of whites used drugs than African-Americans. The highest percentage of current users of heroin were those aged eighteen to twenty-five. Males were 60% of all users.

Hallucinogens, Inhalants, and Psychotherapeutics

About 3.9 million people used hallucinogens in the past year in 2003, down from 4.7 million in 2002. (See Figure 3.8.) Most, according to SAMHSA, were in the youth category dominated by the eighteen- to twenty-five-year segment. American Indians/Alaska Natives generally showed the highest usage measured in percentage, while Asians were usually least involved in use of these drugs.

Lifetime inhalant use leveled off at 9.7% in 2003 (see Table 3.4), after increasing from 7.5% to 8.1% of the

FIGURE 3.6

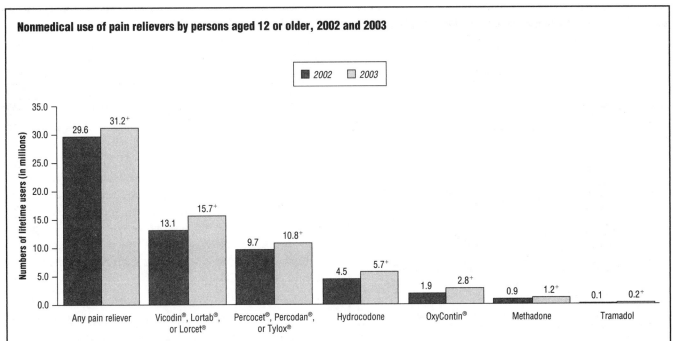

Nonmedical use of pain relievers by persons aged 12 or older, 2002 and 2003

Note: Statistically significant differences (at 0.05 level) between 2002 and 2003 are denoted by "+".

SOURCE: "Figure 2.4. Numbers (in Millions) of Lifetime Nonmedical Users of Selected Pain Relievers among Persons Aged 12 or Older: 2002 and 2003," in *Results from the 2003 National Survey on Drug Use and Health: National Findings*, U.S. Department of Health and Human Services, Substance Abuse and Mental Health Services Administration, Office of Applied Studies, 2004, http://www.oas.samhsa.gov/nhsda/2k3nsduh/2k3ResultsW.pdf (accessed February 10, 2005)

FIGURE 3.7

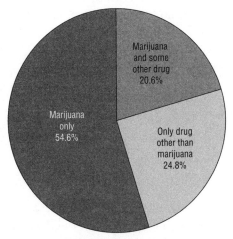

Types of drugs currently used by persons aged 12 and over, 2003

19.5 million illicit drug users

SOURCE: "Figure 2.1. Types of Drugs Used by Past Month Illicit Drug Users Aged 12 or Older: 2003," in *Results from the 2003 National Survey on Drug Use and Health: National Findings*, U.S. Department of Health and Human Services, Substance Abuse and Mental Health Services Administration, Office of Applied Studies, 2004, http://www.oas.samhsa.gov/nhsda/2k3nsduh/2k3ResultsW.pdf (accessed February 10, 2005)

population from 2000 to 2001, according to SAMHSA. Whites were more likely to have used inhalants in their lifetimes than African-Americans. The largest percentages were among American Indians/Alaska Natives and those of more than one race. Past year inhalant use also remained stable between 2002 and 2003, at 0.9%. Among those using inhalants currently, the leading age group was the youngest (twelve to seventeen).

In 2003 some 6.3 million individuals had used prescription medicines in the past month for other than medical purposes (see Table 3.3), those in the eighteen to twenty-five age group more predominantly than those younger or older. In this single category of drug use, female participation in current use was nearly the same as the male, according to the 2003 SAMHSA report. For "any illicit drug" in 2003 (current use) females were far less likely than males to participate—6.5%, compared to 10% for males. (See Table 3.5.)

TRENDS IN DRUG EMERGENCIES

Under Section 505 of the Public Health Services Act, SAMHSA is required to collect data on drug episodes as observed in the emergency rooms of the nation's hospitals. The agency does this under a program called the Drug Abuse Warning Network (DAWN). The data collected by DAWN at six-month intervals are not considered to measure prevalence, but the sample of hospitals used has been chosen to produce what SAMHSA calls "representative estimates of

FIGURE 3.8

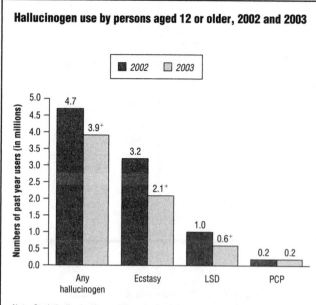

Hallucinogen use by persons aged 12 or older, 2002 and 2003

Note: Statistically significant differences (at 0.05 level) between 2002 and 2003 are denoted by "+".

SOURCE: "Figure 2.3. Numbers (in Millions) of Past Year Users of Selected Hallucinogens among Persons Aged 12 or Older: 2002 and 2003," in *Results from the 2003 National Survey on Drug Use and Health: National Findings,* U.S. Department of Health and Human Services, Substance Abuse and Mental Health Services Administration, Office of Applied Studies, 2004, http://www.oas.samhsa.gov/nhsda/2k3nsduh/2k3ResultsW.pdf (accessed February 10, 2005)

E[mergency] D[epartment] drug episodes and drug mentions for the coterminous United States and for 21 metropolitan areas" (*Emergency Department Trends from the Drug Abuse Warning Network, Preliminary Estimates January–June 2002*, DAWN Series: D-22, DHHS Publication No. [SMA] 03-3779, Rockville, MD: SAMHSA, 2002). What DAWN counts, in other words, are the medical emergencies caused by drugs used alone or in combination. Hospitals report to DAWN the emergency room visits involving conditions of intentional drug abuse, addiction, and suicide attempts. Visits that involve chronic health conditions due to drug abuse are also included, as are intentional abuses of prescription and over-the-counter drugs. But DAWN does not include cases that are simply accidents without intentional abuse of a drug.

Patients counted in DAWN's survey usually mention more than one drug. The average is about two different drugs per visit. About a third of cases also involve the use of some drug used in combination with alcohol. Drug episodes and drug mentions are thus a way of tracking the relative importance of different drugs over time, alone or in combination, in causing distress enough to send people to the hospital. Cocaine, marijuana, heroin, and amphetamines are the leading substances DAWN classifies as "major substances of abuse." In most cases that result in death, the leading drugs as of 2002 were heroin and cocaine—usually used in combination with other drugs and alcohol.

DAWN's most recent data (in Table 3.6) provide selected drug-related emergency room visits from 1995–2002. Almost all of the selected major drugs shown display a rising involvement in episodes during this period, though in some cases the change was not statistically significant. The fastest growing hallucinogenic drug has been Ecstasy; related emergency room visits increased by 856.3% between 1995 and 2002, though they tapered off considerably in the final year of that period. Ecstasy is an unusual synthetic drug in that it combines the effects of a stimulant and of a hallucinogen. As episodes involving Ecstasy were growing, the previous leading hallucinogen in terms of emergency room visits, LSD, declined dramatically. PCP ("angel dust"), the second most important of the synthetic hallucinogens in terms of emergency room visits, has been on the rise in recent years, representing about 3,600 more emergency department visits than Ecstasy in 2002.

Marijuana mentions have nearly tripled between 1995 and 2002, a much greater increase than in mentions of cocaine and heroin. While marijuana is very often mentioned, DAWN reporting points out that a mention does not indicate that a drug is the cause of the emergency episode; in the case of marijuana, other drugs are usually also involved. In fact, there is little if any evidence that marijuana is capable at all of causing a medical emergency on its own.

Two other drugs that showed notable growth in mentions were Ketamine and GHB. GHB (gamma hydroxy butyrate) is a depressant but is known as a strength enhancer and a euphoriant. Ketamine hydrochloride is a dissociative anesthetic; it produces hallucinogenic states and impairs perception. Both drugs are synthetics known as date-rape drugs, because they can be used in incapacitating victims who are then sexually assaulted.

TRENDS IN DRUG-RELATED DEATHS

SAMHSA's DAWN program also collects data on drug-related mortality. The data are collected and published for metropolitan areas and counties. According to DAWN, its locally collected data cannot be used for national estimates of drug abuse-related mortality because, among other reasons, the samples are skewed toward urban areas and are also incomplete. National data, however, are available from the National Center for Health Statistics (NCHS), a part of the Centers for Disease Control and Prevention, an agency of the U.S. Department of Health and Human Services.

According to NCHS data, in 1979 the death rate related to drugs was 3.2 deaths per one hundred thousand of population, or 7,101 total drug deaths, split about evenly by gender. (See Table 3.7.) The death rate and total deaths have been climbing steadily since 1980,

TABLE 3.6

Selected drug-related emergency department visits, 1995–2002

ED trends from DAWN

Drug category	Total 1995	Total 1996	Total 1997	Total 1998	Total 1999	Total 2000	Total 2001	Total 2002	% change* 1995, 2002	% change* 2000, 2002	% change* 2001, 2002
Major substances of abuse	**457,773**	**478,387**	**510,284**	**548,582**	**575,163**	**623,999**	**669,340**	**681,957**	**49.0**		
Alcohol-in-combination	166,897	166,166	171,894	184,989	196,178	204,500	217,940	207,395	24.3		
Cocaine	135,711	152,420	161,083	172,011	168,751	174,881	193,034	199,198	46.8		
Heroin	69,556	72,980	70,712	75,688	82,192	94,804	93,064	93,519	34.5		
Marijuana	45,259	53,770	64,720	76,842	87,068	96,426	110,512	119,472	164.0	23.9	16.6
Amphetamines	9,581	9,772	10,496	12,183	12,496	17,134	18,555	21,644	125.9		
Methamphetamine	15,933	11,002	17,154	11,486	10,447	13,505	14,923	17,696			
MDMA (ecstasy)	421	319	637	1,143	2,850	4,511	5,542	4,026	856.3		
Ketamine	⋯	81	⋯	209	396	263	679	260			
LSD	5,682	4,569	5,219	4,982	5,126	4,016	2,821	891	−84.3	−77.8	−68.4
PCP	5,963	3,441	3,626	3,436	3,663	5,404	6,102	7,648	28.3	41.5	25.3
Miscellaneous hallucinogens	1,463	1,600	1,629	1,849	1,533	1,849	1,788	1,428			
Flunitrazepam (Rohypnol)	⋯	⋯	⋯	⋯	⋯	⋯	⋯	⋯			
GHB	145	638	762	1,282	3,178	4,969	3,340	3,330	2,196.6	−33.0	186.6
Inhalants	736	1,030	1,539	1,735	650	1,141	522	1,496			
Combinations NTA	163	383	201	125	94	127	298	⋯			

*This column denotes statistically significant (p < 0.05) increases and decreases between estimates for the periods noted.

Note: These estimates are based on a representative sample of non-Federal, short-stay hospitals with 24-hour emergency departments in the coterminous U.S. Dots (…) indicate that an estimate with an RSE greater than 50% has been suppressed.

ED=emergency department, GHB=gamma hydroxy butyrate, LSD=lysergic acid diethylamide, MDMA=methylenedioxymethamphetamine, NTA=not tabulated above, PCP=phencyclidine

SOURCE: Adapted from "Table 2.2.0. ED Mentions for Selected Drug Categories, Total ED Drug Episodes and Mentions, and Total ED Visits: Estimates for the Coterminous U.S. by Year," in *Emergency Department Trends from the Drug Abuse Warning Network, Final Estimates 1995–2002*, U.S. Department of Health and Human Services, Substance Abuse and Mental Health Services Administration, Office of Applied Studies, July 2003, http://dawninfo.samhsa.gov/old_dawn/pubs_94_02/edpubs/2002final/files/EDTrendFinal02AllText.pdf (accessed March 8, 2005)

TABLE 3.7

Drug deaths, by sex and race, 1979–2001

Year	Both sexes	Male	Female	White	All non-white	Black
1979	7,101	3,656	3,445	6,116	985	897
1980	6,900	3,771	3,129	5,814	1,086	1,006
1981	7,106	3,835	3,271	5,863	1,243	1,152
1982	7,310	4,130	3,180	5,991	1,319	1,212
1983	7,492	4,145	3,347	6,187	1,305	1,194
1984	7,892	4,640	3,252	6,309	1,583	1,480
1985	8,663	5,342	3,321	6,946	1,717	1,600
1986	9,976	6,284	3,692	7,948	2,028	1,906
1987	9,796	6,146	3,650	7,547	2,249	2,101
1988	10,917	7,004	3,913	8,409	2,508	2,395
1989	10,710	6,895	3,815	8,336	2,374	2,236
1990	9,463	5,897	3,566	7,603	1,860	1,703
1991	10,388	6,593	3,795	8,204	2,184	2,037
1992	11,703	7,766	3,937	9,360	2,343	2,148
1993	13,275	9,052	4,223	10,394	2,881	2,688
1994	13,923	9,491	4,432	10,895	3,028	2,780
1995	14,218	9,909	4,309	11,173	3,045	2,800
1996	14,843	10,093	4,750	11,903	2,940	2,682
1997	15,973	10,991	4,982	12,863	3,110	2,816
1998	16,926	11,462	5,464	13,811	3,115	2,831
1998 ICD-10	20,227	13,697	6,529	16,504	3,722	3,383
1998 ICD-10	19,102	12,873	6,229	15,694	3,408	3,094
2000 ICD-10	19,698	13,125	6,573	16,371	3,327	3,032
2001 ICD-10	21,683	14,244	7,439	18,176	3,507	3,163

Note: In 1999, cause of death coding was revised to ICD-10. Modified figures for 1998 were calculated based on comparability ratios for drug-induced deaths according to ICD-9 and ICD-10. The new coding scheme yields 19.5 percent more drug-induced deaths compared to the old system using 1998 data. The implementaion of ICD-10 represents a break in the trend data.

SOURCE: "Table 26. Number of Deaths from Drug-Induced Causes, by Sex and Race, 1979–2001," in *National Drug Control Strategy: Data Supplement*, The White House, March 2004, http://www.whitehousedrugpolicy.gov/publications/policy/ndcs04/data_suppl_2004.pdf (accessed March 31, 2005)

reaching a record high of 7.2 deaths per one hundred thousand in 2001, an increase of 125%. The total number of drug deaths that year was 21,683.

NCHS death rate measurements are not exclusively restricted to the use of illegal drugs or the use of legal drugs in nonmedical applications. NCHS data also include accidental poisonings and assaults by drugs. The anthrax poisoning deaths of late 2001, for instance, would be included, but documented murders by poisoning would not. The inclusion of accidents and chemical assaults where intent is unknown somewhat weaken the data for tracking drug abuse trends, but the majority of cases are related to the use of drugs.

Another possible explanation for sharply rising drug-related deaths is the increasing use of dangerous new synthetic drugs. Along with heroin and cocaine, death rates are often related to use of the new synthetics, or combinations of these, as shown for instance by DAWN's mortality survey, (*Mortality Data from the Drug Abuse Warning Network, 2002*, Rockville, MD: SAMHSA, January 2004).

According to the above DAWN report, drug-related deaths, more narrowly construed and excluding accidental deaths or "assaults," consist of deaths said to be *induced* by one or more drugs in combination and of deaths that are said to be *drug-related*. In the first case, the person dies of an overdose, for instance; in the second, the drug may be responsible for a terminal medical condition, may have made the individual reckless, or may have brought the person to a psychological state that led to suicide. In the 2002 DAWN mortality survey, in twenty-five out of the thirty-one metropolitan areas studied, drug-induced deaths, such as overdoses, accounted for the majority of the drug-related deaths reported to DAWN. Deaths reported to DAWN, however, are not limited to drug overdoses. Reports also include deaths in which drug abuse was a contributing factor, but not the primary cause. In six of the thirty-one metropolitan areas (Birmingham, Buffalo, Kansas City, Miami, Omaha, and St. Louis), drug-related deaths were more commonly reported than drug-induced deaths.

CHAPTER 4

DRUG USE BY SELECTED POPULATION GROUPS

PREGNANT WOMEN AND UNBORN CHILDREN

Drug use during pregnancy places both mother and infant at risk for serious health problems. A child may become addicted to heroin in its mother's womb—provided the child is born at all (fetal death is a possibility). Cocaine use by the pregnant mother carries similar risks to the fetus and may kill the mother too. LSD use may lead to birth defects. PCP users may have smaller-than-normal babies who later turn out to have poor muscle control. Learning disabilities are associated with children born to pregnant women using cocaine, Ketamine, and Ecstasy. Smoking marijuana may prevent an embryo from attaching to the uterine wall and halt pregnancies. Pregnant women who smoke tobacco and drink alcohol further handicap their unborn child in its development.

The National Institute of Drug Abuse (NIDA) conducted its first national survey of drug use during pregnancy in 1992 by interviewing 2,613 women all over the United States ("NIDA Survey Provides First National Data on Drug Use During Pregnancy," *NIDA Notes*, January/February 1995, http://www.drugabuse.gov/NIDA_Notes/NNVol10N1/NIDASurvey.html). Data projected from this national sample suggested that 221,000 women in 1992 used illegal drugs while pregnant. Of these women, 119,000 had used marijuana and 45,000 had taken cocaine. Substantially larger numbers smoked at some point during their pregnancy (820,000); some 757,000 drank alcohol. Regarding racial/ethnic categories, the NIDA survey found as follows:

Overall, 11.3% of African-American women, 4.4% of white women, and 4.5% of Hispanic women used illicit drugs while pregnant. While African Americans had higher rates of drug use, in terms of actual number of users, most women who took drugs while they were pregnant were white. The survey found that an estimated 113,000 white women, 75,000 African-American women, and 28,000 Hispanic women used illicit drugs during pregnancy.

NIDA's survey was a one-time study not repeated since, but the Substance Abuse and Mental Health Services Administration (SAMHSA) has been collecting similar data annually in its *National Survey on Drug Use and Health* (formerly called the *National Household Survey on Drug Abuse*). The latest survey available, *2003 National Survey on Drug Use and Health (NSDUH)*, was published in September of 2004 (http://www.oas.samhsa.gov/nhsda/2k3nsduh/2k3ResultsW.pdf). Among other things, the survey determines the drug use of pregnant women within the last thirty days of the actual survey date; the data are thus somewhat narrower in definition than those used in the 1992 NIDA study. Data for 1994–2001 are presented in Figure 4.1. The graphic shows that 62,000 pregnant women (2.3% of all pregnant women) had taken some kind of illegal drug in the 1994–95 period (the data are two-year averages). Over time, SAMHSA's observations show a variable rate of drug use by pregnant women, but with a definite upward trend, so that in the 2002–03 time frame 105,000 pregnant women were using drugs, or 4.3% of all pregnant women. (See Table 4.1 and Table 4.2.)

Data for drug use during the 2002–03 period are shown in Table 4.3 for all women, subdivided into total, pregnant, and not pregnant categories by demographic characteristics. The data are for women ranging in age from fifteen to forty-four. Pregnant women in this group are much less likely to be using drugs than women who are not pregnant (4.3% versus 10.4% of those not pregnant). That gap is smallest in the fifteen-to-seventeen age group: 12.8% of those pregnant are involved with drugs versus 16.5% of those who are not pregnant: pregnancy, in this age

FIGURE 4.1

TABLE 4.1

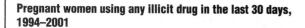

Pregnant women using any illicit drug in the last 30 days, 1994–2001

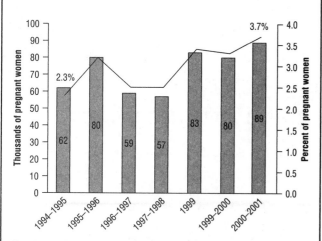

Note: Any illicit drug includes marijuana/hashish, cocaine, heroin, hallucinogens, inhalants, and psychotherapeutic drugs used in a non-medical fashion. Data for all periods except 1999 are averages of two years. The left scale shows the intervals for the bars, the right scale for the curve.

SOURCE: Adapted from "Substance Use among Pregnant Women during 1999 and 2000," in *National Household Survey on Drug Abuse (NHSDA)*, Substance Abuse and Mental Health Services Administration (SAMHSA), May 2002, and "Illicit Drug Use," *2001 NHSDA*, SAMHSA, 2003

Annual average drug use by women, by pregnancy status 2002–03

[Numbers in thousands]

Drug	Total[a]	Pregnancy status	
		Pregnant	Not pregnant
Any illicit drug[b]	6,300	105	6,152
Marijuana and hashish	4,575	86	4,452
Cocaine	601	8	587
Crack	116	1	115
Heroin	34	1	32
Hallucinogens	354	6	344
LSD	35	0	35
PCP	15	2	14
Ecstasy	223	4	217
Inhalants	131	1	130
Nonmedical use of any psychotherapeutic[c]	2,329	30	2,285
Pain relievers	1,630	21	1,596
Tranquilizers	692	5	684
Stimulants	492	7	483
Methamphetamine	207	1	205
Sedatives	124	2	123
Any illicit drug other than marijuana[b]	2,961	35	2,907

[a]Estimates in the total column are for all females aged 15 to 44, including those with unknown pregnancy status.
[b]Any illicit drug includes marijuana/hashish, cocaine (including crack), heroin, hallucinogens, inhalants, or any prescription-type psychotherapeutic used nonmedically. Any illicit drug other than marijuana includes cocaine (including crack), heroin, hallucinogens, inhalants, or any prescription-type psychotherapeutic used nonmedically.
[c]Nonmedical use of any prescription-type pain reliever, tranquilizer, stimulant, or sedative; does not include over-the-counter drugs.

SOURCE: "Table 7.62A. Illicit Drug Use in the Past Month among Females Aged 15 to 44, by Pregnancy Status: Numbers in Thousands, Annual Averages Based on 2002 and 2003 NSDUHs," in *Index for 2003 NSDUH: Detailed Tables*, U.S. Department of Health and Human Services, Substance Abuse and Mental Health Services Administration, Office of Applied Studies, 2004, http://www.oas.samhsa.gov/nhsda/2k3tabs/PDFindex.htm (accessed February 11, 2005)

group, may be the consequence of the same behavioral patterns that lead to drug use. In fact, for the 2000–01 period, according to SAMHSA's report from that year, a higher percentage of pregnant fifteen-to-seventeen-year-olds used drugs than of their nonpregnant peers.

Drug use among pregnant women is highest in the youngest group and decreases with age. Based on averages from SAMHSA's 2002 and 2003 surveys, 12.8% of pregnant women aged fifteen to seventeen had recently used some kind of illegal drug. In the 2002–03 period pregnant African-American women had the highest rates of illicit drug use at 8.0%, compared to 4.4% and 3.0% for whites and Hispanics, respectively. Survey numbers were too imprecise to permit estimates for other races.

Drug use among pregnant women is highest in the first trimester (7.7%) and drops thereafter. Still, an estimated 18,000 women were taking drugs in the third trimester of pregnancy (2.3%).

Marijuana was by far the drug most used by pregnant women on drugs. (See Table 4.1 and Table 4.2.) The next most-used category was psychotherapeutic drugs taken without medical supervision. Within that category, use of pain relievers lead in frequency. The National Institutes of Health has

shown that marijuana use can terminate pregnancies in some cases; marijuana use also leads to low birth weight in babies. In the 2002–03 period, eight thousand pregnant women used cocaine and, of those, one thousand smoked crack. SAMHSA reported one thousand pregnant heroin users, but reporting of heroin use is, according to SAMHSA, least reliable because the survey respondents often withhold such information. Six thousand pregnant women reported using hallucinogens (four thousand of those using Ecstasy) and one thousand said that they had used methamphetamine.

Babies of women who are using cocaine, heroin, hallucinogenics, and methamphetamines are most at risk for major health problems. The Center for the Evaluation of Risks to Human Reproduction, an element of the National Institutes of Health, reports that cocaine use can cause miscarriage or trigger premature labor ("Cocaine Use During Pregnancy" http://cerhr.niehs.nih.gov/genpub/topics/drugs-ccae.html). The

TABLE 4.2

Annual average drug use by pregnant females, 2002–03

[Numbers are percentages]

| Drug | Total[a] | Pregnancy status | |
		Pregnant	Not pregnant
Any illicit drug[b]	10.2	4.3	10.4
Marijuana and hashish	7.4	3.5	7.6
Cocaine	1.0	0.3	1.0
Crack	0.2	0.0	0.2
Heroin	0.1	0.0	0.1
Hallucinogens	0.6	0.3	0.6
LSD	0.1	0.0	0.1
PCP	0.0	0.1	0.0
Ecstasy	0.4	0.1	0.4
Inhalants	0.2	0.0	0.2
Nonmedical use of any psychotherapeutic[c]	3.8	1.2	3.9
Pain relievers	2.6	0.9	2.7
Tranquilizers	1.1	0.2	1.2
Stimulants	0.8	0.3	0.8
Methamphetamine	0.3	0.0	0.3
Sedatives	0.2	0.1	0.2
Any illicit drug other than marijuana[b]	4.8	1.4	4.9

[a]Estimates in the total column are for all females aged 15 to 44, including those with unknown pregnancy status.
[b]Any illicit drug includes marijuana/hashish, cocaine (including crack), heroin, hallucinogens, inhalants, or any prescription-type psychotherapeutic used nonmedically. Any illicit drug other than marijuana includes cocaine (including crack), heroin, hallucinogens, inhalants, or any prescription-type psychotherapeutic used nonmedically.
[c]Nonmedical use of any prescription-type pain reliever, tranquilizer, stimulant, or sedative; does not include over-the-counter drugs.

SOURCE: "Table 7.62B. Illicit Drug Use in the Past Month among Females Aged 15 to 44, by Pregnancy Status: Percentages, Annual Averages Based on 2002 and 2003 NSDUHs," in *Index for 2003 NSDUH: Detailed Tables*, U.S. Department of Health and Human Services, Substance Abuse and Mental Health Services Administration, Office of Applied Studies, 2004, http://www.oas.samhsa.gov/nhsda/2k3tabs/PDFindex.htm (accessed February 11, 2005)

TABLE 4.3

Annual average drug use by pregnant females, by demographic characteristics, 2002–03

[Numbers in percentages]

| Demographic characteristic | Total[a] | Pregnancy status | |
		Pregnant	Not pregnant
Total	**10.2**	**4.3**	**10.4**
Age			
15–17	16.5	12.8	16.5
18–25	16.4	7.5	16.9
26–44	6.8	1.6	7.0
Hispanic origin and race			
Not Hispanic or Latino	10.8	4.7	11.0
White	11.4	4.4	11.6
Black or African American	9.5	8.0	9.4
American Indian or Alaska Native	15.4	*	16.3
Native Hawaiian or other Pacific Islander	12.6	*	12.8
Asian	4.3	*	4.4
Two or more races	15.4	*	15.9
Hispanic or Latino	7.2	3.0	7.4
Trimester[b]			
First	N/A	7.7	N/A
Second	N/A	3.2	N/A
Third	N/A	2.3	N/A

*Low precision; no estimate reported.
N/A: Not applicable.
Note: Any illicit drug includes marijuana/hashish, cocaine (including crack), heroin, hallucinogens, inhalants, or any prescription-type psychotherapeutic used nonmedically.
[a]Estimates in the Total column are for all females aged 15 to 44, including those with unknown pregnancy status.
[b]Pregnant females aged 15 to 44 not reporting trimester were excluded.

SOURCE: "Table 7.63B. Any Illicit Drug Use in the Past Month among Females Aged 15 to 44, by Pregnancy Status and Demographic Characteristics: Percentages, Annual Averages Based on 2002 and 2003 NSDUHs," in *Index for 2003 NSDUH: Detailed Tables*, U.S. Department of Health and Human Services, Substance Abuse and Mental Health Services Administration, Office of Applied Studies, 2004, http://www.oas.samhsa.gov/nhsda/2k3tabs/PDFindex.htm (accessed February 11, 2005)

unborn baby may die or have a stroke or suffer irreversible brain damage. Low birth weight is the consequence of blocked flow of oxygen and nutrients to the fetus; babies may have smaller heads and brains. Birth defects are more likely. Mothers who use cocaine early in the pregnancy, for instance, are five times as likely to give birth to babies with malformed urinary tracts than mothers who do not use the drug.

DRUG USE BY YOUTHS

Drug use may begin before birth, but habituation tends to start in school. Appropriately enough, the nation's most comprehensive survey of drug use in youth is called *Monitoring the Future* (MTF). It is conducted annually by the Institute for Social Research at the University of Michigan under the sponsorship of the National Institute on Drug Abuse. The survey began in 1975 and initially focused on seniors in high school; it was then known as the National High School Senior Survey. Since 1991,

MTF has also surveyed the drug use behavior of eighth and tenth graders and of young adults aged nineteen to twenty-eight. MTF, in effect, surveys drug use in the age categories that use drugs most intensively. The latest MTF chronicles findings from 2004 (http://www.monitoringthefuture.org/pubs/monographs/overview2004.pdf). As shown earlier from data collected by SAMHSA, drug use is principally a youth phenomenon if legal drugs (alcohol and tobacco) are excluded.

Prevalence

A picture of drug use is presented in Figure 4.2 and Figure 4.3 from 1975 to 2003 for high school seniors and from 1991 to 2003 for eighth and tenth graders. The data in Figure 4.3 show the percentage of youths in these categories who used any illicit drug within the last twelve months of each year's survey date. According to the survey, the pattern mirrors that of the population as a whole. Drug use as measured here peaked for seniors in

FIGURE 4.2

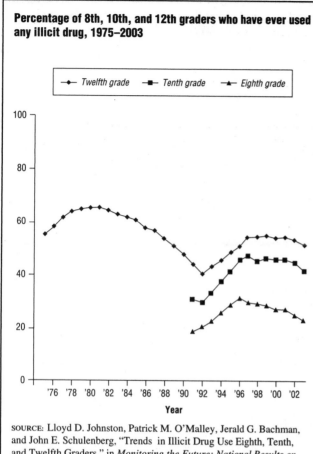

Percentage of 8th, 10th, and 12th graders who have ever used any illicit drug, 1975–2003

Twelfth grade   *Tenth grade*   *Eighth grade*

Year

SOURCE: Lloyd D. Johnston, Patrick M. O'Malley, Jerald G. Bachman, and John E. Schulenberg, "Trends in Illicit Drug Use Eighth, Tenth, and Twelfth Graders," in *Monitoring the Future: National Results on Adolescent Drug Use—Overview of Key Findings, 2003*, The University of Michigan, Institute for Social Research and U.S. Department of Health and Human Services, Public Health Service, National Institutes of Health, National Institute on Drug Abuse, June 2004, http://www.monitoringthefuture.org/pubs/monographs/overview2003.pdf (accessed February 10, 2005)

FIGURE 4.3

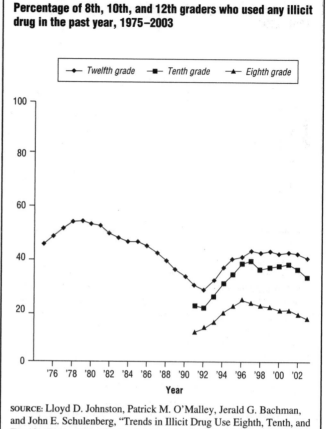

Percentage of 8th, 10th, and 12th graders who used any illicit drug in the past year, 1975–2003

Twelfth grade   *Tenth grade*   *Eighth grade*

Year

SOURCE: Lloyd D. Johnston, Patrick M. O'Malley, Jerald G. Bachman, and John E. Schulenberg, "Trends in Illicit Drug Use Eighth, Tenth, and Twelfth Graders," in *Monitoring the Future: National Results on Adolescent Drug Use—Overview of Key Findings, 2003*, The University of Michigan, Institute for Social Research and U.S. Department of Health and Human Services, Public Health Service, National Institutes of Health, National Institute on Drug Abuse, June 2004, http://www.monitoringthefuture.org/pubs/monographs/overview2003.pdf (accessed February 10, 2005)

1979, when more than half of all seniors (54.2%) used some kind of drug; usage then declined steadily to 1992, when 27.1% of seniors used drugs. Thereafter, usage increased again and reached a second peak for seniors in 1997 (42.4%). Thereafter use of any illicit drugs by seniors has been declining gradually as measured by MTF in 2003.

The White House's 2004 National Drug Control Strategy tracks a similar curve in drug usage by eighth, tenth, and twelfth graders combined, beginning in 1991. Figure 4.4 demonstrates that use of any illicit drug in the past month peaked in 1996 and steadily declined thereafter. MTF also collected data for eighth and tenth graders beginning in 1991. As demonstrated in Figure 4.2 and Figure 4.3, the youngest age group—eighth graders—appears to "lead" usage trends. This group signaled the new increase in drug usage a year before it began for tenth graders and seniors. Eighth graders reached their peak a year

ahead of tenth graders in 1996; since that time eighth-grade use of any illicit drug has been decreasing every year.

Race and Gender

Data for high school seniors, for whom more than a quarter century of observations are available, show that drug use by African-American youths follows the same up-and-down patterns as use by whites and Hispanics, but African-American youths use drugs less than the other two major groups. According to MTF, over the 1977–2003 time frame, using two-year averages, white seniors used illicit drugs more than the other two groups except in 1992, when Hispanic senior drug use matched whites, and in 2000, when Hispanic seniors surpassed whites by 2%.

Male seniors consistently used drugs more than female seniors, but the overall pattern of use was similar

FIGURE 4.4

Percent of secondary school students using illicit drugs, 1991–2003

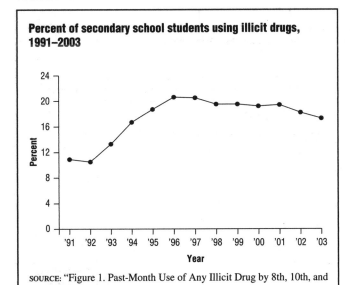

SOURCE: "Figure 1. Past-Month Use of Any Illicit Drug by 8th, 10th, and 12th Graders Combined," in *National Drug Control Strategy: Update*, The White House, March 2004, http://www.whitehousedrugpolicy.gov/ publications/policy/ndcs04/2004ndcs.pdf (accessed March 31, 2005)

FIGURE 4.5

Illicit drug use by high school seniors, by sex, 1975–2003

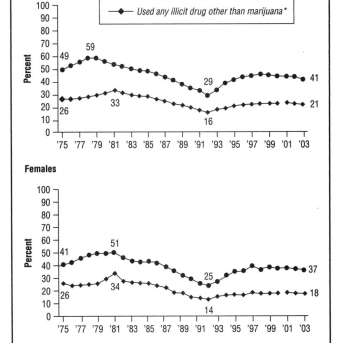

*Beginning in 2001, revised set of questions on other hallucinogen and tranquilizer use were introduced. Data for "any illicit drug other than marijuana" are affected by these changes. From 2001 on, data points are based on the revised questions.

SOURCE: Lloyd D. Johnston, Patrick M. O'Malley, Jerald G. Bachman, and John E. Schulenberg, "Figure 5-7. Trends in Annual Prevalence of an Illicit Drug Use Index for Twelfth Graders by Gender," in *Monitoring the Future: National Survey Results on Drug Use, 1975–2003—Vol. 1: Secondary School Students, 2003*, The University of Michigan, Institute for Social Research and U.S. Department of Health and Human Services, National Institutes of Health, National Institute on Drug Abuse, August 2004, http://www.monitoringthefuture .org/pubs/monographs/vol1_2003.pdf (accessed February 10, 2005)

during the 1975 to 2003 period. (See Figure 4.5.) The difference between females and males was smallest in 1981 (2.8%) and largest in 1978, when 58.6% of males but only 48.7% of females used some illegal drug in the year before, according to data in MTF.

Patterns of Drug Use

Of eighth, tenth, and twelfth graders tracked by the MTF program who had used drugs, more had used marijuana than any other illicit drug in 2003. (See Figure 4.6.) The survey tracks info for those in these grades using various substances from 1991 to 2003. (See Table 4.4.) In 2003, 7.5% of eighth graders had smoked marijuana in the thirty days before the survey; 17.0% of tenth graders had done so, and 21.2% of seniors. The next category of drugs used came at some distance. Among eighth graders, inhalants were sniffed by 4.1%. Among both tenth and twelfth graders, amphetamines were consumed by 4.3 and 5.0%, respectively. About 0.9% of eighth graders, 1.3% of tenth graders, and 2.1% of seniors reported using cocaine. Heroin use was lowest, at 0.3-0.4% of all three groups. Use of marijuana among eighth, tenth, and twelfth graders is demonstrated over the years in Figure 4.7, inhalants in Figure 4.8, cocaine in Figure 4.9, heroin in Figure 4.10, and Ecstasy in Figure 4.11.

The data displayed in Table 4.4 through 2002 are graphed in Figure 4.12 for each age group using the same scale so that both progression over time and the differences between the three age groups can be

assessed at a glance. As noted earlier, 1992 was a low point in general drug use followed by a new upsurge. The graphic begins on the left by showing the last part of the dip down and then the rise, flattening, and downturn of drug use late in the 1991–2002 period. That pattern is observable in all three age groups, with the exception of eighth graders who began to increase drug consumption one year before the older classes.

Comparing the three groups to each other, several things stand out. First is the dramatic rise in marijuana consumption with age, involving about a tenth of the youngest group at its peak year of use, a fifth of the tenth graders, and nearly a quarter of the seniors. Second, in all three of the age groups, use of the other drugs involved no more than 6% of

FIGURE 4.6

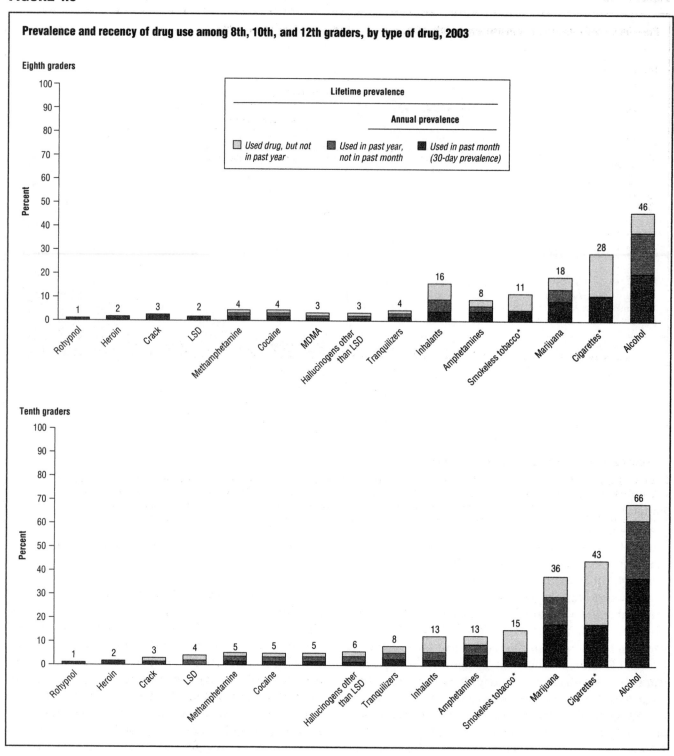

Prevalence and recency of drug use among 8th, 10th, and 12th graders, by type of drug, 2003

the students in each class in 2002. In the eighth grade inhalants were used by almost 5% of the students on average between 1991 and 2002. Among tenth graders, stimulants are the next most-used drugs, at over 5% since 1995. Among seniors, stimulants showed growth from 1991 to 2002. Also, among tenth graders and seniors, cocaine gained in usage over time, increasing between 2001 and 2002, the

only drug category to do so in that year of declining usage of other drugs.

Disapproval

As part of its survey work, MTF also measures its respondents' views of others who take drugs, of respondents' perceptions of the risks involved in using drugs, and their opinion on the ease or difficulty of obtaining drugs.

FIGURE 4.6

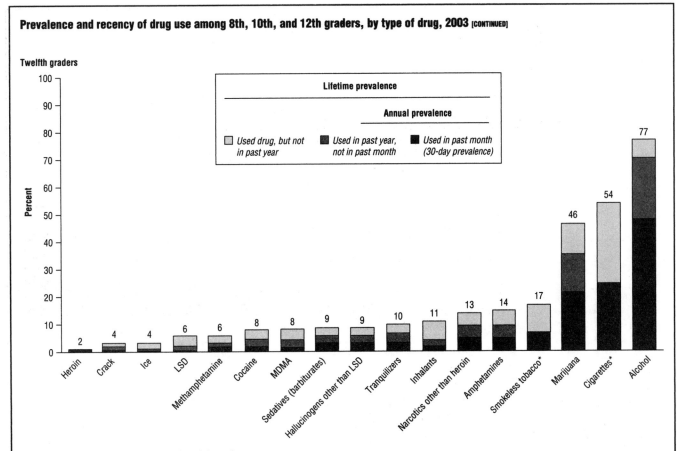

Prevalence and recency of drug use among 8th, 10th, and 12th graders, by type of drug, 2003 [CONTINUED]

*Annual use not measured for cigarettes and smokeless tobacco.

SOURCE: Lloyd D. Johnston, Patrick M. O'Malley, Jerald G. Bachman, and John E. Schulenberg, "Figure 4-1. Prevalence and Recency of Use of Various Types of Drugs for Eighth, Tenth, and Twelfth Graders, 2003," in *Monitoring the Future: National Survey Results on Drug Use, 1975–2003—Vol. 1: Secondary School Students, 2003,* The University of Michigan, Institute for Social Research and U.S. Department of Health and Human Services, National Institutes of Health, National Institute on Drug Abuse, August 2004, http://www.monitoringthefuture.org/pubs/monographs/vol1_2003.pdf (accessed February 10, 2005)

Disapproval ratings—the percentage of those who disapprove of others who use drugs—are the inverse of use. (See Table 4.5.) In 2003, for example, 78.7% of seniors disapproved of those who smoked marijuana regularly. In that year, 21.2% of twelfth graders reported using marijuana or hashish within the last thirty days. (See Table 4.4.) These two percentages, added together, result in 99.9%. Those who do not use the drugs generally disapprove of those who do.

Perceptions of risk (to be discussed below) also appear to influence disapproval ratings; in 2003, among seniors, the lowest disapproval rating was associated with trying marijuana once or twice (53.4% disapproved) and the highest with taking heroin regularly (97.1%). Between 1990 and 2003, disapproval of marijuana use has dropped more than 10% for all categories of use; disapproval of heroin use has remained almost unchanged between 1990 and 2003.

High school students' disapproval ratings for two activities, marijuana smoking and using crack, are shown in Figure 4.13 and Figure 4.14, respectively. Eighth graders' disapproval ratings for marijuana smoking are decisively higher than those of tenth and twelfth graders. Interestingly, eighth graders' disapproval of using crack once or twice is not higher than that of students in later grades—probably reflecting eighth graders' ignorance of risks. But disapproval ratings for crack are uniformly higher than for marijuana.

Risk Perception

In 1991, 83.8% of eighth graders, 82.1% of tenth graders, and 78.6% of seniors said that "great risk" was associated with smoking marijuana regularly, according to MTF. Only 5.2 points separated the risk ratings of twelfth graders from those of eighth graders. Twelve years later, the "great risk" ratings of eighth, tenth, and twelfth graders were 74.2, 63.9, and 54.9%

TABLE 4.4

Prevalence of drug use within previous month among 8th, 10th, and 12th graders, by type of drug, 1991–2003

	1991	1992	1993	1994	1995	1996	1997	1998	1999	2000	2001	2002	2003	'02–'03 change
Any illicit drug														
8th grade	5.7	6.8	8.4	10.9	12.4	14.6	12.9	12.1	12.2	11.9	11.7	10.4	9.7	-0.7
10th grade	11.6	11.0	14.0	18.5	20.2	23.2	23.0	21.5	22.1	22.5	22.7	20.8	19.5	-1.3
12th grade	16.4	14.4	18.3	21.9	23.8	24.6	26.2	25.6	25.9	24.9	25.7	25.4	24.1	-1.2
Any illicit drug other than marijuana														
8th grade	3.8	4.7	5.3	5.6	6.5	6.9	6.0	5.5	5.5	5.6‡	5.5	4.7	4.7	0.0
10th grade	5.5	5.7	6.5	7.1	8.9	8.9	8.8	8.6	8.6	8.5‡	8.7	8.1	6.9	-1.2s
12th grade	7.1	6.3	7.9	8.8	10.0	9.5	10.7	10.7	10.4	10.4‡	11.0	11.8	10.4	-1.0
Any illicit drug including inhalants														
8th grade	8.8	10.0	12.0	14.3	16.1	17.5	16.0	14.9	15.1	14.4	14.0	12.6	12.1	-0.6
10th grade	13.1	12.6	15.5	20.0	21.6	24.5	24.1	22.5	23.1	23.6	23.6	21.7	20.5	-1.2
12th grade	17.8	15.5	19.3	23.0	24.8	25.5	26.9	26.6	26.4	26.4	26.5	25.9	24.6	-1.3
Marijuana/hashish														
8th grade	3.2	3.7	5.1	7.8	9.1	11.3	10.2	9.7	9.7	9.1	9.2	8.3	7.5	-0.8
10th grade	8.7	8.1	10.9	15.8	17.2	20.4	20.5	18.7	19.4	19.7	19.8	17.8	17.0	-0.8
12th grade	13.8	11.9	15.5	19.0	21.2	21.9	23.7	22.8	23.1	21.6	22.4	21.5	21.2	-0.3
Inhalants														
8th grade	4.4	4.7	5.4	5.6	6.1	5.8	5.6	4.8	5.0	4.5	4.0	3.8	4.1	+0.3
10th grade	2.7	2.7	3.3	3.6	3.5	3.3	3.0	2.9	2.6	2.6	2.4	2.4	2.2	-0.1
12th grade	2.4	2.3	2.5	2.7	3.2	2.5	2.5	2.3	2.0	2.2	1.7	1.5	1.5	+0.1
Nitrites														
8th grade	—	—	—	—	—	—	—	—	—	—	—	—	—	—
10th grade	—	—	—	—	—	—	—	—	—	—	—	—	—	—
12th grade	0.4	0.3	0.6	0.4	0.4	0.7	0.7	1.0	0.4	0.3	0.5	0.6	0.7	+0.1
Hallucinogens														
8th grade	0.8	1.1	1.2	1.3	1.7	1.9	1.8	1.4	1.3	1.2‡	1.6	1.2	1.2	-0.1
10th grade	1.6	1.8	1.9	2.4	3.3	2.8	3.3	3.2	2.9	2.3‡	2.1	1.6	1.5	-0.2
12th grade	2.2	2.1	2.7	3.1	4.4	3.5	3.9	3.8	3.5	2.6‡	3.3	2.3	1.8	-0.5
LSD														
8th grade	0.6	0.9	1.0	1.1	1.4	1.5	1.5	1.1	1.1	1.0	1.0	0.7	0.6	-0.1
10th grade	1.5	1.6	1.6	2.0	3.0	2.4	2.8	2.7	2.3	1.6	1.5	0.7	0.6	-0.1
12th grade	1.9	2.0	2.4	2.6	4.0	2.5	3.1	3.2	2.7	1.6	2.3	0.7	0.6	-0.1
Hallucinogens other than LSD														
8th grade	0.3	0.4	0.5	0.7	0.8	0.9	0.7	0.7	0.6	0.6‡	1.1	1.0	1.0	0.0
10th grade	0.4	0.5	0.7	1.0	1.0	1.0	1.2	1.4	1.2	1.2‡	1.4	1.4	1.2	-0.2
12th grade	0.7	0.5	0.8	1.2	1.2	1.6	1.7	1.6	1.6	1.7‡	1.9	2.0	1.5	-0.5ss

TABLE 4.4

Prevalence of drug use within previous month among 8th, 10th, and 12th graders, by type of drug, 1991–2003 [CONTINUED]

	1991	1992	1993	1994	1995	1996	1997	1998	1999	2000	2001	2002	2003	'02–'03 change
PCP														
8th grade	—	—	—	—	—	—	—	—	—	—	—	—	—	—
10th grade	—	—	—	—	—	—	—	—	—	—	—	—	—	—
12th grade	0.5	0.6	1.0	0.7	0.6	1.3	0.7	1.0	0.8	0.9	0.5	0.4	0.6	+0.2
MDMA (Ecstasy)														
8th grade	—	—	—	—	—	1.0	1.0	0.9	0.8	1.4	1.8	1.4	0.7	−0.7sss
10th grade	—	—	—	—	—	1.8	1.3	1.3	1.8	2.6	2.6	1.8	1.1	−0.7ss
12th grade	—	—	—	—	—	2.0	1.6	1.5	2.5	3.6	2.8	2.4	1.3	−1.1sss
Cocaine														
8th grade	0.5	0.7	0.7	1.0	1.2	1.3	1.1	1.4	1.3	1.2	1.2	1.1	0.9	−0.2
10th grade	0.7	0.7	0.9	1.2	1.7	1.7	2.0	2.1	1.8	1.8	1.3	1.6	1.3	−0.3
12th grade	1.4	1.3	1.3	1.5	1.8	2.0	2.3	2.4	2.6	2.1	2.1	2.3	2.1	−0.2
Crack														
8th grade	0.3	0.5	0.4	0.7	0.7	0.8	0.7	0.9	0.8	0.8	0.8	0.8	0.7	−0.1
10th grade	0.3	0.4	0.5	0.6	0.9	0.8	0.9	1.1	0.8	0.9	0.7	1.0	0.7	−0.2s
12th grade	0.7	0.6	0.7	0.8	1.0	1.0	0.9	1.0	1.1	1.0	1.1	1.2	0.9	−0.3
Other cocaine														
8th grade	0.5	0.5	0.6	0.9	1.0	1.0	0.8	1.0	1.1	0.9	0.9	0.8	0.7	−0.2
10th grade	0.6	0.6	0.7	1.0	1.4	1.3	1.6	1.8	1.6	1.6	1.2	1.3	1.1	−0.3
12th grade	1.2	1.0	1.2	1.3	1.3	1.6	2.0	2.0	2.5	1.7	1.8	1.9	1.8	−0.1
Heroin														
8th grade	0.3	0.4	0.4	0.6	0.6	0.7	0.6	0.6	0.6	0.5	0.6	0.5	0.4	0.0
10th grade	0.2	0.2	0.3	0.4	0.6	0.5	0.6	0.7	0.7	0.5	0.3	0.5	0.3	−0.2
12th grade	0.2	0.3	0.2	0.3	0.6	0.5	0.5	0.5	0.5	0.7	0.4	0.5	0.4	−0.1
With a needle														
8th grade	—	—	—	—	0.4	0.5	0.4	0.5	0.4	0.3	0.4	0.3	0.3	0.0
10th grade	—	—	—	—	0.3	0.3	0.3	0.4	0.3	0.3	0.2	0.3	0.2	−0.1
12th grade	—	—	—	—	0.3	0.4	0.3	0.2	0.2	0.2	0.2	0.3	0.3	0.0
Without a needle														
8th grade	—	—	—	—	0.3	0.4	0.4	0.3	0.4	0.3	0.4	0.3	0.3	−0.1
10th grade	—	—	—	—	0.3	0.3	0.4	0.5	0.5	0.4	0.2	0.4	0.2	−0.1
12th grade	—	—	—	—	0.6	0.4	0.6	0.4	0.4	0.7	0.3	0.5	0.4	0.0
Other narcotics														
8th grade	—	—	—	—	—	—	—	—	—	—	—	—	—	—
10th grade	—	—	—	—	—	—	—	—	—	—	—	—	—	—
12th grade	1.1	1.2	1.3	1.5	1.8	2.0	2.3	2.4	2.6	2.9	3.0‡	4.0	4.1	+0.2
OxyContin														
8th grade	—	—	—	—	—	—	—	—	—	—	—	—	—	—
10th grade	—	—	—	—	—	—	—	—	—	—	—	—	—	—
12th grade	—	—	—	—	—	—	—	—	—	—	—	—	—	—

TABLE 4.4

Prevalence of drug use within previous month among 8th, 10th, and 12th graders, by type of drug, 1991–2003 [CONTINUED]

	1991	1992	1993	1994	1995	1996	1997	1998	1999	2000	2001	2002	2003	'02–'03 change
Vicodin														
8th grade	—	—	—	—	—	—	—	—	—	—	—	—	—	—
10th grade	—	—	—	—	—	—	—	—	—	—	—	—	—	—
12th grade	—	—	—	—	—	—	—	—	—	—	—	—	—	—
Amphetamines														
8th grade	2.6	3.3	3.6	3.6	4.2	4.6	3.8	3.3	3.4	3.4	3.2	2.8	2.7	−0.1
10th grade	3.3	3.6	4.3	4.5	5.3	5.5	5.1	5.1	5.0	5.4	5.6	5.2	4.3	−0.9ss
12th grade	3.2	2.8	3.7	4.0	4.0	4.1	4.8	4.6	4.5	5.0	5.6	5.5	5.0	−0.5
Ritalin														
8th grade	—	—	—	—	—	—	—	—	—	—	—	—	—	—
10th grade	—	—	—	—	—	—	—	—	—	—	—	—	—	—
12th grade	—	—	—	—	—	—	—	—	—	—	—	—	—	—
Methamphetamine														
8th grade	—	—	—	—	—	—	—	—	1.1	0.8	1.3	1.1	1.2	+0.1
10th grade	—	—	—	—	—	—	—	—	1.8	2.0	1.5	1.8	1.4	−0.4
12th grade	—	—	—	—	—	—	—	—	1.7	1.9	1.5	1.7	1.7	+0.1
Ice														
8th grade	—	—	—	—	—	—	—	—	—	—	—	—	—	—
10th grade	—	—	—	—	—	—	—	—	—	—	—	—	—	—
12th grade	0.6	0.5	0.6	0.7	1.1	1.1	0.8	1.2	0.8	1.0	1.1	1.2	0.8	−0.4
Sedatives (barbiturates)														
8th grade	—	—	—	—	—	—	—	—	—	—	—	—	—	—
10th grade	—	—	—	—	—	—	—	—	—	—	—	—	—	—
12th grade	1.4	1.1	1.3	1.7	2.2	2.1	2.1	2.6	2.6	3.0	2.8	3.2	2.9	−0.3
Methaqualone														
8th grade	—	—	—	—	—	—	—	—	—	—	—	—	—	—
10th grade	—	—	—	—	—	—	—	—	—	—	—	—	—	—
12th grade	0.2	0.4	0.1	0.4	0.4	0.6	0.3	0.6	0.4	0.2	0.5	0.3	0.4	0.0
Tranquilizers														
8th grade	0.8	0.8	0.9	1.1	1.2	1.5	1.2	1.2	1.1	1.4‡	1.2	1.2	1.4	+0.3
10th grade	1.2	1.5	1.1	1.5	1.7	1.7	2.2	2.2	2.2	2.5‡	2.9	2.9	2.4	−0.5s
12th grade	1.4	1.0	1.2	1.4	1.8	2.0	1.8	2.4	2.5	2.6‡	2.9	3.3	2.8	−0.5s
Rohypnol														
8th grade	—	—	—	—	—	0.5	0.3	0.4	0.3	0.3	0.4	0.2	0.1	−0.1
10th grade	—	—	—	—	—	0.5	0.5	0.4	0.5	0.4	0.2	0.4	0.2	−0.1
12th grade	—	—	—	—	—	0.5	0.3	0.3	0.3	0.4	0.3	—	—	—
GHB														
8th grade	—	—	—	—	—	—	—	—	—	—	—	—	—	—
10th grade	—	—	—	—	—	—	—	—	—	—	—	—	—	—
12th grade	—	—	—	—	—	—	—	—	—	—	—	—	—	—
Ketamine														
8th grade	—	—	—	—	—	—	—	—	—	—	—	—	—	—
10th grade	—	—	—	—	—	—	—	—	—	—	—	—	—	—
12th grade	—	—	—	—	—	—	—	—	—	—	—	—	—	—

TABLE 4.4

Prevalence of drug use within previous month among 8th, 10th, and 12th graders, by type of drug, 1991–2003 [CONTINUED]

	1991	1992	1993	1994	1995	1996	1997	1998	1999	2000	2001	2002	2003	'02–'03 change
Alcohol any use														
8th grade	25.1	26.1‡	24.3	25.5	24.6	26.2	24.5	23.0	24.0	22.4	21.5	19.6	19.7	+0.1
10th grade	42.8	39.9‡	38.2	39.2	38.8	40.4	40.1	38.8	40.0	41.0	39.0	35.4	35.4	0.0
12th grade	54.0	51.3‡	48.6	50.1	51.3	50.8	52.7	52.0	51.0	50.0	49.8	48.6	47.5	−1.0
Flavored alcoholic beverages ("alcopops")														
8th grade	—	—	—	—	—	—	—	—	—	—	—	—	—	—
1th grade	—	—	—	—	—	—	—	—	—	—	—	—	—	—
12th grade	—	—	—	—	—	—	—	—	—	—	—	—	—	—
Been drunk														
8th grade	7.6	7.5	7.8	8.7	8.3	9.6	8.2	8.4	9.4	8.3	7.7	6.7	6.7	+0.1
10th grade	20.5	18.1	19.8	20.3	20.8	21.3	22.4	21.1	22.5	23.5	21.9	18.3	18.2	−0.1
12th grade	31.6	29.9	28.9	30.8	33.2	31.3	34.2	32.9	32.9	32.3	32.7	30.3	30.9	+0.6
Cigarettes any use														
8th grade	14.3	15.5	16.7	18.6	19.1	21.0	19.4	19.1	17.5	14.6	12.2	10.7	10.2	−0.5
10th grade	20.8	21.5	24.7	25.4	27.9	30.4	29.8	27.6	25.7	23.9	21.3	17.7	16.7	−1.0
12th grade	28.3	27.8	29.9	31.2	33.5	34.0	36.5	35.1	34.6	31.4	29.5	26.7	24.4	−2.3s
Bidis														
8th grade	—	—	—	—	—	—	—	—	—	—	—	—	—	—
10th grade	—	—	—	—	—	—	—	—	—	—	—	—	—	—
12th grade	—	—	—	—	—	—	—	—	—	—	—	—	—	—
Kreteks														
8th grade	—	—	—	—	—	—	—	—	—	—	—	—	—	—
10th grade	—	—	—	—	—	—	—	—	—	—	—	—	—	—
12th grade	—	—	—	—	—	—	—	—	—	—	—	—	—	—
Smokeless tobacco														
8th grade	6.9	7.0	6.6	7.7	7.1	7.1	5.5	4.8	4.5	4.2	4.0	3.3	4.1	+0.9
10th grade	10.0	9.6	10.4	10.5	9.7	8.6	8.9	7.5	6.5	6.1	6.9	6.1	5.3	−0.8
12th grade	—	11.4	10.7	11.1	12.2	9.8	9.7	8.8	8.4	7.6	7.8	6.5	6.7	+0.2
Steroids														
8th grade	0.4	0.5	0.5	0.5	0.6	0.4	0.5	0.5	0.7	0.8	0.7	0.8	0.7	−0.1
10th grade	0.6	0.6	0.5	0.6	0.6	0.5	0.7	0.6	0.9	1.0	0.9	1.0	0.8	−0.3s
12th grade	0.8	0.6	0.7	0.9	0.7	0.7	1.0	1.1	0.9	0.8	1.3	1.4	1.3	−0.1

Note: Level of significance of difference between the two most recent classes: s = .05, ss = .01, sss = .001.

SOURCE: Adapted from Lloyd D. Johnson, Patrick M. O'Malley, Jerald G. Bachman, and John E. Schulenberg, "Table 2. Trends in Annual and 30-Day Prevalence of Use of Various Drugs for Eighth, Tenth, and Twelfth Graders," in *Monitoring the Future: National Results on Adolescent Drug Use—Overview of Key Findings, 2003*, The University of Michigan, Institute for Social Research and U.S. Department of Health and Human Services, Public Health Service, National Institutes of Health, National Institute on Drug Abuse, June 2004, http://www.monitoringthefuture.org/pubs/monographs/overview2003.pdf (accessed February 10, 2005)

FIGURE 4.7

Percentage of 8th, 10th, and 12th graders who used marijuana in the past year, 1975–2003

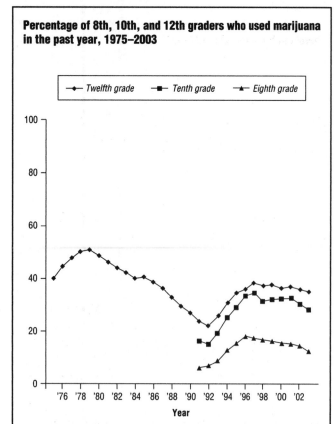

SOURCE: Lloyd D. Johnston, Patrick M. O'Malley, Jerald G. Bachman, and John E. Schulenberg, "Marijuana: Trends in Annual Use, Risk, Disapproval, and Availability, Eighth, Tenth, and Twelfth Graders," in *Monitoring the Future: National Results on Adolescent Drug Use— Overview of Key Findings, 2003*, The University of Michigan, Institute for Social Research and U.S. Department of Health and Human Services, Public Health Service, National Institutes of Health, National Institute on Drug Abuse, June 2004, http://www.monitoringthefuture .org/pubs/monographs/overview2003.pdf (accessed February 10, 2005)

FIGURE 4.8

Percentage of 8th, 10th, and 12th graders who used inhalants in the past year, 1975–2003

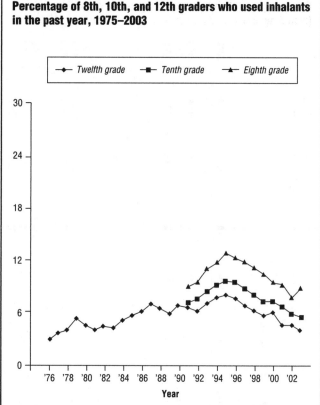

SOURCE: Lloyd D. Johnston, Patrick M. O'Malley, Jerald G. Bachman, and John E. Schulenberg, "Inhalants: Trends in Annual Use, Risk, Disapproval, and Availability, Eighth, Tenth, and Twelfth Graders," in *Monitoring the Future: National Results on Adolescent Drug Use— Overview of Key Findings, 2003*, The University of Michigan, Institute for Social Research and U.S. Department of Health and Human Services, Public Health Service, National Institutes of Health, National Institute on Drug Abuse, June 2004, http://www.monitoringthefuture .org/pubs/monographs/overview2003.pdf (accessed February 10, 2005)

respectively; in 2003, 19.3 points separated eighth graders from seniors. This downward trend in risk perception is shown, along with risk perceptions relating to using cocaine (for twelfth graders only), in Figure 4.15 and Figure 4.16. Cocaine is viewed by youths as more risky. More than 60% of all twelfth-grade students saw great risk in taking it, even if only occasionally.

Availability of Drugs

"How difficult do you think it would be for you to get each of the following types of drugs, if you wanted some?"

The MTF project puts this question to students in its annual survey. The question is followed by a list of substances, including alcohol and cigarettes. According to the 2003 MTF, the two substances students have consistently judged "easy" or "fairly easy" to get have been alcohol and cigarettes, in that order. In 2003 the least

available drug reported by eighth graders was PCP, followed by the crystalline form of methamphetamine ("crystal meth" or "ice"); 13.7% reported that it was easy or fairly easy for them to get this PCP, and 14.1% to get ice. Heroin was least available to tenth graders (19.9% reporting it easy/fairly easy to get). Seniors put amyl and butyl nitrites into the "least available" category; these nitrites are inhalants with intoxicating effects. In 2003, 87.1% of twelfth graders thought that they could easily get marijuana. (See Figure 4.17.)

Trends in availability have been fairly flat during the 1992 to 2003 period as reported by MTF. There are some exceptions. Availability of marijuana shows a slight upward trend, most notably for tenth graders. Among eighth graders, between 45 and 55% of students have reported marijuana easy to get during this time; since 1995, more than 75% of tenth graders and more than 85% of seniors have reported easy access to marijuana.

FIGURE 4.9

FIGURE 4.10

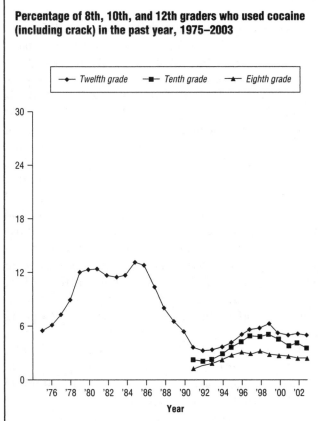

Percentage of 8th, 10th, and 12th graders who used cocaine (including crack) in the past year, 1975–2003

SOURCE: Lloyd D. Johnston, Patrick M. O'Malley, Jerald G. Bachman, and John E. Schulenberg, "Cocaine (Including Crack): Trends in Annual Use, Risk, Disapproval, and Availability, Eighth, Tenth, and Twelfth Graders," in *Monitoring the Future: National Results on Adolescent Drug Use—Overview of Key Findings, 2003*, The University of Michigan, Institute for Social Research and U.S. Department of Health and Human Services, Public Health Service, National Institutes of Health, National Institute on Drug Abuse, June 2004, http://www .monitoringthefuture.org/pubs/monographs/overview2003.pdf) accessed February 10, 2005)

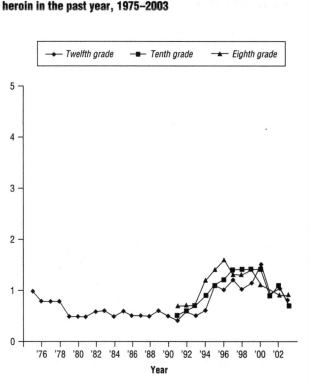

Percentage of 8th, 10th, and 12th grade students who used heroin in the past year, 1975–2003

SOURCE: Lloyd D. Johnston, Patrick M. O'Malley, Jerald G. Bachman, and John E. Schulenberg, "Heroin: Trends in Annual Use, Risk, Disapproval, and Availability, Eighth, Tenth, and Twelfth Graders," in *Monitoring the Future: National Results on Adolescent Drug Use—Overview of Key Findings, 2003*, The University of Michigan, Institute for Social Research and U.S. Department of Health and Human Services, Public Health Service, National Institutes of Health, National Institute on Drug Abuse, June 2004, http://www.monitoringthefuture .org/pubs/monographs/overview2003.pdf (accessed February 10, 2005)

Perceived availability of cocaine powder shows a slight downward trend by each age group tracked by MTF. Over the 1992–2003 period, one in four eighth graders reported it easy to get powdered cocaine, compared with about one in three tenth graders, and just under 45% of seniors. These, of course, are reported perceptions of availability rather than reports of purchases. Only 0.9% of eighth graders and 2.1% of seniors actually reported using cocaine in the most recent thirty days, and, according to MTF, only 3.6% of eighth graders and 7.7% of seniors had ever used cocaine.

DRUGS IN THE WORKPLACE

Drug use in the workplace is tracked by SAMHSA in its national survey that captures the employment status of its survey respondents (http://www.oas.samhsa.gov/ NHSDA/A-11/TOC.htm). The SAMHSA survey is based on self-reporting. The results of drug tests performed on behalf of private and public employers are another lens through which drug use in the workplace can be viewed. Drug testing results are published periodically by Quest Diagnostics Incorporated ("The Drug Testing Index," http://www.questdiagnostics.com/). Quest Diagnostics is the nation's leading provider of drug testing services.

In recent years SAMHSA has collected data by those employed full time, part time, those unemployed, and an "other" category that includes the retired, disabled, homemakers, students, and others to whom the employment/unemployment categories do not apply. Data for the most recent year show (as data in past surveys also consistently show) that the youngest age group in the work-age population, those eighteen to twenty-five, use drugs at higher rates than do those twenty-six years old and older. In this category of users, as in all others, marijuana largely accounted for the majority of uses whereas only small proportions of the population used the more dangerous drugs.

FIGURE 4.11

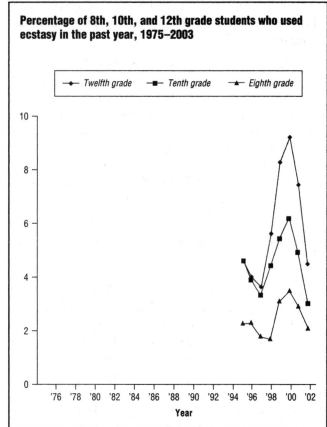

Percentage of 8th, 10th, and 12th grade students who used ecstasy in the past year, 1975–2003

SOURCE: Lloyd D. Johnston, Patrick M. O'Malley, Jerald G. Bachman, and John E. Schulenberg, "MDMA (Ecstasy): Trends in Annual Use, Risk, Disapproval, and Availability, Eighth, Tenth, and Twelfth Graders," in *Monitoring the Future: National Results on Adolescent Drug Use—Overview of Key Findings, 2003*, The University of Michigan, Institute for Social Research and U.S. Department of Health and Human Services, Public Health Service, National Institutes of Health, National Institute on Drug Abuse, June 2004, http://www.monitoringthefuture.org/pubs/monographs/overview2003.pdf (accessed February 10, 2005)

Use rates are higher for part-time workers than full-time workers and highest for the unemployed for the eighteen-to-twenty-five group. In the older age group, the unemployed used drugs at the highest rates as well, but those in the older age group were less likely to have used drugs overall.

Table 4.6 and Table 4.7 provide data on drug use and employment status. In 2003 nearly two-thirds of full-time workers ages eighteen to twenty-five had used illicit drugs in their lifetime, and about one-third in that age group had used drugs in the past year. For full-time workers aged twenty-six and older, the figures were 55.7% and 12.2%. The percentages in each employment status category remained relatively stable between 2002 and 2003.

Demographic and Occupational Profile

Using data from the 2000 household survey, SAMHSA completed and published a special analysis showing data for full-time workers aged eighteen to forty-nine by gender, age groups, occupation, and employing sector. (See Table 4.8.)

In 2000 men working full time were 1.5 times more likely to be using drugs than women (past-thirty-days usage) and twice as likely to have been dependent upon or abusing drugs (past-year usage). When the eighteen-to-forty-nine age group is segmented into three groups, drug use is highest among those eighteen to twenty-five (14.9% current use), lower among those twenty-six to thirty-four (7.9%), and lowest among those thirty-five to forty-nine (5.5%)—once more demonstrating that drug use diminishes with age. Within occupational groupings, production, craft, and repair workers had the highest current usage (11.2%) and those practicing some professional specialty had the lowest (4.7%). Executive/administrative occupations were toward the low end (6.5%), and those in the service industry at the higher end (9.7%). By type of industry, people working in construction and mining had the highest rate of drug use, at 12.3%, followed by those in the wholesale and retail sector, at 10.8%. The two lowest rated groups were government employees (3.7% using drugs currently) and those providing professional services (5%).

Drug Testing of Employees

Another view of drug use in the workplace is presented by actual counts of people who tested positive for illicit drugs, known in the testing industry as "positivity rates." People are tested as a condition of employment, periodically, on return to duty, or at random—all such tests based on corporate or government agency policy. People are also tested for cause when behavioral deviations from the norm suggest their involvement with drugs; tests are also performed after accidents. According to the American Management Association's annual survey of workplace medical testing (http://www.amanet.org/research/pdfs/Medical_testing_04.pdf), 61.8% of companies surveyed engaged in employee drug testing in 2004; 54.5% of these companies test new employees, including qualified applicants who have been offered a job pending results of a physical. Under federal law, the U.S. Department of Transportation and the Nuclear Regulatory Commission require the testing of "safety-sensitive" workers; pilots, bus drivers, and truck drivers fall into this category as do people who work in nuclear power plants.

Positivity rates as measured by Quest Diagnostics' 2003 drug testing index have been dropping. (See Table 4.9 and Table 4.10.) In 1988, 13.6% of employees undergoing tests showed positive results. The rate had been nearly halved by 1994 to

FIGURE 4.12

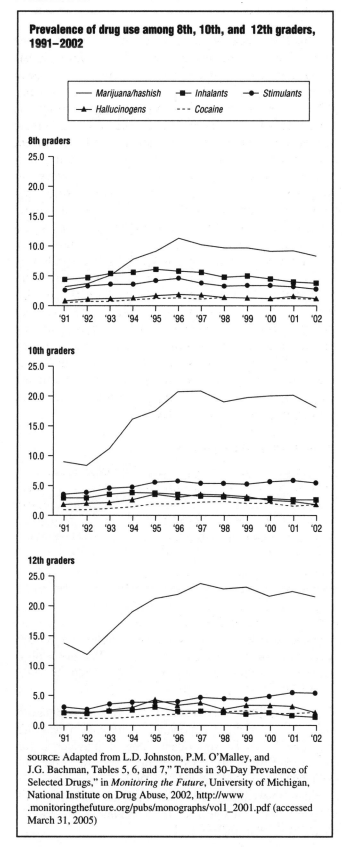

Prevalence of drug use among 8th, 10th, and 12th graders, 1991–2002

— Marijuana/hashish   ■ Inhalants   ● Stimulants
▲ Hallucinogens   --- Cocaine

8th graders

10th graders

12th graders

SOURCE: Adapted from L.D. Johnston, P.M. O'Malley, and J.G. Bachman, Tables 5, 6, and 7," Trends in 30-Day Prevalence of Selected Drugs," in *Monitoring the Future*, University of Michigan, National Institute on Drug Abuse, 2002, http://www .monitoringthefuture.org/pubs/monographs/vol1_2001.pdf (accessed March 31, 2005)

7.5%; Quest Diagnostics' most recent compilation showed that the rate was down to 4.5% in 2003. The types of drugs used by those testing positively

has changed from 1999 to 2003, with use of amphetamines, methadone, and opiates, for example, rising, and use of barbiturates, cocaine, and marijuana decreasing.

1988–2003 data from SAMHSA's national household survey show that in the period 1988 through 1993, full-time workers reporting on their own drug use were a consistently lower percentage of the workforce than as measured by drug testing results. Both SAMHSA and Quest Diagnostics, however, showed a dropping prevalence of drug use. After 1993, self-reported rates were consistently higher than those shown by drug testing results. The Quest Diagnostics index measures *very* current drug use, current enough so that the drugs are still detectable in blood or urine samples, whereas the SAMHSA data include drug use within the past thirty days.

Drug test outcomes for the workforce population tested, as reported by Quest Diagnostics, showed that in 2003 marijuana was the leading cause for a positive result in 55% of cases, followed by cocaine (13.8% of positives), amphetamines (9.0%, a fairly large jump from previous years) and opiates (6.3%). (See Table 4.10.) Heroin is in the opiate category. According to Quest Diagnostics, in 1997 the leading categories were the same, but opiates held the third rank and amphetamines came in fourth.

DRUGS IN THE MILITARY

The U.S. Department of Defense (DOD), through the Office of the Assistant Secretary of Defense for Health, conducts surveys of drug use in the military at three- to four-year intervals. The DOD surveys go back to 1980, with the latest available data being for 2002. Military personnel are concentrated in the younger age groups most prone to use drugs; the military may also be said to be one of the most disciplined voluntary bodies in the U.S. workforce. The military thus presents a unique window on drug use.

In 2002 drug use in the military was down sharply from 1980, a year in which military personnel used drugs at high rates. (See Table 4.11.) In 1980 nearly 28% of all service personnel had used drugs in the last thirty days and more than a third (36.7%) had used drugs in the past twelve months. The highest rate was observed in the U.S. Marine Corps: 37.7% had used drugs during the past month and 48% during the past year. The U.S. Air Force had the lowest rates, 14.5% in the past month and 23.4% in the last year. The high usage rate of drugs in the military in 1980 reflects the high prevalence of drugs in the population as a whole: past-month use in the eighteen-to-twenty-five age

TABLE 4.5

Disapproval of drug use by 12th graders, 1990–2003

QUESTION: "DO YOU DISAPPROVE OF PEOPLE (WHO ARE 18 OR OLDER) DOING EACH OF THE FOLLOWING?"

| | Percentage "disapproving"* | | | | | | | | | | | | | | '02–'03 change |
| | Class of: | | | | | | | | | | | | | | |
	1990	1991	1992	1993	1994	1995	1996	1997	1998	1999	2000	2001	2002	2003	
Try marijuana once or twice	67.8	68.7	69.9	63.3	57.6	56.7	52.5	51.0	51.6	48.8	52.5	49.1	51.6	53.4	+1.8
Smoke marijuana occasionally	80.5	79.4	79.7	75.5	68.9	66.7	62.9	63.2	64.4	62.5	65.8	63.2	63.4	64.2	+0.8
Smoke marijuana regularly	91.0	89.3	90.1	87.6	82.3	81.9	80.0	78.8	81.2	78.6	79.7	79.3	78.3	78.7	+0.4
Try LSD once or twice	89.8	90.1	88.1	85.9	82.5	81.1	79.6	80.5	82.1	83.0	82.4	81.8	84.6	85.5	+0.9
Take LSD regularly	96.3	96.4	95.5	95.8	94.3	92.5	93.2	92.9	93.5	94.3	94.2	94.0	94.0	94.4	+0.3
Try MDMA (ecstasy) once or twice	—	—	—	—	—	—	—	82.2	82.5	82.1	81.0	79.5	83.6	84.7	+1.1
Try cocaine once or twice	91.5	93.6	93.0	92.7	91.6	90.3	90.0	88.0	89.5	89.1	88.2	88.1	89.0	89.3	+0.4
Take cocaine regularly	96.7	97.3	96.9	97.5	96.6	96.1	95.6	96.0	95.6	94.9	95.5	94.9	95.0	95.8	+0.8
Try crack once or twice	92.3	92.1	93.1	89.9	89.5	91.4	87.4	87.0	86.7	87.6	87.5	87.0	87.8	86.6	−1.2
Take crack occasionally	94.3	94.2	95.0	92.8	92.8	94.0	91.2	91.3	90.9	92.3	91.9	91.6	91.5	90.8	−0.7
Take crack regularly	94.9	95.0	95.5	93.4	93.1	94.1	93.0	92.3	91.9	93.2	92.8	92.2	92.4	91.2	−1.1
Try cocaine powder once or twice	87.9	88.0	89.4	86.6	87.1	88.3	83.1	83.0	83.1	84.3	84.1	83.3	83.8	83.6	−0.3
Take cocaine powder occasionally	92.1	93.0	93.4	91.2	91.0	92.7	89.7	89.3	88.7	90.0	90.3	89.8	90.2	88.9	−1.3
Take cocaine powder regularly	93.7	94.4	94.3	93.0	92.5	93.8	92.9	91.5	91.1	92.3	92.6	92.5	92.2	90.7	−1.5
Try heroin once or twice	95.1	96.0	94.9	94.4	93.2	92.8	92.1	92.3	93.7	93.5	93.0	93.1	94.1	94.1	0.0
Take heroin occasionally	96.7	97.3	96.8	97.0	96.2	95.7	95.0	95.4	96.1	95.7	96.0	95.4	95.6	95.9	+0.4
Take heroin regularly	97.5	97.8	97.2	97.5	97.1	96.4	96.3	96.4	96.6	96.4	96.6	96.2	96.2	97.1	+0.9
Try heroin once or twice without using a needle	—	—	—	—	—	92.9	90.8	92.3	93.0	92.6	94.0	91.7	93.1	92.2	−0.9
Take heroin occasionally without using a needle	—	—	—	—	—	94.7	93.2	94.4	94.3	93.8	95.2	93.5	94.4	93.5	−0.8
Try amphetamines once or twice	85.3	86.5	86.9	84.2	81.3	82.2	79.9	81.3	82.5	81.9	82.1	82.3	83.8	85.8	+2.0
Take amphetamines regularly	95.5	96.0	95.6	96.0	94.1	94.3	93.5	94.3	94.0	93.7	94.1	93.4	93.5	94.0	+0.4
Try barbiturates once or twice	90.5	90.6	90.3	89.7	87.5	87.3	84.9	86.4	86.0	86.6	85.9	85.9	86.6	87.8	+1.2
Take barbiturates regularly	96.4	97.1	96.5	97.0	96.1	95.2	94.8	95.3	94.6	94.7	95.2	94.5	94.7	94.4	−0.3
Try one or two drinks of an alcoholic beverage (beer, wine, liquor)	29.4	29.8	33.0	30.1	28.4	27.3	26.5	26.1	24.5	24.6	25.2	26.6	26.3	27.2	+0.9
Take one or two drinks nearly every day	77.9	76.5	75.9	77.8	73.1	73.3	70.8	70.0	69.4	67.2	70.0	69.2	69.1	68.9	−0.3
Take four or five drinks nearly every day	91.9	90.6	90.8	90.6	89.8	88.8	89.4	88.6	86.7	86.9	88.4	86.4	87.5	86.3	−1.3
Have five or more drinks once or twice each weekend	68.9	67.4	70.7	70.1	65.1	66.7	64.7	65.0	63.8	62.7	65.2	62.9	64.7	64.2	−0.5
Smoke one or more packs of cigarettes per day	72.8	71.4	73.5	70.6	69.8	68.2	67.2	67.1	68.8	69.5	70.1	71.6	73.6	74.8	+1.2
Take steroids	90.8	90.5	92.1	92.1	91.9	91.0	91.7	91.4	90.8	88.9	88.8	86.4	86.8	86.0	−0.8
Approx. N=	**2566**	**2547**	**2645**	**2723**	**2588**	**2603**	**2399**	**2601**	**2545**	**2310**	**2150**	**2144**	**2160**	**2442**	

Notes: Level of significance of difference between the two most recent classes: s=.05, ss=.01, sss=.001. '—' indicates data not available. Any apparent inconsistency between the change estimate and the prevalence of use estimates for the two most recent classes is due to rounding error.

*Answer alternatives were: (1) Don't disapprove, (2) Disapprove, and (3) Strongly disapprove. Percentages are shown for categories (2) and (3) combined.

SOURCE: Lloyd D. Johnston, Patrick M. O'Malley, Jerald G. Bachman, and John E. Schulenberg, "Table 8-4. Long-Term Trends in Disapproval of Drug Use by Twelfth Graders," in *Monitoring the Future: National Survey Results on Drug Use, 1975–2003—Vol. 1: Secondary School Students, 2003*, The University of Michigan, Institute for Social Research and U.S. Department of Health and Human Services, National Institutes of Health, National Institute on Drug Abuse, August 2004, http://www.monitoringthefuture.org/pubs/monographs/vol1_2003.pdf (accessed February 10, 2005)

group nationally was 38% in 1979 and past-year use by this same age group was 45.5%. (See Table 3.2 in Chapter 3.)

By 2002 past-month drug use across the military services had declined to 3.4% and past-year usage to 6.9%, though it should be noted that these figures are slightly higher than those found during the 1990s. In 2002 the U.S. Army had the highest rate at 4.8% for the past thirty days and 10.4% for the past year. Air Force personnel consistently used drugs least between 1980 and 2002. Declines in drug use were greatest in the 1980 to 1988 period (22.8% change for past-month use DOD-wide) and grew slightly after 1998.

When one compares the military population with civilians, both populations displayed a declining prevalence of drug use, but military personnel consistently displayed a substantially lower rate of use, less than half that of the civilian population in 1988, 1992, and 1995, and a little more than half since then, according to data from the DOD and SAMHSA.

In the military services, as in the general population and in the working-age population, marijuana was the drug that produced significant rates of prevalence for past-month use in 2002. (See Table 4.12.) According to the DOD survey, about half of DOD-wide current use prevalence was accounted for by marijuana smoking. Use of painkillers (analgesics) in a nonmedical manner ranked second in the military.

A profile of military drug use within the last twelve months is presented in Table 4.13 using a variety of categories. Men used drugs more than women (7.2% of men, 5.5% of women). Hispanic service people were most prone to have used drugs in the last year, 8.3%,

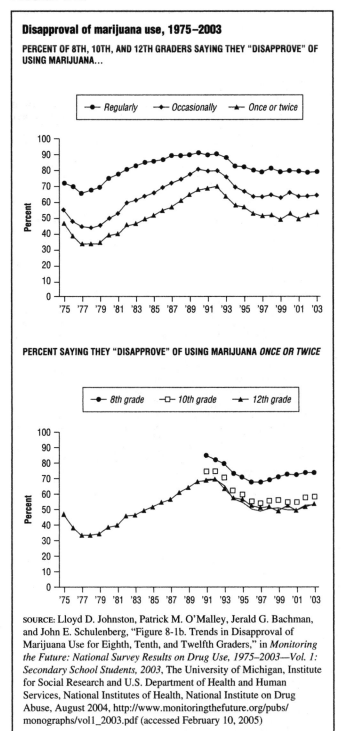

FIGURE 4.13

Disapproval of marijuana use, 1975–2003

PERCENT OF 8TH, 10TH, AND 12TH GRADERS SAYING THEY "DISAPPROVE" OF USING MARIJUANA...

Legend: ● Regularly ◆ Occasionally ▲ Once or twice

PERCENT SAYING THEY "DISAPPROVE" OF USING MARIJUANA *ONCE OR TWICE*

Legend: ● 8th grade □ 10th grade ▲ 12th grade

SOURCE: Lloyd D. Johnston, Patrick M. O'Malley, Jerald G. Bachman, and John E. Schulenberg, "Figure 8-1b. Trends in Disapproval of Marijuana Use for Eighth, Tenth, and Twelfth Graders," in *Monitoring the Future: National Survey Results on Drug Use, 1975–2003—Vol. 1: Secondary School Students, 2003*, The University of Michigan, Institute for Social Research and U.S. Department of Health and Human Services, National Institutes of Health, National Institute on Drug Abuse, August 2004, http://www.monitoringthefuture.org/pubs/monographs/vol1_2003.pdf (accessed February 10, 2005)

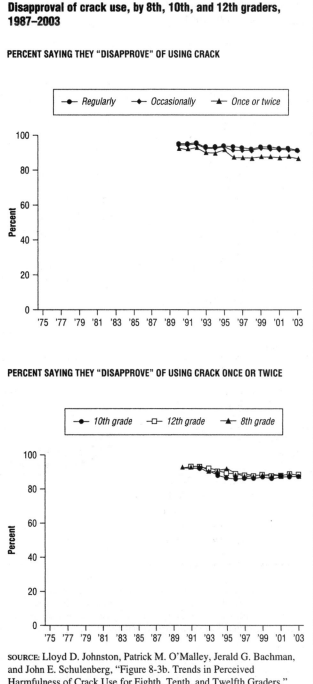

FIGURE 4.14

Disapproval of crack use, by 8th, 10th, and 12th graders, 1987–2003

PERCENT SAYING THEY "DISAPPROVE" OF USING CRACK

Legend: ● Regularly ◆ Occasionally ▲ Once or twice

PERCENT SAYING THEY "DISAPPROVE" OF USING CRACK ONCE OR TWICE

Legend: ● 10th grade □ 12th grade ▲ 8th grade

SOURCE: Lloyd D. Johnston, Patrick M. O'Malley, Jerald G. Bachman, and John E. Schulenberg, "Figure 8-3b. Trends in Perceived Harmfulness of Crack Use for Eighth, Tenth, and Twelfth Graders," in *Monitoring the Future: National Survey Results on Drug Use, 1975–2003—Vol. 1: Secondary School Students, 2003*, The University of Michigan, Institute for Social Research and U.S. Department of Health and Human Services, National Institutes of Health, National Institute on Drug Abuse, August 2004, http://www.monitoringthefuture.org/pubs/monographs/vol1_2003.pdf (accessed February 10, 2005)

with both African Americans and whites at 6.7%. The lower the educational level of the service person, the higher his or her drug use. Those abroad or afloat on ships used drugs more than those stationed in the contiguous forty-eight states of the nation. Drug use rates declined with age from 14.1% of those twenty or younger to 2.2% of those thirty-five or older. Single personnel used drugs more than those who were married, and among those married, those whose spouse was present

used drugs less than those whose spouse was absent. Drug use was lowest among senior enlisted personnel (pay grades E7-E9) and warrant officers (such as technical specialists like helicopter pilots or demolitions experts, pay grades W1-W5 in Table 4.13.)

FIGURE 4.15
FIGURE 4.16

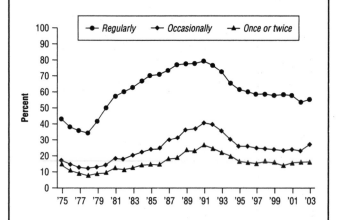

Perception of harmfulness of marijuana, by 8th, 10th, and 12th graders, 1975–2003

PERCENT SAYING "GREAT RISK" FROM USING MARIJUANA...

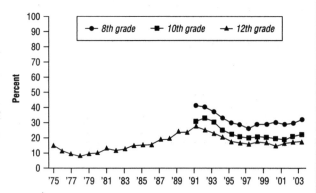

PERCENT SAYING "GREAT RISK" FROM USING MARIJUANA ONCE OR TWICE

SOURCE: Lloyd D. Johnston, Patrick M. O'Malley, Jerald G. Bachman, and John E. Schulenberg, "Figure 8-1a. Trends in Perceived Harmfulness of Marijuana Use for Eighth, Tenth, and Twelfth Graders," in *Monitoring the Future: National Survey Results on Drug Use, 1975–2003—Vol. 1: Secondary School Students, 2003,* The University of Michigan, Institute for Social Research and U.S. Department of Health and Human Services, National Institutes of Health, National Institute on Drug Abuse, August 2004, http://www .monitoringthefuture .org/pubs/monographs/vol1 _2003.pdf (accessed February 10, 2005)

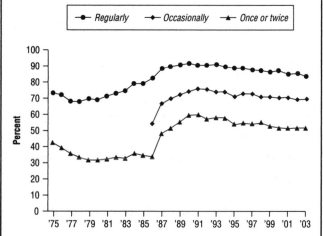

Trends in perceived risk of cocaine use among 12th graders, 1975–2003

PERCENT SAYING "GREAT RISK" FROM USING COCAINE...

Note: Data not available for 8th and 10th graders.

SOURCE: Lloyd D. Johnston, Patrick M. O'Malley, Jerald G. Bachman, and John E. Schulenberg, "Figure 8-2a. Trends in Perceived Harmfulness of Cocaine Use for Twelfth Graders," in *Monitoring the Future: National Survey Results on Drug Use, 1975–2003—Vol.1: Secondary School Students, 2003*, The University of Michigan, Institute for Social Research and U.S. Department of Health and Human Services, National Institutes of Health, National Institute on Drug Abuse, August 2004, http://www.monitoringthefuture.org/pubs/ monographs/vol1_2003.pdf (accessed February 10, 2005)

Current drug use in the military was significantly lower than in the full-time work force in 2002, but patterns of drug use in the services were similar to patterns in the general population: more of those in the youngest age groups used drugs than those in the oldest, and use was lowest among those with the highest skill qualifications. Males in the military were also more likely to use drugs than females, as in the general population.

FIGURE 4.17

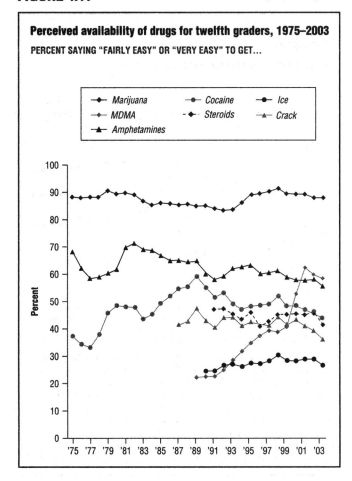

Perceived availability of drugs for twelfth graders, 1975–2003

PERCENT SAYING "FAIRLY EASY" OR "VERY EASY" TO GET...

FIGURE 4.17

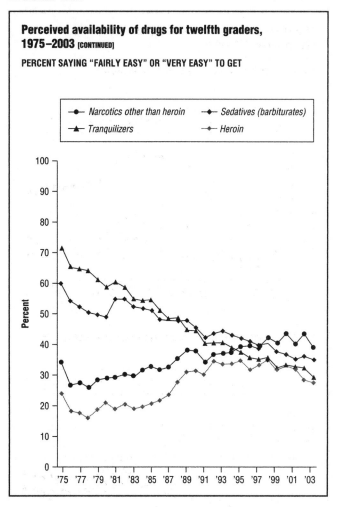

Perceived availability of drugs for twelfth graders, 1975–2003 [CONTINUED]

PERCENT SAYING "FAIRLY EASY" OR "VERY EASY" TO GET

FIGURE 4.17

Perceived availability of drugs for twelfth graders, 1975–2003 [CONTINUED]

PERCENT SAYING "FAIRLY EASY" OR "VERY EASY" TO GET...

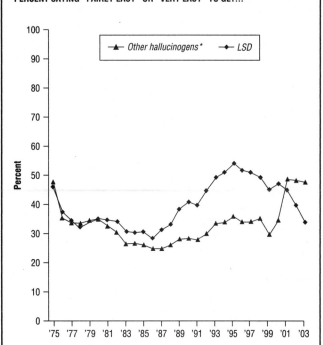

*In 2001 the question text was changed from "other psychedelics" to "other hallucinogens," and "shrooms" was added to the list of examples. These changes likely explain the discontinuity in the 2001 results.

SOURCE: Lloyd D. Johnston, Patrick M. O'Malley, Jerald G. Bachman, and John E. Schulenberg, "Figures 9-5a, b, and c. Trends in Perceived Availability of Drugs for Twelfth Graders," in *Monitoring the Future: National Survey Results on Drug Use, 1975–2003—Vol. 1: Secondary School Students, 2003,* The University of Michigan, Institute for Social Research and U.S. Department of Health and Human Services, National Institutes of Health, National Institute on Drug Abuse, August 2004, http://www.monitoringthefuture.org/pubs/monographs/vol1_2003.pdf (accessed February 10, 2005)

TABLE 4.6

Drug use by demographic characteristics, ages 18–25, 2002 and 2003

[In percentages]

	Time period					
	Lifetime		**Past year**		**Past month**	
Demographic characteristic	**2002**	**2003**	**2002**	**2003**	**2002**	**2003**
Total	**59.8**	**60.5**	**35.5**	**34.6**	**20.2**	**20.3**
Gender						
Male	62.6	63.6	39.3	38.6	24.0	24.0
Female	57.1	57.4	31.6	30.5	16.4	16.5
Hispanic origin and race						
Not Hispanic or Latino	61.8	62.3	37.3	36.1	21.5	21.3
White	64.9	65.1	39.6	38.2	22.9	22.5
Black or African American	53.7	54.6	30.9	30.6	18.2	18.2
American Indian or Alaska Native	79.2	77.9	49.4	44.2	29.5	31.0
Native Hawaiian or other Pacific Islander	—	—	—	—	—	—
Asian	34.9[a]	43.1	18.6	22.1	8.9	11.8
Two or more races	76.3	71.4	48.8	45.4	29.3	29.2
Hispanic or Latino	50.7	52.2	27.0	27.5	14.2	15.6
Education						
<High school	59.5	59.7	36.7	36.8	22.5	23.0
High school graduate	60.6	60.6	34.7	34.4	19.8	20.1
Some college	60.6	61.6	37.7	35.5	21.0	20.6
College graduate	56.3	58.8	29.7	28.9	15.0	15.3
Current employment						
Full-time	62.1	63.0	34.4	33.1	19.7	19.2
Part-time	58.1	58.8	36.7	36.8	20.5	21.6
Unemployed	64.9	66.6	43.7	44.1	26.2	27.6
Other[c]	54.6	54.2	33.0	31.1	18.5	17.9

—Low precision; no estimate reported.
Note: Any illicit drug includes marijuana/hashish, cocaine (including crack), heroin, hallucinogens, inhalants, or any prescription-type psychotherapeutic used nonmedically.
[a]Difference between estimate and 2003 estimate is statistically significant at the 0.05 level.
[b]Difference between estimate and 2003 estimate is statistically significant at the 0.01 level.
[c]Retired person, disabled person, homemaker, student, or other person not in the labor force.

SOURCE: "Table G.9. Any Illicit Drug Use in Lifetime, Past Year, and Past Month among Persons Aged 18 to 25, by Demographic Characteristics: Percentages, 2002 and 2003," in *Results from the 2003 National Survey on Drug Use and Health: National Findings*, U.S. Department of Health and Human Services, Substance Abuse and Mental Health Services Administration, Office of Applied Studies, September 2004, http://www.oas,samhsa.gov/nhsda/2k3nsduh/2k3ResultsW.pdf (accessed February 10, 2005)

TABLE 4.7

Drug use by demographic characteristics, age 26 or older, 2002 and 2003

	Time period					
	Lifetime		Past year		Past month	
Demographic characteristic	2002	2003	2002	2003	2002	2003
Total	45.7	46.1	10.4	10.3	5.8	5.6
Gender						
Male	51.3	51.8	12.9	12.6	7.5	7.2
Female	40.7	40.8	8.1	8.1	4.2	4.3
Hispanic origin and race						
Not Hispanic or Latino	46.8	47.6	10.4	10.3	5.9	5.7
White	48.1	49.0	10.2	10.5	5.9	5.8
Black or African American	44.4	45.1	13.5	11.3	7.8	6.4
American Indian or Alaska Native	—	63.2	10.5	11.0	4.3	6.8
Native Hawaiian or other Pacific Islander	—	—	—	—	—	—
Asian	25.0	22.8	4.8	3.5	2.2	1.9
Two or more races	53.9	63.8	13.7	14.2	6.9	7.9
Hispanic or Latino	37.2	33.9	10.5	9.7	4.5	5.2
Education						
<High school	32.0	33.2	10.2	9.8	6.0	5.8
High school graduate	43.6	43.7	10.1	10.3	5.8	6.0
Some college	53.4	53.2	11.6	12.1	6.4	6.6
College graduate	50.1	50.5	9.8	9.0	5.0	4.4
Current employment						
Full-time	55.8	55.7	12.3	12.2	6.5	6.3
Part-time	48.7	48.5	11.3	11.2	6.5	6.4
Unemployed	59.8	59.9	22.3	21.0	13.2	13.5
Other*	23.8	25.1	5.3	5.0	3.3	3.2

—Low precision; no estimate reported.
Note: Includes marijuana/hashish, cocaine (including crack), heroin, hallucinogens, inhalants, or any prescription-type psychotherapeutic used nonmedically.
*Retired person, disabled person, homemaker, student, or other person not in the labor force.

SOURCE: "Table G.10. Any Illicit Drug Use in Lifetime, Past Year, and Past Month among Persons Aged 26 or Older, by Demographic Characteristics: Percentages, 2002 and 2003," in *Results from the 2003 National Survey on Drug Use and Health: National Findings*, U.S. Department of Health and Human Services, Substance Abuse and Mental Health Services Administration, Office of Applied Studies, September 2004, http://www.oas.samhsa.gov/nhsda/ 2k3nsduh/2k3ResultsW.pdf (accessed February 10, 2005)

TABLE 4.8

Drug use by full-time workers aged 18–49, 2000

	Estimated total population (000s)	Rates of use (%) Past month any illicit drug use	Rates of use (%) Past year dependence or abuse of illicit drugs
Total	**87,672**	**7.8**	**1.9**
Male	50,466	9.2	2.4
Female	37,206	5.9	1.2
Age groups			
18–25	15,190	14.9	5.3
26–34	24,464	7.9	1.8
35–49	48,017	5.5	1.0
By type of occupation			
Executive, administrative, and managerial	14,822	6.5	1.1
Professional specialty	13,222	4.7	1.4
Technical and sales support	13,239	8.0	1.8
Administrative support	10,714	6.9	1.9
Services	10,047	9.7	2.3
Precision production, craft and repair	10,786	11.2	2.5
Operators, fabricators, and laborers	12,428	8.6	3.0
By type of industry			
Construction and mining	8,267	12.3	3.6
Manufacturing	14,610	6.7	1.7
Transportation, communications, and other public utilities	6,541	7.2	1.4
Whole sale and retail	15,881	10.8	2.9
Services—business and repairs	7,883	9.0	1.9
Finance, insurance, real estate, and other services (personal and recreation)	8,320	7.7	1.7
Services—professional	19,125	5.0	1.3
Government	4,252	3.7	0.6

Note: Total population is the count of all individuals in a category of which the percentiles shown are involved in drug use.

SOURCE: Adapted from "Table 1. Prevalence of Substance Use, Abuse or Dependence among Full-Time Employed Workers Aged 18 to 49: 2000 NHSDA," in *The NHSDA Report*, Substance Abuse and Mental Health Services Administration, September 2002

TABLE 4.9

Drug testing positivity rates, combined U.S. workforce, 1988–2003

[More than 7.1 million tests from January to December 2003]

Year	Drug positive rate
1988	13.6%
1989	12.7%
1990	11.0%
1991	8.8%
1992	8.8%
1993	8.4%
1994	7.5%
1995	6.7%
1996	5.8%
1997	5.0%
1998	4.8%
1999	4.6%
2000	4.7%
2001	4.6%
2002	4.4%
2003	4.5%

SOURCE: "Annual Positivity Rates (for Combined U.S. Workforce)," in *Increased Use of Amphetamines Linked to Rising Workplace Drug Use, According to Quest Diagnostics' 2003 Drug Testing Index*, Quest Diagnostics Incorporated, July 22, 2004, http://phx.corporate-ir.net/phoenix.zhtml?c=82068&p=irol-newsArticle&ID=594794&highlight=workplace%20drug%20use (accessed March 31, 2005)

TABLE 4.10

Drugs in the workforce, by drug category, 1999–2003

[More than 5.9 million tests from January to December 2003]

Drug category	2003	2002	2001	2000	1999
Acid/base	0.16%	0.25%	0.23%	0.07%	0.14%
Amphetamines	9.0%	6.7%	5.5%	4.8%	4.3%
Barbiturates	2.8%	2.9%	3.2%	3.5%	3.7%
Benzodiazepines	5.1%	5.0%	5.0%	4.2%	3.3%
Cocaine	13.8%	13.9%	13.2%	13.9%	15.8%
Marijuana	55.0%	57.7%	60.9%	63.0%	62.6%
Methadone	1.6%	1.2%	0.98%	0.89%	0.45%
Methaqualone	0.00%	0.00%	0.00%	0.00%	0.00%
Opiates	6.3%	5.3%	5.5%	5.2%	5.1%
Oxidizing adulterants (incl. Nitrites)	0.16%	0.48%	0.51%	0.88%	1.6%
PCP	0.51%	0.47%	0.46%	0.45%	0.35%
Propoxyphene	5.0%	5.6%	4.0%	2.5%	2.0%
Substituted	0.58%	0.54%	0.48%	0.56%	0.80%

SOURCE: "Positivity Rates by Drug Category (for General U.S. Workforce, as a Percentage of All Positives)," in *Increased Use of Amphetamines Linked to Rising Workplace Drug Use, According to Quest Diagnostics' 2003 Drug Testing Index*, Quest Diagnostics Incorporated, July 22, 2004, http://phx.corporate-ir.net/phoenix.zhtml?c=82068&p=irol-newsArticle&ID=594794&highlight=workplace%20drug%20use (accessed March 31, 2005)

TABLE 4.11

Current and past year prevalence of drug use in the military services, 1980–2002

Service/period of use	Year of survey							
	1980	1982	1985	1988	1992	1995	1998	2002
Army								
Past 30 days	30.7	26.2	11.5	6.9	3.9	4.0	4.5	4.8
Past 12 months	39.4	32.4	16.6	11.8	7.7	9.2	9.8	10.4
Navy								
Past 30 days	33.7	16.2	10.3	5.4	4.0	3.6	1.8	3.7
Past 12 months	43.2	28.1	15.9	11.3	6.6	7.3	4.2	7.1
Marine Corps								
Past 30 days	37.7	20.6	9.9	4.0	5.6	3.6	3.3	3.8
Past 12 months	48.0	29.9	14.7	7.8	10.7	7.3	7.2	7.9
Air Force								
Past 30 days	14.5	11.9	4.5	2.1	1.2	1.0	1.2	1.0
Past 12 months	23.4	16.4	7.2	3.8	2.3	2.5	2.4	1.8
Total DoD								
Past 30 days	27.6	19.0	8.9	4.8	3.4	3.0	2.7	3.4
Past 12 months	36.7	26.6	13.4	8.9	6.2	6.5	6.0	6.9

Note: Table entries are percentages. Estimates have not been adjusted for sociodemographic differences among services.

SOURCE: "Table 5.1. Trends in Any Illicit Drug Use, Past 30 Days and Past 12 Months, by Service, 1980–2002," in *2002 Department of Defense Survey of Health Related Behaviors among Military Personnel*, U.S. Department of Defense, November 2003, http://dodwws.rti.org/2002WWFinalReportComplete05-04.pdf (accessed February 14, 2005)

TABLE 4.12

Military drug use, by drug and service, 2002

Drug/period of use	Army	Navy	Marine Corps	Air Force	Total DoD
Marijuana					
Past 30 days	2.5	2.1	1.8	0.3	1.7
Past 12 months	6.8	4.8	5.5	0.8	4.5
Cocaine					
Past 30 days	0.9	1.1	0.5	0.1	0.7
Past 12 months	2.0	1.8	2.0	0.2	1.5
PCP					
Past 30 days	0.5	0.7	0.1	**	0.4
Past 12 months	0.7	0.9	0.3	**	0.5
LSD/hallucinogens					
Past 30 days	0.7	0.7	0.5	0.2	0.5
Past 12 months	1.5	1.3	1.8	0.2	1.2
Amphetamines/stimulants					
Past 30 days	1.1	1.3	0.3	0.1	0.8
Past 12 months	1.7	1.7	0.9	0.2	1.2
Tranquilizers					
Past 30 days	1.1	0.8	0.6	0.2	0.7
Past 12 months	1.7	1.0	1.2	0.3	1.1
Barbiturates/sedatives					
Past 30 days	0.8	0.8	0.3	0.2	0.6
Past 12 months	1.1	1.0	0.7	0.2	0.7
Heroin/other opiates					
Past 30 days	0.5	0.8	0.2	**	0.4
Past 12 months	0.7	0.9	0.4	**	0.5
Analgesics					
Past 30 days	1.2	1.5	1.1	0.4	1.0
Past 12 months	2.0	1.9	1.4	0.5	1.5
Inhalants					
Past 30 days	0.8	0.9	0.6	0.2	0.6
Past 12 months	1.3	1.2	0.9	0.3	1.0
"Designer" drugs					
Past 30 days	1.0	1.0	0.7	**	0.7
Past 12 months	2.5	1.6	2.0	0.1	1.6
Any illicit drug[a]					
Past 30 days	4.8	3.7	3.8	1.0	3.4
Past 12 months	10.4	7.1	7.9	1.8	6.9
Any illicit drug except marijuana[b]					
Past 30 days	3.3	2.8	2.7	0.8	2.4
Past 12 months	6.6	4.4	5.2	1.2	4.4
Anabolic steroids					
Past 30 days	0.9	1.0	0.7	0.1	0.7
Past 12 months	1.1	1.1	1.2	0.2	0.9
Gamma hydroxy butyrate					
Past 30 days	0.5	0.7	0.2	**	0.4
Past 12 months	0.6	0.9	0.5	**	0.5

Note: Table entries are percentages. Estimates have not been adjusted for sociodemographic differences among services.
**Estimate rounds to zero.
[a]Nonmedical use one or more times of any of the above classes of drugs, excluding steroids.
[b]Nonmedical use one or more times of any of the above classes of drugs, excluding marijuana and steroids.

SOURCE: "Table 5.3. Any Illicit Drug Use, Past 30 Days and Past 12 Months, by Drug and Service," in *2002 Department of Defense Survey of Health Related Behaviors among Military Personnel*, U.S. Department of Defense, November 2003, http://dodwws.rti.org/2002WWFinalReportComplete05-04 .pdf (accessed February 14, 2005)

TABLE 4.13

Drug use in the military services within the last year, by user characteristics, 2002

Sociodemographic characteristic	Prevalence	Odds ratio[a] Adjusted
Service		
Army	10.4	6.35[b]
Navy	7.1	3.56[b]
Marine Corps	7.9	2.94[b]
Air Force	1.8	1.00
Gender		
Male	7.2	1.41[b]
Female	5.5	1.00
Race/ethnicity		
White, non-Hispanic	6.7	1.00
African American, non-Hispanic	6.7	0.86
Hispanic	8.3	1.10
Other	9.1	1.31
Education		
High school or less	11.2	2.04[b]
Some college	5.8	1.93[b]
College graduate or higher	1.7	1.00
Age		
20 or younger	14.1	1.66[b]
21–25	10.8	1.75
26–34	3.1	0.69
35 or older	2.2	1.00
Family status		
Not married[c]	10.1	1.50[b]
Married, spouse not present	8.6	1.51[b]
Married, spouse present	4.0	1.00
Pay grade		
E1-E3	13.9	2.66[b]
E4-E6	6.8	1.60
E7-E9	0.9	0.34[b]
W1-W5	1.3	0.40
O1-O3	1.8	1.08
O4-O10	1.4	1.00
Region		
CONUS[d]	6.4	1.03
OCONUS[e]	8.0	1.00
Total	**6.9**	

Note: Prevalence estimates are percentages.
[a]Odds ratios were adjusted for service, gender, race/ethnicity, education, age, family status, pay grade, and region.
[b]Odds ratio is significantly different from the reference group.
[c]Estimates by family status after 1998 are not strictly comparable to those from previous survey years. Personnel who reported that they were living as married (in 1998 and 2002) were classified as "not married." Before 1998, the marital status question did not distinguish between personnel who were married and those who were living as married.
[d]Refers to personnel who were stationed within the 48 contiguous states in the continental United States.
[e]Refers to personnel who were stationed outside the continental United States or aboard afloat ships.

SOURCE: Table 5.4. Sociodemographic Correlates of Any Illicit Drug Use, Past 12 Months, Total DoD, in *2002 Department of Defense Survey of Health Related Behaviors among Military Personnel*, U.S. Department of Defense, November 2003, http://dodwws.rti.org/2002WWFinalReport Complete05-04.pdf (accessed February 14, 2005)

CHAPTER 5
DRUGS AND THE JUSTICE SYSTEM

The United States justice system has been affected since the early 1900s by attempts to eradicate various drugs. The first legislation aimed at drugs was the Harrison Act of 1914, which outlawed opiates and cocaine. Following that act, laws were passed or amended at intervals, but the war on drugs began in earnest in the early 1970s after Congress passed the Comprehensive Drug Abuse and Control Act in 1970. The phrase "war on drugs" dates to 1971, during the first Nixon administration. A national effort was launched after that to bring drug use under control. It is still very much under way and has lasted much longer than an earlier movement to control another substance—alcohol.

Alcohol was prohibited by the Eighteenth Amendment to the Constitution, ratified in 1919. According to the U.S. Department of Justice's Bureau of Justice Statistics (BJS) ("Homicide Rates, 1900–2000"), during Prohibition (1920–33) criminal activity peaked and the homicide rate reached record levels (9.7 murders per one hundred thousand people in 1933) that were not surpassed again until 1974 (about ten per one hundred thousand), when the war on drugs was underway. (See Figure 5.1.) The rate remained high throughout the 1980s and early 1990s before beginning a decline. Alcohol was legalized again with the passage of the Twenty-first Amendment to the Constitution, ratified in 1933. Tobacco, another legal substance, has also captured public interest. Efforts are underway to persuade people to give up smoking, but tobacco remains a legal product that may be purchased by adults.

Public efforts to influence or prohibit the use of substances that change the mood or enhance attention have had mixed results. Prohibition came to an end because of massive public disobedience. Data from the *National Survey on Drug Use and Health (formerly the National Household Survey on Drug Abuse)* conducted by the Substance Abuse and Mental Health Administra-

tion (SAMHSA), an agency of the U.S. Department of Health and Human Services, suggests a similar public response to laws that prohibit use of drugs. In 2003, 46.4% of people aged twelve or older, more than 110 million individuals, had used drugs at some time in their lives. About thirty-five million had done so in the last twelve months, and nearly 19.5 million had used drugs in the past thirty days. (See Table 3.4 and Table 3.3 in Chapter 3.) The percentage of lifetime users increased during the twenty-five preceding years; it was 31% of the twelve-and-older population in 1979, according to SAMHSA.

In some ways, efforts to control the use of substances appear to be inconsistent with direct harm caused. Tobacco and alcohol, both legal substances, cause many more deaths per year than drugs. The Centers for Disease Control and Prevention estimated during the 1990s that 430,000 people die yearly as a result of smoking cigarettes, and 81,000 die as a result of drinking alcohol, not including motor vehicle deaths caused by drunken driving. Drug use produces 14,000 deaths a year. The vast majority of these fatalities occur, according to SAMHSA mortality data, as a result of heroin, cocaine, and synthetic drug use, with or without the involvement of alcohol. Marijuana, which is preponderantly the drug used by the majority of those classified as drug users, causes few fatalities, and virtually none by itself (*Mortality Data from the Drug Abuse Warning Network 2002*, SAMHSA, January 2004). Such facts are behind efforts to legalize marijuana.

THE RELATIONSHIP BETWEEN DRUGS AND CRIME

Despite the fact that drug use accounts for few fatalities per year, there is evidence to support a strong relationship between drug use and criminal behavior. There are two types of drug offenders: those who pass through

FIGURE 5.1

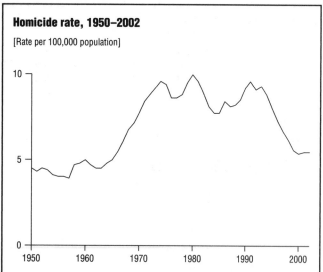

Homicide rate, 1950–2002

[Rate per 100,000 population]

SOURCE: James Alan Fox, and Marianne W. Zawitz, "Homicide Victimization, 1950–2002," in *Homicide Trends in the United States: 2002 Update*, U.S. Department of Justice, Bureau of Justice Statistics, November 2004, http://www.ojp.usdoj.gov/bjs/abstract/htus02.htm (accessed February 14, 2005)

TABLE 5.1

Homicides related to drugs, 1987–2003

Year	Number of homicides	Percent drug related
1987	17,963	4.9%
1988	17,971	5.6
1989	18,954	7.4
1990	20,273	6.7
1991	21,676	6.2
1992	22,716	5.7
1993	23,180	5.5
1994	22,084	5.6
1995	20,232	5.1
1996	16,967	5.0
1997	15,837	5.1
1998	14,276	4.8
1999	13,011	4.5
2000	13,230	4.5
2001	14,061	4.1
2002	14,263	4.7
2003	14,408	4.6

SOURCE: "Drug-Related Homicides," in *Drugs and Crime Facts*, U.S. Department of Justice, Bureau of Justice Statistics, 2004, http://www.ojp.usdoj.gov/bjs/dcf/contents.htm (accessed February 14, 2005)

the judicial system because they have violated drug laws and those who enter the system because they have committed a crime while under the influence of drugs or in order to get money to pay for drugs. These two themes frequently overlap.

There are usually three reasons given for the correlation between drugs and crime:

- Drugs may reduce inhibitions or stimulate aggression and interfere with the ability to earn legitimate income.

- Persons who develop a dependence on an illegal drug need a substantial income to pay for them and may commit crimes in order to fund their habit.

- Drug trafficking may lead to such crimes as extortion, aggravated assault, and homicide. Table 5.1 shows the number of homicides related to drugs from 1987 to 2003.

In *Adult Patterns of Criminal Behavior* (Washington, DC: National Institute of Justice, 1996), University of Nebraska researchers Julie Horney, D. Wayne Osgood, and Ineke Haen Marshall studied 658 newly convicted male prisoners sentenced to the Nebraska Department of Correctional Services during 1989–90. The researchers wanted to determine if changes in life circumstances, such as being unemployed or living with a wife or girlfriend, influenced their criminal behavior. Among their conclusions, they found that "use of illegal drugs was related to all four measures of offending (any crime, property crime, assault, and drug crime). For example, during months of drug use, the odds of committing a

property crime increased by 54%; the odds of committing an assault increased by over 100%. Overall, illegal drug use increased the odds of committing any crime sixfold."

According to the BJS, in *Drug Use, Testing, and Treatment in Jails*, published in May 2000, in 1998 an estimated 138,000 convicted jail inmates (36%) were under the influence of drugs at the time of the offense. An estimated 61,000 convicted jail inmates (13.3%) said they had committed their offense to get money for drugs. Of convicted property and drug offenders, about one in four had committed their crimes to get money for drugs.

The U.S. Department of Justice, using data from the Uniform Crime Reporting Program (UCR) of the Federal Bureau of Investigation (FBI), reported that in 2003, 4.6% of the 14,408 homicides in which circumstances were known were narcotics related, including those committed during drug trafficking or manufacturing. (See Table 5.1.)

DRUGS AND ALCOHOL PLAY A MAJOR ROLE IN ARRESTS

As estimated by the FBI in its annual *Crime in the United States* report, nearly 13.7 million total arrests took place in 2003; about 1.7 million people, or about 12%, were arrested for drug abuse violations. (See Table 5.2; Table 5.3 breaks these arrests down by region of the country.) Driving under the influence accounted 1.4 million (or 10.5%) of total arrests; drunkenness, 548,616 (4%); and liquor law violations, 612,079 (4.5%). These 4.3 million arrests accounted for 31% of all arrests. In addition, arrests for disorderly conduct (639,371), vagrancy (28,948), and vandalism (273,431) often involved drug and alcohol abuse.

TABLE 5.2

Estimated arrests, 2003

Totalª	13,639,479
Murder and nonnegligent manslaughter	13,190
Forcible rape	26,350
Robbery	107,553
Aggravated assault	449,933
Burglary	290,956
Larceny-theft	1,145,074
Motor vehicle theft	152,934
Arson	16,163
Violent crimeᵇ	597,026
Property crimeᵇ	1,605,127
Other assaults	1,246,698
Forgery and counterfeiting	111,823
Fraud	299,138
Embezzlement	16,826
Stolen property; buying, receiving, possessing	126,775
Vandalism	273,431
Weapons; carrying, possessing, etc.	167,972
Prostitution and commercialized vice	75,190
Sex offenses (except forcible rape and prostitution)	91,546
Drug abuse violations	1,678,192
Gambling	10,954
Offenses against the family and children	136,034
Driving under the influence	1,448,148
Liquor laws	612,079
Drunkenness	548,616
Disorderly conduct	639,371
Vagrancy	28,948
All other offenses	3,665,543
Suspicion	7,163
Curfew and loitering law violations	136,461
Runaways	123,581

ªDoes not include suspicion.
ᵇViolent crimes are offenses of murder, forcible rape, robbery, and aggravated assault. Property crimes are offenses of burglary, larceny-theft, motor vehicle theft, and arson.

SOURCE: Table 29. Estimated Number of Arrests: United States, 2003, in *Crime in the United States, 2003*, U.S. Department of Justice, Federal Bureau of Investigation, October 27, 2004, http://www.fbi.gov/ucr/03cius .htm (accessed February 14, 2005)

TABLE 5.3

Drug arrests by region, 2003

Drug abuse violations	United States total	Northeast	Midwest	South	West
Total*	**100.0**	**100.0**	**100.0**	**100.0**	**100.0**
Sale/manufacturing:	19.4	25.7	19.2	20.1	15.9
Heroin or cocaine and their derivatives	8.8	17.1	4.8	9.8	5.8
Marijuana	5.5	6.4	7.7	5.3	4.2
Synthetic or manufactured drugs	1.5	1.0	1.4	2.8	0.7
Other dangerous nonnarcotic drugs	3.6	1.2	5.2	2.3	5.2
Possession:	80.6	74.3	80.8	79.9	84.1
Heroin or cocaine and their derivatives	21.5	24.3	11.4	22.3	23.8
Marijuana	39.5	42.3	51.7	46.3	26.2
Synthetic or manufactured drugs	3.1	1.8	3.1	4.3	2.6
Other dangerous nonnarcotic drugs	16.6	5.7	14.7	6.9	31.5

*Because of rounding, the percentages may not add to 100.0.

SOURCE: "Table 4.1. Arrests for Drug Abuse Violations by Region, 2003," in *Crime in the United States*, U.S. Department of Justice, Federal Bureau of Investigation, October 27, 2004, http://www.fbi.gov/ucr/03cius.htm (accessed February 14, 2005)

FIGURE 5.2

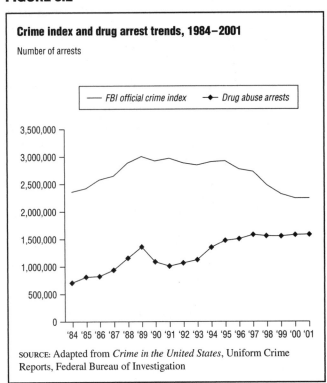

Crime index and drug arrest trends, 1984–2001

Number of arrests

— FBI official crime index   ◆ Drug abuse arrests

SOURCE: Adapted from *Crime in the United States*, Uniform Crime Reports, Federal Bureau of Investigation

According to the FBI, total arrests were about 0.5% lower than two years earlier in 2001, but drug arrests rose nearly 6% over that two-year span. They also increased as a percentage of all arrests, from 11.6% in 2001 to 12.3% in 2003. In 2003 more people were arrested for drug and alcohol violations than were arrested for murder, rape, robbery, aggravated assault, burglary, theft, car theft, arson, forgery, fraud, embezzlement, prostitution and vice, gambling, offenses against family and children (usually domestic violence), and curfew/loitering-law violations combined.

Data for these two years are the continuation of a longer trend. (See Figure 5.2.) The official crime rate, which was climbing through 1989, began to decline slowly, if not uniformly, after that year. Drug arrests also dropped at first, but then resumed their upward direction between 1991 and 1992 and have been rising since that time.

ARRESTEE DRUG USE

The National Institute of Justice annually publishes the *Arrestee Drug Abuse Monitoring* (ADAM) report, formerly called *Drug Use Forecasting* (DUF). The latest report contains information up to 2000 and was published in 2003 (http://www.ojp.usdoj.gov/nij/adam/welcome.html). In 2000 the report surveyed arrestees in thirty-five urban sites about drug use in the past year and conducted urinalyses to determine if ten different drugs had been used recently (each drug has a different number of days in which it can still be detected by urinalysis). ADAM reported on drugs in six categories: cocaine (crack or powder), marijuana, opiates, methamphetamine, phencyclidine (PCP), and "any drug," which could include the remainder of the other five drugs. The 2000 report states that "people who come to the attention of the criminal justice system by being arrested are more often than not users of drugs and/or alcohol." To support this claim, in half of the ADAM sites in 2000, urinalysis showed that more than 64% of adult male arrestees had used at least one of five drugs: marijuana, cocaine, opiates, methamphetamine, or PCP. Use ranged from a low of 52% of arrestees in Anchorage, Alaska, to a high of 80% in New York, but was consistently a majority of those arrested. In half the sites, at least 21% tested positive for more than one drug, with a low of 10% in Anchorage and Albany, New York, and a high of 34% in Chicago.

Though data on females was more limited, ADAM found that in half of the twenty-nine sites where data on females was analyzed, more than 63% of women had used one of the five drugs mentioned above. The rates ranged from a low of 31% in Laredo, Texas, to 80% in Chicago. For many locations and drugs, female arrestees were more likely to have used drugs than male arrestees. Two factors may explain the higher rates for women: fewer females are arrested, which may raise the rates; and females are more likely than males to be arrested for offenses that carry a high likelihood of drug use, such as prostitution.

Only nine ADAM sites survey and conduct urinalysis on juveniles (and only eight have results for female juveniles), but there were similarities at those sites, with at least 41% of juvenile arrestees at all sites testing positive for drug use. The highest use rate was 55% in Phoenix, Arizona. Consistent with the SAMHSA survey, marijuana was the most commonly used drug among juveniles. FBI data showed that juvenile offenses decreased 15% between 1996 and 2000, but that arrests for driving under the influence, liquor law violations, and curfew violations rose (to 36, 31, and 9% respectively). The charge faced by most juveniles in 2000 was a "condition of release" violation (such as probation), with the most common offense being larceny-theft, followed by drug possession.

Marijuana Use

Marijuana use among arrestees is high, according to the ADAM report; often one-third or more report using the drug within days of their arrest. In general, men were more likely than women to test positive for marijuana, and younger arrestees (fifteen to twenty-five years of age) were much more likely to test positive than older respondents.

Alcohol was the substance most frequently used with marijuana. However, respondents also reported using marijuana with powder cocaine, crack, methamphetamine, and PCP.

Overall, almost 41% of all adult males tested positive for marijuana in 2000, according to the ADAM report, whereas 26.7% of females tested positive. The proportion of adult male respondents who tested positive for marijuana use ranged from a high of 57% in Oklahoma City, Oklahoma, to a low of 28.5% in Laredo, Texas. The proportion of female arrestees with marijuana-positive tests ranged from 44.7% in Oklahoma City to 17.2% in Laredo.

Cocaine Use

According to the 2000 ADAM report, almost one-third of all adult arrestees tested positive for cocaine. Female arrestees were more likely to have used cocaine than male arrestees (30.9% of males versus 33.1% of females). Based on self-reports, female arrestees were more likely than male arrestees to use crack cocaine. Drug testing cannot yet distinguish crack from powder cocaine, so researchers must rely on self-reported data to track trends in crack use.

In 2000 the percentage of adult male arrestees who tested positive for recent cocaine use ranged from a high of 48.8% in New York to a low of 11% in Des Moines, Iowa. Male cocaine users reported recent crack use twice as frequently as they reported recent powder-cocaine use.

The percentage of adult female arrestees who tested positive for recent cocaine use ranged from a high of 59.2% in New York City to a low of 7.8% in San Jose. Participation in the crack cocaine market was reported by a higher percentage of females than males (23% of females and 15% of males). ADAM data suggest significant crack use among female arrestees in urban areas.

Opiate Use

The use of opiates—including heroin, codeine, and morphine—is relatively low compared with that of cocaine and marijuana use. Though current screening methods cannot distinguish heroin from other opiates, preliminary results from another project indicate that more than 97% of ADAM arrestees who tested positive for opiates were heroin users. Older arrestees used opiates at higher rates than did younger arrestees. In a few locations, however, the youngest groups were more likely to test positive. There has been recent concern that opiate use may increase among the young as the price of heroin decreases and purity increases.

Female arrestees were more likely than male arrestees to test positive for opiate use (7.2 versus 6.5%). Opiate-positive rates of adult male arrestees ranged from a high of 27% in Chicago to a low of 1.9% in the

Charlotte metro area of North Carolina, while among adult female respondents, opiate-positive rates ranged from 40% in Chicago to 1.3% in Omaha, Nebraska.

Methamphetamine Use

Methamphetamine prevalence varied wildly by geographical site. In more than half of the thirty-five sites where ADAM tested adult male arrestees, prevalence rates were less than 2%, while they exceeded 20% in six sites. Sites in the West and Northwest had considerably higher rates of methamphetamine use than those in the Northeast, South, or Midwest. Surprisingly, despite reports of active methamphetamine production in, and trafficking from, Mexico, most sites along the Southwest border and in Texas showed considerably lower levels of methamphetamine use than sites in the West and Northwest.

A greater proportion of female arrestees than male arrestees tested positive for methamphetamine in most sites (1.6 versus 3%). Methamphetamine-positive rates for male and female arrestees were 0% at several sites, but Honolulu, Hawaii, had the highest rate of methamphetamine use for both male and female arrestees, at 35.9% and 47.2%, respectively.

ARRESTS FOR DRUG VIOLATIONS

As mentioned above, the FBI's UCR report estimated that there were 1.7 million arrests for drug violations in 2003. Drug violations are defined by the FBI as "state and/or local offenses relating to the unlawful possession, sale, use, growing, manufacturing, and making of narcotic drugs including opium or cocaine and their derivatives, marijuana, synthetic narcotics, and dangerous non-narcotic drugs such as barbiturates."

A history of drug arrests is presented in Figure 5.3; Figure 5.4 separates drug arrests of adults from those of juveniles. Juveniles are defined in most jurisdictions as those younger than eighteen. Drug arrests increased during the Nixon-Ford (1973–76), Reagan (1981–88), and Clinton (1993–2000) administrations and dropped during the Carter (1977–80) and the George H. W. Bush (1989–92) administrations. Growth in drug arrests is attributable largely to the arrest of adults. In 1970 juveniles represented 22.4% of those arrested. That percentage peaked in 1973 at 26.3%, a level not reached since then. According to the Bureau of Justice Statistics, 1.48 million adults and 201,400 juveniles were arrested for drug violations in 2003.

Total drug arrests nearly tripled between 1980 and 2003, from 580,900 to 1.68 million, according to the Bureau of Justice Statistics. Adult arrests alone more than tripled, while juvenile arrests increased only slightly, and have leveled off since the mid-1990s.

FIGURE 5.3

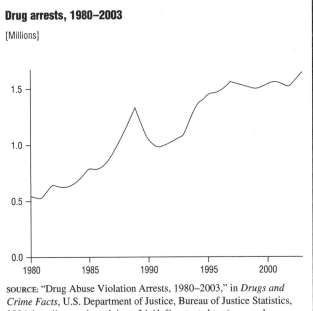

Drug arrests, 1980–2003

[Millions]

SOURCE: "Drug Abuse Violation Arrests, 1980–2003," in *Drugs and Crime Facts*, U.S. Department of Justice, Bureau of Justice Statistics, 2004, http://www.ojp.usdoj.gov/bjs/dcf/contents.htm (accessed February 14, 2005)

FIGURE 5.4

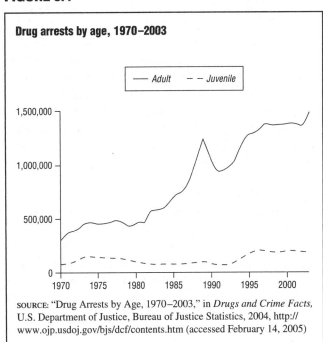

Drug arrests by age, 1970–2003

— Adult   – – Juvenile

SOURCE: "Drug Arrests by Age, 1970–2003," in *Drugs and Crime Facts*, U.S. Department of Justice, Bureau of Justice Statistics, 2004, http://www.ojp.usdoj.gov/bjs/dcf/contents.htm (accessed February 14, 2005)

Possession versus Sale

Most of those arrested for drug offenses are charged with possession rather than with the sale or manufacture of drugs. (See Figure 5.5.) According to FBI data as reported by the Bureau of Justice Statistics, in 1982 four-fifths (80%) of those arrested for drug offenses were held for carrying some kind of drug; that proportion was

FIGURE 5.5

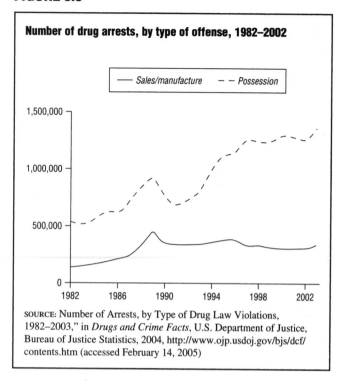

Number of drug arrests, by type of offense, 1982–2002

SOURCE: Number of Arrests, by Type of Drug Law Violations, 1982–2003," in *Drugs and Crime Facts*, U.S. Department of Justice, Bureau of Justice Statistics, 2004, http://www.ojp.usdoj.gov/bjs/dcf/contents.htm (accessed February 14, 2005)

FIGURE 5.6

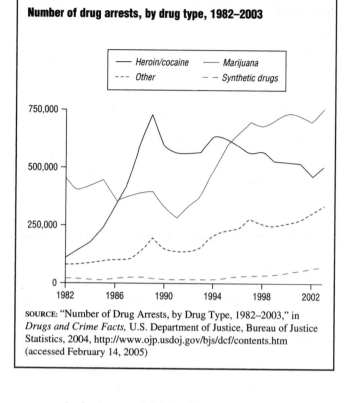

Number of drug arrests, by drug type, 1982–2003

SOURCE: "Number of Drug Arrests, by Drug Type, 1982–2003," in *Drugs and Crime Facts*, U.S. Department of Justice, Bureau of Justice Statistics, 2004, http://www.ojp.usdoj.gov/bjs/dcf/contents.htm (accessed February 14, 2005)

slightly higher in 2003. This percentage had been lower in the middle of the 1982–2003 period, having declined gradually from 80% in 1980 to 67% in 1991. The ratio began to increase again, eventually matching the 1980 level in 2001. Arrests for possession have grown at an annual rate slightly higher than arrests for sales/manufacture in the entire period, 4.6 versus 4.4% a year, but if measured from 1989 forward, arrests for sales/manufacture actually declined at the rate of 2.9% whereas arrests for possession increased 2.4% a year.

Arrest Trends by Drug Category

In 1982, 71% of all drug arrests were for the possession or sale of marijuana, according to the BJS. By 2003 marijuana-related arrests were just 45% of the total, but were still the largest number overall—about three-quarters of a million arrests out of 1.59 million. (See Figure 5.6.) Between 1982 and 2003 arrests linked to drugs fluctuated somewhat. In 1989, for instance, 54% of arrests were related to heroin/cocaine and only 29% to marijuana, police or public interest in the one rising sharply, while dropping in the other. But marijuana became important again, topping arrests once more in 1996. During the entire period shown in the figure (1982–2003), heroin/cocaine arrests increased at an annual rate of 9.8%; "other" drugs at the rate of 6.7% a year; synthetic drugs at 4.7%; and marijuana at 2.1% a year.

Synthetics, as the FBI defines the category, include all manufactured narcotic drugs, whether made for drug users exclusively or originally for medical purposes. The "other" category includes dangerous non-narcotic drugs like barbiturates and benzedrine.

Arrest records at the national level are a mix of use patterns and enforcement strategies that may be quite different from city to city; it is impossible to discern which drives which—use patterns resulting in arrests or police initiatives targeting specific user/seller groups. Supply systems, pricing, and demographics of drug use are highly variable; police tactics and approaches are both different and change over time. Data for the 1982–2003 period shown indicate great interest in heroin/cocaine peaking in 1989 and leveling off thereafter; a decreasing emphasis on marijuana until 1991, followed by a steady increase; and a persistent interest in non-narcotic drugs labeled "other" by the FBI.

Alcohol and Drug Trends

According to the UCR program of the FBI, arrest trends from 1984–2003 indicate that alcohol-related offenses, while remaining dominant, dropped, while drug-related offenses grew in importance. In 1984, 3.4 million people were arrested for alcohol-related offenses (drunkenness, driving under the influence, drug law violations); that year 708,400 were arrested for drug violations. Nineteen years later, in 2003, there were 2.6 million alcohol-related arrests and 1.7 million drug arrests. Alcohol consumption has been dropping, according to the National Institute on Alcohol Abuse and Alcoholism, an element of the U.S. Department of Health and Human Services. Per capita

TABLE 5.4

Drug arrests by race, 2002

[By offense charged, age group, and race. 10,370 agencies; 2002 estimated population 205,108,615.]

Offense charged	Total arrests					Percent[a]				
	Total	White	Black	American Indian or Alaskan Native	Asian or Pacific Islander	Total	White	Black	American Indian or Alaskan Native	Asian or Pacific Islander
Drug abuse violations	1,101,547	728,797	357,725	6,848	8,177	100.0	66.2	32.5	0.6	0.7

[a]Because of rounding, percents may not add to total.

SOURCE: Adapted from "Table 4.10. Arrests by Offense Charged, Age Group, and Race, United States, 2002," in *Sourcebook of Criminal Justice Statistics Online*, U.S. Department of Justice, Bureau of Justice Statistics, 2002, http://www.albany.edu/sourcebook/pdf/section4.pdf (accessed February 15, 2005)

consumption of all alcoholic beverages among those aged fourteen and older decreased from 2.65 gallons in 1984 to 2.19 gallons in 1998. Consumption of spirits fell from 0.94 gallons to 0.63 gallons (*Apparent Per Capita Alcohol Consumption*, Washington, DC: NIAAA, December 2000). Consumption of marijuana, heroin, and methamphetamines has increased in tonnage based on data from the Office of National Drug Control Policy (to be discussed later); physical quantities of cocaine have decreased. But while alcohol is legal, drugs are not.

Arrests and Race

Enforcing the official public policy on drugs has an important impact on the nation's justice system—local policing, the courts, and the state and federal corrections systems. A relatively small percentage of total users are arrested, but at increasing rates. Sentencing policies have changed to require mandatory incarceration of those who possess, not just those who sell, drugs. Prison populations have swollen as a consequence, putting pressure on prison capacities. Arrest rates, sentencing, and incarceration have been different for whites and African-Americans.

Most of those arrested for drug abuse violations are white. Of the 1.1 million persons identified by race in 2002 (records do not always capture the race/ethnicity category), 728,797 were white, accounting for 66.2% of all arrests. (See Table 5.4.) That year 357,725 African-Americans were arrested according to FBI data, 32.5% of the total; Asians/Pacific Islanders made up 0.7% of arrestees; and American Indians/Alaska Natives, 0.5%. According to the BJS, since 1993 arrests of African-Americans were down, whereas arrests of all the other racial categories rose. The most rapid growth in the 1993–2002 period was experienced by Asians and American Indians. Arrests of whites grew at a 2.9% rate; African-American arrests declined at the rate of 0.7% yearly.

When arrest rates are normalized by population—expressed as a ratio to the racial group as a whole—

African-Americans are arrested with greater frequency than any other group. In 2000, 390 whites were arrested for each one hundred thousand people in the eighteen-and-older population of whites. The corresponding rate for African-Americans was 1,460, for Asians it was 93, and for American Indians/Alaska Natives it was 342. An African-American person was nearly four times as likely to be arrested as a white person, more than fifteen times as likely as an Asian, and more than four times as likely to be arrested as an American Indian. Ratios for 1993 were even higher. One possible explanation for this is that law enforcement efforts are concentrated in areas of predominantly African-American settlement, not because African-Americans used drugs more than the other racial groups.

In 2003, 49.2% of whites aged twelve and over had used drugs in their lifetime, compared with 44.6% of African-Americans, 25.6% of Asians, and 62.4% of American Indians. (See Table 3.5 in Chapter 3.) Drug use in the past month was slightly lower for whites (8.3%) than African-Americans (8.7%), according to data obtained by SAMHSA in their *2003 National Survey on Drug Use and Health (NSDUH)*. The highest rates of past-month and past-year drug use was reported by American Indians in 2003, but their arrests rates were lower than those for whites. Use of drugs by those of Hispanic origin are shown, but arrest data are not broken down for Hispanics in the FBI statistics.

CONVICTION AND SENTENCING TRENDS

According to SAMHSA data, in 2003 nearly thirty-five million people aged twelve and older had used drugs in the past year. (See Table 3.3 in Chapter 3.) That year, as shown in Table 5.2, almost 1.7 million people were arrested for drug abuse violations, equivalent to about 5% of all estimated past-year users. According to data from the BJS, of the just-over one million people convicted by state courts for felonies in 2002, 32% were convicted for drug felonies (*State Court Sentencing of Convicted Felons, 2002*, Washington, DC: BJS, April

TABLE 5.5

Felony convictions and sentences in state courts relative to number of arrests, 2002

[For 100 arrests]

Offense	Felony conviction	Incarcerations	Prison sentences
Murder*	70	67	64
Robbery	47	41	34
Aggravated assault	23	17	10
Burglary	50	36	23
Motor vehicle theft	18	14	7
Drug trafficking	80	54	34

*Includes nonnegligent manslaughter.

SOURCE: "Felony Convictions and Sentences in State Courts Relative to the Number of Arrests, 2002," in *Drugs and Crime Facts*, U.S. Department of Justice, Bureau of Justice Statistics, December 2004, http://www.ojp.usdoj .gov/bjs/dcf/contents.htm (accessed February 14, 2005)

TABLE 5.6

Sentence length and time served, by offenses, 2002

[In months]

Most serious conviction offense	Mean state prison sentence	Estimated time to be served*
Murder	225	142
Sexual assault	100	64
Robbery	91	53
Aggravated assault	54	36
Burglary	50	24
Larceny	34	18
Drug offenses		
Possession	35	14
Trafficking	55	24

*Derived by multiplying the percentage of sentence to be served by the mean sentence imposed.

SOURCE: "Mean State Prison Sentence and Estimated Time to Be Served in Prison, by Offenses, 2002," in *Drugs and Crime Facts*, U.S. Department of Justice, Bureau of Justice Statistics, 2004, http://www.ojp.usdoj.gov/bjs/dcf/ contents.htm (accessed February 14, 2005)

2005 http://www.ojp.usdoj.gov/bjs/dcf/contents.htm). Of these, nearly two-thirds were convicted for trafficking—85% were males and nearly half were in their twenties. The number of those convicted of possession was less than 1% of the total number of users of drugs. For every one hundred arrests for drug trafficking, eighty of those arrestees were convicted of a felony in state courts, and thirty-four were sentenced to state prison. (See Table 5.5.) Table 5.6 shows the average length of those sentences.

Convictions and Race

Minorities represent a significant and growing portion of American prisoners, with the growth rate of incarcerations due to drug offenses from 1995–2001 committed by African-Americans at 23%, opposed to that of whites at 18%. (See Table 5.7.) According to BJS data, of the 266,465 adults arrested for drug trafficking in 2002, 212,810 were convicted. According to the BJS, of those convicted, 85% were male, 51% were white, and 47% were African-American. In absolute numbers, more whites are arrested and convicted for drug violations than African-Americans, but African-Americans are much more likely to be arrested and convicted in proportion to their representation in the population.

Once convicted for drug offenses, more African-Americans, on average, are incarcerated than whites, and more whites on average receive milder jail sentences (less than a year) than blacks or get probation or split sentences, as shown in Table 5.8. Of all whites convicted of drug offenses in 2000, 63% were incarcerated, versus 73% of all African-Americans convicted of drug offenses. Among convicted whites, 30% went to prison (sentences of a year or longer), and among African-Americans this figure was 48%. About one-third (32%) of whites got the milder jail sentence, versus 25% of African-Americans. More whites received nonincarceration sentences (37%) than African-Americans (28%). Similarly, more whites received probation (32%) than African-Americans (24%). The "other" category shown in the table includes split sentences and other disposition of the cases.

Truth-in-Sentencing

Sentence lengths for all offenses moved upward in U.S. district courts for almost half a century, from 1945 to 1991. Average sentence lengths for drug offenses also showed an upward trend during this time, except for a few slight dips over the years. (See Table 5.9.) A slight downward trend in sentence lengths for drug offenses took place during the 1990s through 2001, followed by an upturn in 2002 and 2003.

Sentence lengths, however, do not fully convey the picture. The time actually served for an offense is a better indicator of the actual "price" society extracts for an offense. Thus, for instance, a person sentenced to five years who serves 60% of his sentence and is then paroled serves as long as a person sentenced to four years who serves 75% of her sentence. In both cases, time served will be three years. Public perceptions in the late 1970s that felons were sentenced only to walk free after doing a brief stint in prison culminated in the "truth-in-sentencing" movement, an attempt at the state and federal levels to reform sentencing practices. The State of Washington passed the first truth-in-sentencing statute in 1984. Congress established the U.S. Sentencing Commission in the same year with the purpose of setting mandatory sentence lengths. The consequence of these actions (42 states and the District of Columbia have passed truth-in-sentencing laws since 1984) was an increase in

TABLE 5.7

Total growth of state prison population, by race and offense, 1995–2001

	White		Black		Hispanic	
	Increase, 1995–2001	Percent of total	Increase, 1995–2001	Percent of total	Increase, 1995–2001	Percent of total
Total	90,700	100%	83,200	100%	35,300	100%
Violent	53,000	59	47,400	57	29,900	82
Property	3,000	3	0	—	−100	—
Drug	16,200	18	19,100	23	−1,400	—
Public-order	18,000	20	16,800	20	6,800	18

SOURCE: "Total Growth of Sentenced Prisoners under State Jurisdiction, by Offense, Race, and Hispanic Origin, 1995–2001," in *Drugs and Crime Facts*, U.S. Department of Justice, Bureau of Justice Statistics, July 2003, http:// www.ojp.usdoj.gov/bjs/dcf/contents.htm (accessed February 14, 2005)

TABLE 5.8

Felony sentencing, by type, as percent of total, imposed by state courts, 1998 and 2000

	Total	Incarceration						Nonincarceration					
		Total		Prison		Jail		Total		Probation		Other	
		1998	2000	1998	2000	1998	2000	1998	2000	1998	2000	1998	2000
Whites													
Drug offenses	100	65	63	33	30	32	32	35	37	32	32	3	6
Possession	100	67	62	31	27	36	35	33	38	30	31	3	7
Trafficking	100	64	63	35	33	29	31	36	37	33	32	3	4
Blacks													
Drug offenses	100	73	73	51	48	23	25	27	28	24	24	2	3
Possession	100	72	72	47	48	25	24	28	28	25	25	2	4
Trafficking	100	74	73	52	48	21	25	26	27	24	24	2	3

Note: Detail may not sum to total because of rounding. Racial categories include Hispanics. Shaded areas are those where one racial group is less represented than the other.

SOURCE: Adapted from Ann L. Pastore, and Kathleen Maguire, "Table 4.10. Arrests," in *Sourcebook of Criminal Justice Statistics, 1996–2001*, U.S. Bureau of Justice Statistics; original data obtained from successive editions of *Crime in the United States*, Federal Bureau of Investigation

time served even as, in some areas, the average length of the formal sentences grew shorter.

The effects of truth-in-sentencing at the state level are illustrated using data for 1990 and 1999 for all categories of offenses. (See Table 5.10.) The average sentence length for all offenses went down from sixty-nine months in 1990 to sixty-five months in 1999. Total time served went up from twenty-eight months to thirty-four months, a consequence of the fact that the percent of sentence served increased from 38% in 1990 to 48.7% in 1999.

In the drug offense category, state prison sentence length for possession dropped from sixty-one to fifty-six months from 1990 to 1999, but time served increased from eighteen to twenty-five months. Sentence length for drug trafficking increased from sixty to sixty-four months; actual time served went up from twenty-two to twenty-nine months. As these data show, there remained in this period a fairly wide gap between the average sentence imposed and the actual time served, but time served was up. Under federal sentencing guidelines, persons sentenced are required to serve 85% of the imposed sentence. At the state level in 1999, the percent of time served was well below 85%: 42.4% for possession, and 42% for trafficking. Those selling drugs, in effect, served slightly less of their imposed sentences than those caught carrying drugs, though percentage of time served was up from 1990, when those convicted of possession served only 29% and those convicted of trafficking served only 34.8%.

DRUGS' IMPACT ON PRISONS

According to the BJS, on December 31, 2003, there were 2,085,620 prisoners held in federal or state prisons or in local jails. The total had increased 2.6% from year-end 2002. Of those held in state prisons in 2003, about one in five were in prison for drug offenses. Drug offenders outnumbered those held for burglary, larceny, auto theft, fraud, and all other property crimes. Between 1995 and 2001, 15% of the total growth in the number of prisoners was attributable to the increasing number of drug offenders, while 63% was attributable to violent offenders.

Prisoners incarcerated for drug violations have become the second-most-populous category over a period of twenty years at the state level and the largest group in the federal prison system, as illustrated in Figure 5.7 and Table 5.11. Persons incarcerated in state prison systems for drug offenses increased more than 1,000% between 1980 and 2001. Incarcerations for public order offenses, which include weapons violations grew nearly as fast. In the federal system, drug offenders make up more than half the prison population. Here, the number of drug offense cases handled quadrupled between 1980 and 2000.

According to the BJS, persons in prison for drug offenses were 6.5% of the state prison population in 1980. By 1990 they had topped 20% of the prison population and have remained at that level since then, reaching

TABLE 5.9

Drug charges, by type and sentence lengths, in U.S. District Courts, 1945–2003

[By type and length of sentence]

					Type of sentence							
			Imprisonment									
			Regular sentences[a]									
	Total	Total regular	1 through 12 months	13 through 35 months	36 through 60 months	Over 60 months	Life sentences	Other[b]	Probation	Fine and other[c]	Average sentence to imprisonment (in months)[d]	Average sentence to probation (in months)[e]
1945	861	X	308	360	140	53	NA	X	287	37	22.2	NA
1946	949	X	430	377	108	34	NA	X	369	20	18.7	NA
1947	1,128	X	471	452	161	44	NA	X	504	38	19.7	NA
1948	1,048	X	488	408	122	30	NA	X	411	23	18.6	NA
1949	1,187	X	541	451	152	43	NA	X	398	13	18.9	NA
1950	1,654	X	595	736	218	105	NA	X	471	11	21.9	NA
1951	1,659	X	473	671	328	187	NA	X	345	24	27.1	NA
1952	1,551	X	221	652	402	276	NA	X	312	6	35.2	NA
1953	1,586	X	108	789	358	331	NA	X	403	14	38.4	NA
1954	1,483	X	72	681	360	370	NA	X	411	16	41.3	NA
1955	1,457	X	47	648	360	402	NA	X	329	17	43.5	NA
1956	1,258	X	30	511	341	376	NA	X	250	13	45.8	NA
1957	1,432	X	16	326	248	842	NA	X	220	2	66.0	NA
1958	1,351	X	25	167	141	1,018	NA	X	282	8	69.4	NA
1959	1,151	X	43	126	95	887	NA	X	224	3	74.2	NA
1960	1,232	X	33	145	148	906	NA	X	271	3	72.8	NA
1961	1,258	X	42	126	105	985	NA	X	252	5	74.0	NA
1962	1,173	X	38	129	106	900	NA	X	217	13	70.5	NA
1963	1,085	X	39	144	113	789	NA	X	304	17	70.1	NA
1964	1,076	X	28	142	157	749	NA	X	309	23	63.7	NA
1965	1,257	X	53	186	197	821	NA	X	480	18	60.3	NA
1966	1,272	X	85	154	276	757	NA	X	589	13	61.3	NA
1967	1,180	X	83	139	245	713	NA	X	620	22	62.0	NA
1968	1,368	X	93	141	293	841	NA	X	728	33	64.4	NA
1969	1,581	X	110	179	500	892	NA	X	1,110	18	63.7	NA
1970	1,283	X	101	166	276	740	NA	X	1,156	22	64.8	NA
1971	1,834	X	249	300	428	857	NA	X	1,258	70	58.5	NA
1972	3,050	X	882	396	789	983	NA	X	2,068	130	46.4	NA
1973	5,097	X	1,445	744	1,343	1,565	NA	X	2,591	126	45.5	NA
1974	5,125	X	1,547	792	1,390	1,396	NA	X	3,039	81	43.7	NA
1975	4,887	X	1,366	706	1,441	1,374	NA	X	3,209	55	45.3	NA
1976	5,039	X	1,221	790	1,544	1,484	NA	X	2,927	75	47.6	NA
1977	5,223	X	1,505	886	1,366	1,466	NA	X	2,324	88	47.3	NA
1978	4,119	3,605	885	623	956	1,141	NA	514	1,630	68	51.3	38.6
1979	3,641	2,820	369	614	868	969	NA	821	1,379	47	50.8	37.8
1980	3,479	2,547	281	565	792	909	NA	932	1,232	38	54.5	38.7
1981	3,856	2,865	403	578	748	1,136	NA	991	1,371	119	55.5	36.6
1982	4,586	3,516	383	729	966	1,438	NA	1,070	1,617	133	61.4	34.1
1983	5,449	4,150	447	890	1,011	1,802	NA	1,299	1,893	148	63.8	33.7
1984	5,756	4,306	354	845	1,173	1,934	NA	1,450	1,584	119	65.7	43.2
1985	6,786	5,207	411	1,103	1,459	2,234	NA	1,579	2,039	238	64.8	36.2
1986	8,152	6,601	506	1,271	1,808	3,016	NA	1,551	2,353	259	70.0	38.7
1987	9,907	8,188	613	1,491	2,049	4,035	NA	1,719	2,680	112	73.0	39.9
1988	9,983	8,560	708	1,466	1,577	4,809	NA	1,423	3,042	137	78.0	33.4
1989	11,626	10,838	1,270	2,343	1,844	5,381	NA	788	2,358	155	73.8	32.8
1990	13,838	13,462	1,490	3,047	1,801	7,124	NA	376	2,135	215	79.3	32.3
1991	14,382[f]	14,286	1,687	2,828	3,063	6,708	34	61	1,896	68	95.7	53.4
1992	16,040	15,775	1,810	3,423	3,397	7,145	80	185	2,011	194	87.8	38.7
1993	16,995[f]	16,639	2,097	3,383	4,128	7,031	186	169	1,943	310	83.2	35.8
1994	15,623	15,130	1,836	3,074	3,798	6,422	238	255	1,908	73	84.3	34.4
1995	14,157	13,734	1,606	2,716	3,311	6,101	150	273	1,597	107	88.7	33.6
1996	18,333	16,684	1,643	3,334	4,025	7,113	197	372	1,534	112	82.5	35.0
1997	18,231[f]	17,456	1,687	4,166	4,445	7,158	228	546	1,523	79	79.3	34.9
1998	19,809	19,062	2,100	4,443	4,517	8,002	180	567	1,629	91	78.0	34.9
1999	22,443[f]	21,513	2,670	5,074	5,240	8,529	205	724	1,719	85	74.6	34.2

TABLE 5.9

Drug charges, by type and sentence lengths, in U.S. District Courts, 1945–2003 [CONTINUED]

[By type and length of sentence]

		Type of sentence										Average sentence to imprisonment (in months)[d]	Average sentence to probation (in months)[e]
		Imprisonment											
		Regular sentences[a]											
	Total	Total regular	1 through 12 months	13 through 35 months	36 through 60 months	Over 60 months	Life sentences	Other[b]	Probation	Fine and other[c]			
2000	23,120	22,207	2,523	5,095	5,452	9,137	148	765	1,591	75		75.7	35.1
2001	24,011	23,127	2,780	5,350	5,670	9,327	122	762	1,671	133		73.8	34.5
2002	25,031	23,838	2,825	5,250	5,727	10,036	168	1,025	1,947	148		75.9	33.4
2003	25,060	23,937	2,632	4,781	5,967	10,557	157	966	1,781	145		80.2	32.2

Note: Data for 1945–91 are reported for the 12-month period ending June 30. Beginning in 1992, data are reported for the federal fiscal year, which is the 12-month period ending September 30.
[a]Includes sentences of more than 6 months that are to be followed by a term of probation (mixed sentences). Beginning in 1991, includes sentences of at least 1 month that may be followed by a term of probation.
[b]From 1978–88, "other" includes split sentences, indeterminate sentences, and Youth Corrections Act and youthful offender sentences. In 1989 and 1990, the category includes split sentences and indeterminate sentences. Beginning in 1991, "other" includes deportation, suspended and sealed sentences, imprisonment of 4 days or less, and no sentence.
[c]Includes supervised release, probation of 4 days or less, suspended sentences, sealed sentences, and no sentence.
[d]From 1978–90, split sentences, Youth Corrections Act and youthful offender sentences, and life sentences are not included in computing average sentence. Beginning in 1991, life sentences, death sentences, deportation, suspended and sealed sentences, imprisonment of 4 days or less, and no sentence also are not included in computing average sentence.
[e]From 1986–90, split sentences, indeterminate sentences, and Youth Corrections Act and youthful offender sentences are not included in computing average sentence. Beginning in 1991, supervised release, probation of 4 days or less, suspended sentences, sealed sentences, and no sentence also are not included in computing the average sentence.

SOURCE: "Table 5.38. Defendants Sentenced for Violation of Drug Laws in U.S. District Courts by Type and Length of Sentence, 1945–2003," in *Sourcebook of Criminal Justice Statistics Online*, U.S. Department of Justice, Bureau of Justice Statistics, 2002, http://www.albany.edu/sourcebook/pdf/t538.pdf (accessed February 15, 2005)

TABLE 5.10

Sentence length and time served for first releases from state prisons, 1990 and 1999

	Mean sentence length[a]		Mean time served in —				Total time served[c]		Percent of sentence served[d]	
			Jail[b]		Prison					
	1990	1999	1990	1999	1990	1999	1990	1999	1990	1999
All offenses	69 mo	65 mo	6 mo	5 mo	22 mo	29 mo	28 mo	34 mo	38.0%	48.7%
Violent offenses	99 mo	87 mo	7 mo	6 mo	39 mo	45 mo	46 mo	51 mo	43.8%	55.0%
Murder[e]	209	192	9	10	83	96	92	106	43.1	53.1
Manslaughter	88	102	5	6	31	49	37	56	41.0	52.5
Rape	128	124	7	6	55	73	62	79	45.5	58.3
Other sexual assault	77	76	5	6	30	42	36	47	43.8	57.0
Robbery	104	97	7	6	41	48	48	55	42.8	51.6
Assault	64	62	6	6	23	33	30	39	43.9	58.7
Property offenses	65 mo	58 mo	6 mo	5 mo	18 mo	25 mo	24 mo	29 mo	34.4%	45.6%
Burglary	79	73	6	5	22	31	29	36	33.9	44.3
Larceny/theft	52	45	6	4	14	19	20	24	35.5	46.9
Motor vehicle theft	56	44	7	5	13	20	20	25	33.1	52.5
Fraud	56	49	6	4	14	19	20	23	33.2	41.7
Drug offenses	57 mo	59 mo	6 mo	5 mo	14 mo	22 mo	20 mo	27 mo	32.9%	42.8%
Possession	61	56	6	5	12	20	18	25	29.0	42.4
Trafficking	60	64	6	5	16	24	22	29	34.8	42.0
Public-order offenses	40 mo	42 mo	5 mo	4 mo	14 mo	19 mo	18 mo	23 mo	42.6%	51.1%

Note: Based on prisoners with a sentence of more than 1 year who were released for the first time on the current sentence. Excludes prisoners released from prison by escape, death, transfer, appeal, or detainer.
[a]Maximum sentence length for the most serious offense. Excludes sentences of life, life without parole, life plus additional years, and death.
[b]Time served in jail and credited toward the current sentence.
[c]Based on time served in jail and in prison. Detail may not add to total because of rounding.
[d]Based on total sentence length (not shown) for all consecutive sentences.
[e]Includes nonnegligent manslaughter.

SOURCE: Timothy A. Hughes, Doris James Wilson, and Allen J. Beck, "Table 5. Sentence Length and Time Served for First Releases from State Prison, 1990 and 1999," in *Trends in State Parole, 1990–2000*, in U.S. Bureau of Justice Statistics, October 2001

FIGURE 5.7

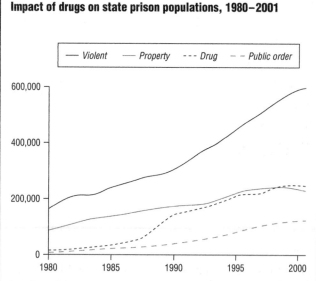

Impact of drugs on state prison populations, 1980–2001

Note: From 1995 to 2001 the number of drug offenders in state prison increased by 30,600 inmates (15%).

SOURCE: "State Prison Population by Offense Type, 1980–2001," in *Drugs and Crime Facts*, U.S. Department of Justice, Bureau of Justice Statistics, July 2003, http://www.ojp.usdoj.gov/bjs/dcf/contents.htm (accessed February 14, 2005)

TABLE 5.11

Federal prisoners by type of offense, 2004

Drug offenses:	88,960 (53.8%)
Weapons, explosives, arson:	21,475 (13.0%)
Immigration:	18,325 (11.1%)
Robbery:	10,078 (6.1%)
Burglary, larceny, property offenses:	6,784 (4.1%)
Extortion, fraud, bribery:	6,856 (4.1%)
Homicide, aggravated assault, and kidnapping offenses:	5,326 (3.2%)
Miscellaneous:	3,478 (2.1%)
Sex offenses:	1,732 (1.0%)
Banking and Insurance, counterfeit, embezzlement:	1,013 (0.6%)
Courts or corrections:	709 (0.4%)
Continuing criminal enterprise:	603 (0.4%)
National security:	103 (0.1%)

SOURCE: "Type of Offenses," in *Federal Bureau of Prisons Quick Facts*, U.S. Department of Justice, Federal Bureau of Prisons, March 2005, http://www.bop.gov//about/facts.jsp#2 (accessed February 15, 2005)

a peak of 21.8% in 1990, dropping slightly to 20.9% in 2000. Data for federal cases handled show that drug-related cases were already fairly high, 18.2%, in 1980. They more than doubled to 36.9% by 2000.

A more recent look at federal prisoners shows that as of March 2005 the number of drug offenders held in federal prison had grown to 88,960, or 53.8% of the total federal inmate population, according to data from the Bureau of Prisons. (See Table 5.11.)

The much larger state prison population of drug offenders (246,100 individuals in 2001) were overwhelmingly male, 90.2%. The majority of these prisoners were African-American, about a quarter were white, and nearly one fifth were Hispanic, according to BJS statistics.

Crowded Prisons and Growing Costs

State prisons have been operating at 100% of capacity for several years, and federal prisons are "overbooked." In 2001 the statistics were much the same; state prisons operated at 101% of capacity and federal prisons continued to operate at 131% of capacity. Pressures on correctional facilities are the result of growing rates of drug arrests that result in felony convictions combined with truth-in-sentencing policies that cause actual time served to increase.

According to the BJS (*Sourcebook of Criminal Justice Statistics 2001*, Washington, DC: BJS, 2002), state expenditures on corrections were $4.55 billion in 1980 at a time when persons serving time for drug offenses were 6.5% of all state prisoners. In 1980, therefore, about $293 million was used to house, hold, guard, feed, clothe, and to provide medical care for drug-law offending prisoners. By 2001, costs of state corrections had risen to $35.8 billion. Drug offenders were nearly one quarter of state prison populations at this time, meaning that nearly $8.9 billion was spent to imprison them.

CHAPTER 6
DRUG TRAFFICKING

In America, all matters relating to public health receive careful attention. No other country gives such careful study to questions that affect it, or makes such determined efforts to improve it and raise it to a higher level. In the last few years our attention has been drawn to a condition which has now become a grave menace to our nation's welfare, something which is extraneous, artificial, and wholly uncalled for, yet which is assuming such proportions that we must recognize it as a threatening danger. This is the great increase of the drug habit. To meet this danger, most drastic laws regulating the sale and distribution of drugs have been in force for a number of years; yet we see these laws, theoretically perfect, totally unable to cope with the situation.

—Ellen N. LaMotte, writing in *The Atlantic Monthly*, June 1922

While the accuracy of the above statement is debatable, there's no question that many policy makers see drugs as a major threat to our national well-being and accordingly propose strong measures to combat that perceived threat. Figure 6.1 and Figure 6.2 present contrasting maps of the perceived drug threat in the 1990s and in the new century.

CRIMINAL PENALTIES FOR TRAFFICKING
Federal Penalties

The Controlled Substances Act (PL 91-513, 1970, last amended in 2000) provides penalties for the unlawful manufacture, distribution, and dispensing (or trafficking) of controlled substances, based on the schedule (rank) of the drug or substance. Generally, the more dangerous the drug and the larger the quantity involved, the stiffer the penalty. Trafficking of heroin, cocaine, LSD, and PCP, all Schedule I or II drugs (see Table 2.1 in Chapter 2), includes mandatory jail time and fines. A person caught selling at least five hundred grams but less than five kilograms of cocaine powder (seventeen ounces to just under eleven pounds) will receive a minimum of five years in prison

and may be fined up to $2 million for a first offense. (See Table 6.1.) The same penalty is imposed for the sale of five to forty-nine grams of cocaine base ("crack"). Five grams are equal to the weight of six plain M&Ms candies, and forty-nine grams are a little more than a bag of M&Ms candies (47.9 grams). The high penalty for selling crack is an expression of the unusual severity with which legislators are trying to curb the use of this drug.

Penalties double with the second offense to ten years in prison and up to $4 million in fines. When higher quantities are involved (five or more kilograms of cocaine powder, fifty grams or more of crack, etc.), penalties for the first offense are ten years, and fines up to $4 million may be levied. For the second offense, twenty years and up to $8 million in fines are given, and the third offense results in mandatory life imprisonment. These examples are for an individual. Higher penalties apply if an organized group is involved or if a death or injury is associated with the arrest event.

These penalties apply also to the sale of fentanyl (a powerful painkiller medicine) or like-acting drugs, heroin, LSD, methamphetamine, and PCP. The smallest amount, which can earn someone a minimum sentence of five years in prison and a fine of up to $2 million, involves trafficking in LSD, where a one-gram amount carries a five-year minimum sentence in prison.

Punishments for marijuana, hashish, and hashish oil are shown in Table 6.2. Special penalties exist for marijuana trafficking, since it may be traded in large quantities or grown in substantial amounts. The lower the amounts sold or the fewer the plants grown, the lower the sentence. A person cultivating one to forty-nine plants or selling less than fifty kilograms of marijuana mixture, ten kilograms or less of hashish, or one kilogram or less of hashish oil may get a

FIGURE 6.1

Drug smuggling in the 1990s

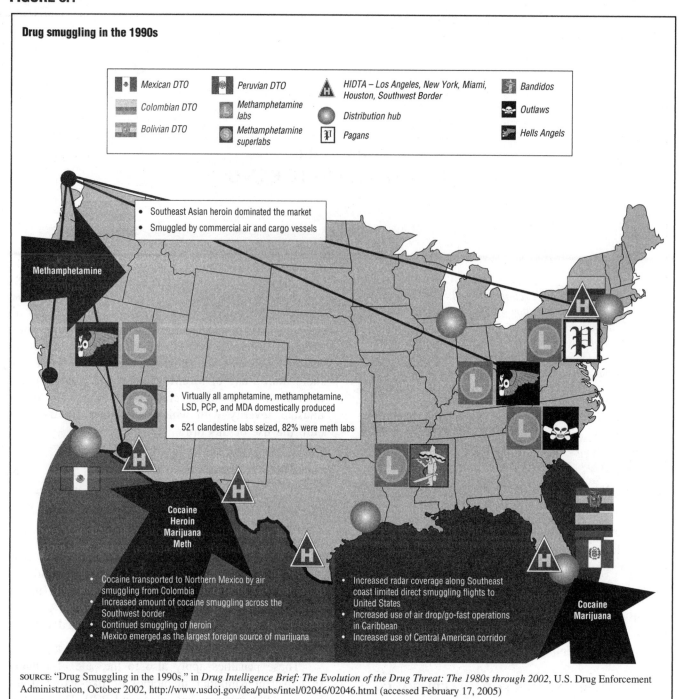

SOURCE: "Drug Smuggling in the 1990s," in *Drug Intelligence Brief: The Evolution of the Drug Threat: The 1980s through 2002*, U.S. Drug Enforcement Administration, October 2002, http://www.usdoj.gov/dea/pubs/intel/02046/02046.html (accessed February 17, 2005)

maximum sentence of five years in prison and a maximum fine of $250,000. Sentences for second offenses involving large amounts of marijuana may earn the trafficker up to life imprisonment.

State Laws

The states have the discretionary power to make their own drug laws. Possession of marijuana may be a misdemeanor in one state but a felony in another. Prison sentences can also vary for the same charges in different states—distribution of five hundred grams of cocaine as a Class C felony may specify ten to fifty years in one state and twenty-four to forty years in another.

Changes in 1990 to the Controlled Substances Act (PL 101-647) led to more than 450 new drug laws in forty-four states and the District of Columbia. Most states have followed the model of the Controlled Substances Act and have enacted laws that facilitate seizure of drug-trafficking profits, specify greater penalties for trafficking, and promote "user accountability" by punishing drug users.

FIGURE 6.2

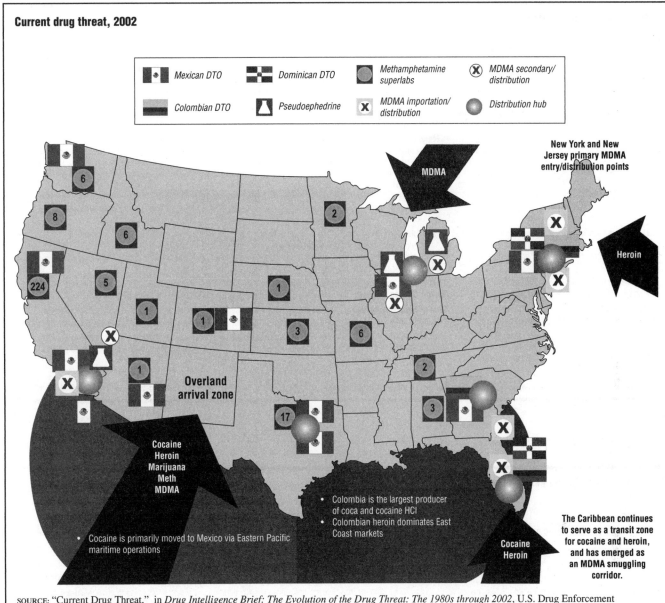

Current drug threat, 2002

Legend:
- Mexican DTO
- Colombian DTO
- Dominican DTO
- Pseudoephedrine
- Methamphetamine superlabs
- MDMA importation/distribution
- MDMA secondary/distribution
- Distribution hub

MDMA

New York and New Jersey primary MDMA entry/distribution points

Heroin

Overland arrival zone

Cocaine
Heroin
Marijuana
Meth
MDMA

• Cocaine is primarily moved to Mexico via Eastern Pacific maritime operations

• Colombia is the largest producer of coca and cocaine HCl
• Colombian heroin dominates East Coast markets

Cocaine
Heroin

The Caribbean continues to serve as a transit zone for cocaine and heroin, and has emerged as an MDMA smuggling corridor.

SOURCE: "Current Drug Threat," in *Drug Intelligence Brief: The Evolution of the Drug Threat: The 1980s through 2002*, U.S. Drug Enforcement Administration, October 2002, http://www.usdoj.gov/dea/pubs/intel/02046/02046.html (accessed February 17, 2005).

IS THE PROFIT WORTH THE RISK?

> *Only in the illicit drug industry can seizures of between 10 and 30% of production, the forfeiture of a (small) percentage of financial and other assets and the loss, through death or imprisonment, of a percentage of operatives, impose merely an imperceptible or short-term impact on retail price and still allow large net profits at every stage of the distribution chain.*
>
> —*World Drug Report*, United Nations Drug Programme, New York, 1997

Despite the possibility of long prison terms—up to life imprisonment—many drug dealers evidently consider the enormous potential profits worth the risk. The media often report drug "busts" and indictments of persons involved in multimillion- or billion-dollar operations. Paying fines of hundreds of thousands of dollars, or even millions of dollars, becomes part of doing business when the profits are so high. Exact figures on the amount of money made from drug trafficking and sales are not available.

SUBSTANTIAL WORLD AND U.S. TRADE

The United Nations, in its *Economic and Social Consequences of Drug Abuse and Illicit Drug Trafficking* (New York: International Drug Programme, 1998), estimated the total revenue of the world drug trade at about $400 billion.

TABLE 6.1

Federal trafficking penalties*

Drug/schedule	Quantity	Penalties	Quantity	Penalties
Cocaine (schedule II) Cocaine base (schedule II) Fentanyl (schedule II) Fentanyl Analogue (schedule I) Heroin (schedule I)	500–4999 gms 5–49 gms mixture 40–399 gms mixture 10–99 gms mixture 100–999 gms mixture	**First offense:** Not less than 5 years, and not more than 40 years. If death or serious injury, not less than 20 or more than life. Fine of not more than $2 million if an individual, $5 million if not an individual	5 kgs or more 50 gms or more mixture 400 gms or more mixture 100 gms or more mixture 1kg or more mixture	**First offense:** Not less than 10 years, and not more than life. If death or serious injury, not less than 20 or more than life. Fine of not more than $4 million if an individual, $10 million if not an individual.
LSD (schedule I) Methamphetamine (schedule II) PCP (schedule II)	1–9 gms mixture 5–49 gms pure or 50–499 gms mixture 10–99 gms pure or 100–999 gms mixture	**Second offense:** Not less than 10 years, and not more than life. If death or serious injury, life imprisonment. Fine of not more than $4 million if an individual, $10 million if not an individual	10 gms or more mixture 50 gms or more pure or 500 gms or more mixture 100 gms or more pure or 1 kg or more mixture	**Second offense:** Not less than 20 years, and not more than life. If death or serious injury, life imprisonment. Fine of not more than $8 million if an individual, $20 million if not an individual. **Two or more prior offenses:** Life imprisonment.
Other schedule I & II drugs	Any amount	**First offense:** Not more than 20 years. If death or serious injury, not less than 20 years, or more than life. Fine $1 million if an individual, $5 million if not an individual.		
Flunitrazepam (schedule IV)	1 gm or more	**Second offense:** Not more than 30 years. If death or serious injury, not less than life. Fine $2 million if an individual, $10 million if not an individual.		
Other schedule III drugs Flunitrazepam (schedule IV)	Any amount 30 to 999 mgs	**First offense:** Not more than 5 years. Fine not more than $250,000 if an individual, $1 million if not an individual. **Second offense:** Not more than 10 years. Fine not more than $500,000 if an individual, $2 million if not an individual.		
All other schedule IV drugs Flunitrazepam (schedule IV)	Any amount Less than 30 mgs	**First offense:** Not more than 3 years. Fine not more than $250,000 if an individual, $1 million if not an individual. **Second offense:** Not more than 6 years. Fine not more than $500,000 if an individual, $2 million if not an individual.		
All other schedule V drugs	Any amount	**First offense:** Not more than 1 year. Fine not more than $100,000 if an individual, $250,000 if not an individual. **Second offense:** Not more than 2 years. Fine not more than $200,000 if an individual, $500,000 if not an individual.		

*Does not include marijuana, hashish, or hash oil.

SOURCE: "Federal Trafficking Penalties," U.S. Drug Enforcement Administration, http://www.usdoj.gov/dea/agency/penalties.htm (accessed February 15, 2005)

TABLE 6.2

Federal drug trafficking penalties—marijuana

Description	Quantity	1st offense	2nd offense
Marijuana	1,000 kg or more mixture; or 1,000 or more plants	• Not less than 10 years, not more than life • If death or serious injury, not less than 20 years, not more than life • Fine not more than $4 million individual, $10 million other than individual	• Not less than 20 years, not more than life • If death or serious injury, mandatory life • Fine not more than $8 million individual, $20 million other than individual
Marijuana	100 kg to 999 kg mixture; or 100–999 plants	• Not less than 5 years, not more than 40 years • If death or serious injury, not less than 20 years, not more than life • Fine not more than $2 million individual, $5 million other than individual	• Not less than 10 years, not more than life • If death or serious injury, mandatory life • Fine not more than $4 million individual, $10 million other than individual
Marijuana	More than 10 kgs hashish; 50–99 plants More than 1 kg of hashish oil; 50–99 plants	• Not more than 20 years • If death or serious injury, not less than 20 years, not more than life • Fine $1 million individual, $5 million other than individual	• Not more than 30 years • If death or serious injury, mandatory life • Fine $2 million individual, $10 million other than individual
Marijuana Hashish Hashish oil	1–49 plants; less than 50 kg mixture 10 kg or less 10 kg or less 1 kg or less	• Not more than 5 years • Fine not more than $250,000, $1 million other than individual	• Not more than 10 years • Fine $500,000 individual, $2 million other than individual

Note: Marijuana is a schedule I controlled substance.

SOURCE: "Federal Trafficking Penalties—Marijuana," U.S. Drug Enforcement Administration, http://www.usdoj.gov/dea/agency/penalties.htm (accessed February 15, 2005)

The *World Drug Report 2004* (United Nations Office on Drugs and Crime, 2005, http://www.unodc.org/unodc/en/world_drug_report.html) estimates that 185 million people—4.7% of the world's population ages fifteen to sixty-four—were users of illicit drugs during the period from 2001 to 2003. The survey concluded that about nine million used heroin; thirteen million used cocaine; 146 million used cannabis; and thirty million used amphetamine-type stimulants.

TABLE 6.3

Total expenditures on illicit drugs, 1988–2000

[In billions]

Year	Cocaine	Heroin	Marijuana	Meth-amphetamine	Other drugs	Total
1988	107.0	26.1	12.1	5.8	3.3	154
1989	88.4	24.3	11.0	5.8	2.8	132
1990	69.9	22.5	15.0	5.7	2.2	115
1991	57.1	20.3	14.0	3.7	2.3	97
1992	49.9	17.2	14.6	4.8	1.5	88
1993	45.0	13.8	12.0	5.1	1.5	77
1994	42.8	13.2	12.2	7.6	2.6	78
1995	40.0	13.2	10.2	9.2	2.7	75
1996	39.2	12.8	9.5	10.1	2.7	74
1997	34.7	11.4	10.5	9.3	2.5	68
1998	34.9	11.1	10.8	8.0	2.3	67
1999	35.6	10.1	10.6	5.8	2.6	65
2000*	35.3	10.0	10.5	5.4	2.4	64

Note: Amounts are in constant 2000 dollars.

SOURCE: "Table 41. Total U.S. Expenditures on Illicit Drugs, 1988–2000," in *National Drug Control Strategy: Data Supplement*, The White House, March 2004, http://www.whitehousedrugpolicy.gov/publications/policy/ndcs04/data_suppl_2004.pdf (accessed March 31, 2005)

According to the White House's Office of National Drug Control Policy (ONDCP), the U.S. share of drug expenditures in 2000 was $64 billion. (See Table 6.3.) In 1998, by way of comparison, states spent about half that sum and the federal government one-fourth on various programs and efforts to control drugs.

WORLD PRODUCTION

The Bureau for International Narcotics and Law Enforcement Affairs, an element of the U.S. State Department, reports data on the amount of land cultivated to raise opium poppy, coca leaf, and cannabis, the hemp plant from which marijuana and hashish are derived (*International Narcotics Control Strategy Report* [INCSR], Washington, DC, March 2004). From estimates and observations in INCSR of the land cultivated, the bureau develops estimates of potential production.

According to the State Department, the largest amount of cultivated land was dedicated to the production of coca leaf, followed by opium poppy and cannabis. (See Table 6.4. Note that because of reporting changes, 2003 coca cultivation in Columbia—the biggest producer of coca—is not included in the graphic, making the 2003 totals for coca cultivation misleading.) In 2003, 59,600 hectares of land were used growing coca, a sharp decrease from 205,450 the previous year. A hectare is 2.47 acres. Opium poppy was cultivated on 127,030 hectares; the largest producer was Afghanistan, which supplanted the previous year's leader, Burma. Cannabis cultivation, which excludes what is grown domestically in the United States in this tabulation, took place on 5,000 hectares in 2003. Over the fifteen-year period from 1987–2002, opium cultivation was higher than coca leaf cultivation, measured in hectares, in all but five years. Cannabis cultivation is a distant third, reflecting the much lower value of marijuana than of opium, cocaine, and their derivatives.

Data on production of opium gum, coca leaf, and cannabis are shown for recent years in Table 6.5. Production is measured in metric tons. The largest tonnage of drug material is coca leaf, followed by opium and cannabis. Results for the year 2000 are the most comparable because Colombia, overwhelmingly the largest producer, has been left unstated in the years since then because of a change in reporting. In 2000, 664,200 metric tons of coca were produced, 14,500 tons of cannabis, and 5,004 tons of opium gum. Leading producer countries were Colombia for coca, Afghanistan for opium, and Mexico for cannabis.

COCAINE

Price, Purity, and Supply

In its report entitled *Illegal Drug Price and Purity Report* (Washington, DC: DEA-02058, April 2003, http://www.usdoj.gov/dea/pubs/intel/02058/02058.html), the U.S. Drug Enforcement Administration (DEA) reached the conclusion that cocaine was readily available in the United States: "Cocaine prices at the kilogram level remained relatively low in the primary importation/distribution centers, such as Los Angeles, Miami, and New York City, as well as in most other major U.S. cities. ... Cocaine prices nationwide have remained relatively stable over the time period [1998–2001], particularly for ounce and gram quantities, suggesting that cocaine was readily available to the user."

Price ranges going back to 1993 from a 2003 DEA report and from an earlier report by the National Narcotics Intelligence Consumers Committee (NNICC) are shown in Table 6.6. The data suggest that prices have been fairly stable, with a slight decline since 1993. In 1993, for instance, a kilogram (2.2 pounds) of cocaine went for $10,500 to $40,000 on average nationwide. In 2001 the average price was $10,000 to $36,000. Cocaine prices per gram were $20 to $200 nationwide in 2001 and lowest in New York where the price range was $20 to $30 per gram.

The U.S. government's policy of drug control is three-pronged: public education to prevent drug use before it happens; interdiction of supply is aimed at producers and distributors of drugs; and demand reduction is aimed at the user, employing law-enforcement on the one hand and treatment/rehabilitation on the other. If

TABLE 6.4

Worldwide illicit drug cultivation, 1996–2003

[In hectares]

	2003	2002	2001	2,000	1999	1998	1997	1996
Opium								
Afghanistan	61,000	30,750	1,685	64,510	51,500	41,720	39,150	37,950
India								3,100
Iran								
Pakistan		622	213	515	1,570	3,030	4,100	3,400
Total SW Asia	61,000	31,372	1,898	65,025	53,070	44,750	45,300	44,450
Burma	47,130	78,000	105,000	108,700	89,500	130,300	155,150	163,100
China								
Laos	18,900	23,200	22,000	23,150	21,800	26,100	28,150	25,250
Thailand		750	820	890	835	1,350	1,650	2,170
Vietnam		1,000	2,300	2,300	2,100	3,000	6,150	3,150
Total SE Asia	66,030	102,950	130,120	135,040	114,235	160,750	191,100	193,670
Colombia		6,500	6,500	7,500		6,100	6,600	6,300
Lebanon								
Guatemala								
Mexico		2,700	4,400	1,900	3,600	5,500	4,000	5,100
Total other		9,200	10,900	9,400	11,100	11,600	10,600	11,490
Total opium	127,030	143,522	142,918	209,465	178,405	217,100	247,000	249,610
Coca								
Bolivia*	28,450	24,400	19,900	14,600	21,800	38,000	45,800	48,100
Colombia		144,450	169,800	136,200	122,500	101,800	79,500	67,200
Peru	31,150	36,600	34,000	34,200	38,700	51,000	68,800	94,400
Ecuador								
Total coca	59,600	205,450	223,700	185,000	183,000	190,800	194,100	209,700
Cannabis								
Mexico		3,900	3,900	3,900	3,700	4,600	4,800	6,500
Colombia	5,000	5,000	5,000	5,000	5,000	5,000	5,000	5,000
Jamaica								527
Total cannabis	5,000	8,900	8,900	8,900	8,700	9,600	10,117	12,027

*Beginning in 2001, U.S. government surveys of Bolivian coca take place over the period June to June.

SOURCE: "Worldwide Illicit Drug Cultivation, 1996–2003 (All Figures in Hectares)," in *International Narcotics Control Strategy Report, 2003*, U.S. Department of State, Bureau for International Narcotics and Law Enforcement Affairs, March 1, 2004, http://www.state.gov/g/inl/rls/nrcrpt/2003/ (accessed February 15, 2005)

interdiction was successful while heavy demand continued, prices would be expected to go up. If demand for the drugs decreased because people gave up their habits, prices would be expected to drop. Prices in 2001 continued a slight downturn, while at the same time 858,000 more people reported having used cocaine in the past year based on the *National Survey* conducted annually by the Substance Abuse and Mental Health Administration (SAMHSA). Since demand has not softened the steady or decreasing prices suggest increased supplies and/or decreased purities. Distributors, of course, can increase supplies by diluting the active ingredient.

Cocaine purity decreased from 1993 to 2001. (See Table 6.7.) At the kilogram level, purity was 82% in 1993 and had declined to 69% by 2001; at the ounce level the drop was from 70% to 53% and at the gram level from 63 to 56% from 1993 to 2001. At lower weights, purity usually declines because more filler is added to the drug.

Making and Distributing Cocaine

The coca plant, from which cocaine is produced, is grown primarily in the Andean region of Colombia, Peru, and Bolivia, with Columbia's production increasing from 1991 to 2001 while that of Peru and Bolivia has decreased. (See Figure 6.3.) According to the INCSR, 930 metric tons of cocaine were potentially available from the Andean region in 2001, 125 metric tons more than the year before. (See Figure 6.4.) More than three-quarters (78.5%) of the base came from Colombia, which produced 730 metric tons. The Bureau for International Narcotics and Law Enforcement Affairs (BINLA) stresses the fact that these quantities are "potentials" and that actual results may be lower. The same estimating methods are used, however, one year to the next, suggesting that cocaine supplies were increasing.

Once the cocaine is converted into base, it is then transported from the jungles of Bolivia and Peru to southern Colombia, where it is processed into cocaine

TABLE 6.5

Worldwide potential illicit drug production, 1996–2003

[In metric tons]

	2003	2002	2001	2,000	1999	1998	1997	1996
Opium gum								
Afghanistan	2,865	1,278	74	3,656	2,861	2,340	2,184	2,174
India								47
Iran								
Pakistan		5	5	11	37	66	85	75
Total SW Asia	**2,865**	**1,283**	**79**	**3,667**	**2,898**	**2,406**	**2,299**	**2,296**
Burma	484	630	865	1,085	1,090	1,750	2,365	2,560
China								
Laos	200	180	200	210	140	140	210	200
Thailand		9	6	6	6	16	25	30
Vietnam		10	15	15	11	20	45	25
Total SE Asia	**684**	**829**	**1,086**	**1,316**	**1,247**	**1,926**	**2,645**	**2,815**
Colombia						61	66	63
Lebanon								
Guatemala								
Mexico		47	71	21	43	60	46	54
Total other		**47**	**71**	**21**	**118**	**121**	**112**	**118**
Total opium	**3,549**	**2,159**	**1,236**	**5,004**	**4,263**	**4,453**	**5,056**	**4,285**
Coca leaf								
Bolivia[a]	17,210	19,800	20,200	26,800	22,800	52,900	70,100	75,100
Colombia[b]				583,000		437,600	347,000	302,900
Peru		52,700	52,600	54,400	69,200	95,600	130,200	174,700
Ecuador								
Total coca[c]	**17,210**	**72,500**	**72,800**	**664,200**	**613,400**	**586,100**	**547,300**	**552,700**
Cannabis								
Mexico		7,900	7,400	7,000	3,700	8,300	8,600	11,700
Colombia		4,000	4,000	4,000	4,000	4,000	4,133	4,133
Jamaica								356
Belize								
Other	3,500	3,500	3,500	3,500	3,500	3,500	3,500	3,500
Total cannabis	**3,500**	**15,400**	**14,900**	**14,500**	**11,200**	**15,800**	**16,447**	**19,689**

[a]Beginning in 2001, U.S. government surveys of Bolivian coca take place over the period June to June.
[b]Since leaf calculation is by fresh leaf weight in Colombia, in contrast to dry weight elsewhere, these boxes are blank.
[c]2002 and 2001 totals do not include Colombia. See footnote 2 above.

SOURCE: "Worldwide Potential Drug Production, 1996–2003 (All Figures in metric Tons)," in *International Narcotics Control Strategy Report, 2003*, U.S. Department of State, Bureau for International Narcotics and Law Enforcement Affairs, March 1, 2004, http://www.state.gov/g/inl/rls/nrcrpt/2003/ (accessed February 15, 2005)

TABLE 6.6

Cocaine price ranges, 1993–2001

[In dollars per kilogram]

Year	National	Miami	New York City	Chicago	Los Angeles
1993	10,500–40,000	16,000–24,000	17,000–25,000	20,000–30,000	14,000–20,000
1994	10,500–40,000	16,000–22,000	16,000–23,000	21,000–25,000	15,000–20,000
1995	10,500–36,000	15,000–25,000	17,000–27,000	21,000–25,000	15,000–20,000
1996	10,500–36,000	14,000–25,000	16,000–25,000	18,000–25,000	12,500–20,000
1997	10,000–36,000	12,500–28,000	17,000–42,000	18,000–32,000	12,000–17,500
1998	10,000–36,000	12,500–28,000	15,300–30,000	21,000–25,000	13,000–17,000
1999	9,000–40,000	17,000–20,000	16,000–24,000	21,000–25,000	13,000–18,000
2000	9,000–42,000	17,000–29,000	21,000–28,000	18,000–25,000	12,500–18,500
2001	10,000–36,000	16,500–23,000	20,000–30,000	18,000–25,000	12,500–18,000

SOURCE: "Cocaine Price Ranges (per Kilogram)," in *The NNICC Report 1997: The Supply of Illicit Drugs to the United States*, National Narcotics Intelligence Consumers Committee, 1998, and "Cocaine 1998–2001 Price Data," in *Illegal Drug Price and Purity Report*, U.S. Drug Enforcement Administration, April 2003

TABLE 6.7

Cocaine purity, 1993–2001

[Annual national average in percent]

Year	Kilogram	Ounce	Gram
1993	82	70	63
1994	83	74	63
1995	83	65	61
1996	82	67	61
1997	80	64	64
1998	82	69	69
1999	79	63	63
2000	72	56	59
2001	69	53	56

SOURCE: "Cocaine Purity (Annual National Average—Percent)," in *The NNICC Report 1997: The Supply of Illicit Drugs to the United States*, National Narcotics Intelligence Consumers Committee, 1998, and "Cocaine 1998–2001 Purity Data," in *Illegal Drug Price and Purity Report*, U.S. Drug Enforcement Administration, April 2003

hydrochloride (white powder) at clandestine drug laboratories. Recently, small, independent Bolivian and Peruvian trafficking groups have also been processing cocaine. After processing, the powder is shipped to the United States and Europe.

Caribbean and Central American countries serve as transit countries for the shipment of drugs into the United States. Drug traffickers shift routes according to law enforcement and interdiction pressures. Recently, drug flow has been steadily increasing through the Central American countries. In the late 1990s Central American governments stepped up antidrug operations in response.

The Colombian government has disrupted the activities of two major drug-trafficking organizations, the Medellin and Cali cartels, by either capturing or killing their key leaders. Nonetheless, this disruption has not reduced drug-trafficking activities. Independent traffickers, as well as splinter groups from the Cali cartel, have increasingly moved into the market, and huge volumes of cocaine are still being shipped to the United States through the Caribbean.

MOST COCAINE ENTERS THE U.S. THROUGH MEXICO. Much South American cocaine is sent to Mexican traffickers who smuggle the drug into the United States. As Mexican traffickers have become more sophisticated, it is suspected that many are bypassing their Colombian contacts and dealing directly with Peruvian and Bolivian producers.

Almost all drugs, especially cocaine, once entered the United States through Florida. Florida was a major entry point mainly because of its thousands of miles of coastline, where boats could secretly dock, and the millions of acres in the Everglades, where planes could

covertly land. Though intensive law enforcement efforts make it more difficult to land drugs in Florida, cocaine continues to be transported through the Caribbean, Puerto Rico, the Dominican Republic, and Haiti to Florida from Colombia. According to the DEA's *Drug Trafficking in the United States* (http://www.usdoj.gov/dea/concern/ drug_trafficking.html), Haiti and Jamaica are growing transport points for Colombian cocaine destined for eastern U.S. markets. Because of Jamaica's location between South America and the United States, it is increasingly significant. Cocaine is smuggled into Jamaica primarily by sea, then into the Bahamas, and finally to the Florida coast using speed-boats, pleasure craft, and fishing vessels.

Because of efforts to cease drug flow to Florida, nearly 65% of the cocaine sold in the United States today passes through Mexico and across the Mexico–U.S. border. The two-thousand-mile border is patrolled by a relatively small number of Immigration and Naturalization Service (INS) officers, who must divide their limited time between illegal aliens trying to cross the border and drug traffickers trying to smuggle drugs into the United States. The United States has introduced soldiers into the area to assist the INS, although some observers question whether soldiers trained to fight wars have the correct preparation to patrol a border populated by farmers and ranchers.

Mexico, the main transit and distribution hub for drugs moving to the United States, now rivals Colombia for dominance of the Western Hemisphere drug trade. Powerful Mexican drug syndicates have become dominant in the cocaine trade and the U.S. wholesale market. The Mexican government has intensified its investigations of the four largest drug-trafficking organizations—the Juarez cartel, the Tijuana cartel, the Gulf cartel, and the Caro Quintero organization.

Most cocaine destined for the United States is transported from South American countries to northern Mexico. In the early 1990s traffickers used aircraft to deliver cocaine, but over the past few years they have shifted to the maritime movement of drugs. According to U.S. law enforcement officials, most drugs enter Mexico via ship or small boat through the Yucatan Peninsula and Baja California regions. In addition, more drugs are moving overland into Mexico, primarily through Guatemala.

After the drugs have been unloaded, the cocaine is transported, usually by truck, to warehouses in cities such as Guadalajara or Juarez, which are operating bases for the major drug organizations. Mexican smugglers, often with experience smuggling illegal workers, and who frequently have family or friends in the United States, are paid to carry the drugs across the border. Sometimes the drugs are carried across the

FIGURE 6.3

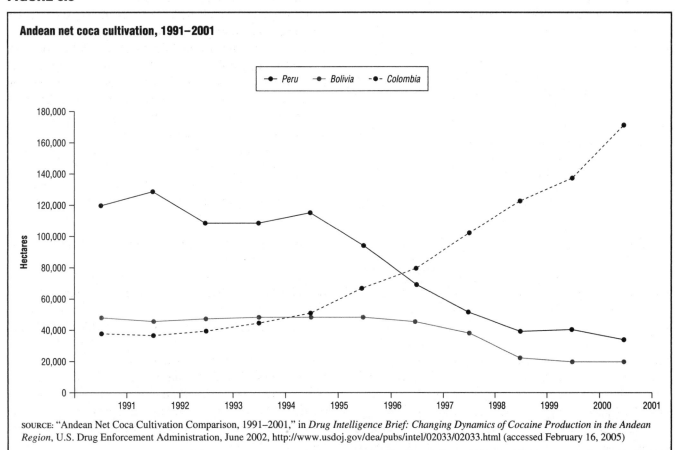

Andean net coca cultivation, 1991–2001

● Peru ● Bolivia -●- Colombia

Hectares

180,000
160,000
140,000
120,000
100,000
80,000
60,000
40,000
20,000
0

1991 1992 1993 1994 1995 1996 1997 1998 1999 2000 2001

SOURCE: "Andean Net Coca Cultivation Comparison, 1991–2001," in *Drug Intelligence Brief: Changing Dynamics of Cocaine Production in the Andean Region*, U.S. Drug Enforcement Administration, June 2002, http://www.usdoj.gov/dea/pubs/intel/02033/02033.html (accessed February 16, 2005)

FIGURE 6.4

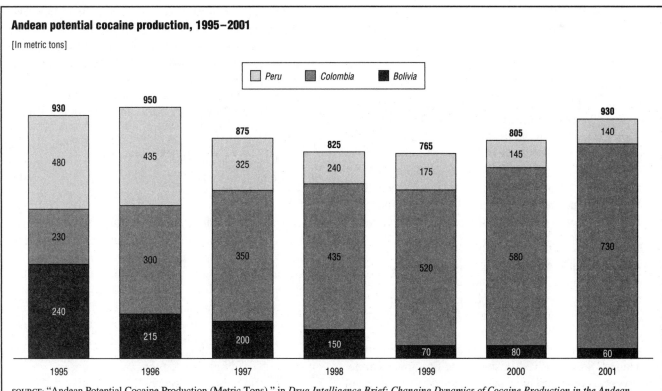

Andean potential cocaine production, 1995–2001

[In metric tons]

☐ Peru ▨ Colombia ■ Bolivia

	1995	1996	1997	1998	1999	2000	2001
Total	930	950	875	825	765	805	930
Peru	480	435	325	240	175	145	140
Colombia	230	300	350	435	520	580	730
Bolivia	240	215	200	150	70	80	60

SOURCE: "Andean Potential Cocaine Production (Metric Tons)," in *Drug Intelligence Brief: Changing Dynamics of Cocaine Production in the Andean Region*, U.S. Drug Enforcement Administration, June 2002, http://www.usdoj.gov/dea/pubs/intel/02033/02033.html (accessed February 16, 2005) border in backpacks; sometimes they are hidden in cars and trucks; and, occasionally, they are flown into the United States.

In Mexico, where unemployment is high and the value of the peso dropped sharply in the mid-1990s, the hundreds or thousands of dollars to be earned from drug smuggling can be very attractive. Few of the smugglers know any more about the makeup of the drug ring than the identity of the individual who gives them the drugs; capturing them does not significantly restrict the flow of drugs.

Drug syndicates have become very powerful in Mexico, and Mexican traffickers use their vast wealth to corrupt and influence public officials. For example, in 1997 the head of Mexico's National Institute to Combat Drugs, General Jesus Gutierrez Rebello, was arrested for taking money and gifts from drug dealers. General Barry McCaffrey, the U.S. drug coordinator at the time, had recently praised the general for his integrity and commitment to the drug war.

Mexican drug organizations have been implicated in dozens of political assassinations in Tijuana since the mid-1990s. In 1994 a presidential candidate and Tijuana's police chief were assassinated, and a second police chief, Alfredo de la Torre Marquez, was assassinated in 1999. In 2000 the murders of two federal prosecutors and an army captain were among the many that American officials suspect were ordered by drug cartels. Other high-profile victims have included lawyers, police officers, judges, and prosecutors—anyone who might stand in the way of the high-stakes trafficking enterprise.

A major obstacle to joint law enforcement and prosecution efforts is the widespread corruption of Mexican officials, especially police. According to the INCSR, the Mexican authorities arrested forty-three corrupt police officials in 2002 who had been providing protection to the Arellano Felix Organization (AFO), another powerful drug cartel. The AFO was known to have made payments amounting to $1 million a week to Mexican federal, state, and local officials. A number of high-ranking AFO operatives were also arrested, and one was killed in a shoot-out. But corruption is very difficult to root out because drug profits are high and poverty widespread.

SMUGGLERS WILL USE ANY METHOD. In 1993 Mexican police discovered an elaborate cocaine-smuggling tunnel that extended fourteen hundred feet from Tijuana, Mexico, to the outskirts of San Diego, California. Short tunnels have been found in the past, but nothing like this air-conditioned, well-lighted tunnel that would have provided a secret, comfortable route for transporting tons of cocaine. Those involved in smuggling find innumerable ways to get cocaine into the United States. The profits from even relatively small amounts of the drug are considered worth the risk of being caught.

Drug couriers will go to extreme lengths, including swallowing packets of drugs and excreting them after they have entered the United States. One courier had half a pound of cocaine surgically implanted under the skin of each of his thighs. Panamanian cocaine smugglers have developed a new technology that combines cocaine with vinyl, which is then incorporated into luggage and sneakers. The cocaine is separated after it reaches its destination.

The U.S. Customs Service and the U.S. Fish and Wildlife Service seized several kilograms of cocaine within a shipment of boa constrictors. The smugglers had wrapped the cocaine in rubber containers and forced them down the snakes' throats. Cocaine was found implanted in dogs' stomachs, and liquid cocaine was discovered in a shipment of tropical fish.

Cocaine may be hidden in the walls and support beams of cargo containers or mixed in with legal cargo such as coffee. Fishing vessels with hidden compartments often conceal cocaine. Cocaine is hidden in the walls of planes flying regularly scheduled flights. Other smugglers drop the cocaine by parachute to waiting accomplices below. Some traffickers have bought old, propeller-driven airplanes to fly in cocaine. And, with the price of aging jet aircraft dropping sharply, some smugglers have even bought Boeing 727 jets to haul in large amounts of drugs. Sixty-five pounds of cocaine was once found hidden inside the cockpit of an American Airlines Boeing 757 jetliner.

AFTER COCAINE REACHES THE UNITED STATES. The primary entry ports into the United States are southern Florida, southern California, Arizona, and Texas. Colombia-based traffickers continue to control wholesale-level distribution throughout the northeastern United States and along the eastern seaboard in cities such as Boston, Miami, Newark, New York City, and Philadelphia, often employing Dominican criminals as subordinates. Mexico-based traffickers operate out of Chicago and control the western and midwestern United States in such cities as Chicago, Dallas, Denver, Houston, Los Angeles, Phoenix, San Diego, San Francisco, and Seattle.

From these distribution cities, drug carriers transport cocaine throughout the country in commercial and private vehicles, including trains, buses, airplanes, and even postal trucks. U.S. law enforcement officials have encountered smuggling operations that use concealed compartments within campers, recreational vehicles, tractor trailers, and vans. Modern communications have made it difficult to catch the drug dealers. They keep in touch using beepers and pay phones in efforts to avoid getting caught.

Many observers note that drug traffickers have little difficulty funneling drugs north through Mexico because

TABLE 6.8

Cocaine, heroin, methamphetamine, and cannabis seizures, by the federal government and selected foreign countries, 1989–2003

[In kilograms]

Year	Cocaine	Heroin	Methamphetamine	Cannabis Marijuana	Cannabis Hashish
1989	114,903	1,311	—	393,276	23,043
1990	96,085	687	—	233,478	7,683
1991	128,247	1,448	—	224,603	79,110
1992	120,175	1,251	—	344,899	111
1993	121,215	1,502	7	409,922	11,396
1994	129,378	1,285	178	474,856	561
1995	111,031	1,543	369	627,776	14,470
1996	128,555	1,362	136	638,863	37,851
1997	101,495	1,624	1,099	698,799	756
1998	118,436	1,458	2,559	827,149	241
1999	132,063	1,151	2,779	1,075,154	797
2000	106,619	1,674	3,470	1,235,938	10,867
2001	105,748	2,496	4,051	1,214,188	161
2002	102,711	2,773	2,521	1,100,439	621
2003	115,725	2,351	3,573	1,224,213	155

—Data not available.

SOURCE: "Table 44. Federalwide Cocaine, Heroin, Methamphetamine, and Cannabis Seizures, 1989–2003 (Kilograms)," in *National Drug Control Strategy: Data Supplement*, The White House, February 2004, http://www.whitehousedrugpolicy.gov/publications/policy/ndcs04/table44.doc (accessed March 31, 2005)

of Mexico's weak political and law enforcement institutions, but traffickers appear to have an equally easy time moving drugs across the United States.

HOW MUCH COCAINE IS SEIZED? To give an idea of how enormous the challenge is to find smuggled drugs, U.S. Customs and Border Protection (a part of the Department of Homeland Security created via the 2003 merger of the U.S. Customs Service and the Border Patrol) reported in its annual report (*Performance and Annual Report, Fiscal Year 2003*, Washington, DC: U.S. Customs and Border Protection, Department of Homeland Security, http://www.customs.gov/linkhandler/cgov/toolbox/publications/admin/accountability_report_2003.ctt/cbpAnnualReportMarch04.pdf) that during fiscal year 2003, 70.9 million people entered the country on commercial airlines. Another fifteen million came by sea and 327 million by land through more than three hundred ports of entry. The Service also handled over 130 million trucks, aircraft, boats, and ships.

Customs and Border Protection estimates that two-thirds of all cocaine entering the United States crosses through a border facility manned by a government agent. Most of it is hidden in some way in the huge number of tractor trailers and passenger vehicles. Customs estimates that it seizes only 10% of smuggled drugs. Many experts believe it seizes much less.

For the United States, interdiction, or stopping drugs at the border, has been a high-priority, high-visibility

effort in the war against drugs. In 2003 all federal cocaine seizures were 115,725 kilograms. (See Table 6.8.) In fiscal year 2003 the Customs Service seized or assisted in seizing 76,300 pounds of cocaine, a reduction from previous years due, according to the Customs Service, to lower traffic overall and heightened vigilance.

HEROIN

Heroin users represent the smallest group using a major drug: 3.7 million lifetime and 314,000 past-year users in 2003. (See Table 3.3 in Chapter 3.) For traffickers, heroin is a stable commodity. In its 1999 INCSR, the State Department summed up the attractiveness of heroin for traffickers as follows:

> Though cocaine dominates the U.S. drug scene, heroin is lurking conspicuously in the wings. . . . Heroin has a special property that appeals to the drug trade's long range planners: as an opiate, it allows many addicts to develop a long-term tolerance to the drug. Where constant cocaine or crack use may kill a regular user in five years, a heroin addiction can last for a decade or more, as long as the addict has access to a regular maintenance "fix." This pernicious property of tolerance potentially assures the heroin trade of a long-term customer base of hard-core addicts.

Heroin users have been increasing based on data collected by SAMHSA, although at a slowing rate. The number of lifetime heroin users increased annually at a rate of 8.9% between 1990 and 1995 and a rate of 3.4% between 1995 and 2003. According to the ONDCP, 12.9 metric tons of heroin were used in the United States in 2001, up from 11.4 tons in 1995.

Purity and Price

The purity of the typical kilogram of heroin increased between 1998 and 2001. (See Table 6.9.) At the same time, however, purity levels have dropped at the ounce and the gram level to 53% from 57% for the average ounce and from 55% to 51% for the average gram. Despite the drop, these are very high purity products in comparison with the average of 27% in 1991 and 7% in 1987.

The rise in purity has been tied to the increased availability of high-purity South American heroin. Colombian

TABLE 6.9

Heroin purity, 1998–2001

[National average in percent]

Quantity	1998	1999	2000	2001
Kilogram	68	63	64	69
Ounce	57	53	55	53
Gram	55	53	52	51

SOURCE: "Heroin: 1998–2001 Purity Data," in *Illegal Drug Price/Purity Report*, U.S. Drug Enforcement Administration, April 2003

TABLE 6.10

Heroin price range, 1998–2001

Amount and source	1998	1999	2000	2001
Kilogram				
Mexican black tar	$20,000–$100,000	$20,000–$100,000	$15,000–$100,000	$15,000–$65,000
South America	50,000–160,000	65,000–160,000	55,000–120,000	60,000–125,000
Southeast Asia	80,000–180,000	70,000–180,000	120,000–175,000	90,000–120,000
Southwest Asia	55,000–190,000	55,000–190,000	70,000–190,000	35,000–115,000
Unidentified source	N/R	90,000–150,000	48,000–200,000	35,000–180,000
Ounce				
Mexican black tar	$400–$6,500	$300–$6,000	$400–$7,000	$350–$6,400
South America	N/R	2,000–12,000	1,200–9,000	2,000–5,500
Southeast Asia	N/R	2,000–9,000	2,000–9,000	2,600–9,000
Southwest Asia	N/R	3,800–8,000	7,000–12,000	N/R
Unidentified source	N/R	2,400–11,000	1,200–8,500	1,000–10,500
Gram				
Mexican black tar	$80–$600	$50–$500	$40–$500	$50–$400
South America	N/R	50–400	50–600	60–300
Southeast Asia	N/R	100–600	100–500	90–500
Southwest Asia	N/R	175–450	N/R	N/R
Unidentified source	N/R	75–600	90–900	50–500

N/R=Not reported

SOURCE: "Heroin," in *Illegal Drug Price/Purity Report*, U.S. Drug Enforcement Administration, April 2003

drug traffickers have been trying to break into the heroin market by producing a very high-quality drug. This has forced heroin producers from other areas to improve the purity of their product. Purer product has led to a change in the way many people take the drug. Injecting heroin into an artery is the most effective way to get the most out of low-purity heroin. Higher-purity heroin has made it easier to smoke or snort the drug, which has also made heroin more attractive to potential users who feel uncomfortable using needles. The potential of being infected by HIV is also removed. Despite these "advantages," an estimated three in five heroin users continue to inject the drug.

Heroin is more lucrative for dealers than most other drugs. While a kilogram of cocaine might fetch between $10,000 and $35,000, a kilo of heroin could be worth as much as $180,000. (See Table 6.10.) According to the DEA, the price of a gram of heroin ranged from $50 to $500 in 2001. A relative beginner in heroin use will inject between five to ten milligrams of heroin. A gram thus delivers between one hundred and two hundred doses. Street prices for a single dose run $10 to $20 per bag, and a kilogram of heroin converts into a small fortune. Compared with earlier years shown, prices are generally down despite improving purity levels. The Mexican "black tar" variety of heroin is called that because of its color; heroin from other sources range from white to brown in coloration.

Heroin Production and Distribution

PRODUCTION PROCESS. After the leaves of the poppy fall off, only the round poppy pods remain. Heroin production begins by scoring the poppy pod with a knife. A gummy substance begins to ooze out. This material is then scraped off later and collected. The process, thereafter, is described as follows on a CIA web page (*From Flowers to Heroin*, CIA Homepage for Kids, Central Intelligence Agency, http://www.cia.gov/cia/publications/heroin/flowers_to_heroin.htm):

Once the opium gum is transported to a refinery, it is converted into morphine, an intermediate product. This conversion is achieved primarily by chemical processes and requires several basic elements and implements. Boiling water is used to dissolve opium gum; 55-gallon drums are used for boiling vessels; and burlap sacks are used to filter and strain liquids. When dried, the morphine resulting from this initial process is pressed into bricks. The conversion of morphine bricks into heroin is also primarily a chemical process. The main chemical used is acetic anhydride, along with sodium carbonate, activated charcoal, chloroform, ethyl alcohol, ether, and acetone. The two most commonly produced heroin varieties are No. 3 heroin, or smoking heroin, and No. 4 heroin, or injectable heroin.

This generic process produces heroin that may be 90% pure. Variations in the process are introduced as the heroin is diluted, "cut" to increase its bulk and thus also the profits. The pure heroin is mixed with various substances including caffeine, baking soda, powdered milk, and quinine.

OVERVIEW OF THE TRADE. Opium poppies are intensely cultivated in three regions of the world—Southeast Asia, Southwest Asia, and Mexico and South America. In 2003 (see Table 6.5) Southwest Asia, particularly Afghanistan, accounted for 80.7% of known opium gum production. Opium gum is the intermediate from which heroin is made. Afghanistan's production was

3,656 metric tons in 2000, then dropped to seventy-four tons in 2001 as a consequence of steps taken by the Taliban to suppress the trade. According to the INCSR, production went up again to 1,278 metric tons in 2002 after the Taliban fell, and more than doubled to 2,865 metric tons in 2003.

The DEA conducts the Heroin Signature Program (HSP). The name of the program comes from the fact that each producing region uses a unique process for deriving heroin from opium and the heroin thus has a unique "signature."

Under this program, heroin seized by federal authorities is analyzed in order to determine the purity of the heroin and its origin. In its most recent formal work-up of these data, *Drug Intelligence Brief: Heroin Signature Program: 2002*, the agency determined that 80% of all heroin seized in 2002 came from South America, 9% from Mexico, 1% from Southeast Asia, and 10% from Southwest Asia. (See Table 6.11.) The DEA's analysis is that HSP results can be projected to determine the actual origin of all heroin sold in the United States. The implication is that while Latin America represents about 3% of opium gum production, it supplies most of the heroin used here. Much Asian heroin is used in the country in which it was produced, in nearby countries, or in Europe. The government's concentrated effort to interdict drug supplies from "south of the border" are informed by such analyses, which, according to the United Nation's *World Drug Report*, show that most of the major drugs come to the U.S. from the south rather than from Asia.

MEXICO AND COLOMBIA. The bulk of heroin from Latin America comes from Mexico and Colombia. Mexico produces a variety of heroin called "black tar" because it looks like roofing tar. It was once considered inferior to Colombian and Asian heroin, but it has reached a level of purity high enough so that it can be snorted or smoked. Mexican heroin is targeted almost exclusively to the American market. The long Mexico–U.S. land border provides many opportunities for drug smugglers to cross. Female couriers are used more frequently than males. Mexican heroin is smuggled in cars, trucks, and buses and may also be hidden on or in the body of the smuggler. Many smugglers send their drugs by overnight-package express services.

Many Colombian coca traffickers have been requiring their dealers to accept a small amount of heroin along with their normal deliveries of coca. This has allowed the Colombian producers to use an existing network to introduce a very pure grade of heroin into the U.S. market. Much of the growing Colombian heroin production is sent through Central America and Mexico by smugglers traveling on commercial airline flights into the United States. These smugglers hide the drugs in false-sided luggage, clothing, hollowed-out

TABLE 6.11

Heroin seizures by source region, 1977–2002

[In percent]

	Mexico[a]	Southeast Asia	Southwest Asia	South America
1977	89	9	2	NA
1978	82	15	3	NA
1979	48	13	51	NA
1980	38	11	51	NA
1981	36	10	54	NA
1982	34	14	47	NA
1983	33	19	48	NA
1984	32	17	51	NA
1985	39	14	47	NA
1986	42	22	36	NA
1987	42	25	33	NA
1988	29	46	25	NA
1989	27	56	17	NA
1990	21	56	23	NA
1991	21	58	21	NA
1992	10	58	32	NA
1993	8	68	9	15[b]
1994	5	57	6	32
1995	5	17	16	32
1996	20	8	20	52
1997	14	5	6	75
1998	17	14	4	65
1999	24	10	6	60
2000	17	8	16	59
2001	30	7	7	56
2002	9	1	10	80

[a]The percentages are based on samples for which a signature was identified. In 2002, approximately 90 percent of the samples were classified.
[b]The signature for heroin from South America was not developed until July 1993; therefore, this figure represents only partial-year data.
Not Applicable (The signature for heroin from South America was not developed until 1993.)

SOURCE: "Figure 4. Heroin Signature Program Data: 1977–2002 Geographic Source Area Distribution (in percent) Based on Net Weight of Heroin Seized and Analyzed," in *Drug Intelligence Brief: Heroin Signature Program 2002*, U.S. Drug Enforcement Administration, March 2004, http://www.usdoj.gov/dea/pubs/intel/04005/04005.html (accessed March 1, 2005)

shoe soles, or inside their bodies. The Colombia-based heroin traffickers have established distribution outlets throughout the eastern half of the United States.

SOUTHWEST ASIA (THE GOLDEN CRESCENT). At one time, perhaps half the heroin shipped into the United States came from Iran, Afghanistan, and Pakistan—a region referred to as the Golden Crescent. Currently, however, only a small percentage is thought to come to the United States from this area; most of the Southwest Asian production is shipped to Europe.

Opium is Afghanistan's largest cash crop, and now, in the wake of the Taliban's fall, the country appears to be succeeding again in capturing the lion's share of the world's opium market.

By 2000, after strong pressure from the United States, the Pakistani government had nearly eliminated opium cultivation. Iran also grows very few opium poppies, perhaps as a result of an Iranian government crackdown on heroin users. It is generally believed that Iran's opium production provides barely enough for native drug users and that Iran imports heroin from neighboring Afghanistan.

Drug users in Southwest and Central Asia use some of the opium grown in the Southwest Asian region, but most of the region's opium is shipped to Turkey to be transformed into heroin in secret laboratories.

According to the INCSR, about 80% of the heroin from Southwest Asia is shipped to the European market from Turkey along the "Balkan Route." This supply line originates in Afghanistan and Pakistan, passes through Turkey, and splits into branches. The northern route carries heroin to Romania, Hungary, the Czech and Slovak Republics, and points north. The southern branch crosses through Croatia, Slovenia, the former Yugoslav republic of Macedonia, Greece, and Albania to the countries of Western Europe. Every country along the route now faces serious domestic drug problems. Turkish drug syndicates, which control distribution in a large number of European cities, dominate most of the Balkan Route drug business.

The growth of corruption and criminal organizations in Russia has led to a growth of drug trafficking and drug abuse there. Russian drug traffickers transport Southwest Asian heroin through Central Asia to Russia and on to Europe. Russian authorities have noted a huge increase in domestic drug use in Russia and estimate that there are more than two million users in the country, although the figure could well be higher.

SOUTHEAST ASIA (THE GOLDEN TRIANGLE). Burma supplied an estimated 14% of the opium produced in the world in 2003, according to the INCSR. Its share of world production has decreased annually since the mid-1990s, when it outproduced Afghanistan. The opium produced in Burma, Thailand, and Laos (the Golden Triangle) has traditionally gone by sea from Thailand to Hong Kong or Taiwan, where it was processed into heroin for local use or shipped on to the United States. Trafficking through China is on the increase, and much Golden Triangle opium is being processed into heroin in that country. A growing amount of heroin has been moving through Singapore and Malaysia, despite their strict drug laws.

NIGERIA—A MAJOR TRANSSHIPMENT BASE. According to the State Department in the INCSR, "Nigeria remains a worldwide hub of narcotics trafficking and money laundering activity. Nigerian organized criminal groups dominate the African drug trade, and transport narcotics to markets in the United States, Europe, Asia, and Africa." The nation's continuing political corruption and turbulence have made it easier for criminal organizations to develop and use Nigeria as a transshipment point for Asian heroin.

Before 1997 Nigerian drug traffickers paid couriers between $2,000 and $5,000 (what an average Nigerian would earn in sixteen years) to transport a pound or two of heroin into the United States. In the late 1990s traffickers began using Express Mail Services (EMS) to ship heroin, concealing it in such items as pots and pans, children's books, and decorative figurines. The use of EMS is far cheaper than couriers, and packages can be mailed anonymously, with less chance of tracing them back to the trafficker if the heroin is discovered. Nigerian traffickers often use Thailand as a base of operation for their heroin trafficking. Most parcels seized originate in Thailand.

MARIJUANA

The ONDCP conducts an annual survey of drug use called the Pulse Check. ONDCP gets reports from law-enforcement and epidemiologic/ethnographic sources across the country (ninety-four sources in twenty-five cities for its 2004 edition of Pulse Check). These sources reported that marijuana was readily available everywhere. Domestically grown, Mexican, hydroponically grown Canadian, and the potent seedless marijuana were all available; the domestic variety was the most common (*Pulse Check: Trends in Drug Abuse*, Washington, DC: ONDCP, January 2004).

Marijuana is made from the flowering tops and leaves of the cannabis plant; these are collected, trimmed, dried, and then smoked in a pipe or as a cigarette. Many users smoke "blunts," named after the inexpensive blunt cigars from which they are made. Blunt cigars are approximately five inches long and can be purchased at any store that sells tobacco products. A marijuana blunt is made from the emptied cigar casing, which is then stuffed with marijuana or a marijuana/tobacco mixture. A blunt may contain as much marijuana as six regular marijuana cigarettes. In some cases, blunt users add crack cocaine or PCP to the mixture to make it more potent. These are sometimes called "turbos," "woolies," or "woolie blunts."

THC Content and Price

The active ingredient in marijuana is tetrahydrocannabinol, THC, which is most concentrated in the flowering tops of the plants also known as colas or buds. The flowering tops of female plants have no seeds and produce sinsemilla (literally, "without seed"), a mixture with the highest THC content.

During the 1970s and 1980s, the THC content of commercial-grade marijuana averaged less than 2%. By 1998 potency had increased to 4.2% for commercial grade and 12.3% for sinsemilla. The most recent measurements conducted by the DEA (2001) put commercial THC content at 4.7% and sinsemilla at 9%. (See Table 6.12.) Improving marijuana potency may be the reason for the growing popularity of marijuana across most regions of the nation, as reported by ONDCP's Pulse Check.

TABLE 6.12

Marijuana price ranges and potency, 1998–2001

[National average in dollars]

	1998	1999	2000	2001
Commercial grade				
Pound	250–3,200	100–6,000	100–4,000	70–1,200
Ounce	30–450	35–750	50–650	25–600
THC content	4.21%	4.19%	4.68%	4.72%
Sinsemilla				
Pound	850–6,000	500–7,000	900–8,000	600–4,000
Ounce	160–600	160–600	100–600	80–1,200
THC content	12.33%	13.38%	12.82%	9.03%

SOURCE: "Marijuana: 1998–2001 Price and Potency Data," in *Illegal Drug Price/Purity Report*, U.S. Drug Enforcement Administration, April 2003

FIGURE 6.5

Cross-border marijuana distribution

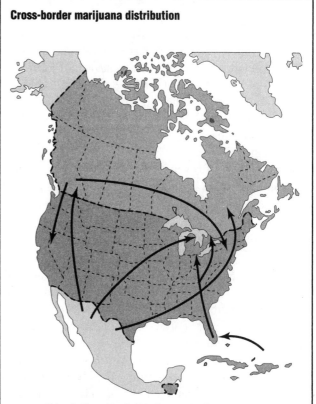

SOURCE: "Map 1. Cross-Border Marijuana Distribution," in *United States–Canada Border Drug Threat Assessment*, U.S. Department of Justice, National Drug Intelligence Center, December 2001

THC levels may rise even higher. Marijuana with a THC content of more than 20% has appeared in the Netherlands and Latin America (called "skunk," "skunk-weed," or "nederweed"). Raids in Alaska have also uncovered marijuana with THC content well above 20%. This marijuana is grown by indoor cultivators who focus their efforts on hybridizing, cloning, and growing high-potency marijuana.

Prices have been moving downward, as shown in Table 6.12. A pound of commercial-grade marijuana sold for as little as $250 and for as much as $3,200 in 1998. The reported price range in 2001, as determined by the DEA, was from $70 to $1,200 a pound. Sinsemilla pricing, while generally higher, has also dropped. ONDCP's 2001 Pulse Check cited street level ounce prices in the range of $50 (Denver) to $1,200 (the high range for New York City) without specifying the type of marijuana purchased; the values agree with those determined by the DEA.

Foreign Production

Morocco is one of the largest producers of marijuana in the world. Virtually all of its production is exported to other North African nations and Europe. Traffickers in Nigeria and Kenya export large amounts of marijuana to Europe. In 1997 South Africa was one of the world's largest producers of marijuana. Although most of the marijuana produced in South Africa was for domestic or regional use, some was smuggled to Australia, the Netherlands, and the United Kingdom. Brazil is also a major producer of marijuana, most of which is consumed in Brazil.

Most foreign marijuana available in the United States comes from Mexico, though the National Drug Intelligence Center (NDIC) (part of the U.S. Department of Justice) states that significant quantities also originate in Colombia, Jamaica, and Canada. Though the amount arriving from Canada is smaller than from the other three

countries, it is usually extremely high-grade and in high demand, creating a profitable market. Some marijuana arrives on the U.S. West Coast from Asia, most notably Thailand and Cambodia.

Mexican marijuana enters the United States mainly by land, although some of it is smuggled in by private aircraft. Almost all Colombian marijuana is shipped by noncommercial vessels or is transshipped through northern Mexico. Most Jamaican marijuana arrives by cargo vessel, pleasure boat, or fishing boat. Most marijuana enters the United States in Florida, except the Mexican variety, which usually comes through Texas and California. (Figure 6.5.)

According to the ONDCP, between 1990 and 2001 Mexico eradicated on average 21,434 hectares of marijuana; annual eradication levels rose each year during this period, from 6,750 hectares in 1990 to 33,300 in 2001. During this same period, an average of 21,460 hectares were under cultivation, but this number decreased from 41,800 in 1990 to 11,500 in 2001. As authorities eradicate plants, growers engage in replanting, but in Mexico cultivation generally has been decreasing. In Bolivia and Peru, land dedicated to growing marijuana also has been shrinking. Efforts to control marijuana trafficking by eradicating the plant have not been equally successful elsewhere. The ONDCP determined that cultivation increased dramatically in Colombia despite eradication efforts. In 2000, 183,000 hectares were under cultivation, up from 41,000 hectares in 1990. Eradication affected 900 hectares in 1990 and 47,000 in 2000. Large parts of Colombia are under the control of insurgents, the Revolutionary Armed Forces of Colombia (FARC), the National Liberation Army (ELN), and the United Self-Defense Forces of Colombia (AUC). The drug trade is a source of revenues for these insurgent groups and Colombia, as a consequence, has become a major supplier of cocaine, heroin, and marijuana.

Domestic Production

Today, a large portion of the marijuana used in the United States is grown within its borders. Whereas U.S. agencies have data on marijuana cultivation in a number of foreign countries (Mexico, Colombia, Bolivia, Peru, etc.), information about domestic production is not available. In its *National Drug Threat Assessment 2004* (http://www.usdoj.gov/ndic/pubs8/8731/marijuana.htm), the National Drug Intelligence Center, an element of the U.S. Department of Justice, states: "The amount of marijuana produced domestically, although currently not quantified, is insufficient to meet the high demand for the drug in the United States. Consequently, drug markets throughout the country are supplied with marijuana produced domestically and in foreign source areas. ... Domestic cannabis cultivation occurs throughout the country and ranges from a few plants grown for personal use to thousands mass-cultivated by organized criminal groups, from outdoor plots to indoor operations, and from computerized hydroponics to organic grows. Small-scale operations in cities and smaller towns and communities across the country produce marijuana, in immeasurable amounts, that helps fill demand in localized drug markets or within peer distribution networks. Larger amounts of marijuana sufficient to supply high-volume drug markets for state, regional, or national distribution are produced on private and public lands in many areas of the country as well." There is no doubt that significant amounts are being produced domestically; as the Pulse Check program reports, domestically cultivated marijuana is the most common kind available.

OUTDOOR PRODUCTION. Domestic growers grow cannabis in remote areas in order to avoid detection by law-enforcement agencies. They surround their plots with camouflaging crops like corn or soybeans. Based on eradication data collected by the DEA, California, Appalachia (Kentucky and Tennessee), Hawaii, and, to a somewhat lesser extent, the Pacific Northwest (Washington and Oregon) are the primary domestic marijuana source areas. (See Figure 6.6.) Growers also plant cannabis in suburban and rural gardens interspersed with legitimate crops. Cannabis also grows in the wild. Wild-growing cannabis is known in law-enforcement circles as ditchweed. Some growers start with and cultivate ditchweed, but it produces a low-potency flower and leaf.

INDOOR PRODUCTION. Cannabis will grow indoors under sufficient light. Controlled conditions can also enhance the potency of the products derived from the plants. According to the DEA, a healthy indoor-grown sinsemilla plant can produce up to a pound of high-THC-content marijuana.

Indoor cultivation permits year-round production in a variety of settings. Growers may cultivate a handful of plants grown in a closet or operate elaborate, specially constructed (sometimes underground) greenhouses where thousands of plants grow under intense electric lighting or in sunlight. Indoor cultivators often use such advanced growing practices as hydroponics, in which light, water, and fertilizers are automatically adjusted; the atmosphere may also be enriched with carbon dioxide.

Domestic Marijuana Eradication

The domestic cannabis eradication program accounts for its success by counting plants destroyed rather than hectares sprayed. In 2003 law-enforcement agencies destroyed a total of 247 million plants, including 3.4 million commercial-grade plants cultivated out of doors and 223,183 plants grown indoors. By far the largest category of hemp plant destroyed in 2003 was ditchweed, some 243 million plants, accounting for 98% of all plants eradicated. (See Table 6.13, Table 6.14, and Table 6.15.)

The Domestic Cannabis Eradication and Suppression Program is sponsored by the DEA and involves a number of federal, state, and local organizations that cooperate in destroying marijuana plants on both private and public lands. Among these are the Civil Air Patrol, the National Guard, the U.S. military, the U.S. Fish and Wildlife Service, the National Park Service, and the Bureau of Indian Affairs.

Marijuana Seizures

In 2002 the DEA seized 195,644 kilograms of marijuana, some 76,000 kilograms less than the year before. The history of DEA marijuana seizures from 1986 through 2002 is shown in Table 6.16. In 1986, 599,166 kilograms were seized, followed the year after by a record in this sixteen-year period, 629,892 kilograms. Seizures then began to drop to the low in this

FIGURE 6.6

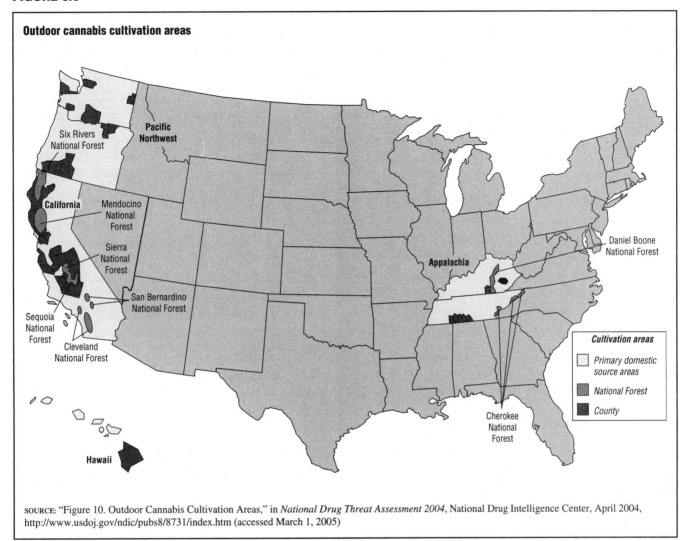

Outdoor cannabis cultivation areas

SOURCE: "Figure 10. Outdoor Cannabis Cultivation Areas," in *National Drug Threat Assessment 2004*, National Drug Intelligence Center, April 2004, http://www.usdoj.gov/ndic/pubs8/8731/index.htm (accessed March 1, 2005)

period of 98,601 kilograms in 1991. A smaller secondary peak came in 1999 with the DEA seizing 337,832 kilograms. The overall trend in this period is down. The overall pattern of seizures, however, reflects past-month marijuana usage by the population as shown in Chapter 3. The more people who use the substance, the more of it is seized.

METHAMPHETAMINES

Methamphetamine ("meth," or "ice" in its crystalline rather than powdered form) is the leading drug in the synthetic stimulants category (cocaine being the leading stimulant derived from a plant). According to SAMHSA, 1.3 million people had used methamphetamines in the past year in 2003. The drug was first synthesized in 1919 and has been a factor on the drug market since the 1960s. The effect of meth is similar to that of cocaine, but the onset of the drug is slower and its effects are longer lasting. Meth is widely manufactured in the United States in rural laboratories. Over the period 1995–2002 clandes-

tine labs producing methamphetamines were discovered and seized in every state of the union other than Vermont, according to DEA seizure data.

Production

According to the Bureau for International Narcotics and Law Enforcement Affairs, an element of the U.S. Department of State, in the 1999 INCSR: "Methamphetamine's great advantage is its relative ease of manufacture from readily available chemicals. Like other synthetics, methamphetamine appeals to large and small criminal enterprises alike, as it frees them from dependence on vulnerable crops such as coca or opium poppy. Even a small organization can control the whole process, from manufacture to sale on the street. The drugs can be made almost anywhere and generate large profit margins."

Ingredients for making meth are lithium from batteries, acetone from paint thinner, and lye and ephedrine/

TABLE 6.13

Eradicated domestic cannabis plants, 2003

State	Total cultivated plants eradicated	Outdoor operations		Indoor operations		Bulk processed marijuana (in pounds)	Ditchweed[b] eradicated	Number of arrests	Number of weapons seized	Value of assets seized
		Plots eradicated	Cultivated plants eradicated[a]	Grows seized	Cultivated plants eradicated					
Total	3,651,106	34,362	3,427,923	2,678	223,183	56,283	243,430,664	8,480	4,176	$25,062,874
Alabama	51,137	1,160	50,917	4	220	0	NA	90	NA	0
Alaska	7,350	4	74	111	7,276	44	NA	157	81	243,278
Arizona	19,574	5	19,339	114	235	5	8	127	31	112,549
Arkansas	72,565	254	71,630	14	935	7	NA	56	45	113,329
California	1,181,957	1,880	1,109,066	451	72,891	9,026	NA	812	869	2,378,403
Colorado	13,981	31	6,618	84	7,363	1	220,217	241	133	1,672,189
Connecticut	3,027	31	1,393	10	1,634	6	NA	16	10	43,100
Delaware	200	5	200	NA	NA	132	NA	4	26	3,806
Florida	37,744	393	21,442	227	16,302	2,100	NA	403	187	503,852
Georgia	46,985	675	46,762	6	223	220	NA	80	98	378,467
Hawaii	392,422	9,662	388,903	9	3,519	553	NA	969	25	36,669
Idaho	13,664	29	8,560	20	5,104	196	NA	71	22	239,210
Illinois	41,806	752	39,440	54	2,366	338	701,503	127	54	210,806
Indiana	31,192	1,715	23,816	166	7,376	636	219,124,925	1,021	96	925,894
Iowa	1,257	18	368	10	889	22	181,421	17	38	17,800
Kansas	14,471	42	13,338	29	1,133	389	619,049	45	23	78,486
Kentucky	527,775	8,264	519,986	56	7,789	6,552	NA	647	590	3,579,876
Louisiana	5,090	127	4,319	36	771	2	NA	80	3	6,750
Maine	16,258	208	14,052	30	2,206	114	NA	165	55	191,463
Maryland	3,445	170	3,409	7	36	14	NA	85	45	101,641
Massachusetts	1,937	61	1,802	3	135	0	NA	10	NA	0
Michigan	24,524	241	21,942	53	2,582	0	NA	140	131	555,512
Minnesota	2,967	8	357	29	2,610	305	3,095,172	37	68	363,760
Mississippi	2,984	53	2,812	11	172	3	NA	55	NA	46,800
Missouri	14,285	346	12,825	70	1,460	805	4,489,850	398	104	614,295
Montana	404	3	210	10	194	271	NA	25	46	1,300
Nebraska	2,632	3	2,056	16	576	83	362,313	26	19	17,429
Nevada	1,877	4	23	19	1,854	38	NA	18	91	64,364
New Hampshire	547	20	332	11	215	123	NA	27	4	1,000
New Jersey	1,260	43	726	19	534	96	NA	39	NA	40,250
New Mexico	1,507	7	1,068	5	439	9	NA	10	1	29,500
New York	99,423	384	95,385	97	4,038	4	387	281	49	1,491,747
North Carolina	34,283	848	32,793	23	1,490	185	NA	125	38	64,877
North Dakota	1,811	4	1,116	19	695	12	3,200,000	31	4	0
Ohio	44,597	1,429	41,183	43	3,414	107	NA	41	87	41,875
Oklahoma	4,297	184	3,008	12	1,289	52	9,995,153	73	96	230,050
Oregon	32,346	316	16,402	199	15,944	914	NA	231	333	2,957,171
Pennsylvania	5,622	318	3,833	49	1,789	46	NA	97	1	21,599
Rhode Island	76	2	16	2	60	28	NA	2	3	198,919
South Carolina	15,038	138	13,396	7	1,642	23	NA	66	59	37,983
South Dakota	340	NA	340	NA	NA	0	33,010	8	NA	74,905
Tennessee	679,105	2,506	678,635	9	470	26,411	NA	476	7	234,760
Texas	33,404	256	21,682	107	11,722	1,897	448,000	86	48	460,138
Utah	173	NA	NA	2	173	1	NA	2	NA	0
Vermont	3,427	191	2,351	25	1,076	606	NA	77	2	11,171
Virginia	11,419	290	8,981	33	2,438	3,396	0	203	35	45,040
Washington	65,675	228	42,118	196	23,557	308	NA	355	379	6,132,981
West Virginia	74,690	793	73,345	46	1,345	131	34,000	114	35	26,933
Wisconsin	8,523	261	5,554	121	2,969	70	925,656	209	105	460,947
Wyoming	33	NA	NA	4	33	2	NA	5	NA	0

Note: These data were collected by the Drug Enforcement Administration (DEA) in conjunction with the Domestic Cannabis Eradication/Suppression Program. This program is a joint federal and state effort in which the DEA contributes funding, training, equipment, investigative, and aircraft resources to the participating States in the effort to eradicate domestically cultivated marijuana.

[a]May include tended ditchweed; see footnote b.

[b]Ditchweed is a type of marijuana that grows wild.

SOURCE: "Table 4.38. Number of Marijuana Plants Eradicated and Seized, Arrests Made, Weapons Seized, and Value of Assets Seized, under the Drug Enforcement Administration's Domestic Cannabis Eradication/Suppression Program, by State, 2003," in *Sourcebook of Criminal Justice Statistics Online*, U.S. Department of Justice, Bureau of Justice Statistics, http://www.albany.edu/sourcebook/pdf/t438.pdf (accessed February 15, 2005)

pseudoephedrine available in pharmacies. Anhydrous ammonia used as fertilizer can be used to dry the drug and cuts the production cycle by ten hours. The process produces ten pounds of toxic waste for every pound of meth. Making meth creates a big stench, forcing producers into remote areas to avoid arousing the suspicion of those living downwind; explosions and fires are also very common.

TABLE 6.14

Eradicated domestic cannabis plants, by plant type, 1982–2002

[In thousands]

	Cultivated plants outdoors*	Cultivated indoor plants
1982	2,590	—
1983	3,794	—
1984	3,803	—
1985	3,961	—
1986	4,673	—
1987	7,433	—
1988	5,344	—
1989	5,636	—
1990	7,329	—
1991	5,257	283
1992	7,490	349
1993	4,049	290
1994	4,032	220
1995	3,054	243
1996	2,843	217
1997	3,827	224
1998	2,283	233
1999	3,205	208
2000	2,598	217
2001	3,069	236
2002	3,129	213

Note: Data for eradication supported through DEA Office of Domestic Cannabis Eradication and Suppression Program.
—Data not available.
*May include tended ditchweed.

SOURCE: "Table 45. Eradicated Domestic Cannabis by Plant Type, 1982–2002 (Plants in Thousands)," in *National Drug Control Strategy: Data Supplement*, The White House, March 2004, http://www .whitehousedrugpolicy.gov/publications/policy/ndcs04/data_suppl_2004.pdf (accessed March 31, 2005)

Ephedrine is the key ingredient for making methamphetamines. In 1989 the Chemical Diversion and Trafficking Act gave the DEA authority to regulate bulk sales of ephedrine, but over-the-counter sales were not included. As a result, manufacturers simply bought ephedrine at drugstores and then used it to manufacture meth.

The passage of the Domestic Chemical Diversion Control Act of 1993 (PL 103-200) made it illegal to sell ephedrine over the counter as well, but pseudoephedrine, a substitute, was not included in the ban. Pseudoephedrine is found in more than one hundred over-the-counter drugs, including Sudafed and Actifed. Manufacturers have been able to use pseudoephedrine taken from these drugs to make methamphetamines, often for less than they could with ephedrine. By 2005 a number of states were considering legislation that would make it more difficult to purchase large quantities of over-the-counter medication containing pseudoephedrine. Big purchases of such medications have long caught the eye of law enforcement as evidence of a potential methamphetamine operation.

The Comprehensive Methamphetamine Control Act of 1996 (PL 104-237) made it illegal to knowingly possess certain chemicals (known as precursor chemicals) used in the preparation of methamphetamines, and doubled the possible penalty for manufacturing and/or distribution from ten to twenty years. The Methamphetamine Trafficking Penalty Enhancement Act of 1998 (PL 105-277), signed into law as part of the omnibus spending agreement for 1999, further increased penalties for trafficking in meth. Authorities are targeting companies that knowingly supply chemicals essential to methamphetamine producers, domestically and internationally. The importance of controlling precursor chemicals has been established in international treaties and laws.

Clandestine laboratories in the United States are usually operated as temporary facilities. Drug producers make a batch, tear down the lab, and either store it for later use or rebuild it at another site. This constant assembling and disassembling of laboratories is necessary to avoid detection by law enforcement authorities.

Seizures

Data for the seizure of clandestine labs from 1995 through 2003 is shown in Table 6.17. Seizures increased annually from 912 in 1995 to a peak of 9,180 in 2002, before sliding slightly back to 8,502 in 2003. In the peak year the leading state was California, with 1,130 labs seized, followed by Missouri, with 1,055 lab seizures. In 2003 Missouri led with 967 seizures, followed by California with 779. The map shown in Figure 6.7 illustrates seizures in 2004 and expands it to include not only labs but also dumpsites and abandoned equipment.

Seizures of product by the DEA are shown for 1986–2002 in Table 6.16. The largest number of doses of methamphetamines were seized in 1989, about 175 million. Some 118 million doses were seized in 2002. Whereas seizure trends for marijuana have been down, seizures of methamphetamines showed an upward trend in this time period.

Methamphetamine Prices

Prices of methamphetamine appeared to be stable or slightly down in the 1998–2001 period. (See Table 6.18.) Prices per pound were $3,500 to $30,000 in 1998, lower in 1999 ($2,000 to $21,000), and up again in 2000 and 2001 to $3,000 to $23,000.

Continuing activity by the DEA intended to locate and seize meth labs across the country clearly affects local pricing patterns. Prices vary quite substantially from year to year. The low price per ounce in Houston was $750 in 1999, dropped to $350 per ounce in 2000, and was then up again to $500 per ounce in 2001. Prices in Seattle for the same years varied much

TABLE 6.15

Eradicated domestic cannabis plants, by plant type and state, 2002

State or jurisdiction	Total Cultivated plants eradicated	Outdoor Plots eradicated	Outdoor Cultivated plants eradicated*	Indoor Grows seized	Indoor Cultivated plants eradicated	Bulk processed marijuana
Total national	3,341,840	33,329	312,800	2,504	213,040	24,209
Alabama	60,444	1,146	60,294	8	150	558
Alaska	8,616	6	271	143	8,345	84
Arizona	3,837	19	3,345	19	492	237
Arkansas	32,537	184	31,940	21	597	61
California	1,267,771	2,104	1,208,672	477	59,099	6,314
Colorado	15,127	128	11,597	39	3,530	150
Connecticut	2,935	62	1,772	18	1,163	1
Delaware	108	1	3	5	105	36
Florida	37,854	369	19,506	181	18,348	1,467
Georgia	75,770	476	75,259	8	511	15
Hawaii	435,789	9,865	435,475	3	314	1,798
Idaho	1,449	21	570	27	879	201
Illinois	15,852	163	14,289	52	1,563	448
Indiana	15,551	946	7,957	158	7,594	877
Iowa	1,036	5	251	9	785	1,728
Kansas	4,879	69	3,772	15	1,107	961
Kentucky	378,036	7,803	373,117	41	4,919	672
Louisiana	5,299	126	4,403	38	896	1
Maine	7,169	133	4,815	33	2,354	336
Maryland	2,582	234	1,814	16	768	77
Massachusetts	2,371	85	1,888	3	483	0
Michigan	26,443	201	9,947	89	16,496	4
Minnesota	6,929	19	1,400	20	5,529	565
Mississippi	3,973	154	3,709	13	264	503
Missouri	12,612	210	10,919	50	1,693	142
Montana	513	2	98	15	415	7
Nebraska	4,302	6	3,225	22	1,077	41
Nevada	1,513	1	16	26	1,497	543
New Hampshire	1,055	45	876	8	179	4
New Jersey	2,302	48	957	18	1,345	8
New Mexico	2,568	9	2,086	6	482	10
New York	14,414	459	12,289	50	2,125	764
North Carolina	112,017	1,111	110,628	17	1,389	0
North Dakota	1,543	22	1,414	9	129	1
Ohio	41,090	1,873	39,975	24	1,115	26
Oklahoma	5,149	213	5,120	4	29	27
Oregon	45,458	391	32,453	194	13,005	841
Pennsylvania	7,308	359	6,508	79	800	10
Rhode Island	551	17	551	NA	NA	183
South Carolina	27,013	118	26,549	9	464	182
South Dakota	NA	NA	NA	NA	NA	718
Tennessee	485,819	1,976	485,751	1	68	41
Texas	53,175	586	32,712	143	20,463	1,359
Utah	7,820	13	6,180	11	1,640	350
Vermont	2,302	103	2,009	11	293	382
Virginia	17,888	435	15,343	31	2,545	368
Washington	45,159	136	22,510	189	22,649	413
West Virginia	30,887	688	30,166	39	721	136
Wisconsin	6,993	189	4,399	107	2,594	558
Wyoming	32	NA	NA	5	32	0

—Data not available.
*May include tended ditchweed.

SOURCE: "Table 72. Eradicated Domestic Cannabis by Plant Type, by State, 2002 (Number of Plants)," in *National Drug Control Strategy: Data Supplement*, The White House, March 2004, http://www.whitehousedrugpolicy.gov/publications/policy/ndcs04/data_suppl_2004.pdf (accessed March 31, 2005)

less at the low end of the range, $350 per ounce in 1999 and $325 per ounce in 2000 and 2001. DEA data for the second quarter of 2003, as reported by the ONDCP in 2004 (http://www.whitehousedrugpolicy.gov/ publications/ price_purity/price_purity.pdf), put the average national price of methamphetamine at $4,410 per ounce, which converts to $155 dollars per gram.

TABLE 6.16

Drug seizures by DEA, 1986–2002

Calendar year	Cocaine kgs	Heroin kgs	Marijuana kgs	Methamphetamine dosage units	Hallucinogens dosage units
2002	61,594	705	195,644	118,049,279	11,532,704
2001	59,426	752	271,785	124,532,740	13,756,939
2000	58,627	546	331,964	129,622,961	29,306,453
1999	36,167	351	337,832	76,621,124	1,716,954
1998	34,448	371	262,176	62,907,212	1,075,257
1997	28,630	399	215,348	116,143,493	1,100,912
1996	44,765	320	190,453	74,648,735	1,719,096
1995	45,326	876	219,830	139,540,464	2,768,165
1994	75,051	491	157,182	139,500,284	1,366,817
1993	55,158	616	143,030	92,608,266	2,710,063
1992	69,323	722	201,507	48,498,483	1,305,177
1991	67,016	1,170	98,601	21,882,289	1,295,874
1990	57,031	532	127,694	46,358,120	2,826,966
1989	73,592	758	286,167	174,849,333	13,125,010
1988	60,826	730	347,306	108,919,418	16,706,442
1987	49,668	512	629,892	24,179,401	6,556,884
1986	30,333	371	599,166	32,602,774	4,146,224

SOURCE: "DEA Drug Seizures," in *Statistics*, U.S. Drug Enforcement Administration, http://www.usdoj.gov/dea/statistics.html (accessed February 17, 2005)

TABLE 6.17

Methamphetamine laboratory seizures, by state, 1995–2003

State	1995	1996	1997	1998	1999	2000	2001	2002	2003*
Alabama	2	5	5	1	30	81	136	198	209
Alaska	0	2	1	6	22	20	11	30	19
Arizona	17	88	116	226	379	372	288	207	79
Arkansas	19	73	126	232	329	216	357	423	605
California	622	1,627	1,679	1,749	2,090	1,631	1,329	1,130	779
Colorado	14	16	25	51	104	130	173	325	181
Connecticut	0	0	0	0	0	0	0	1	0
Delaware	1	0	1	0	0	1	0	0	2
District of Columbia	0	0	1	0	0	0	0	0	0
Florida	3	0	1	6	22	15	28	111	128
Georgia	3	5	9	6	27	52	44	93	159
Hawaii	0	12	13	4	7	4	3	8	2
Idaho	3	3	3	35	132	89	85	69	42
Illinois	0	7	3	54	124	114	205	338	400
Indiana	0	1	3	5	152	218	304	392	506
Iowa	4	10	17	20	349	208	316	365	450
Kansas	15	47	34	74	209	382	423	329	282
Kentucky	1	3	1	19	67	87	126	215	322
Louisiana	1	1	1	5	8	15	15	60	61
Maine	0	0	0	1	0	2	2	0	0
Maryland	0	0	0	0	1	0	2	1	2
Massachusetts	0	0	0	3	0	0	0	0	1
Michigan	11	13	9	34	99	103	102	165	159
Minnesota	3	1	3	3	10	18	76	146	138
Mississippi	0	1	0	14	57	97	139	285	206
Missouri	38	246	293	395	432	647	827	1,055	967
Montana	1	1	2	2	26	20	49	55	45
Nebraska	1	1	1	10	17	39	108	87	51
Nevada	23	36	17	16	291	244	194	80	68
New Hampshire	0	0	0	1	0	1	2	1	1
New Jersey	1	1	1	0	2	0	1	3	0
New Mexico	4	7	16	29	47	48	74	109	148
New York	0	0	0	0	1	1	4	19	8
North Carolina	0	0	2	1	6	14	28	36	89
North Dakota	1	2	1	1	11	22	48	95	62
Ohio	0	1	6	6	14	27	68	61	70
Oklahoma	8	74	103	162	404	302	615	475	527
Oregon	14	60	98	240	221	238	460	397	247
Pennsylvania	2	13	6	5	1	8	7	19	40
Rhode Island	0	0	0	0	0	0	2	0	1
South Carolina	0	0	0	3	6	4	6	22	24
South Dakota	1	1	3	0	2	7	16	21	20
Tennessee	2	2	21	55	135	225	378	438	550
Texas	10	13	19	43	176	350	468	401	220
Utah	30	62	86	105	240	203	144	109	42
Vermont	0	0	0	0	0	0	0	0	0
Virginia	0	1	2	1	8	1	5	10	21
Washington	54	69	85	173	495	712	811	678	447
West Virginia	0	0	0	1	5	3	16	40	51
Wisconsin	2	3	0	1	5	11	24	24	48
Wyoming	1	1	0	13	18	10	27	54	23
Total	912	2,509	2,813	3,811	6,781	6,992	8,546	9,180	8,502

Note: Federal seizures only.
*2003 data as of January 15, 2004.

SOURCE: "Table 73. Methamphetamine Lab Seizures, by State, 1995–2003," in *National Drug Control Strategy: Data Supplement*, The White House, March 2004, http://www.whitehousedrugpolicy.gov/publications/policy/ndcs04/data%5Fsuppl%5F2004.pdf (accessed March 31, 2005)

FIGURE 6.7

Methamphetamine laboratory incidents, 2004

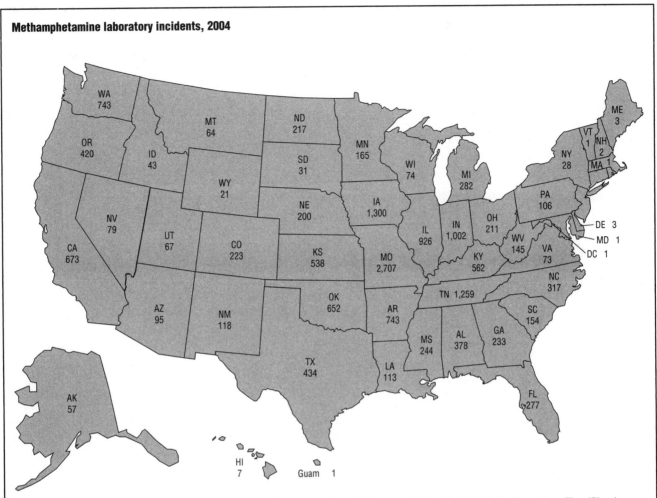

SOURCE: "Total of All Methamphetamine Incidents," in *Maps of Meth Clandestine Laboratory Incidents Including Labs, Dumpsites, Chem/Glass/ Equipment, Calendar Year 2004*, U.S. Drug Enforcement Administration, 2005, http://www.dea.gov/concern/map_lab_seizures.html (accessed February 17, 2005)

TABLE 6.18

Methamphetamine price ranges, 1998–2001

[National and metropolitan area ranges in dollars]

Quantity	Division	1998	1999	2000	2001
Pound	National	3,500–30,000	2,000–21,000	3,000–23,000	3,000–23,000
Ounce	National	450–2,500	350–3,000	300–2,500	300–2,200
	Houston	750–2,000	750–1,400	350–1,200	500–800
	Phoenix	500–800	500–800	300–600	300–600
	San Francisco	450–800	500–1,000	450–1,100	450–1,500
	Seattle	Not reported	350–900	325–650	325–550
	St. Louis	800–1,600	800–1,600	700–1,300	700–1,400
Grams	National	20–200	20–200	20–300	20–300
	Houston	100–125	70–100	85–100	85–100
	Phoenix	80–135	50–60	48–55	48–55
	San Francisco	Not reported	Not reported	Not reported	80–100
	Seattle	Not reported	20–60	20–60	20–60
	St. Louis	37–100	Not reported	100–200	100–150

SOURCE: "Methamphetamine Powder," in *Illegal Drug Price and Purity Report*, U.S. Drug Enforcement Administration, April 2003

CHAPTER 7
THE INTERNATIONAL WAR ON DRUGS

CONVERGING WARS

In the aftermath of the September 11, 2001, terrorist attacks on the United States, the federal government's approach to combating drug production and trade beyond our borders—the subject of this chapter—has come to merge with the war on terror. The principal agency charged with this effort is the Bureau of International Narcotics and Law Enforcement Affairs (which abbreviates its name as INL). The INL is a part of the U.S. Department of State. The case for the convergence between the war on drugs and the war on terror is made in the Bureau's *Fiscal Year 2004 Budget Congressional Justification* (www.state.gov/documents/organization/22061.pdf) as follows:

The September 11 attacks and their aftermath highlight the close connections and overlap among terrorists, drug traffickers, and organized crime groups. The nexus is far-reaching. In many instances, such as Colombia, the groups are the same. Drug traffickers benefit from terrorists' military skills, weapons supply, and access to clandestine organizations. Terrorists gain a source of revenue and expertise in the illicit transfer and laundering of money for their operations. All three groups seek out weak states with feeble justice and regulatory sectors where they can corrupt and even dominate the government. September 11 demonstrated graphically the direct threat to the United States by a narco-terrorist state such as Afghanistan where such groups once operated with impunity. Although the political and security situation in Colombia is different from the Taliban period in Afghanistan—the central government is not allied with such groups but rather is engaged in a major effort to destroy them—the narco-terrorist linkage there poses perhaps the single greatest threat to the stability of Latin America and the Western Hemisphere and potentially threatens the security of the United States in the event of a victory by the insurgent groups. The bottom line is that such groups invariably jeopardize international peace and freedom, undermine the rule of law, menace local and regional stability, and threaten both the United States and our friends and allies.

The same theme is also sounded in INL's *International Narcotics Control Strategy Report, 2003* (Washington, DC: Bureau of International Narcotics and Law Enforcement Affairs, March 2004, http://www.state.gov/g/inl/rls/nrcrpt/2003/):

The U.S. campaign against global terrorism since September of 2001 has highlighted the importance of our international drug control programs. As the single greatest source of illegal revenue, the drug trade has long been the mainstay of violent political insurgencies, rogue regimes, international criminal organizations, and terrorists of every stripe. Whether through the heroin that financed the former Taliban regime in Afghanistan or the cocaine that sustains the decades-old insurgency in Colombia, the drug trade generates the money that is the lifeblood of the violence that increasingly threatens global peace and stability.

The President's National Drug Control Strategy (*National Drug Control Strategy*, Washington, DC: The White House, March 2004, http://www. whitehousedrugpolicy. gov/ publications/ policy/ ndcs04/) sets out three national priorities: 1) stopping the use of drugs before it starts; 2) healing America's drug users; and 3) disrupting the market. The first two priorities are clearly aimed at a goal that is sometimes labeled "demand reduction." The INL is responsible for the international aspects of the third priority, often referred to as "interdiction," a role it shares with the Drug Enforcement Administration, which is responsible for market disruption domestically. There are several other agencies involved in the international effort, including the U.S. Agency for International Development (USAID), an independent government entity that promotes the planting of legal crops to replace drug crops. Also, the new Department of Homeland Security (DHS) has charge of border security and the U.S. Coast Guard operates under its jurisdiction. Finally, the U.S. Department of Defense is active in various roles in Afghanistan, for instance, and elsewhere providing advisors and trainers in counterinsurgency.

The linkage between organized crime, insurgency overseas, and drugs has always been well understood. The linkage to terrorism is a contemporary emphasis. In the older conceptualization, the "recipe" for the drug phenomenon has included as its main ingredients demand for drugs, which acts as the principal motive, and poverty in underdeveloped areas of the world where weak central governments and/or strong tribal loyalties result in corruption fostered by criminal organizations flush with the rich profits of the drug trade.

DRUG ECONOMICS

According to the United Nations' International Narcotics Control Board (INCB), only a very small portion of drug wealth actually ends up in underdeveloped countries (*Report of the International Narcotics Control Board for 2004*, http://www.incb.org/incb/en/annual_report_2004.html). Only one cent of every dollar spent on drugs at the street level by a user ends up in the hands of a farmer who grows illicit crops; 99 cents go to traffickers and those who provide services to them or purchase intermediate chemicals.

The INCB report points out that farmers' income from coca and opium production (approximately $1.1 billion in 2001) was equivalent to 2% of global development assistance expenditures of $53.7 billion in 2000. This might suggest that a 2% increase in development funds, channeled to farmers who now grow poppy and coca, could eliminate opium and cocaine production. By way of comparison, according to the Office of National Drug Control Policy (ONDCP), costs in the United States related to drugs were projected to be about $181 billion in 2002, including $129 billion in lost productivity and $16 billion in health care expenditures related to drug use (*The Economic Costs of Drug Abuse in the United States, 1992–2002*, Washington, DC: Executive Office of the President, December 2004).

INCB reports that the growing of drug plants and local distribution of drugs in producing countries averaged less than 1% of Gross Domestic Product (GDP) in most countries in 2000, and even in countries where the proportion was high, it is less than 20%. In Afghanistan and Myanmar, the opium trade was estimated to have been between 10 and 15% of GDP, in Colombia (coca) and the Lao People's Republic (opium) between 2 and 3%, and in Bolivia (coca) slightly over 1%.

The INCB's conclusion is that, measured in flows of money, the bulk of the drug trade is international in character and most of the profit is realized in the developed countries where drugs are sold rather than in the underdeveloped or developing countries where they are initially produced.

INTERDICTION STRATEGY

The federal effort internationally is concentrated on what INL calls the Andean Ridge, the northwestern part of South America where Colombia, Ecuador, and Peru, running north to south, touch the Pacific and where land-locked Bolivia lies east of Peru. According to the INL, an estimated 90% of all cocaine and 40% of heroin entering the United States comes from Colombia. The remaining cocaine comes from Bolivia and Peru. INL also concentrates on Mexico, not only because the country is a major transmission route of drugs to the United States, but because Mexico is a significant source of heroin, marijuana, and methamphetamine. The centerpiece of the effort is eradication of coca and poppy by providing airplanes and funds for spraying herbicides that kill the plants. Efforts also include assisting law enforcement and, delivered by USAID, financial support for planting licit crops and improving infrastructure for delivering farm goods to market (roads and bridges).

Elsewhere INL is concentrating on South Asia (Afghanistan and Pakistan). The INL programs, however, extend to some 150 countries the world over and involve assistance in law enforcement and in the fight against money laundering. What follows is a brief encapsulation of the INL strategy in selected high-focus areas.

Colombia

According to the INL, the U.S.-assisted aerial eradication program destroyed 122,000 hectares of coca in Colombia in 2002, up 45% over 2001, which was also a record year. Around three thousand hectares of opium poppy were also destroyed. Colombian military forces captured 129 cocaine processing labs and 1,247 cocaine base labs (where precursors are made). Data on how these moves affected coca leaf production, however, were not published by INL because, beginning in 2001, measurements of leaf production in Colombia were not compatible with reports from other countries; in Colombia leaf weight was calculated as fresh weight and elsewhere as dry weight.

Along with eradication, USAID has also been active in Colombia. This agency conducts what is known as the "alternative development" program aimed at providing drug farmers with alternative crops. USAID began operations in the country late in 2000. Since then, the agency has helped twenty thousand families, supported the planting of fifteen thousand hectares of legal crops, and has funded two hundred infrastructure projects, including roads, bridges, sewer facilities, and school rehabilitations.

Colombia, however, illustrates some of the fundamental dilemmas of interdiction. The drug trade there is in part a symptom of a festering civil war. The CIA's *The World Factbook 2005* (http://www.cia.gov/cia/publications/factbook/geos/co.html) provides this summary:

> A 40-year insurgent campaign to overthrow the Colombian Government escalated during the 1990s, undergirded in part by funds from the drug trade. Although the violence is deadly and large swaths of the countryside are under guerrilla influence, the movement lacks the military strength or popular support necessary to overthrow the government. An anti-insurgent army of paramilitaries has grown to be several thousand strong in recent years, challenging the insurgents for control of territory and the drug trade, and also the government's ability to exert its dominion over rural areas.

With an internal conflict that has managed to last more than forty years, quite some time may pass before civil order is restored in Colombia and economic development has advanced enough to make drug plant cultivation unattractive.

Bolivia and Peru

Similar problems, if not outright insurrection, have hampered efforts to bring coca production under control in Bolivia. The country is very poor and has had an unsettled history (nearly two hundred coups since its independence in 1825). The country has been under democratic rule since the 1980s, but successive governments have been reluctant to support eradication programs energetically. Coca growing is traditional and coca leaf is chewed by the inhabitants; eradication has resulted in a popular antiestablishment movement. Despite ongoing eradication efforts in 2002, coca cultivation in that year increased 23% according to the INL. Eradication efforts are paralleled by replanting, and eradication is sometimes violently opposed by the population.

Peru also has organized bodies of *cocaleros* (coca growers) who enjoy sufficient popular support to hamper government action. In 2002, for example, cocaleros succeeded, for a time, in halting eradication efforts in places, although by year's end some seven thousand hectares had been put out of commission. In Peru, as in Bolivia, replanting frequently follows eradication efforts. In both Bolivia and Peru USAID has active alternative development programs.

Mexico

INL estimates that twenty-seven hundred hectares in Mexico were dedicated to the cultivation of opium poppy in 2002. Climate and terrain are such that up to three growing seasons are possible and capable of producing—despite active eradication programs—eleven tons of black tar heroin. The Mexican government, under President Vicente Fox, has been energetic both in the eradication of the poppy crop and in the arrest and prosecution of members of drug cartels, though efforts have been hampered by the dispersed nature and small size of most poppy fields, requiring manual eradication.

Afghanistan

Under the Taliban, poppy acreage cultivated dropped precipitously from 64,510 hectares in 2000 to 1,685 hectares in 2001, and estimated production of opium latex (the poppy's white milky substance from which opium is made) fell from 3,656 metric tons to seventy-four metric tons in the same two years. With the fall of the Taliban, control over outlying regions of the country slipped from the fingers of the relatively weak U.S.-backed government. Poppy cultivation resumed, rising to 30,750 hectares in 2002 and production to 1,278 metric tons, the highest in the world. According to the INL, these figures rose even higher in 2003: 61,000 hectares and 2,685 metric tons. Recultivation of poppy was in part a response to continuing drought in the region: opium poppy is hardy and can grow under adverse conditions.

Afghanistan's new government officially banned opium poppy cultivation and has pressured its regional governors to suppress the drug trade. USAID has been active in the country, mounting alternative development programs. The United Kingdom has conducted some eradication efforts. Germany has provided training and equipment to establish an Afghan security force; Italy has been involved in strengthening the country's judicial system; and the UK has also been active in establishing a counternarcotics mobile force.

Despite these efforts, the situation in Afghanistan was, in the immediate post-Taliban era, similar to the situation in Colombia, with a weak central government unable to assert itself in areas where autonomous warlords hold de facto power. For a brief period only, the Taliban, by draconian methods, almost stopped poppy cultivation.

TRANSIT-ZONE AGREEMENTS

Other countries are frequently reluctant to cooperate with the United States to stop drug traffickers. In the Caribbean Basin, while most of the islands have bilateral agreements with the United States, these agreements are limited to maritime matters that permit American ships to seize traffickers in the territorial waters of particular Caribbean islands. Other problems revolve around the transit zone, the area between the South American continent and the twelve-mile contiguous zone offshore the United States within which U.S. interdiction forces can operate. Very few transit-zone countries permit American planes to fly in their airspace to force suspected traffickers to land.

Twelve transit-zone countries have no maritime agreements with the United States, including Ecuador and Mexico.

Bilateral agreements are not the same in each country, and some provide very limited rights to U.S. law enforcement authorities. For example, a U.S.–Belize agreement allows the U.S. Coast Guard to board suspected Belizean vessels on the high seas without prior notification. The agreement with Panama requires U.S. Coast Guard vessels in Panamanian waters to be escorted by a Panamanian government ship.

DRUG CERTIFICATION PROCESS

To promote international cooperation to control drug production and trafficking, the United States uses the drug certification process, which involves the threat of, or application of, sanctions for noncompliance. Sanctions range from suspension of U.S. foreign assistance and preferential trade benefits to curtailment of air transportation. Another major sanction is public criticism for failing the standard.

Sections 489 and 490 of the Foreign Assistance Act (FAA) of 1961 (PL 87-195), as amended, established the drug certification process. The process was most recently amended as a result of the Foreign Relations Authorization Act, 2002–2003, signed into law on September 30, 2002. The president is required to submit to Congress an annual list of major drug-producing and drug-transiting countries, and also to certify the countries that have been fully cooperative with U.S. or United Nations (UN) narcotics-reduction goals (and are, therefore, fully eligible to receive U.S. foreign aid). Congress has the option of disapproving the president's certification within thirty days. If Congress does that, financial aid permitted to flow under the president's certification may be stopped by Congress.

In 2003 President George W. Bush determined that twenty-three countries were major drug-producing or drug-transiting countries: Afghanistan, the Bahamas, Bolivia, Brazil, Burma, China, Colombia, Dominican Republic, Ecuador, Guatemala, Haiti, India, Jamaica, Laos, Mexico, Nigeria, Pakistan, Panama, Paraguay, Peru, Thailand, Venezuela, and Vietnam. In 2001 Cambodia had been on the list. President Bush also determined all but three of these countries to be in full compliance with the goals and objectives of the 1988 United Nations Convention against Illicit Traffic in Narcotic Drugs and Psychotropic Substances. Burma, Guatemala, and Haiti were designated as failing demonstrably "to adhere to their obligations under international counternarcotics agreements and take the measures set forth in section 489(a)(1) of the FAA" (Presidential Determination No. 2003-14, The White House, January 31, 2003, http://www.whitehouse.gov/news/releases/2003/01/20030131-7.html). The president further determined that assistance to Guatemala and Haiti were of vital interest to the United States, thus denying aid only to Burma.

Two years earlier, in the first months of 2001, Afghanistan as well as Burma were denied aid by the certification process. Since that time, the Taliban ruling Afghanistan was removed from power and a government cooperating with U.S. and international objectives was elected by a tribal process under UN supervision. The new administration, led by Hamid Karzai in Kabul, the capital, had not been able to stop the opium trade as of 2005. The certification process, however, appears to reward or to punish other countries not for actual performance, but for their attempts. Under the Taliban, a regime hostile to the United States, poppy growing had been all but eliminated, whereas poppy cultivation reached new highs under the Karzai regime. At the same time, most of the cocaine and heroin reaching the United States now comes from Colombia and Mexico, but both of these countries have been actively involved with the United States in eradication and alternative development programs, both of which require U.S. aid.

HAVE INTERDICTION AND ERADICATION HELPED?
Budgetary Perspective

The federal budget request to Congress for all drug control activities for fiscal year 2005 was $12.6 billion. (See Table 7.1.) The two largest components of the requested overall program were treatment, including research ($3.7 billion, 29.4%) and domestic law enforcement ($3.2 billion, 25.3%). Again, still looking at the big picture, the majority of federal funds are dedicated to stopping the supply (nearly $7 billion, 55%) rather than curbing of demand for drugs ($5.7 billion, 45%). The 2005 budget request distributes funding among federal departments in the following way: $3.7 billion to the Department Health and Human Services; $2.7 billion to the Department of Justice; and $2.5 billion to the Department of Homeland Security. The Departments of State, Defense, Education, and Veterans Affairs are also targeted for significant funding. (See Table 7.2.)

Of the total federal budget request for all drug control activities for fiscal year 2005, $1.15 billion (9.1%) was requested for international operations, and of that, according to the ONDCP, $731 million was for the Andean Counterdrug Initiative (ACI). The ACI includes the lion's share of the government's international eradication and interdiction programs; the government requested $54.3 million for all regional programs for Asia, Africa and the Middle East for fiscal year 2005. Eradication and interdiction are thus enfolded in pockets of funding that make up a very small portion of the total federal drug control program.

TABLE 7.1

Distribution of federal drug control spending, 2003–05

[Budget authority in millions]

Function:	FY 2003 final	FY 2004 enacted	FY 2005 request	FY 04–FY 05 change	
Treatment (w/research)	$3,223.9	$3,392.1	$3,717.3	$325.2	9.6%
Percent	28.3%	28.1%	29.4%		
Prevention (w/research)	1,966.4	1,985.3	1,977.7	(7.6)	(0.4%)
Percent	17.3%	16.4%	15.6%		
Domestic law enforcement	2,954.1	3,080.5	3,201.1	120.6	3.9%
Percent	25.9%	25.5%	25.3%		
Interdiction	2,147.5	2,490.6	2,602.7	112.1	4.5%
Percent	18.8%	20.6%	20.6%		
International	1,105.1	1,133.9	1,149.9	16.0	1.4%
Percent	9.7%	9.4%	9.1%		
Total	**$11,397.0**	**$12,082.3**	**$12,648.6**	**$566.3**	**4.7%**
Supply/demand split					
Supply	$6,206.7	$6,705.0	$6,953.7	$248.6	3.7%
Percent	54.5%	55.5%	55.0%		
Demand	5,190.3	5,377.3	5,694.9	317.6	5.9%
Percent	45.5%	44.5%	45.0%		
Total	**$11,397.0**	**$12,082.3**	**$12,648.6**	**$566.3**	**4.7%**

SOURCE: "Table 1. Federal Drug Control Spending by Function, FY 2003–FY 2005 (Budget Authority in Millions)," in *National Drug Control Strategy: FY 2005 Budget Summary*, The White House, Office of National Drug Control Policy, March 2004, http://www.whitehousedrugpolicy.gov/publications/policy/budgetsum04/budgetsum05.pdf (accessed March 31, 2005)

The overall federal budget for drug control has roughly doubled since 1996. (See Table 7.3.) The greatest growth in terms of percentage of the federal budget has been in international operations, which made up 3.9% of the budget in 1996 and 9.1% in the 2005 request. Demand reduction, domestic law enforcement, and interdiction as percentages of the overall drug control budget have all remained fairly stable. The question arises whether this increased focus on international operations is stimulated by the government's concern with terrorism or whether it is a sign that eradication/interdiction programs overseas are working.

Past History Shows Poor Results

According to a paper published in 1998 (Phillip Coffin, "Foreign Policy in Focus: Coca Eradication," *Foreign Policy in Focus*, October 1998), drug crop eradication proposals in the U.S. go back to 1925 and have been used in the Andes since the 1970s. Since that time, cocaine production has increased enormously in South America and cultivation of the heroin poppy has been introduced. Coca leaf production appears to be climbing, not declining, despite energetic eradication efforts. Opium gum production dropped briefly between 2000 and 2001. This was due to the ruthless actions of the Taliban rulers of Afghanistan—the only case on record of a brief but successful eradication effort. Since the Taliban's departure, things in Afghanistan have "returned to normal."

The rise of Colombia as a major drug producer has drawn the attention of Congress to that country. Congress has requested the U.S. Government Accountability Office

(GAO) to conduct a number of studies of developments there. One report, published in 1999, suggested that eradication and interdiction programs have not had much success (*Drug Control: Narcotics Threat from Colombia Continues to Grow*, Washington, DC: GAO, June 22, 1999). Another, published in 2004, suggested that some headway was being made in Colombia but that the program suffered from management and budget oversight problems and called its sustainability into doubt. ("U.S. Nonmilitary Assistance to Colombia Is Beginning to Show Intended Results but Programs Are Not Readily Sustainable," GAO, August 2004, http://www.gao.gov/new.items/d04726.pdf).

The 2004 GAO report concluded that U.S. strategy, based on a combination of interdiction, aerial eradication, and alternative development, has "resulted in a 33% reduction in the amount of coca cultivated in Colombia over the last 2 years—from 169,800 hectares in 2001 to 113,850 hectares in 2003—and a 10% reduction in the amount of opium poppy cultivated over the last year. However, according to Drug Enforcement Administration officials and documents, cocaine prices nationwide have remained relatively stable—indicating that cocaine is still readily available—and Colombia dominates the market for heroin in the northeastern United States."

Some of the problems reported by the GAO provide an insight into the difficulties faced by a country attempting to work its will on another distant country, which is itself embroiled in an insurgency. Among those cited by GAO were 1) widespread corruption, e.g., the seizure of

TABLE 7.2

Agency funding for drug control, 2003–05

[Budget authority in millions]

	FY 2003 final	FY 2004 enacted	FY 2005 request
Department of Defense	$905.9	$908.6	$852.7
Department of Education	644.0	624.5	611.0
Department of Health and Human Services			
National Institute on Drug Abuse	960.9	990.8	1,019.1
Substance Abuse and Mental Health Services Administration	2,354.3	2,488.7	2,637.7
Total HHS	**3,315.2**	**3,479.5**	**3,656.8**
Department of Homeland Security			
Immigration and customs enforcement	518.0	538.7	575.8
Customs and border protection	873.9	1,070.5	1,121.4
U.S. Coast Guard	648.1	773.7	822.3
Total HLS	**2,040.0**	**2,382.9**	**2,519.4**
Department of Justice			
Bureau of Prisons	43.2	47.7	49.3
Drug Enforcement Administration	1,639.8	1,703.0	1,815.7
Interagency crime and drug enforcement[a]	477.2	550.6	580.6
Office of justice programs	269.6	181.3	304.3
Total Department of Justice	**2,429.8**	**2,482.7**	**2,749.9**
Office of National Drug Control Policy (ONDCP)			
Operations	26.3	27.8	27.6
High Intensity Drug Trafficking Area Program	226.0	225.0	208.4
Counterdrug Technology Assessment Center	46.5	41.8	40.0
Other federal drug control programs	221.8	227.6	235.0
Total ONDCP	**520.6**	**522.2**	**511.0**
Department of State			
Bureau of International Narcotics and Law Enforcement Affairs	874.3	914.4	921.6
Department of Veterans Affairs			
Veterans Health Administration	663.7	765.3	822.8
Other presidential priorities[b]	**3.4**	**2.2**	**3.5**
Total, federal drug budget	**$11,397.0**	**$12,082.3**	**$12,648.6**

[a]Prior to FY 2004, funds for the interagency crime and drug enforcement programs were appropriated into two accounts, one in the Justice Department and one in the Treasury Department. Beginning in FY 2004 those accounts were consolidated. In this table funding is shown as combined for all three years.
[b]Includes the Small Business Administration's Drug Free Workplace grants and the National Highway Traffic Safety Administration's Drug Impaired Driving Program.

SOURCE: "Table 2. Drug Control Funding: Agency Summary, FY 2003–FY 2005 (Budget Authority in Millions)," in *National Drug Control Strategy: FY 2005 Budget Summary*, The White House, Office of National Drug Control Policy, March 2004, http://www.whitehousedrugpolicy.gov/publications/policy/budgetsum04/budgetsum05.pdf (accessed March 31, 2005).

a Colombian Air Force plane in Florida carrying cocaine and heroin ferried by officers and enlisted persons of the Colombian Air Force; 2) human rights violations by the Colombian military, which have made it difficult to support Colombian military efforts; and 3) control by insurgents (Revolutionary Armed Forces of Colombia and the National Liberation Army) of areas where coca and heroin poppy are grown.

Measurement Is Difficult

A UN report (*Global Illicit Drug Trends 2003*, New York, NY: United Nations Office for Drug Control and Crime Prevention, 2003) points out a problem with accurate reporting—namely that total production may be underestimated by governments reporting to the UN, thus potentially distorting data on the effect of interdiction programs. The report states that in 2001 the amount of cocaine reported seized was equivalent to 44% of estimated world production. The amount of opiates (heroin and precursors) seized was 45% of supply, a much higher percentage than in previous years, but largely due to dramatically decreased production. The agency gave as its opinion that actual production of cocaine may have been well over what was reported by member states.

When estimates are too low, amounts seized can give the public a false sense of progress. In data reported by the State Department's INL for coca leaf production, Colombian production was omitted for 2001 through 2003 because measurement had changed from dry to fresh weight in Colombia. But this omission causes a serious gap in statistical measurement in that Colombia is, by far, the largest producer of coca leaf in the world.

Another indication of the measurement problem—in tracking the success of eradication programs—is that no

TABLE 7.3

Federal drug control spending by functional areas, 1995–2005

[Budget authority in millions]

Functional areas*	FY 1996 actual	FY 1997 actual	FY 1998 actual	FY 1999 actual	FY 2000 final	FY 2001 final	FY 2002 final	FY 2003 final	FY 2004 enacted	FY 2005 request
Demand reduction										
Drug abuse treatment	$1,928.7	$2,132.7	$1,947.4	$2,175.6	$2,241.6	$2,491.6	$2,544.7	$2,612.5	$2,775.3	$3,084.8
Drug abuse prevention	902.0	1,106.9	1,330.8	1,407.6	1,445.8	1,540.8	1,639.0	1,583.6	1,579.2	1,566.1
Treatment research	281.6	309.6	322.2	373.5	421.6	489.0	547.8	611.4	616.7	632.5
Prevention research	187.4	206.5	219.6	249.9	280.8	326.8	367.4	382.9	406.0	411.5
Total demand reduction	3,299.7	3,755.6	3,819.9	4,206.6	4,389.7	4,848.3	5,098.9	5,190.3	5,377.3	5,694.9
Percentage	52.6%	49.9%	50.1%	45.7%	43.2%	49.4%	46.8%	45.5%	44.5%	45.0%
Domestic law enforcement	1,624.1	1,836.3	1,937.5	2,100.6	2,238.3	2,462.8	2,794.7	2,954.1	3,080.5	3,201.1
Percentage	25.9%	24.4%	25.4%	22.8%	22.0%	25.1%	25.7%	25.9%	25.5%	25.3%
Interdiction	1,106.7	1,549.3	1,406.5	2,155.6	1,904.4	1,895.3	1,913.7	2,147.5	2,490.6	2,602.7
Percentage	17.6%	20.6%	18.4%	23.4%	18.8%	19.3%	17.6%	18.8%	20.6%	20.6%
International	243.6	389.9	464.0	746.3	1,619.2	617.3	1,084.5	1,105.1	1,133.9	1,149.9
Percentage	3.9%	5.2%	6.1%	8.1%	15.9%	6.3%	10.0%	9.7%	9.4%	9.1%
Totals	$6,274.1	$7,531.2	$7,628.0	$9,209.1	$10,151.5	$9,823.8	$10,891.9	$11,397.0	$12,082.3	$12,648.6

*Consistent with the restructured drug budget, ONDCP has adjusted the amounts reported for fiscal years 1996–2002 to eliminate the BYRNE grant funding from this table and has included funding for the National Highway Traffic Safety Administration's Drug Impaired Driving program.

SOURCE: "Table 3. Historical Drug Control Funding by Function, FY 1996–2005 (Budget Authority in Millions)," in *National Drug Control Strategy: FY 2005 Budget Summary*, The White House, Office of National Drug Control Policy, March 2004, http://www.whitehousedrugpolicy.gov/publications/policy/ budgetsum04/budgetsum05.pdf (accessed March 31, 2005)

data have ever been produced for estimating marijuana production domestically in the United States against which U.S. eradication efforts can be measured. Furthermore, U.S. marijuana eradication is tallied by plant whereas Mexican eradication is counted by hectare, so that U.S. and Mexican efforts cannot be compared effectively.

Cost-Effectiveness Critique

In a 1994 study, *Controlling Cocaine: Supply versus Demand Programs* (http://www.rand.org/publications/ MR/MR331/), the RAND Corporation took a look at different public policy options for controlling cocaine. The study was funded by the Office of National Drug Control Policy, the U.S. Army, and RAND's Drug Policy Research Center with support from the Ford Foundation. The study concluded that the least costly program for decreasing cocaine use would be treatment of individuals, and the most costly would be what RAND's analysts called source-country control; next highest in cost was the option of interdicting the drugs at the borders. Based on this study, the question is not whether eradication and interdiction work but how cost-effective they are. According to the study, treatment of individuals appears to be the most effective, eradication the least.

The study was controversial. In 1999 the National Research Council (NRC) published a critique of the RAND study, which RAND in turn answered by saying that the NRC did not fully grasp RAND's model. The NRC critique is available as *Assessment of Two Cost-Effectiveness Studies on Cocaine Control Policy* (Washington, DC: National Academies Press, 1999, http://books.nap.edu/html/cocaine_control/).

The RAND study continues to play a role in the policy debate between those who favor supply eradication and those who favor a treatment-based approach to the drug problem. The budgetary presentation at the beginning of this section appears to indicate that in federal expenditures at least, treatment receives a much larger share of resources than international eradication/ interdiction programs.

WHY IS THE "WAR ON DRUGS" SO DIFFICULT?

The goal of the international "war on drugs" is to stop the flow of a product that is in high demand, generally cheap to produce, and offers enormous profits. While certain traffickers may dominate for a time, the drug trade is generally characterized by a large number of participants. Capturing one or two major figures or hundreds of lesser traffickers does little to slow the trade.

Production costs are so low and the profit so great that even if a trafficker loses most of his product, he can earn a huge amount of money on the remainder. When one drug policy is put in place, drug traffickers change their operations to circumvent it. When one route is blocked or one method of production shut down, traffickers change to another.

Since 90 to 95% of the street price of drugs is directly based on the costs of wholesale and retail distribution within the United States, even if half the cultivated drugs were destroyed and the price of coca leaf doubled, this doubling would probably not be reflected in the street price of the drug.

Furthermore, if the United States cannot successfully interdict the flow of drugs through its closest neighbors, upon which the United States can exert substantial political and economic influence and even introduce advisors and equipment, how successful can it be in attempts to stop the trafficking of drugs in places like Afghanistan or Burma? The resurgence of opium production in Afghanistan after the U.S.-engineered regime change there is an indication of the limits of U.S. reach when dealing with distant, inaccessible parts of the world dominated by very different cultures.

Finally, foreign countries—the producing nations—are being asked to solve a problem that is America's own dilemma. Americans want drugs, are affluent, and thus create a vast market for drugs. So long as this demand persists, suppliers will find a way to deliver the product. Many producer nations feel that a "war on drugs" would be more successful if it focused on lowering demand rather than eradicating or interdicting the supply.

MONEY LAUNDERING

Background

Money laundering is a special aspect of the war on drugs. Simply put, money laundering is the attempt to make funds earned illegally appear as if they were earned legally. The cash that drug traffickers collect, usually in small-denomination bills (five, tens, and twenties), must be deposited in banks so that the funds can be transferred, paid out again, spent, or invested. Traffickers cannot simply haul their cash to banks by the truckload for deposit without arousing suspicion. Money launderers hide the fact that funds deposited in banks have been illegitimately obtained. The U.S. attorney general defines money laundering as "all activities designed to conceal the existence, nature, and final disposition of funds gained through illicit activities." The crime is codified under Title 18 of the U.S. Code, Section 1956. Money laundering can range from things as simple as mailing a packet of money out of the country or as complex as a series of international bank transactions involving speed-of light transfer of money by wire.

Before 1986, the Bank Secrecy Act of 1970 (PL 91-508) served as the main tool against money laundering. The act required financial institutions to file a currency transaction report (CTR) on all cash deposits of more than $10,000. Institutions also had to file reports on international transactions exceeding $10,000. Launderers avoided these regulations by keeping each transaction under $10,000 (known as "smurfing"). They would, for

instance, split a $100,000 deposit into twelve smaller deposits. Smurfing is now illegal as well. Until the early 1980s, bank compliance with the law was lax and penalties were lenient. As a result of the Eduardo Orozco case (Orozco laundered approximately $151 million in drug profits through eighteen New York banks), compliance became stricter.

The Money Laundering Control Act of 1986 (PL 99-570) made laundering a federal crime. The act prohibits engaging in financial transactions or transfers of funds or property derived from "specified unlawful activity" and engaging in monetary transactions in excess of $10,000 with property derived from proceeds of "specified unlawful activity." In addition, the act prohibits the structuring of currency transactions to evade the CTR reporting requirement.

Increasingly, the government has been monitoring all transactions of those known or suspected of money laundering or drug trafficking—and, since 9/11, those suspected of terrorist linkages. U.S. banks today must have "know your customer" policies. They must verify the business of a new account holder and monitor the activity of all business customers so that activities inconsistent with a client's type of business can be spotted.

The Mechanics of Laundering

Drug dealing creates a lot of cash. Drug users don't like to pay by check or credit card (even if they could), lest their habits become known. To hide the illegitimate origin of drug funds, dealers pass them through legitimate businesses, which pretend, for a cut of the profits, that these funds were earned legitimately. Dealers also deposit money in cooperating offshore banks, or smuggle cash out of the country. Once drug cash has been deposited without detection in the legitimate banking system, it can be used freely. While the actual amount of drug money laundered in the United States is unknown, federal law enforcement officials across agencies estimated in 2003 that drug traffickers laundered between $100 billion and $300 billion, much of it through legal financial institutions.

A preliminary step in laundering is to convert masses of small bills into larger bills by exchanging them at a bank, post office, or check cashing service. The larger bills are then smuggled out of the country or deposited in a domestic financial institution. The usual route is to deposit funds into foreign accounts. Getting the money into the financial system is called the placement stage. Laundered money is most vulnerable at this stage. Regulations and reporting requirements are designed to detect unusual deposits.

After the funds are in the financial system, they are moved from institution to institution to hide their source and ownership. This is known as the layering stage. To circumvent the reporting requirements, numerous deposits just under the $10,000 cash transaction threshold may be made. The high volume of wire transfers and the speed with which they are accomplished make it difficult to distinguish an illegal transfer from a legal one except by patterns of activity such as frequent transfers when made by or at the behest of unlikely individuals. A typical major bank in New York will handle about forty thousand transfers every day, moving about $3 billion.

The third stage involves the investment of illegal funds into legitimate businesses, known as the integration stage. It must be possible for drug lords to extract this money again as "profits" dividends, commissions, bonuses, salaries, or in the form of property. Drug organizations create and maintain dummy or "front" corporations for this purpose. Such "fronts" can be art dealerships, precious metal stores, casinos, jewelry shops, real estate investment companies, car and boat dealerships, or banking institutions—any type of business that can easily justify the pay-out of large amounts of money.

Targeting the consolidated earnings of drug kingpins is the most effective way to reach the top layers or at least to disrupt their operations. Drug lords are well insulated from street-level dealers but must keep close to their money. Laundering invariably leaves a paper/electronic trail of transactions that authorities can trace, although such tracing may involve massive investigative effort.

Operation Casablanca, completed in 1998 by the U.S. Treasury and the U.S. Department of Justice, was such an operation, dubbed by Treasury "the largest drug money laundering case in U.S. history" ("Operation Casablanca Continues Its Sweep," Press Release, U.S. Department of the Treasury, May 20, 1998, http://www.treas.gov/press/releases/rr2467.htm). The indictment charged Mexican bank officials and Venezuelan bankers. Several American banks, including Citibank and Bank of America, testified or were cited for failure to supervise their own operations. The international ring was linked to the Colombian Cali cartel. The operation seized more than $100 million in domestic bank accounts and cash.

Operation Casablanca resulted in more than 160 arrests, including those of dozens of Mexican and Venezuelan bankers. In May 1998, forty-four individuals were arrested in the final takedown. Of these, forty-one either pled guilty or were convicted. In addition, two Mexican banks pled guilty to criminal money laundering charges, and a third forfeited $12 million.

Money Laundering in the Post-9/11 Era

The September 2001 terrorist attacks on the United States produced changes in domestic and international efforts to stop money laundering, making it more difficult for drug traffickers to operate. As noted earlier, U.S. government policy now links drug trafficking and terrorism. The new international rigor came from the fact that terrorists also move money around and must hide its origins. The State Department's INL notes one significant difference between terrorist and drug-related money laundering ("Money Laundering and Financial Crimes," *International Narcotics Control Strategy Report—2002*, Washington, DC, March 2003, http://www.state.gov/g/inl/rls/nrcrpt/2002/html/17952.htm). It is that the amounts of money terrorists need to funnel to their cells are relatively small. The 9/11 attack had estimated funding of $500,000—mere pocket change in the drug world. The implication is that techniques for detecting terrorist money movements must be capable of pinpointing small transactions.

USA PATRIOT ACT. The Patriot Act, passed in October 2001, revised provisions of the Bank Secrecy Act and modified the criminal code. The INL, in the 2002 *International Narcotics Control Strategy Report* cited above, sums up the changes as follows:

> On the financial side, the USA PATRIOT Act expands the scope of pre-existing forfeiture laws; broadens compliance, reporting and record keeping requirements for certain types of financial institutions; encourages information sharing mechanisms between the government and the private sector; and restricts the ability of shell banks to do business in the United States. The USA PATRIOT Act also amends existing law to make it easier to pursue federal prosecutions of money remitters who fail to comply with state licensing or registration requirements.

A "shell" bank is a bank that does not have a physical presence in the country. Regulations implementing the Patriot Act did not issue until 2002; the more demanding provisions of the act are thus very new.

Statistical Tracking in the United States

Under the Bank Secrecy Act, financial institutions are required to file Suspicious Activity Reports (SARs) with the U.S. Department of the Treasury. The SARs reporting system provides a statistical view over time of activities that banks and other financial institutions have felt were of a suspicious nature and the proportion of these judged to be connected with money laundering. (See Table 7.4.)

Based on Treasury data, activities that looked like money laundering are the most reported suspicious activities—and have been increasing. In 1997 (in the months following April 1), 35,625 cases, representing 40.1% of all cases, were reported under the money laundering category. In the first half alone of 2003, 72,462 SARs filed were connected with money laundering suspicions, 47% of all cases.

TABLE 7.4

Suspicious activity reports (SARs) filed with U.S. Treasury, 1997–2003

Violation type	1997	1998	1999	2000	2001	2002	2003
BSA/structuring/money laundering	35,625	47,223	60,983	90,606	108,925	154,000	72,462
Bribery/gratuity	109	92	101	150	201	411	261
Check fraud	13,245	13,767	16,232	19,637	26,012	32,954	16,803
Check kiting	4,294	4,032	4,058	6,163	7,350	9,561	5,333
Commercial loan fraud	960	905	1,080	1,320	1,348	1,879	934
Computer intrusion*	0	0	0	65	419	2,484	3,605
Consumer loan fraud	2,048	2,183	2,548	3,432	4,143	4,435	2,271
Counterfeit check	4,226	5,897	7,392	9,033	10,139	12,575	6,445
Counterfeit credit/debit card	387	182	351	664	1,100	1,246	659
Counterfeit instrument (other)	294	263	320	474	769	791	615
Credit card fraud	5,075	4,377	4,936	6,275	8,393	12,780	6,037
Debit card fraud	612	565	721	1,210	1,437	3,741	4,575
Defalcation/embezzlement	5,284	5,252	5,178	6,117	6,182	6,151	2,887
False statement	2,200	1,970	2,376	3,051	3,232	3,685	2,316
Misuse of position or self dealing	1,532	1,640	2,064	2,186	2,325	2,763	1,564
Mortgage loan fraud	1,720	2,269	2,934	3,515	4,696	5,387	3,649
Mysterious disappearance	1,765	1,855	1,854	2,225	2,179	2,330	1,264
Wire transfer fraud	509	593	771	972	1,527	4,747	4,317
Other	6,675	8,583	8,739	11,148	18,318	31,109	15,854
Unknown/blank	2,317	2,691	6,961	6,971	11,908	7,704	2,290
Totals	**88,877**	**104,339**	**129,599**	**175,214**	**220,603**	**300,733**	**154,141**

*The violation of Computer Intrusion was added to Form TDF 90-22.47 in June 2000. Statistics date from this period.

SOURCE: "Table 1. Frequency Distribution of SAR Filings by Characterization of Suspicious Activity, April 1, 1997 through June 30, 2003," in *International Narcotics Control Strategy Report, 2003*, U.S. Department of State, Bureau for International Narcotics and Law Enforcement Affairs, March 1, 2004, http://www.state.gov/g/inl/rls/nrcrpt/2003/vol2/html/29910.htm (accessed March 31, 2005)

The following is INL's listing of methods used by drug traffickers for decades to hide the sources of their money—the kinds of activities that result in the filing of SARs:

- Financial activity inconsistent with the stated purpose of the business;

- Financial activity not commensurate with stated occupation;

- Use of multiple accounts at a single bank for no apparent legitimate purpose;

- Importation of high dollar currency and traveler's checks not commensurate with stated occupation;

- Significant and even dollar deposits to personal accounts over a short period;

- Structuring of deposits at multiple bank branches to avoid Bank Secrecy Act requirements;

- Refusal by any party conducting transactions to provide identification;

- Apparent use of personal account for business purposes;

- Abrupt change in account activity;

- Use of multiple personal and business accounts to collect and then funnel funds to a small number of foreign beneficiaries;

- Deposits followed within a short period of time by wire transfers of funds;

- Deposits of a combination of monetary instruments atypical of legitimate business activity (business checks, payroll checks, and social security checks); and

- Movement of funds through countries that are on the FATF list of NCCTs.

FATF. Money laundering is an international activity that can be fought only with international cooperation. As more countries have tightened their controls and shared information, narcotics dealers have become more sophisticated in their techniques. International criminals are not tied to geographic boundaries and can operate in jurisdictions that permit, or even encourage, money laundering in their territories. In addition, cyberbanking and digital cash are two methods used by money launderers to keep ahead of legislation.

The 1988 Vienna Convention made the laundering of money an international crime. The Financial Action Task Force on Money Laundering (FATF) is a multilateral governmental organization founded in 1989 with thirty-one member nations from around the world that extended the Vienna Convention to include the proceeds from all crimes. The INL describes the task force as "the flagship of international anti-money laundering/anti-terrorist financing efforts." FATF conducts what is known as the Non-Cooperative Countries and Territories (NCCT) process, under which FATF members can apply sanctions against countries that have failed to pass anti-money laundering legislation and to implement effective enforcement efforts. Following 9/11, FATF imposed sanctions on Nauru (an island in the South Pacific) and Ukraine, which had been on the NCCT list for a long time. In response, and presumably in order to avoid similar sanctions, Dominica, Hungary, Israel, Lebanon, the Marshall Islands, Niue (also in the South Pacific), Russia, and St. Kitts and Nevis introduced changes in their money laundering processes so that they were removed form the NCCT list in 2002. Nigeria had made changes in its legislation earlier at FATF's instigation. The Ukraine responded to sanctions by changing its laws so that it was also removed from the list in 2003.

CHAPTER 8
DRUG TREATMENT

What we're doing is simply a holding action. We've arrested more people than the prosecutors can prosecute, than the judges can convict, than the jails can hold. Until there's a demand reduction—and that means education and treatment—you're not going to see any change.

—Captain Harvey Ferguson, former chief of narcotics enforcement, Seattle, Washington

DRUG ABUSE AND/OR ADDICTION
The Psychiatric View

Though not all experts agree on a single definition of drug addiction, the 2000 *Diagnostic and Statistical Manual of Mental Disorders-IV Text Revision*, or DSM-IV-TR (Washington, DC: American Psychiatric Association, 2000), is the most widely used reference for diagnosing and treating mental illness and substance-related disorders. In the current DSM, the nation's psychiatrists draw a distinction between "substance abuse" on the one hand and "substance dependence" on the other. They stress that these terms should not be used interchangeably.

According to the American Psychiatric Association, substance abuse can be diagnosed only when one of the following conditions has been observed in the past year: The patient has 1) repeatedly failed to live up to major obligations, such as on the job, at school, or in the family, because of drug use; 2) has used the substance in dangerous situations, such as before driving; 3) has had multiple legal problems due to drug use; or 4) has continued to use drugs in the face of interpersonal problems, such as arguments or fights caused by substance use.

The DSM requires that at least three of the following conditions be met in the previous year before a person can be said to be substance dependent: The patient has 1) experienced increased tolerance; 2) experienced withdrawal; 3) had a loss of control over quantity or duration of use; 4) had a continuing wish or inability to

decrease use; 5) spent inordinate amounts of time procuring or consuming drugs or recovering from substance use; 6) given up important goals or activities because of substance use; or 7) has continued to use the substance despite knowledge that he or she has experienced damaging effects.

The psychiatric definition goes beyond the popular conception of addiction which, according to dictionary definitions, is characterized by habituation to an activity, including the consumption of drugs.

The Labeling Process

Since the 1960s one tradition in the field of sociology has been to study the "labeling process" by which people are identified and treated as addicts, a methodology also applied to the classification of mental disease and deviance. In this view a person's social status influences how the same behavior (e.g., drug consumption) is labeled by society. Persons of higher status are presumed to require treatment, and those of lower status are seen as out of control and requiring restraint. Sentencing data for whites and African-Americans give some support to this view: higher proportions of whites receive probation for drug possession violations than African-Americans. Data by race or income on persons sentenced to probation with mandatory treatment are not available, but of those admitted for treatment, non-Hispanic whites are present in lower proportion to their share in the population than non-Hispanic African-Americans. (See Table 8.1.) In 2002 whites admitted for drug treatment were 58.9% of the total admitted to treatment but represented 71.0% of the population; African-Americans were 24.0% of those admitted but 12.3% of the population. The closest match was experienced by Hispanics (who may be of any race): they were 12.7% of those admitted for treatment and 11.5% of the 2002 population.

TABLE 8.1

Percent distribution of admissions for drug/alcohol treatment, 1992–2002

Sex, race/ethnicity, and age at admission	TEDS admissions											U.S. population
	1992	1993	1994	1995	1996	1997	1998	1999	2000	2001	2002	2002
Sex												
Male	71.9	71.6	71.4	70.7	70.5	70.4	70.5	70.5	70.0	69.8	69.9	48.9
Female	28.1	28.4	28.6	29.3	29.5	29.6	29.5	29.5	30.0	30.2	30.1	51.1
Total	1992.0	1993.0	1994.0	1995.0	1996.0	1997.0	1998.0	1999.0	2000.0	100.0	100.0	2002.0
Race/ethnicity												
White (non-Hispanic)	60.2	58.8	58.3	59.0	59.8	59.6	59.5	59.2	58.4	59.2	58.9	71.0
Black (non-Hispanic)	26.2	27.0	27.1	26.7	25.7	25.3	24.9	24.3	24.8	24.3	24.0	12.3
Hispanic	9.9	10.5	11.0	10.7	10.4	10.9	11.3	11.9	12.0	12.0	12.7	11.5
American Indian/Alaska Native	2.5	2.5	2.3	2.3	2.5	2.4	2.4	2.4	2.3	2.2	2.1	0.8
Asian/Pacific Islander	0.5	0.6	0.6	0.6	0.6	0.7	0.7	0.8	0.8	0.8	0.9	4.1
Other	0.6	0.7	0.8	0.8	1.0	1.1	1.2	1.4	1.6	1.5	1.5	0.4
Total	2090.9	2091.7	2092.6	2093.6	2094.4	2095.2	2096.1	2096.8	2097.5	100.0	100.0	2097.6
Age at admission												
Under 12 years	0.3	0.2	0.2	0.2	0.2	0.2	0.2	0.2	0.2	0.2	0.2	16.8
12 to 17 years	6.1	5.9	6.6	7.4	7.9	8.2	8.1	8.0	7.8	8.2	8.3	8.7
18 to 24 years	15.6	14.4	14.0	13.8	13.4	13.8	14.4	15.0	15.7	16.6	17.0	9.8
25 to 34 years	39.9	39.2	37.8	36.1	33.9	32.2	30.3	28.4	27.0	26.0	25.1	13.1
35 to 44 years	26.2	28.1	29.1	29.9	31.0	31.6	32.2	32.6	32.6	31.9	31.1	15.7
45 to 54 years	8.4	8.8	9.1	9.5	10.3	10.8	11.5	12.4	13.2	13.9	14.8	14.0
55 to 64 years	2.7	2.6	2.5	2.4	2.5	2.5	2.6	2.7	2.8	2.7	3.0	9.3
65 years and older	0.9	0.9	0.8	0.7	0.7	0.7	0.7	0.7	0.7	0.6	0.6	12.6
Total	2187.3	2188.3	2189.4	2190.5	2191.1	2191.9	2192.9	2193.4	2194.1	100.0	100.0	2175.6

SOURCE: "Table 2.9b. Admissions by Sex, Race/Ethnicity, and Age at Admission: TEDS 1992–2000 and U.S. Population 2002, Percent Distribution," in *Treatment Episode Data Sets (TEDS) 1992–2002*, Department of Health and Human Services, Substance Abuse and Mental Health Services Administration, September 2004, http://www.dasis.samhsa.gov/teds02/2002_teds_rpt.pdf (accessed March 31, 2005)

The "Disease" Model of Addiction

In the last twenty years of the twentieth century, advances in neuroscience led to new understanding of how people become addicted and why they stay that way. The "disease model" of addiction has been proposed by psychiatric and medical researchers. Addicts, they say, respond to drugs differently than people who are not addicted. Much of the difference is associated with differences in brain functioning and can be linked to genetic factors. Current approaches to treatment emphasize that addiction must be treated in the same way as other chronic diseases.

The *Journal of the American Medical Association* published an article (A. McLellan, D. Lewis, C. O'Brien, and H. Kleber, "Drug Dependence, a Chronic Medical Illness," October 4, 2000) that likened drug dependence to chronic illnesses such as diabetes, hypertension, and asthma. The article reviewed scientific studies of twins and children of parents who were dependent on alcohol or other drugs. The authors reported high degrees of correlation between parental and sibling dependence, suggesting a strong genetic component in addiction and alcoholism. Moreover, people who used drugs over long periods had different patterns of brain function, which seemed to lead them to continue to use drugs.

The National Institute on Drug Abuse (NIDA) also views drug addiction (if not all substance abuse) as a dis-

ease. On its *Frequently Asked Questions* Web page (http://www.nida.nih.gov/tools/FAQ.html), the agency, which is part of the National Institutes of Health, answers the question "What is Drug Addiction?" as follows: "Drug addiction is a complex brain disease. It is characterized by compulsive, at times uncontrollable, drug craving, seeking, and use that persist even in the face of extremely negative consequences. Drug seeking becomes compulsive, in large part as a result of the effects of prolonged drug use on brain functioning and, thus, on behavior. For many people, drug addiction becomes chronic, with relapses possible even after long periods of abstinence."

Elsewhere the agency points out that drug addiction is not only a brain disease but leads to social "illness" as well—and other diseases (*Principles of Drug Addiction Treatment: A Research-Based Guide,* Rockville, MD: NIDA, October 1999, http://www.nida.nih.gov/PODAT/PODATindex.html). The agency states: "Addiction often involves not only compulsive drug taking but also a wide range of dysfunctional behaviors that can interfere with normal functioning in the family, the workplace, and the broader community. Addiction also can place people at increased risk for a wide variety of other illnesses. These illnesses can be brought on by behaviors, such as poor living and health habits, that often accompany life as an addict, or because of [the] toxic effects of the drugs themselves."

NIDA monographs also support the American Psychiatric Association definition that another range of behavior exists short of addiction, which the APA defines as "substance abuse." The view of *Epidemiology of Heroin and Other Narcotics* (NIDA Research Monograph 16, November 1977) regarding addiction is: "A single definition has limited application, and the solution may be to develop an array of alternative definitions to reflect the dispersion of experience. There are, for example, registered clients with methadone-maintenance programs legally addicted to a narcotic; persons who use heroin on weekends only; [and] users who interrupt their use from time to time."

The paper deals in part with analyzing this diversity of users in order "to predict which groups among them are likely to become addicts and, therefore, should be special targets for intervention."

Social and Cultural Influences

Researchers' insistence that a spectrum exists, extending from rare or occasional use all the way to compulsive behavior labeled addiction, is based in part on physiological and in part on sociological observations.

Changes in the brain occur after continued use of drugs and may cause individuals to continue using drugs; but these changes are temporary. Researchers have shown that they do not last more than a few months. Yet addicts are at risk of relapsing months, and even years, after they have quit using drugs—long after their brains have returned to normal functioning. Brain function is important, but sociologists and psychologists argue that it cannot explain why all, or even most, addicts become addicted.

American involvement in the Vietnam conflict in the 1960s and 1970s brought much evidence that social and cultural factors are also at work. Many American soldiers began using heroin while in Vietnam and came back addicted. Yet most of them stopped using heroin after returning. This phenomenon focused attention on users who either do not become addicted or who cycle between abstinence and relapse. Many people use morphine to mitigate pain after operations yet do not become addicted.

Norman Zinberg, a Harvard University professor of psychiatry, was the first to study "controlled users" of marijuana, opiates, and hallucinogens in the 1970s and 1980s (*Drug, Set, and Setting,* New Haven, CT: Yale University Press, 1984). He showed that the social situations in which people use drugs have a profound impact on whether or not they become addicted. People who use heroin with intimate groups of friends and do not interact with hard-core addicts often don't become addicted. Conversely, people who use drugs in risky environments—

such as "shooting galleries" or "crack houses"—use drugs in ways that make it more likely that they will become addicts.

NIDA Research Monograph 12, *Psychodynamics of Drug Dependence* (NIDA, May 1977, http://www.drugabuse.gov/pdf/monographs/download12.html), reviews work conducted with drug-addicted adolescents in impoverished urban areas, showing that, in their case, "use of heroin was 'adaptive and functional,' helping them to overcome crippling adolescent anxieties evoked by the prospect of facing adult role expectations with inadequate preparation, models, and prospects."

An Integrated Approach to Treatment

The modern approach to treatment has come to reflect the complexity of the drug abuse/addiction spectrum and combines medical approaches, behavior modification, education, and social support functions intended to redress imbalances in the patient's total environment. Components of a comprehensive drug treatment approach are shown in Figure 8.1. Arrayed in the center are categories of treatment used alone or in combination and, on the periphery, social service functions that may have to be deployed to solve some of the patient's problems that led to drug use or addiction in the first place.

HOW MANY PEOPLE ARE BEING TREATED? UFDS/N-SSATS Data

The Substance Abuse and Mental Health Services Administration (SAMHSA), an agency of the U.S. Department of Health and Human Services, has been collecting data on substance-abuse facilities since 1976. The program has had various names throughout its history; it was called the Uniform Facility Data Set (UFDS) survey until 2000, when the name was changed to the National Survey of Substance Abuse Treatment Services (N-SSATS). In the course of this program's history, the data collected have changed, introducing discontinuities in reporting. Until 1998, under UFDS, data on clients of treatment services were reported in some detail, were omitted in 1999, and reintroduced in limited format in 2000. The most recent UFDS data on the gender, racial/ethnic, and age characteristics of people in treatment were reported in 1998. Data on these breakdowns of admissions, however, have continued to be available from another SAMHSA source covered below, the Treatment Episode Data Sets (TEDS).

N-SSATS numbers represent a snapshot of the treatment units on a particular day and does not indicate how many people were being treated over the course of the entire year. As of March 31, 2003, N-SSATS reported that the number in treatment stood at 1.09 million, representing a slight increase since 1998

FIGURE 8.1

Components of comprehensive drug abuse treatment

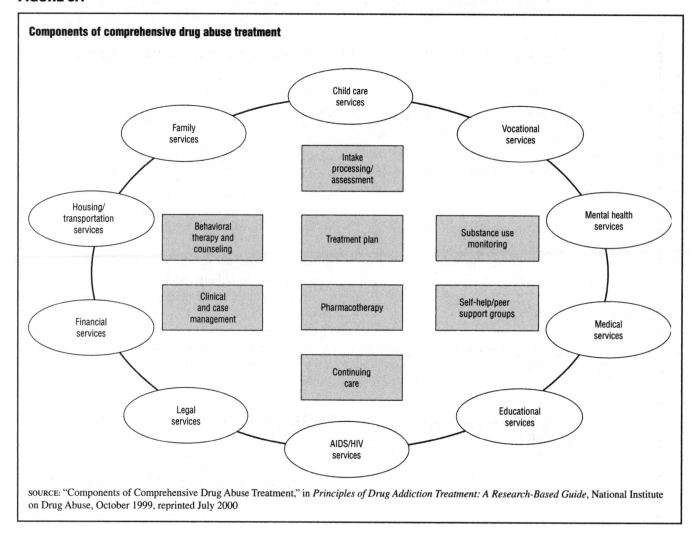

SOURCE: "Components of Comprehensive Drug Abuse Treatment," in *Principles of Drug Addiction Treatment: A Research-Based Guide*, National Institute on Drug Abuse, October 1999, reprinted July 2000

(*National Survey of Substance Abuse Treatment Services (N-SSATS): Data on Substance Abuse Treatment Facilities*, Rockville, MD: SAMHSA). (See Table 8.2.) SAMHSA also includes questions about treatment in its National Survey in order to collect data from the recipients' perspective. Figure 8.2 shows that self-help groups, outpatient rehabilitation facilities, inpatient rehabilitation facilities, and mental health centers are where people most commonly receive treatment. Alcohol is by far the substance that the greatest number of people received treatment for, followed by marijuana, cocaine, and pain relievers. (See Figure 8.3.)

TEDS Data

Another source of data for the drug-treatment population comes from SAMHSA's Treatment Episode Data Set (TEDS). This program counts admissions over the period of a year rather than the number in treatment at a particular moment, and should not be interpreted as a count of unique individuals. When the same person is admitted twice during the same year, he or she is counted twice—whereas in the UFDS/N-SSATS survey, individuals are counted only once.

TEDS data for 1998 showed 1.7 million admissions (versus UFDS' 1.03 million). TEDS admissions in 2002 were up to nearly 1.9 million. To put these numbers in perspective, in 2003, 19.5 million individuals reported using drugs to SAMHSA in the previous month and 35.0 million in the past twelve months.

CHARACTERISTICS OF THOSE ADMITTED

TEDS data from 1992 to 2002 on admissions by sex, race/ethnicity, and age are presented in Table 8.3 and Table 8.1.

Gender

Males represented the majority of those admitted for drug/alcohol treatment, although the proportion of men dropped slightly between 1992 and 2002 (from 71.5 to 69.9%) and that of women increased (from 28.1 to 30.1%). These results in 2002 and data from SAMHSA's household survey of drug use suggest that men abuse drugs more than women. According to SAMHSA, 10% of males were past-month users in 2003, compared to 6% of women.

TABLE 8.2

Clients in substance abuse treatment, as of March 31, 2003

		Number											
		Type of care offered											
		Outpatient						Residential				Hospital inpatient	
State or jurisdiction*	Total	Total outpatient	Regular	Intensive	Day treatment or partial hospitalization	Detox	Methadone or LAAM maintenance	Total residential	Short-term	Long-term	Detox	Total hospital inpatient	Treatment	Detox
Total	**1,092,546**	**968,719**	**587,975**	**128,127**	**27,728**	**11,770**	**213,119**	**108,592**	**22,926**	**76,605**	**9,061**	**15,235**	**8,168**	**7,067**
Alabama	10,749	9,630	1,435	3,608	227	228	4,132	991	304	599	88	128	92	36
Alaska	3,265	2,776	2,002	542	100	42	90	486	104	317	65	3	2	1
Arizona	23,594	21,679	13,024	3,093	364	533	4,665	1,694	380	1,133	181	221	157	34
Arkansas	3,357	2,575	1,821	324	80	33	317	731	450	230	51	51	19	32
California	150,140	128,605	75,643	19,365	4,680	2,434	26,483	20,686	1,985	15,935	2,766	849	541	308
Colorado	31,095	29,420	25,381	1,843	169	115	1,912	1,569	255	1,091	223	106	54	52
Connecticut	20,979	18,342	7,997	1,425	618	280	8,028	2,256	529	1,573	154	381	192	189
Delaware	4,853	4,628	2,596	423	86	—	1,523	209	32	152	25	16	6	10
District of Columbia	5,152	4,488	1,381	673	244	31	2,159	523	47	390	86	141	123	18
Fed. of Micronesia	238	235	232	—	3	—	—	3	—	—	—	3	—	3
Florida	43,032	36,582	23,699	3,023	1,673	653	7,534	5,441	680	4,319	442	1,009	682	327
Georgia	15,483	13,151	6,748	1,522	1,323	159	3,399	1,829	277	1,388	164	503	230	273
Guam	135	135	14	121	—	—	—	—	—	—	—	—	—	—
Hawaii	3,711	3,166	1,449	943	170	59	545	393	38	340	15	152	110	42
Idaho	3,344	3,116	2,435	600	71	10	—	197	74	110	13	31	12	19
Illinois	46,204	42,237	23,259	5,120	931	251	12,676	3,609	722	2,644	243	358	135	223
Indiana	22,739	21,483	12,938	5,598	777	297	1,873	1,024	360	613	51	232	94	138
Iowa	7,311	6,644	5,175	990	183	31	265	617	199	407	11	50	17	33
Kansas	9,332	8,487	6,581	1,096	76	7	727	812	417	340	55	33	7	26
Kentucky	21,323	20,065	17,271	1,354	133	77	1,230	1,105	239	735	131	153	97	56
Louisiana	12,714	11,065	6,079	1,486	154	68	3,278	1,351	293	909	149	298	186	112
Maine	7,063	6,587	4,839	251	84	18	1,395	349	34	315	—	127	59	68
Maryland	35,837	33,286	18,154	3,311	281	616	10,924	2,417	865	1,357	195	134	84	50
Massachusetts	37,369	33,151	20,961	1,347	475	930	9,438	3,544	757	2,365	422	674	200	474
Michigan	45,733	42,366	32,640	2,879	391	233	6,223	3,196	502	2,129	265	171	98	73
Minnesota	8,741	6,037	1,615	2,245	396	30	1,751	2,504	872	1,475	157	200	144	56
Mississippi	6,756	5,281	4,397	664	218	2	—	1,173	180	951	42	302	121	181
Missouri	17,117	15,234	8,822	3,818	779	189	1,626	1,798	1,054	644	100	85	42	43
Montana	2,593	2,349	1,888	429	26	2	4	212	56	149	7	32	19	13
Nebraska	4,573	3,879	3,081	541	46	30	181	634	216	378	40	60	58	2
Nevada	7,376	6,797	3,957	814	42	75	1,909	513	130	308	75	66	25	41
New Hampshire	2,913	2,592	2,146	66	2	147	231	277	64	155	58	44	15	29
New Jersey	31,797	28,498	10,623	4,646	1,179	1,343	10,707	2,661	349	2,265	47	638	427	211
New Mexico	10,877	9,953	6,982	1,078	20	77	1,796	838	167	411	260	86	72	14
New York	128,904	113,498	53,657	14,225	5,520	361	39,735	12,722	2,520	9,578	624	2,684	1,373	1,311
North Carolina	28,870	27,052	19,323	2,915	379	241	4,194	1,494	421	935	138	324	184	140
North Dakota	1,619	1,365	705	315	327	18	—	207	78	123	6	47	44	3
Ohio	34,408	31,063	21,960	5,012	543	180	3,368	2,719	601	2,030	88	626	448	178
Oklahoma	9,373	8,080	6,604	775	144	12	545	1,225	253	873	99	68	14	54
Oregon	19,451	18,417	11,459	4,274	114	109	2,461	998	235	668	95	36	25	11
Palau	48	48	48	—	—	—	—	—	—	—	—	—	—	—

TABLE 8.2

Clients in substance abuse treatment, as of March 31, 2003 [CONTINUED]

		Number												
		Type of care offered												
			Outpatient						Residential				Hospital inpatient	
State or jurisdiction*	Total	Total outpatient	Regular	Intensive	Day treatment or partial hospitalization	Detox	Methadone or LAAM maintenance	Total residential	Short-term	Long-term	Detox	Total hospital inpatient	Treatment	Detox
Pennsylvania	37,928	32,625	18,637	4,763	915	515	7,795	4,841	1,755	2,801	285	462	300	162
Puerto Rico	12,869	7,889	3,269	468	157	301	3,694	4,698	132	4,240	326	282	177	105
Rhode Island	6,355	6,001	2,552	68	84	200	3,097	318	9	288	21	36	9	27
South Carolina	12,646	11,897	9,206	1,164	118	91	1,318	331	123	160	48	418	187	231
South Dakota	2,083	1,489	1,017	414	58	—	—	545	151	343	51	49	48	1
Tennessee	11,527	9,788	5,433	1,242	219	74	2,820	1,377	536	777	64	362	218	144
Texas	35,046	28,357	14,567	4,419	855	185	8,331	5,761	1,652	3,899	210	928	551	377
Utah	9,812	8,663	5,968	1,053	476	101	1,065	1,093	55	973	65	56	26	30
Vermont	2,947	2,804	2,485	182	32	5	100	114	61	37	16	29	14	15
Virgin Islands	157	129	74	37	—	—	18	28	—	28	—	—	—	—
Virginia	20,521	19,287	13,695	1,839	897	196	2,660	1,056	338	580	138	178	90	88
Washington	33,946	32,110	21,568	6,923	338	49	3,232	1,646	682	865	99	190	126	64
West Virginia	4,831	4,375	3,309	325	61	102	578	399	141	226	32	57	9	48
Wisconsin	18,140	16,017	12,364	2,113	435	18	1,087	1,077	153	859	65	1,046	188	858
Wyoming	3,570	3,246	2,816	363	55	12	—	304	99	195	10	20	17	3

*Facilities operated by federal agencies are included in the states in which the facilities are located.

—Quantity is zero.

SOURCE: "Type of Care: Clients in Treatment on March 31, 2003," in *National Survey of Substance Abuse Treatment Services (N-SSATS): 2003*, Department of Health and Human Services, Substance Abuse and Mental Health Services Administration, Office of Applied Studies, September 2004, http://www.dasis.samhsa.gov/03nssats/nssats_rpt_03.pdf (accessed March 31, 2005)

FIGURE 8.2

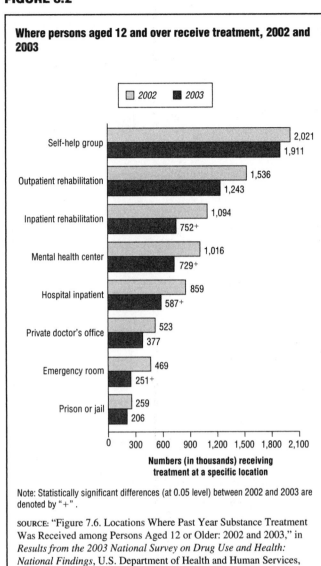

Where persons aged 12 and over receive treatment, 2002 and 2003

Note: Statistically significant differences (at 0.05 level) between 2002 and 2003 are denoted by "+".

SOURCE: "Figure 7.6. Locations Where Past Year Substance Treatment Was Received among Persons Aged 12 or Older: 2002 and 2003," in *Results from the 2003 National Survey on Drug Use and Health: National Findings*, U.S. Department of Health and Human Services, Substance Abuse and Mental Health Services Administration, Office of Applied Studies, September 2004, http://www.oas.samhsa.gov/nhsda/2k3nsduh/2k3ResultsW.pdf (accessed February 10, 2005)

FIGURE 8.3

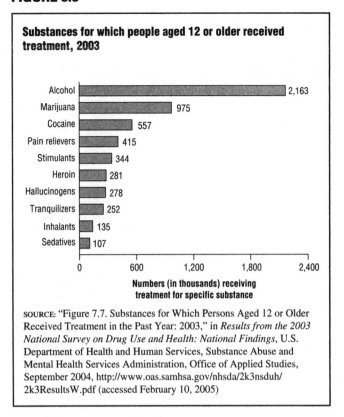

Substances for which people aged 12 or older received treatment, 2003

SOURCE: "Figure 7.7. Substances for Which Persons Aged 12 or Older Received Treatment in the Past Year: 2003," in *Results from the 2003 National Survey on Drug Use and Health: National Findings*, U.S. Department of Health and Human Services, Substance Abuse and Mental Health Services Administration, Office of Applied Studies, September 2004, http://www.oas.samhsa.gov/nhsda/2k3nsduh/2k3ResultsW.pdf (accessed February 10, 2005)

Race/Ethnicity

The largest percentage admitted to treatment were non-Hispanic whites in 2002 (58.9%) followed by non-Hispanic African-Americans (24%). Compared to data from 1992, both whites and African-Americans were proportionately fewer in 2002, whites dropping by 1.3 percentage points, African-Americans dropping by 2.2 percentage points. The largest increase was for Hispanics, whose representation in the treatment population rose from 9.9% in 1992 to 12.7% in 2002. American Indians/Alaska Natives dropped in share of those treated from 2.5% to 2.1% in the 1992–2002 period. Asians/Pacific Islanders increased by 0.4%, but remained less than 1% of the total admissions.

Age

In 1992 the age group with the largest number receiving treatment was aged twenty-five to thirty-four (nearly 40% of total) followed by those aged thirty-five to forty-four (26.2%). Ten years later, these two groups were still the majority, but the older group represented 31.1% of all those seeking treatment and the younger 25.1%. Those sixty-five and older were least represented (not including those under twelve), accounting for 0.9% in 1992 and 0.6% in 2002.

TYPES OF TREATMENT

The treatment that a recovering drug addict receives depends on the types of drugs to which they are addicted. Regardless of the substance they are addicted to most treatment programs involve some form of rehabilitation ("rehab"). For many types of addiction rehab is the only form of treatment that is needed. However those who are addicted to opiates typically must undergo a period of detoxification ("detox") before rehab can begin. In some cases opiate addicts are given opioid substitutes to help them with their addiction in addition to or instead of rehab.

Detox

Individuals addicted to opium-based drugs must usually undergo medical detoxification in an outpatient facility, a residential center, or a hospital. Medical help, including sedation, is provided to manage the painful physical and psychic symptoms of withdrawal. Counseling is always available as well; in many so-called detox centers, group therapy is also available. NIDA, however, describes detoxification as a precursor to treatment (in

TABLE 8.3

Substance abuse treatment admissions, by sex, race/ethnicity, and age group, 1992–2002

Sex, race/ethnicity, and age at admission	1992	1993	1994	1995	1996	1997	1998	1999	2000	2001	2002
Total	1,543,758	1,611,715	1,665,331	1,675,380	1,639,064	1,607,957	1,712,268	1,729,878	1,778,352	1,788,646	1,879,999
Sex											
Male	1,104,492	1,147,004	1,182,286	1,179,563	1,151,527	1,128,154	1,202,608	1,215,478	1,241,677	1,246,642	1,313,303
Female	430,830	455,205	473,884	488,715	481,191	474,350	502,961	508,327	531,542	538,321	565,053
No. of admissions	1,543,758	1,611,715	1,665,331	1,675,380	1,639,064	1,607,957	1,712,268	1,729,878	1,778,352	1,788,646	1,879,999
Race/ethnicity											
White (non-Hispanic)	923,856	939,805	963,257	981,359	973,808	948,992	1,004,115	1,011,066	1,028,144	1,048,230	1,097,962
Black (non-Hispanic)	401,478	431,065	447,945	443,964	418,514	402,619	419,784	415,289	437,320	429,409	446,946
Hispanic	152,488	168,521	181,168	178,269	169,285	173,347	191,484	202,865	211,483	212,424	236,652
American Indian/ Alaska Native	38,531	39,402	38,404	37,704	40,082	38,333	40,511	40,137	40,407	39,373	39,463
Asian/Pacific Islander	7,738	9,010	9,873	9,870	10,197	10,893	11,515	13,619	14,859	14,298	16,552
Other	9,557	11,031	12,896	13,193	16,606	18,263	20,351	24,161	28,588	26,936	27,620
No. of admissions	3,060,111	3,190,508	3,296,105	3,316,676	3,240,753	3,171,248	3,368,162	3,399,235	3,495,706	3,518,082	3,701,022
Age at admission											
Under 12 years	3,926	3,438	3,211	3,616	3,469	3,704	3,390	3,300	3,371	2,952	3,030
12 to 17 years	94,089	95,266	109,122	122,909	129,858	131,194	139,129	137,783	138,660	146,012	156,367
18 to 24 years	239,761	231,869	232,063	230,645	219,406	220,714	245,508	258,551	278,759	295,782	318,758
25 to 34 years	612,220	629,632	628,260	603,148	555,300	516,346	517,297	489,763	478,685	463,098	469,970
35 to 44 years	403,150	450,682	482,401	499,650	507,067	506,624	549,754	561,144	577,897	569,573	583,820
45 to 54 years	128,436	140,865	151,320	159,111	167,899	173,335	197,211	213,867	234,880	247,184	277,512
55 to 64 years	41,076	41,133	41,052	40,390	41,377	40,736	44,096	46,320	48,833	48,732	55,492
65 years and older	13,494	13,691	12,967	11,938	11,535	11,381	11,611	11,484	11,937	11,098	11,054
No. of admissions	4,541,693	4,742,260	4,902,482	4,935,755	4,823,752	4,723,165	5,020,451	5,063,643	5,207,958	5,242,683	5,510,479

SOURCE: "Table 2.9a. Admissions by Sex, Race/Ethnicity, and Age at Admission: TEDS 1992–2002 Number," in *Treatment Episode Data Sets (TEDS) 1992–2002*, Department of Health and Human Services, Substance Abuse and Mental Health Services Administration, September 2004, http://www.dasis .samhsa.gov/teds02/2002_teds_rpt.pdf (accessed March 31, 2005)

Principles of Drug Addiction Treatment, cited above), because actual treatment cannot begin in earnest until the individual's body has been cleared of the drug and a certain equilibrium has been established. A program of rehabilitation usually follows detoxification.

Rehabilitation

Rehab has many forms, but it is always designed to change the behavior of the drug abuser. Changed behavior—achieving independence of drugs or alcohol—requires understanding of the circumstances that led to dependence, faith that the individual can succeed, and changes in lifestyle so that the individual avoids occasions that produced drug-using behavior. Individual counseling, interaction with support groups, and formal education are used in combination with close supervision, incentives, and disincentives (such as, for instance, termination of probation). Certain individuals require a new socialization, achieved by living for an extended time in a structured and supportive environment in which new life-skills can be acquired. Treatment may involve guiding the individual to seek help from other social agencies (as shown in Figure 8.1) to reorder his or her life.

Individuals, of course, may be mentally ill and will then receive, as part of drug rehabilitation, mental health services in outpatient or hospital settings.

Most treatment, as will be discussed below, takes place in outpatient settings, with the individual reporting daily, weekly, or less frequently for periodic treatment and assessment.

OPIOID SUBSTITUTE PROGRAMS. Heroin addicts and those habituated to other opium-based substances follow the treatment programs already described but may, in addition, be prescribed what are known as opioid substitutes. The best known of these is methadone, known as an "agonist," a chemical substance that activates brain receptors. In the case of methadone, these are the same receptors that respond to heroin. Methadone was approved for use in 1972. While heroin addiction disrupts many physiological functions, methadone normalizes those functions. Many studies have shown methadone to be effective; many thousands lead normal lives using this heroin substitute.

LAAM (levo-alpha-acetylmethadol), approved in 1993, is another agonist used in treating drug dependency. While methadone must be taken daily, LAAM can be taken three times a week. Use of LAAM and methadone is not without risk. It is possible to become dependant on them just as it is with heroin and other opioids. However clinical experience with both methadone and LAAM indicates that these medications have a much lower potential for abuse than heroin.

Naltrexone is an "antagonist," a chemical substance that reduces the effect of another chemical substance on the body. Naltrexone blocks the effect of heroin on the brain's receptors and can reduce involuntary compulsive drug craving. It can be prescribed by physicians and is effective both against alcohol dependency and in detoxification. Buprenorphine, which was approved for use by the Food and Drug Administration in 2002, acts as an agonist at lower doses and as an antagonist (a chemical substance that reduces the effect of another chemical substance on the body) at higher doses ("Subutex and Suboxone Approved to Treat Opiate Dependence," *FDA Talk Paper*, T02-38, October 2, 2002, http://www.fda.gov/bbs/topics/ANSWERS/2002/ANS01165.html).

Distribution of Patients

The great majority of patients undergoing treatment in 2003 were receiving outpatient care, 89% of some 1.1 million patients on March 31 of that year. (See Table 8.2.) Of the remainder, 1% received hospital inpatient treatment, and 10% were in residential facilities. Of those under outpatient treatment but not in detox, the majority were receiving what SAMHSA labels regular, or non-intensive, treatment.

Of the total treatment population, 27,898 individuals (2.6% of all patients) were undergoing detox, most in outpatient settings (11,770), the rest in residential facilities (9,061) and hospitals (7,067). Among all patients under treatment, 213,119 (20%) were receiving an opioid substitute; the vast majority of these were on methadone.

About a fifth were being treated for alcohol abuse only, and a third were being treated for drug abuse only. The largest category (47%) was treated for both drug and alcohol abuse. For a small portion of the patients, SAMHSA's survey did not capture the type of treatment (drugs versus alcohol) they were receiving.

Two-thirds of patients were in facilities that specialized in substance abuse, 23% in facilities that combined substance abuse with health care, and 5% were in facilities specializing in mental health treatment.

SAMHSA's N-SSATS survey in 2003 covered 13,623 facilities, with a median of forty clients per facility. Outpatient facilities had a median of forty-five clients, while residential treatment facilities had a median of eighteen. Hospitals had the smallest median number of clients at nine.

STATISTICS ON ADMITTED PATIENTS

Admissions by Substance

Data on admissions by the primary substance of abuse provided by TEDS for 2003 are shown in Table 8.4. From a low of 1.522 million reported by TEDS in 1997, admissions grew to 1.74 million in 2003. Since 1992, the compounded annual increase was less than 1% a year, but much more dramatic increases were posted by admissions caused by different types of substances.

In 2003 alcohol abuse (either alone or in combination with a secondary substance) caused nearly half of all admissions (42.1%), down from 58.8% reported by TEDS in 1992. Total alcohol-related admissions have been declining annually, largely accounting for the relatively flat trend in total admissions. The category showing the largest growth has been stimulants. In 1992 stimulants accounted for 1.4% of all admissions, while in 2003 they accounted for 7.7%. Within the stimulant category, admissions caused by amphetamines (particularly methamphetamine) accounted for the vast majority. Methamphetamine is very addictive and is produced in the rural areas of every state.

Opiate-related admissions have been growing, and cocaine-related admissions have been declining. In 1992 opiate-caused admissions were 11.9% and cocaine-caused admissions 17.5% of the total; eleven years later their roles were nearly reversed, opiates accounting for 17.3% and cocaine for 13.4% of admissions.

Marijuana-related admissions have had the second most rapid growth (after stimulants), representing 15.3% of cases in 2003, up from 6% in as reported by TEDS in 1992. Marijuana is a relatively mild drug. Rapidly rising cases are in part explained by techniques of "lacing" marijuana cigarettes and cigars with crack cocaine and synthetic stimulants or hallucinogens, often without the user's knowledge.

The largest decline of admissions from 1992 to 2003 has been for cases involving inhalants, declining to 0.1% of all admissions in 2003, down from 0.19% in 1992.

Demographics by Substance

A close-up of admissions in 2003 is provided in Table 8.4 showing the distribution of persons admitted by major drug categories, by gender, race/ethnicity, and age at admission.

GENDER. As noted above, total male admissions (69.2%) were higher than total female admissions (30.7%); this trend held in all but two substance categories. Males had the largest separation from females in 2003 in alcohol-only admissions (75.5% of all admissions) and in marijuana-related admissions (74.6%). Females outnumbered men in admissions caused by tranquilizers (52.7%) and sedatives (52.2%).

RACE AND ETHNICITY. Whites were 61.9% of admissions in 2003, African-Americans 23.7%, Hispanics or Latinos (of any race) 13.2%, American Indians and Alaskan Natives 2.3%, Asians and Pacific Islanders

TABLE 8.4

Admissions to drug-alcohol treatment, by individual characteristic and drug type, 2003

		Primary substance															
		Total	Alcohol only	Alcohol with secondary drug	Cocaine (smoked)	Cocaine (other route)	Marijuana	Heroin	Other opiates	PCP	Hallucinogens	Amphetamines	Other stimulants	Tranquilizers	Sedatives	Inhalants	Other/ unknown
Total	No.	1,741,837	407,345	325,399	172,859	61,263	267,277	252,555	49,200	3,951	2,086	131,829	1,083	7,555	4,079	1,099	54,257
	%	100	23.4	18.7	9.9	3.5	15.3	14.5	2.8	0.2	0.1	7.6	0.1	0.4	0.2	0.1	3.1
Sex																	
Male	%	69.2	75.5	73.9	59.4	66.8	74.6	68	53.5	67.1	73.9	55.4	60.3	47.3	47.7	74.5	60.4
Female	%	30.7	24.5	26.1	40.5	33.1	25.4	32	46.4	32.8	26.1	44.6	39.7	52.7	52.2	25.4	39.5
Unknown	%	0	0	0	0	0	0	0	0	0.1	0	0	0	0	0	0.1	0.2
Total	%	100	100	100	100	100	100	100	100	100	100	100	100	100	100	100	100
Age at admission																	
0–11 years	%	0.2	0	0	0	0	0.1	0	0	0	0	0	0	0	0	0.7	4.8
12–17 years	%	8.3	2.4	5.5	0.7	3.1	34.9	0.6	1.8	4	20.1	5	13.7	5	6.7	43.5	19.3
18–20 years	%	6.6	3.7	6	2.1	5.6	15.8	4.3	6.1	11.2	20.3	8.5	8.8	6.4	5.9	7	6.3
21–25 years	%	13.3	9.2	12.6	7	14.1	19.5	13.7	17.8	28.4	26.7	20.5	13.3	12.7	13.6	14.9	12.3
26–30 years	%	11.3	8.8	10.7	10.3	14.4	10.4	12.7	15.3	19.1	12.6	17.8	12.6	11.7	13.1	8.8	10.5
31–35 years	%	13.6	11.7	14.7	19.4	17.2	7.3	15.4	14.8	14.8	7.1	17.7	12.2	12.5	13.1	5.4	11
36–40 years	%	15.7	16	18.5	25	19	5.4	17.2	14.1	11	5.2	14.7	12.1	14.5	14.3	7.5	11.2
41–45 years	%	14.3	17.9	16.6	20.3	14.9	3.6	15.8	13.4	6.9	3.9	10	12.2	14.2	15.1	5.7	10.3
46–50 years	%	9	13.7	9.4	9.9	7.3	1.7	11.7	9.5	3.2	2.3	4.1	8.1	12.3	9.8	4.2	6.8
51–55 years	%	4.5	8.3	3.9	3.6	2.8	0.7	5.9	4.3	0.9	1.2	1.2	3.8	6.1	4.6	1.3	3.7
56–60 years	%	1.8	4.4	1.3	1	0.9	0.2	1.8	1.6	0.3	0.3	0.4	2.1	2.4	1.9	0.5	1.9
61–65 years	%	0.7	2.1	0.4	0.3	0.3	0.1	0.5	0.6	0.2	0	0.1	0.6	1.1	0.8	0.2	0.8
66 years and over	%	0.5	1.6	0.2	0.1	0.1	0	0.2	0.4	0	0.1	0	0.5	0.9	0.9	0.1	0.8
Unknown	%	0.2	0.2	0.2	0.2	0.2	0.2	0.2	0.3	0.2	0.1	0.1	0.1	0.3	0.2	0.3	0.3
Total	%	100	100	100	100	100	100	100	100	100	100	100	100	100	100	100	100
Race																	
White	%	61.9	75.2	60.8	36.9	53.2	57.5	52.1	89.5	23.2	70.5	75	72.6	86.4	83.5	71.6	65.5
Black or African-American	%	23.7	12.7	26.1	55.4	31.1	28.5	24.6	4.7	54.9	16.3	2.7	15.6	5.4	7.5	7.2	24.3
American Indian or Alaska Native	%	2.3	3.4	2.9	0.8	1.4	2	1.2	1.6	3.2	1.9	3.3	3.1	0.9	1.6	5.6	1.7
Asian or Native Hawaiian or other Pacific Islander	%	1.1	0.9	0.8	0.9	0.7	1.3	0.5	0.7	1.1	2.3	3.7	1.8	0.5	0.8	0.2	0.5
Other	%	10	6.5	8.7	5.3	12.5	9.7	20.8	2.9	17.4	8.1	14.4	6.4	6	6.1	13.6	3.7
Unknown	%	1.1	1.4	0.7	0.6	1.1	1.1	0.8	0.6	0.3	0.9	0.8	0.5	0.7	0.5	1.9	4.4
Total	%	100	100	100	100	100	100	100	100	100	100	100	100	100	100	100	100
Ethnicity	%																
Hispanic or Latino	%	13.2	11.5	10.7	7.3	16.4	12.9	24.5	3.4	21.9	9.1	17.3	16.2	7.5	8.4	17.4	5.7
Not Hispanic or Latino	%	83.1	85.1	86.1	89.3	79.6	83.3	72.1	91.8	69.3	87.1	80.3	80.1	89	89.2	79.3	83.8
Unknown	%	3.7	3.5	3.3	3.4	3.9	3.8	3.4	4.8	8.8	3.8	2.4	3.7	3.5	2.4	3.4	10.6
Total	%	100	100	100	100	100	100	100	100	100	100	100	100	100	100	100	100

SOURCE: "Substance Abuse Treatment Admissions by Primary Substance of Abuse, According to Sex, Age Group, Race, and Ethnicity," in *Treatment Episode Data Sets (TEDS)*, Substance Abuse and Mental Health Services Administration, September 2004, http://wwwdasis.samhsa.gov/teds02/2002_teds_rpt.pdf (accessed March 31, 2005)

1.1%, and other races 10%. Whites were highest in all but two categories. African-Americans were highest (with 55.4% of admissions) for smoked-cocaine admissions and 54.9% for PCP-related admissions. African-Americans were uniformly in second place among the racial groups in all other categories, with the exception of methamphetamine/amphetamine-related admissions; in that category, African-Americans came last among the races at 2.7%. It is important to note that the Hispanics or Latinos category is treated as an "ethnicity" rather than a race, and includes both white and black individuals of Latin American ethnicity.

AGE AT ADMISSION. In 2003 most persons admitted for alcohol-only abuse were thirty and older whereas most of those admitted for using inhalants were under eighteen. Those treated for heroin use tended to be twenty and older, with the largest age group of users being thirty-six to forty (17.2%). Crack cocaine treatment recipients clustered in the twenty-six-to-forty-five groupings, with the highest number in the thirty-six-to-forty group (25%). Meth users receiving treatment were younger, the majority falling into the twenty-one-to-forty group, the largest using group aged twenty-one to twenty-five (20.5%). People in treatment for marijuana were in the younger age groups; those twelve to seventeen represented the largest percentage of admissions (34.9%). Those aged twelve to twenty-five made up 70.3% of all those admitted for marijuana use. According to TEDS data for 2002, those treated for hallucinogens had the lowest average age, and those admitted for alcohol use only had the highest.

Type of Treatment

In 2002, 60.6% of those admitted to treatment were admitted into ambulatory treatment facilities; of the remainder, 16.9% went into residential facilities and 22.4% went into residential type (twenty-four-hour) detoxification. (See Table 8.5.)

Among those going into drug-related detoxification, the largest percentages had been admitted for tranquilizer use (35.2%) and heroin (35.0%). Those using marijuana had the highest percentage entering ambulatory care (82.9%). The largest proportions of substance abusers assigned to residential treatment were crack smokers at 28.9%.

Referring Source

Just over one-third of all persons admitted came to get treatment at their own volition (35.1%). The largest referral source (sending 35.9% of individuals) was the criminal justice system, referring people for drug use or driving under the influence of alcohol. Much of the remaining third of all referrals came from substance abuse treatment providers and other health care agencies (10.6 and 6.8% of referrals respectively), referring individuals for specific services. Other referrals came from schools, employers, and community agencies.

Most heroin users (63.3%) and other opiate users (51.5%) sought treatment of their own accord. Justice system sources sent the majority of marijuana users (58.1%), meth users (52.6%), and PCP users (50.4%), along with a good number of hallucinogen users (44.1%) and inhalants users (33.3%), to treatment.

HOW EFFECTIVE IS TREATMENT?

The first major study of drug-treatment effectiveness was the *Drug Abuse Reporting Program* (DARP), which studied more than forty-four thousand clients in more than fifty treatment centers from 1969 to 1973. Program staff then studied a smaller group of these clients six and twelve years after their treatment. A second important study was the *Treatment Outcome Prospective Study* (TOPS) taken during the 1980s. Both DARP and TOPS found major reductions in both drug abuse and criminal activity after treatment.

The Services Research Outcomes Study (SROS)

The *Services Research Outcomes Study*, or SROS (SAMHSA, 1998), confirmed that both drug use and criminal behavior are reduced after drug treatment. With its extended time frame, the SROS provides the best nationally representative data to answer the question, "Does treatment work?" This study, although now several years old and reporting on even older data, has not been repeated and is the most recent assessment available based on a national sample.

During 1995 and 1996 the SROS interviewed 1,799 persons (of a sample of 3,047). The individuals had undergone drug treatment in 1989 and 1990, and the SROS survey was a follow-up. Individuals were not only interviewed but also provided urine samples. The interviews dealt with drug use five years before and five years after the individuals had received drug treatment; other questions established the respondents' criminal behavior and lifestyle changes. A national sample of ninety-nine drug treatment facilities (rural, suburban, and urban) provided the initial list of individuals sampled and also furnished administrative data on their treatment and its duration.

The outcome of the study is shown in Figure 8.4. The number of those reporting using alcohol or a drug is shown for a five-year period before treatment and a five-year period after treatment. Decrease in drug use after treatment as a percent change from before to after is shown as a diamond for each category (measured by the right-hand scale).

TABLE 8.5

Admissions by primary substance of abuse and type of treatment, 2002

Type of service, treatment referral source, and planned use of methadone	All admissions	Alcohol — Alcohol only	Alcohol — With secondary drug	Opiates — Heroin	Opiates — Other opiates	Cocaine — Smoked cocaine	Cocaine — Other route	Marijuana/ hashish	Stimulants — Methamphetamine/ amphetamine	Stimulants — Other stimulants	Tranquilizers	Sedatives	Hallucinogens	PCP	Inhalants	Other/ specified
Total	1,882,584	444,781	363,158	285,667	45,605	176,014	65,685	283,527	124,755	1,308	8,209	4,493	2,795	3,854	1,199	71,534
Type of service																
Ambulatory	60.6	56.5	55.5	52.7	54.2	50.3	60.3	82.9	65.0	62.9	48.5	52.9	62.8	64.9	62.9	79.0
Outpatient	49.0	47.4	46.2	37.7	40.6	37.5	47.2	68.0	53.1	53.5	37.7	42.2	52.6	52.3	48.6	73.3
Intensive outpatient	9.3	8.3	8.9	3.9	9.9	12.1	12.5	14.2	11.8	9.3	9.6	9.6	9.7	12.0	13.6	4.9
Detoxification	2.3	0.8	0.4	11.1	3.7	0.7	0.5	0.7	0.1	0.2	1.1	1.2	0.6	0.5	0.7	0.8
Residential/rehabilitation	16.9	11.3	20.0	12.3	16.1	28.9	25.6	14.5	25.8	18.8	16.3	26.6	26.4	25.3	23.1	11.3
Short-term (<31 days)	8.1	6.4	11.8	5.0	9.4	12.4	10.7	5.9	9.6	4.4	8.6	13.8	9.7	7.9	11.7	3.2
Long-term (31+ days)	8.0	3.9	7.4	6.7	5.6	16.1	13.3	8.0	15.6	11.6	5.7	8.1	15.9	16.7	9.5	4.2
Hospital (non-detox)	0.9	1.0	0.8	0.5	1.2	0.4	1.6	0.6	0.5	2.8	2.0	4.7	0.7	0.7	1.9	3.9
Detoxification (24-hour service)	22.4	32.2	24.5	35.0	29.6	20.9	14.1	2.6	9.2	18.3	35.2	20.5	10.8	9.8	14.0	9.6
Free-standing residential	17.9	27.4	18.7	24.7	23.9	19.0	11.8	2.4	8.9	17.0	21.4	13.8	9.6	9.3	12.9	3.7
Hospital inpatient	4.6	4.9	5.8	10.3	5.7	1.9	2.3	0.2	0.3	1.2	13.8	6.7	1.2	0.5	1.1	6.0
Total	100.0	100.0	100.0	100.0	100.0	100.0	100.0	100.0	100.0	100.0	100.0	100.0	100.0	100.0	100.0	100.0
No. of admissions	1,882,584	444,781	363,158	285,667	45,605	176,014	65,685	283,527	124,755	1,308	8,209	4,493	2,795	3,854	1,199	71,534
Treatment referral source																
Individual	35.1	30.9	31.4	63.3	51.5	40.7	33.8	16.6	24.0	27.8	37.0	38.4	27.0	29.0	30.0	34.3
Criminal justice/DUI	35.9	40.4	34.0	13.0	14.9	26.1	34.1	58.1	52.6	39.2	18.1	23.1	44.1	50.4	33.3	36.0
Substance abuse provider	10.6	10.0	14.7	12.8	14.4	13.9	12.1	5.4	5.0	6.9	15.6	13.5	11.4	6.1	7.0	3.0
Other health care provider	6.8	8.4	7.5	4.5	10.4	7.6	6.9	4.7	4.6	7.2	14.6	12.4	6.9	4.2	12.1	8.7
School (educational)	1.2	0.5	0.8	0.1	0.2	0.1	0.3	4.2	0.4	3.9	0.7	0.7	1.9	0.2	4.7	4.6
Employer/EAP	0.9	1.1	1.0	0.3	1.2	0.7	1.7	1.2	0.5	0.8	0.8	0.9	0.6	0.7	0.5	0.7
Other community referral	9.5	8.6	10.5	6.0	7.5	10.9	11.1	9.8	12.9	14.1	13.1	11.0	8.1	9.4	12.4	12.7
Total	100.0	100.0	100.0	100.0	100.0	100.0	100.0	100.0	100.0	100.0	100.0	100.0	100.0	100.0	100.0	100.0
No. of admissions	516	430,015	352,264	281,525	44,343	170,979	63,013	274,174	120,689	1,272	8,008	4,362	2,688	3,759	1,147	64,659
Methadone use planned as part of treatment																
Yes	6.3	0.1	0.3	35.2	19.2	0.4	0.6	0.4	0.1	0.8	1.3	1.1	1.6	0.8	0.9	0.9
No	93.7	99.9	99.7	64.8	80.8	99.6	99.4	99.6	99.9	99.2	98.7	98.9	98.4	99.2	99.1	99.1
Total	100.0	100.0	100.0	100.0	100.0	100.0	100.0	100.0	100.0	100.0	100.0	100.0	100.0	100.0	100.0	100.0
No. of admissions	13	423,950	343,284	279,973	43,721	170,409	63,528	268,370	112,023	1,298	7,430	3,826	2,547	3,806	1,138	60,131

SOURCE: "Table 3.4. Admissions by Primary Substance of Abuse, according to Type of Service, Treatment Referral Source, and Planned Use of Methadone: TEDS 2002 Percent Distribution," in *Treatment Episode Data Sets (TEDS) 1992–2002*, Department of Health and Human Services, Substance Abuse and Mental Health Services Administration, September 2004, http://www.dasis.samhsa.gov/teds02/2002_teds_rpt.pdf (accessed March 31, 2005)

FIGURE 8.4

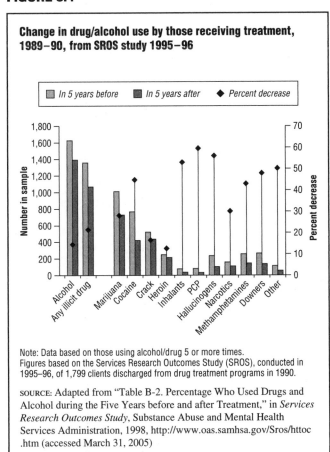

Change in drug/alcohol use by those receiving treatment, 1989–90, from SROS study 1995–96

Note: Data based on those using alcohol/drug 5 or more times.
Figures based on the Services Research Outcomes Study (SROS), conducted in 1995–96, of 1,799 clients discharged from drug treatment programs in 1990.

SOURCE: Adapted from "Table B-2. Percentage Who Used Drugs and Alcohol during the Five Years before and after Treatment," in *Services Research Outcomes Study*, Substance Abuse and Mental Health Services Administration, 1998, http://www.oas.samhsa.gov/Sros/httoc.htm (accessed March 31, 2005)

In this nationally representative sample, alcohol use decreased 14.4% and drug use 21.4%, leading to the following conclusion in SAMHSA's SROS report (Executive Summary, *SROS*, 1998, http://oas.samhsa.gov/Sros/httoc.htm): "A nationally representative survey of 1,799 persons confirms that both drug use and criminal behavior are reduced following inpatient, outpatient and residential treatment for drug abuse."

Decreases varied from drug to drug as shown in the graphic, with heroin use decreasing the least. It went down 13.2%, suggesting that heroin use continued for just under 87% of users. Crack use declined 16.4%, but those treated for snorting cocaine powder did better: 45.4% had abandoned the drug after treatment and continued to do so five years later—but 54.6% were still snorting cocaine. Among marijuana users, 28% had given up the drug, while 72% continued. In all the other drug categories, results were better, but, as the graphic shows, these are also the drugs of limited use by the sample (and the population at large).

Treatment or Time?

SROS did not include a control group of persons using drugs who had not received treatment—which might have been helpful in determining how much of the results achieved were due to treatment and how much

to the passage of time and the aging of the respondents. SROS, however, reported data showing decreases (or increases) in drug use by age groups, suggesting that (among the major drugs at least) success of treatment is higher when users are older. The exception was crack cocaine.

These results are shown in Figure 8.5. Beginning with all illicit drugs tracked by SROS (first set of bars on the left), it is clear that as the age of those interviewed rises, results are better. The first item, marked NS, is for those less than eighteen years of age, where results were "not statistically significant," meaning that changes were small and may have been due to chance. The same pattern is visible for marijuana and for cocaine. In the case of crack, the youngest age group actually increased its drug use after treatment by 202%. In both of the next two age groups, 20% had stopped using crack. The oldest age group (forty years and older) turned in statistically insignificant results. For heroin, finally, the two youngest age groups had NS results, but of the two oldest, those forty and older did better than those aged thirty to thirty-nine.

Type and Length of Treatment

Results by type of treatment have been variable. (See Figure 8.6.) Overall results for any illicit drug show that best results (25% decrease in drug use) were obtained by inpatient (hospital) treatment, followed by residential treatment. Outpatient methadone treatment had less favorable results (10% decrease) than outpatient drug-free treatment (19%). Outpatient methadone treatment consists of receiving methadone during visits to a treatment center; the center may also provide other services, such as counseling. Outpatient "drug-free" treatment consists of counseling, group therapy, and other services, but individuals receive no pharmaceutical support.

Marijuana users who were treated in impatient facilities had better results (35% stopped using the drug) than those in residential (32%) and in methadone treatment (33%). Drug-free outpatient treatment had the lowest success rate (19%). Those using powdered cocaine, on the other hand, benefited almost as much from drug-free outpatient treatment (42% decrease) as from inpatient treatment (47%) and did best in residential settings (55% decrease). Crack users also did best with residential treatment (32% decrease) but had a low response to inpatient care and showed no significant decrease in use from outpatient treatment, whether with methadone or free of drugs. Heroin users responded only to methadone treatment in statistically significant numbers; 27% of those surveyed had stopped using the drug as a consequence of outpatient methadone treatment.

Figure 8.7 shows results based on the length of the treatment received. The same general pattern, with slight

FIGURE 8.5

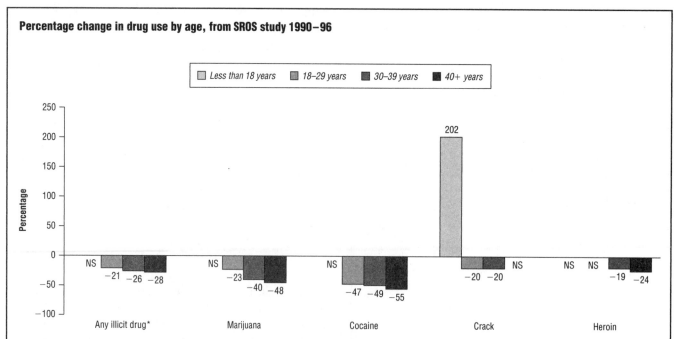

Percentage change in drug use by age, from SROS study 1990–96

☐ *Less than 18 years* ☐ *18–29 years* ■ *30–39 years* ■ *40+ years*

Note: The percentage change is the difference between (a) the percentage using five or more times across the five years after treatment and (b) the percentage using five or more times across the five years before treatment, divided by (b). All percentages shown are significant at the 0.05 level. "NS" means that the difference was not significant. Figures based on the Services Research Outcomes Study (SROS), conducted in 1995–96, of 1,799 clients discharged from drug treatment programs in 1990.
*"Any illicit drug" includes marijuana, cocaine, crack, heroin, inhalants, PCP, other hallucinogens, illegal methadone, narcotics, methamphetamines, downers, and other illicit drugs.

SOURCE: "Figure 3.5. Percentage Change in Drug Use by Age," in *Services Research Outcomes Study*, Substance Abuse and Mental Health Services Administration, 1998, http://www.oas.samhsa.gov/Sros/httoc.htm (accessed March 31, 2005)

FIGURE 8.6

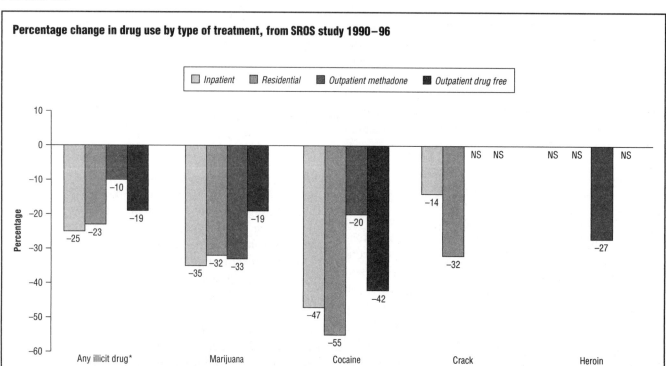

Percentage change in drug use by type of treatment, from SROS study 1990–96

☐ *Inpatient* ☐ *Residential* ■ *Outpatient methadone* ■ *Outpatient drug free*

Note: The percentage change is the difference between (a) the percentage using five or more times across the five years after treatment and (b) the percentage using five or more times across the five years before treatment, divided by (b). All percentages shown are significant at the 0.05 level. "NS" means that the difference was not significant. Figures based on the Services Research Outcomes Study (SROS), conducted in 1995–96, of 1,799 clients discharged from drug treatment programs in 1990.
* "Any illicit drug" includes marijuana, cocaine, crack, heroin, inhalants, PCP, other hallucinogens, illegal methadone, narcotics, methamphetamines, downers, and other illicit drugs.

SOURCE: "Figure 3.6. Percentage Change in Drug Use by Type of Treatment," in *Services Research Outcomes Study*, Substance Abuse and Mental Health Services Administration, 1998, http://www.oas.samhsa.gov/Sros/httoc.htm (accessed March 31, 2005)

FIGURE 8.7

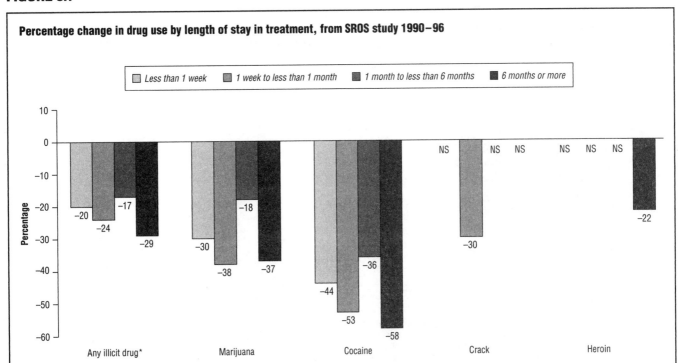

Percentage change in drug use by length of stay in treatment, from SROS study 1990–96

Note: The percentage change is the difference between (a) the percentage using five or more times across the five years after treatment and (b) the percentage using five or more times across the five years before treatment, divided by (b). All percentages shown are significant at the 0.05 level. "NS" means that the difference was not significant. Figures based on the Services Research Outcomes Study (SROS), conducted in 1995–96, of 1,799 clients discharged from drug treatment programs in 1990.
* "Any illicit drug" includes marijuana, cocaine, crack, heroin, inhalants, PCP, other hallucinogens, illegal methadone, narcotics, methamphetamines, downers, and other illicit drugs.

SOURCE: "Figure 3.7. Percentage Change in Drug Use by Length of Stay," in *Services Research Outcomes Study*, Substance Abuse and Mental Health Services Administration, 1998. http://www.oas.samhsa.gov/Sros/httoc.htm (accessed March 31, 2005)

variations, is shown for all drugs, marijuana, and powdered cocaine. Best results for all drugs and cocaine were achieved with treatment that lasted six months or more; this length of treatment was also nearly the top category for marijuana use, missing by one percentage point. The second length with good results (and with the best result for marijuana) was treatment lasting at least one week but less than a month. Results for crack cocaine show statistically significant results only for the "1 week to less than 1 month category." For heroin, only the "6 months or more" treatment duration produced significant decrease in use. Most heroin addicts require long-term methadone treatment (or treatment with a similar prescription drug) to control their habits.

Gender and Racial/Ethnic Differences

Females showed a greater decrease than males in posttreatment substance abuse for any illicit drug and for each of the most frequently used illicit drugs—marijuana, cocaine, crack, and heroin. Figure 8.8 shows the differences. For males, the difference in heroin use before and after treatment was not statistically significant. The total SROS sample was 28.6% female.

Treatment reduced illicit drug use among African-American, white, and Hispanic individuals, although only African-American respondents reduced their crack and heroin use to a statistically significant extent (23% and 18%, respectively). African-Americans were more likely to have used crack and heroin before treatment than whites and Hispanics. The SROS sample was 60.1% white, 28.4% African-American, 8.2% Hispanic of any race, and 3.3% of all other racial categories.

High Death Rates

SROS reported that about 9% of the sample died during the post-treatment phase of the study. Using adjustments for age, sex, and race of the total sample, the investigators calculated, using the overall U.S. death rate, what the expected death rate of the sample would have been and then compared it to the actual observed death rate. The results are shown in Figure 8.9. Each gender and race group within the sample had experienced a substantially higher death rate than expected of a matching group in the population as a whole. The white male death rate was eight times higher than expected, the white female rate eighteen times higher, the African-American male rate five times higher, and the African-American female rate seven times higher than expected—once more documenting the fact that drugs (or more broadly, lifestyles/living conditions that include drug use) are hazardous to health.

FIGURE 8.8

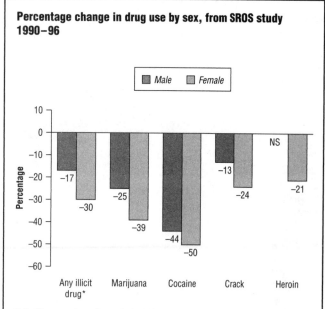

Percentage change in drug use by sex, from SROS study 1990–96

Note: The percentage change is the difference between (a) the percentage using five or more times across the five years after treatment and (b) the percentage using five or more times across the five years before treatment, divided by (b). All percentages shown are significant at the 0.05 level. "NS" means that the difference was not significant.
Figures based on the Services Research Outcomes Study (SROS), conducted in 1995–96, of 1,799 clients discharged from drug treatment programs in 1990.
* "Any illicit drug" includes marijuana, cocaine, crack, heroin, inhalants, PCP, other hallucinogens, illegal methadone, narcotics, methamphetamines, downers, and other illicit drugs.

SOURCE: "Figure 3-4. Percentage Change in Drug Use by Sex," in *Services Research Outcomes Study*, Substance Abuse and Mental Health Services Administration, 1998, http://www.oas.samhsa.gov/Sros/httoc.htm (accessed March 31, 2005)

FIGURE 8.9

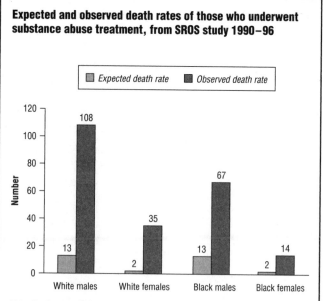

Expected and observed death rates of those who underwent substance abuse treatment, from SROS study 1990–96

Note: Death rates within a sample of 3,047 individuals within a 5-year period of undergoing treatment for substance abuse. The expected rate is the death rate of the general population with the same gender, age, and racial/ethnic composition as the sample. The observed rate is based on the actual deaths in the sample. Figures based on the Services Research Outcomes Study (SROS), conducted in 1995–96, of 1,799 clients discharged from drug treatment programs in 1990.

SOURCE: Adapted from "Table 3.13. Comparison of Expected and Observed Death Rates in the SROS Client Sample," in *Services Research Outcomes Study*, Substance Abuse and Mental Health Services Administration, 1998, http://www.oas.samhsa.gov/Sros/httoc.htm (accessed March 31, 2005)

Criminal Behavior

The SROS, like previous studies, showed that treatment for substance abuse can significantly reduce crime. Criminal activities such as breaking and entering, drug sales, prostitution, driving under the influence, and theft/larceny decreased between 23 and 38% after drug treatment. However, incarceration and parole/probation violations actually increased, by 17 and 26%, respectively. (See Figure 8.10.) Data in the study on those incarcerated or detained were less reliable than other data because of nonresponse to the survey.

How Is Success Measured?

Abstinence is usually the measure of success when treatment providers conduct patient follow-up studies. However, Hazelden Foundation, a nonprofit organization that provides chemical-dependency treatment and education, maintains that abstinence is not the only indicator of successful outcome and suggests that as long as individuals are moving toward abstinence, progress is being made. Other important indicators include the frequency and amount of alcohol/drug use before and after treatment; the patient's quality of life; and decreases in legal, health

care, and job problems. Hazelden measures success by using data self-reported by patients and verified by relatives, friends, and/or laboratory tests (e.g., urinalysis).

Hazelden uses the Minnesota Model of treatment, a program that integrates behavioral treatment concepts with traditional Twelve Step treatment based on Alcoholics Anonymous (AA). A 1998 study (Randy Stinchfield and Patricia Owen, "Hazelden's Model of Treatment and Its Outcome," *Addictive Behaviors,* vol. 23, no. 5) of 1,083 clients using this model found that 53% maintained abstinence during the year after treatment, and an additional 35% reduced their use. Before treatment, 76% of Hazelden's patients used alcohol or drugs daily; one year after treatment, less than 1% used them daily. Between 70 and 80% reported an improved quality of life in such areas as family relationships, job performance, and ability to handle problems. Hazelden considers these findings a treatment success.

Many studies have shown a strong correlation between high abstinence rates and compliance with aftercare and/or participation in Twelve Step programs. These findings confirm that addiction needs to be treated as a chronic illness. In the Stinchfield and Owen study, 72% attended AA or other Twelve Step groups after treatment.

FIGURE 8.10

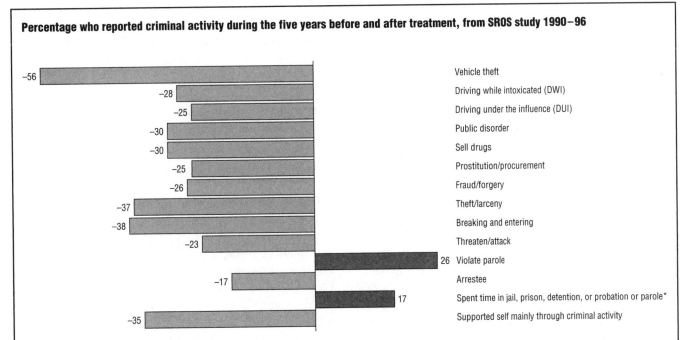

Percentage who reported criminal activity during the five years before and after treatment, from SROS study 1990–96

Value	Activity
−56	Vehicle theft
−28	Driving while intoxicated (DWI)
−25	Driving under the influence (DUI)
−30	Public disorder
−30	Sell drugs
−25	Prostitution/procurement
−26	Fraud/forgery
−37	Theft/larceny
−38	Breaking and entering
−23	Threaten/attack
26	Violate parole
−17	Arrestee
17	Spent time in jail, prison, detention, or probation or parole*
−35	Supported self mainly through criminal activity

Note: Only criminal activities with a statistically significant change were included. Armed robbery, arson, rape, and homicide also decreased, but not at a statistically significant rate.
*There were a large number of cases missing for this variable during the five years after the index episode because of item nonresponse on the five questions that were combined to create this variable.
Figures based on the Services Research Outcomes Study (SROS), conducted in 1995–96, of 1,799 clients discharged from drug treatment programs in 1990.

SOURCE: Adapted from "Table 3-12. Percentage Who Reported Criminal Activity during the Five Years before and after Treatment," in *Services Research Outcomes Study*, Substance Abuse and Mental Health Services Administration, 1998, http://www.oas.samhsa.gov/Sros/httoc.htm (accessed March 31, 2005)

Of the 28% who did not, only 18% remained abstinent, while 57% of those who did attend AA stayed abstinent.

A. Thomas McLellan et al. (*Training about Alcohol and Substance Abuse for All Primary Care Physicians*, New York: Josiah Macy, Jr. Foundation, 1995) maintain that "substance abuse is a real medical disorder. It is a recurring disorder much like diabetes, hypertension, or asthma, with profound and expensive public health and safety implications." These are chronic diseases that have serious consequences for the patient, including death. When substance abuse is treated as a chronic disease, they note that success is similar to that of treatment of other chronic illnesses.

For example, despite the real dangers, less than 50% of diabetics take their medicine properly, and fewer than 30% follow their diet. Within twelve months, 30–50% have to be retreated. Similarly, fewer than 30% of hypertension patients take their medicine properly, and fewer than 30% follow their diet. Within a year, 50–60% must be retreated. Finally, fewer than 30% of asthma sufferers take their medicine properly, and 60–80% must be retreated within twelve months.

Along the same lines, McLellan et al. note that:

Studies of treatment response have shown that patients who comply with the recommended regimen of educa-

tion, counseling, and medication, which characterizes most contemporary forms of treatment, typically have favorable outcomes during treatment and longer-lasting benefits after treatment. Thus, it is discouraging to those in the treatment field that so many substance-dependent patients fail to comply with the recommended course of treatment and subsequently resume substance use. Factors such as low socioeconomic class, co-morbid psychiatric conditions, and lack of family or social supports for continuing abstinence are among the most important variables associated with lack of treatment compliance, and ultimately, to reoccurrence of the disorder following treatment.

HOW MUCH DOES THE NATION SPEND ON DRUG TREATMENT?

The federal government expends substantial sums yearly obtaining data on how many people use drugs, how many are admitted to treatment facilities, how many treatment centers exist, how many hectares of opium poppy or coca bushes are eradicated, how many persons are arrested on drug charges, and on obtaining other similar measurements of progress. Current data on expenditures on treatment or the cost of treatment across the nation, however, are not available. In its 2002 report to Congress (*Report to Congress on the Prevention and Treatment of Co-occurring Substance Abuse Disorders and Mental Disorders*, SAMHSA, 2002, http://alt.samhsa.gov/reports/

congress2002/) SAMHSA stated that the most recent data on national expenditures for substance abuse were from 1997. That year, according to the agency, $11.4 billion was spent on substance abuse by government bodies at all levels and by the private sector. In that year the federal budget for drug treatment was $2.6 billion, or about 23% of the total spent. By 2004 the federal budget for drug treatment had risen to $3.4 billion, according to SAMHSA. Increases between 1997 and 2004 were in part due to higher than average inflation in the medical care services component of the Consumer Price Index (CPI).

Federal Expenditures

In fiscal year (FY) 2004 (which ended September 30), the federal government had authority to spend $12.1 billion on all aspects of drug control. Of this total, $3.4 billion was earmarked for drug treatment, including research to support it, or 28.1% of the total. (See Table 7.1 in Chapter 7.) The federal drug control budget increased from a level of $7.05 billion in FY 1995, growing at an annual rate in this period of 6%. The budget for treatment increased from a level of $2.4 billion, growing 3.8% annually. Treatment funds increased their share from 21.7% of total budget to 28.1% (down slightly from FY 2003), but treatment funds grew at a lower rate than the total budget since FY 1995. The two categories that saw higher than average growth were international programs (growing 21.5% a year) and interdiction of drugs at the borders (growing 7.5% a year). The federal budget has exhibited a slight bias toward control of drugs at the source rather than control of demand at home: the lowest annual growth rate was exhibited by programs of prevention (3.8% a year). Domestic law enforcement expenditures, the second-largest category ($3.1 billion in FY 2004) grew at a rate of 5% yearly. Growth trends by category are shown in Table 7.3 in Chapter 7 from FY 1996 through the requested FY 2005 budget.

The bulk of treatment funds in 2004 were earmarked for SAMHSA, the Department of Veterans Affairs, and the Office of National Drug Control Policy. In addition to the treatment funds it spends, SAMHSA also administers grants to states.

Other Sources of Funding

Based on data published by SAMHSA in 1997 (*Uniform Facility Data Set (UFDS): Data for 1996 and 1980–1996*), 26% of substance abuse treatment funding came from Medicare and Medicaid, 15.8% from private health insurance, and 10.7% from individuals paying for their own services. The rest (48.1%) came from substance abuse programs funded by the federal, state, and local governments. The sources of 4.8% of funds were not known.

STATES AND LOCALITIES. In 2002, according to its report to Congress (cited above), SAMHSA provided $1.725 billion to states under the Substance Abuse Prevention and Treatment (SAPT) block grant program to states, which represented 40% of state expenditures, suggesting a state contribution of $2.6 billion in 2002 as matching funds to the federal program. Total state expenditures are most likely much higher. Data on local government expenditures are not available.

INSURANCE. Insurance coverage of substance abuse treatment depends on the provisions of an individual's health insurance policy. In the 1990s, as health care expenses continued to rise, companies cut back on substance abuse treatment coverage. President Clinton ordered health plans covering federal employees to offer equivalent coverage for physical and mental illness and for substance abuse in 1999. In 2001 Senator Paul Wellstone (D-MN) and Representative Jim Ramstad (R-MN) introduced new legislation to accomplish the same end. The legislation is known as Fairness in Treatment: The Alcohol and Drug Addiction Recovery Act of 2001. Ramstad and Senator Norm Coleman (R-MN), who won the seat formerly held by Wellstone, introduced similar legislation in 2003, called the Help Expand Access to Recovery and Treatment (HEART) Act. As of March of 2005, this "parity" legislation had not yet passed. If passed, it would compel insurers to cover addictive disorders just as they do other illnesses.

Spending by/on Individuals

According to SAMHSA, individuals who have no coverage and cannot qualify for a program could expect to pay somewhere between $2,136 and $8,141 for a regimen of treatment in 2002. These are also the estimated costs that must be borne by insurance or by publicly funded programs. The lower end of the cost range is for "drug-free" outpatient care, costing $18 a day and lasting for 120 days. The high end is for long-term residential treatment at $58 per day for 140 days. The figures go back to the last comprehensive survey conducted by SAMHSA in 1997, updated to 2002 values using the medical care services component of the Consumer Price Index (maintained by the Bureau of Labor Statistics). An intermediate cost of treatment is $4,628 for a person on outpatient methadone treatment ($15 per day lasting 300 days) or for a person participating in short-term residential treatment ($154 per day for thirty days).

IS TREATMENT WORTH THE MONEY?

A study conducted by the RAND corporation in 1994 concluded that treatment was the most effective program available for reducing cocaine consumption (Peter Rydell and Susan Everingham, *Controlling Cocaine: Supply Versus Demand Programs* (Santa Monica, CA: RAND, 1994, http://www.rand.org/publications/MR/MR331/).

The authors studied various drug-control strategies—treatment, domestic enforcement, interdiction, and source country control—and concluded that to achieve a 1% reduction in cocaine consumption in the United States, the country would have to spend either $34 million on treatment, $250 million on domestic enforcement, almost $400 million on interdiction, or around $800 million for source control. Their conclusion was that domestic enforcement was 7.3 times more costly than drug treatment.

The study was criticized on methodological grounds by the National Research Council, to which RAND also responded. The conclusions were controversial, and federal policy makers clearly did not accept the study's findings because budgets have not come to reflect the study's priorities. None of the programs is fully effective, and approaches based entirely on cost effectiveness tend to leave out crucial elements. Treatment, law enforcement, border control, and eradication efforts all continue to have strong proponents.

The issue of cost effectiveness is more frequently discussed by comparing the costs of treatment to the costs of imprisoning drug offenders.

Treatment versus Incarceration

For example, in a somewhat dated analysis (*National Treatment Improvement Evaluation Study (NTIES)*, SAMHSA, 1997), SAMHSA's analysts observed that "treatment appears to be cost-effective, particularly when compared to incarceration, which is often the alternative." The study did not examine the cost of incarceration but referred to a study by the American Correctional Association, which gave the estimated 1994 cost of incarceration as $18,330 per prisoner annually. The most expensive treatment in 1997, according to NTIES, was $6,800 per client for long-term residential programs—just over one-third the cost of a year of incarceration.

If treatment only works in 21.4% of all cases, as shown by SAMHSA data discussed above, results seem to favor incarceration if the object is to remove one person from the drug-using population for some fixed period of time—a year, for example. With treatment working in only 21.4% of cases, nearly five people (4.7) have to be treated to achieve one favorable result. But the analysis would be incomplete. Incarcerating individuals removes them from the drug-using community but does not cure them. Furthermore, many incarcerated individuals must undergo drug treatment while in prison, requiring additional expenditures. Simple answers are not available, one reason why multiple approaches to managing the drug problem survive side by side.

THE ARIZONA EXPERIENCE. In 1996 the voters of Arizona passed Proposition 200, called Drug Medicaliza-tion, Prevention and Control Act of 1996. Under this law, first- and second-time drug offenders not charged with a violent crime are sent to treatment rather than undergoing incarceration. The Arizona Supreme Court conducted a study of the first year of probation with mandatory drug treatment, released in 1999. It estimated that the state's new program saved more than $2.5 million and was likely to show even greater savings in the future. The court estimated the cost of treatment, counseling, and probation at $16.06 a day, compared with $50 a day to keep an inmate in prison (Barbara Broderick, Arizona's director of adult probation, "The Arizona Experience: Probation with Treatment Protects the Community," testimony before the Subcommittee on Criminal Justice, Drug Policy and Human Resources, U.S. House of Representatives, July 1999).

The Arizona program, according to the testimony cited above, is largely paid for by a tax on alcohol. Daily financial savings are not the only benefit of treatment versus incarceration, however. Most addicts, untreated, emerge from prison and quickly return to drug use, often committing crimes to get money for the drugs. Of the 2,622 people treated by the program, 77.5% subsequently tested free of drugs. Arizona drug users on probation are expected to help pay for their treatment; 77.1% made at least one payment. The program, however, does not apply to chronic drug offenders or those who commit violent crimes. It is a partial application of treatment instead of incarceration.

Other Measures of Cost-Effectiveness

DRUG TREATMENT FOR EMPLOYEES. In 1998 John Saylor, manager of Employee Assistance Programs for AMR Corporation (which includes American Airlines), testified before the Senate Committee on Labor and Human Resources about the value of treatment for alcohol and drug addiction for AMR and its employees. Saylor was "charged with the task of ensuring that any AMR-insured person will receive the best available treatment for his/her alcoholism or drug addiction, with no limit on days or sessions, and no limit on dollars other than the lifetime maximum for all medical care (currently at $1,000,000)." He was confident that this corporate investment turned out to be both prudent and highly successful.

Saylor reported that follow-up studies of employees who received alcohol or drug treatment showed that 75–80% remained completely drug and alcohol free during their year of monitoring. He estimated that the average cost to AMR for complete treatment has been between $5,000 and $6,000 per person. With other serious life-threatening diseases, the first day of treatment alone can cost that much, according to Saylor. He is convinced that the expenditure of this "moderate amount of money" reduced accidents, injuries, and diseases.

DRUG TREATMENT FOR WELFARE RECIPIENTS. According to the National Conference of State Legislatures, federal studies estimate that up to 35% of the welfare population is addicted to drugs or alcohol. Welfare recipients who cannot get or keep a job are dropped from the welfare rolls. Therefore, those on the rolls who have substance-abuse problems jeopardize a state's ability to meet strict federal work participation requirements, which could result in financial penalties.

As a result, many states are using a portion of their Temporary Assistance to Needy Families (TANF) money—the welfare reform block grant that replaced Aid to Families with Dependent Children (AFDC) in 1996—in addition to Substance Abuse and Mental Health block grants, to expand their substance-abuse treatment for welfare recipients. Senator Martha Yeager Walker, chair of the West Virginia Senate Health and Human Services Committee, noted at the 1998 National Conference of State Legislature that: "We need to reach these hard-to-serve welfare recipients, those struggling with substance abuse, domestic violence or other impediments to self-sufficiency. Our welfare caseloads are dropping, and those left on the rolls will be parents who need intensive services. It is critical, not only for their individual self-sufficiency, but also for their children." However, as welfare caseloads in many states crept back up in the wake of the 2001 recession and its feeble recovery, fewer TANF dollars were available for these kinds of purposes, as more resources had to be allocated to cash assistance and other core programs. As of 2005, many states' TANF budgets were in crisis, resulting in a contraction of services offered to welfare recipients, including drug treatment, according to reports by such think tanks as the Center on Budget and Policy Priorities, the Center for Law and Social Policy, and others.

WHERE TO GO FOR HELP

God grant me the SERENITY to accept the things I cannot change, the COURAGE to change the things I can, and the WISDOM to know the difference.

—Invocation used in most Twelve Step programs

Many organizations provide assistance for addicts, their families, and friends. Most of the self-help groups are based on the Twelve Step program of Alcoholics Anonymous (AA). While AA is a support group for problem drinkers, Al-Anon/Alateen is for friends and families of alcoholics. Families Anonymous provides support for family members and friends concerned about a loved one's problems with drugs and/or alcohol. Other organizations include Adult Children of Alcoholics, Cocaine Anonymous, and Narcotics Anonymous. For an addict, many of these organizations can provide immediate help. For families and friends, they can provide knowledge, understanding, and support. For contact information for some of these organizations, see the Important Names and Addresses section at the back of this volume.

A chief barrier to seeking help for many persons habitually taking drugs is the recognition that they need help. Users often underestimate the problem and assume that they can manage without seeking professional assistance. Another barrier is the cost of drug abuse treatment, which is not always covered by a person's health insurance. Recognition of these problems has led to new programs both to help individuals recognize the need for help and to fund it.

CHAPTER 9
AIDS AND INTRAVENOUS DRUG USE

Substance abuse and addiction are major underlying causes of preventable morbidity and mortality in the United States. The risks increase when illicit substances are injected, which contributes to multiple health and social problems for IDUs [injection drug users], including transmission of bloodborne infections (e.g., human immunodeficiency virus [HIV] and hepatitis B and C infections) through sharing unsterile drug injection equipment and practicing unsafe sex. In the United States, approximately one third of acquired immunodeficiency syndrome cases and one half of new hepatitis C cases are associated with injection drug use.

—Centers for Disease Control and Prevention, in *Morbidity and Mortality Weekly Report*, vol. 50, no. 19, May 18, 2001

HIV/AIDS—THE BACKGROUND

The human immunodeficiency virus (HIV) was first detected in 1981 and has been claiming lives since then all over the world. The virus causes an infectious disease that, if left untreated, rapidly develops into acquired immunodeficiency syndrome (AIDS). People often use the abbreviations HIV and AIDS interchangeably, but there is a definite progression. HIV infection comes first and AIDS is the last stage of the disease. A small percentage of those testing positive for HIV remain unaffected by the disease and do not develop AIDS. They are known as "non-progressors." In most people HIV progresses to AIDS, and AIDS is still incurable and invariably fatal. The progression to AIDS can be slowed but not yet prevented.

HIV interferes with and ultimately blocks the body's immune system. Infected people have a reduced count of a crucial blood cell called CD4 lymphocyte. When CD4 is present, it prevents the onset of many fatal infections and cancers. In HIV-negative healthy people the CD4 count is between 500 and 1,500 cells per cubic millimeter of blood. CD4 counts below 350 may signal HIV infection; levels below 200 are considered to indicate

the presence of AIDS ("AIDS," MEDLINEplus, a service of the National Library of Medicine and the National Institutes of Health, http://www.nlm.nih.gov/medlineplus/ency/article/000594.htm).

Only a test administered by a qualified health professional can absolutely diagnose HIV infection. In addition to having one or more opportunistic infections (bacterial, fungal, protozoal, and viral agents that take advantage of an immune system weakened by HIV), infected individuals also have other symptoms. They may experience a general malaise, weight loss, nausea, fever, night sweats, swollen lymph glands, persistent cough, unexplained bleeding, watery diarrhea, loss of memory, balance problems, mood changes, blurring or loss of vision, and thrush (a white coating of the tongue and throat). Individuals who die of AIDS die of opportunistic infections and cancers, not of the virus; the effect of the virus is to weaken their bodily defenses.

WAYS HIV IS TRANSMITTED

While much has been done to educate the American public about how HIV is transmitted, many individuals are unaware of, or ignore facts about, the methods of transmission. Some people are in "high risk groups," but they are not the only ones who become infected with HIV.

HIV is transmitted through body fluids, e.g. blood, semen, and vaginal secretions. Most infections occur in the course of anal, vaginal, or oral sexual contact with an infected person. A baby can also acquire the disease from his or her infected mother perinatally, i.e., at some point around the time of birth, or later by drinking her breast milk, another body fluid that carries HIV. People may also be infected through blood transfusions or transplanted organs.

The connection between drug use and HIV arises because intravenous drug users share needles and syringes that have not been sterilized. When these instruments are exposed to infected blood, the disease can pass from an HIV-positive person to another who is not infected. Substantial numbers of individuals are infected with HIV because of drug use. Later they can pass the virus on to others through sexual contacts or more instances of needle-sharing.

In this country the groups at greatest risk, according to the Centers for Disease Control and Prevention (CDC) in *A Glance at the HIV Epidemic* (http://www.cdc.gov/nchstp/od/news/At-a-Glance.pdf), are men who have sex with men, intravenous drug users, and people who have heterosexual contact with infected individuals.

THE DEATH TOLL OF AIDS

Since the onset of the HIV/AIDS epidemic around 1981, a cumulative total of 892,875 adults (including adolescents) have been diagnosed with AIDS in the United States as of the end of 2003. (See Table 9.1.) In the 1981–2003 period, 518,957 people thirteen and older have died of AIDS. (See Table 9.2.) An additional 9,419 children under thirteen were also found to have the disease. (See Table 9.3.) More than five thousand children have died. According to the CDC, for every one hundred persons diagnosed with AIDS, fifty-six have died; for every one hundred children diagnosed, fifty-four have died. The peak in AIDS diagnoses came in 1993 (78,954 persons diagnosed); the peak in deaths came in 1995 (50,876 deaths of adults). Since then both diagnoses and death have been declining, as educational programs have taken hold and curbed unprotected sexual behavior that leads to infection and as treatment programs have been devised to delay the progression of HIV to AIDS. The CDC reports that the peak in children's deaths from AIDS came in 1994, a year ahead of the peak for adults/adolescents.

By Gender, Race/Ethnicity, and Age

2003 AIDS rates by age, race, and sex are shown in Table 9.4, and cumulative totals for AIDS cases and AIDS deaths are shown in Table 9.3 and Table 9.2 respectively. According to the CDC, most adults who have died of AIDS have been males (84.2%).

African-Americans and Hispanics were affected well above their share in the total population by the AIDS epidemic. African-Americans had about half of the total AIDS deaths in 2003 but as of the 2000 U.S. Census made up only 12.3% of the total U.S. population. Hispanics had 21.7% of AIDS deaths in 2003, while representing 11.1% of population three years earlier. Whites, with 71.8% of the population in 2000, experienced 26.5% of total AIDS deaths in 2003. Asians/Pacific Islanders were affected at lower

rates than their share in total populations; they had 0.5% of 2003 AIDS deaths, compared with 3.9% of the 2000 population. American Indians/Alaska Natives had 0.4% of 2003 AIDS deaths; in 2000, they were 0.7% of the total population.

Of those who died of AIDS in 2003, the largest number were aged thirty-five to forty-four (38.7%) followed by those aged forty-five to fifty-four (33.1%). Together, these two age groups accounted for nearly three quarters of all AIDS deaths in 2003. The population of people dying from AIDS seems to be aging. Only 1,928 people aged twenty-five to thirty-four died of AIDS in 2003 (10.7% of the total), compared to 3,258 in 1999 (17.6%), according to CDC data.

SHARING EQUIPMENT

Drug use can lead to HIV infection, then to AIDS, then to death because drug users share equipment contaminated with infected blood. The equipment involved is the syringe, the needle, the "cooker," cotton, and rinse water used to prevent blood from clotting in the needle and syringe.

The syringe and the needle can become contaminated when infected blood is left behind between uses. This can occur when users draw back their own blood into a syringe and then inject the blood again several times in an attempt to capture and inject all of the drug held in the syringe. This practice, known as "booting," does not occur when users practice intramuscular or subcutaneous injection, known as "skin popping."

Tests have shown that bleach, hydrogen peroxide, and alcohol can kill HIV in a test tube (in vitro). These substances can be effective for cleaning a syringe and needle if the solution fills the syringe completely, but using disinfected syringes and needles is still not as safe as using new, sterile equipment.

The "cooker" is any small container, usually a spoon or a bottle cap, used to dissolve the injectable drug, most often a powder. Contamination may occur when infected blood is pushed out of the needle or syringe into the cooker while a new shot of the drug is being drawn up. If the needle and syringe are effectively sterilized, the cooker will not be contaminated. In the event of cooker contamination, heating the cooker between shots can kill the virus.

Drug users sometimes employ a piece of cotton as a strainer to trap any impurities from the cooker solution. They strain the solution through the cotton as they draw solution into the syringe. Instead of disposing of each piece of cotton immediately after use, a user will sometimes "beat the cotton" with a little

TABLE 9.3

Estimated number of AIDS cases, by year of diagnosis and selected characteristics, 1999–2003

	Year of diagnosis					Cumulative through 2003[a]
	1999	**2000**	**2001**	**2002**	**2003**	
Age at diagnosis (years)						
<13	187	117	119	105	59	9,419
13–14	57	56	76	68	59	891
15–24	1,541	1,642	1,625	1,810	1,991	37,599
25–34	11,349	10,385	9,947	9,504	9,605	311,137
35–44	17,165	17,295	16,890	17,008	17,633	365,432
45–54	8,099	8,566	8,929	9,310	10,051	148,347
55–64	2,218	2,422	2,468	2,724	2,888	43,451
≥65	739	783	779	759	886	13,711
Race/ethnicity						
White, not Hispanic	12,626	12,047	11,620	11,960	12,222	376,834
Black, not Hispanic	19,960	20,312	20,291	20,476	21,304	368,169
Hispanic	8,141	8,233	8,204	8,021	8,757	172,993
Asian/Pacific Islander	369	373	409	452	497	7,166
American Indian/Alaska Native	162	186	179	196	196	3,026
Transmission category						
Male adult or adolescent						
Male-to-male sexual contact	16,556	16,272	16,383	16,971	17,969	440,887
Injection drug use	7,710	7,425	6,772	6,406	6,353	175,988
Male-to-male sexual contact and injection drug use	2,323	2,071	2,026	1,942	1,877	62,418
Heterosexual contact	4,243	4,299	4,578	4,890	5,133	56,403
Other[b]	328	319	315	308	281	14,191
Subtotal	31,159	30,387	30,074	30,517	31,614	749,887
Female adult or adolescent						
Injection drug use	3,448	3,498	3,269	3,024	3,096	70,558
Heterosexual contact	6,350	7,011	7,119	7,380	8,127	93,586
Other[b]	212	254	251	261	276	6,535
Subtotal	10,010	10,763	10,639	10,666	11,498	170,679
Child (<13 yrs at diagnosis)						
Perinatal	185	115	116	103	58	8,749
Other[c]	3	2	3	3	1	670
Subtotal	187	117	119	105	59	9,419
Region of residence						
Northeast	11,885	12,516	11,350	10,551	11,461	285,040
Midwest	4,069	4,139	4,094	4,337	4,498	91,926
South	17,224	16,757	17,693	18,482	19,609	337,409
West	6,892	6,661	6,468	6,843	6,667	186,100
U.S. dependencies, possessions, and associated nations	1,286	1,194	1,228	1,075	935	29,511
Total[d]	**41,356**	**41,267**	**40,833**	**41,289**	**43,171**	**929,985**

Note: These numbers do not represent reported case counts. Rather, these numbers are point estimates, which result from adjustments of reported case counts. The reported case counts are adjusted for reporting delays and for redistribution of cases in persons initially reported without an identified risk factor. The estimates do not include adjustment for incomplete reporting.

[a]Includes persons with a diagnosis of AIDS from the beginning of the epidemic through 2003.
[b]Includes hemophilia, blood transfusion, perinatal, and risk factor not reported or not identified.
[c]Includes hemophilia, blood transfusion, and risk factor not reported or not identified.
[d]Includes persons of unknown race or multiple races and persons of unknown sex. Cumulative total includes 1796 persons of unknown race or multiple races and 1 person of unknown sex. Because column totals were calculated independently of the values for the subpopulations, the values in each column may not sum to the column total.

SOURCE: "Table 3. Estimated Numbers of AIDS Cases, by Year of Diagnosis and Selected Characteristics of Persons, 1999–2003—United States," in *HIV/AIDS Surveillance Report: Cases of HIV Infection and AIDS in the United States, 2003*, Department of Health and Human Services, Centers for Disease Control and Prevention, December 2004, http://www.cdc.gov/hiv/stats/2003SurveillanceReport.pdf (accessed March 31, 2005)

Throughout the entire history of the AIDS epidemic through 2003, of a total of 929,985 infections on record, 317,713 were drug-related infections, or 34.2%, according to the CDC's *HIV/AIDS Surveillance Report*.

Race/Ethnicity

MALES. In 2003 Hispanic males and African-American males with AIDS were twice as likely to have been infected by injecting drug use (18% of cases among each of those groups) than white males (9%). (See Table 9.6.) In this and subsequent tabulations, whites and African-Americans exclude Hispanics, who may be of any race. Men having sex with men and also injecting drugs were proportionally most numerous among American Indians/Alaska Natives and whites.

FEMALES. As noted above, a larger percentage of AIDS cases among women result from injecting drugs than is the case among men. In 2003 American

TABLE 9.4

AIDS cases, by race, age, and sex, 2003

| | Adults or adolescents | | | | | | Children (<13 yrs) | | Total | |
| | Males | | Females | | Total | | | | | |
Race/ethnicity	No.	Rate	No.	Rate	No.	Rate	No.	Rate	No.	Rate
White, not Hispanic	10,450	12.8	1,725	2.0	12,175	7.2	9	0.0	12,184	6.1
Black, not Hispanic	13,624	103.8	7,551	50.2	21,174	75.2	40	0.5	21,214	58.2
Hispanic	6,087	40.3	1,744	12.4	7,831	26.8	7	0.1	7,839	20.0
Asian/Pacific Islander	408	8.3	86	1.6	494	4.8	0	0	494	4.0
American Indian/Alaska Native	150	16.2	46	4.8	196	10.4	0	0	196	8.1
Total*	30,851	26.6	11,211	9.2	42,062	17.7	58	0.1	42,120	14.5

Note: These numbers do not represent reported case counts. Rather, these numbers are point estimates, which result from adjustments of reported case counts. The reported case counts are adjusted for reporting delays. The estimates do not include adjustment for incomplete reporting.

Data exclude cases from the U.S. dependencies, possessions, and associated nations, as well as cases in persons whose state or area of residence is unknown, because of the lack of census information by race and age categories for these areas. Rate is per 100,000 population.

*Includes persons of unknown race or multiple races. Total includes 193 persons of unknown race or multiple races. Because column totals were calculated independently of the values for the subpopulations, the values in each column may not sum to the column total.

SOURCE: "Table 5. Estimated Numbers of Cases and Rates (per 100,000 population) of AIDS, by Race/Ethnicity, Age Category, and Sex, 2003—50 States and the District of Columbia," in *HIV/AIDS Surveillance Report: Cases of HIV Infection and AIDS in the United States, 2003*, Department of Health and Human Services, Centers for Disease Control and Prevention, 2003, http://www.cdc.gov/hiv/stats/2003SurveillanceReport.htm (accessed March 31, 2005)

TABLE 9.5

Estimated number of pediatric AIDS cases, by race/ethnicity, year of diagnosis, and transmission category, 1999–2003

| | Year of diagnosis | | | | | Cumulative through 2003[a] |
	1999	2000	2001	2002	2003	
Race/ethnicity						
White, not Hispanic	18	12	15	13	9	1,620
Black, not Hispanic	133	86	78	68	40	5,562
Hispanic	34	17	24	22	7	2,128
Asian/Pacific Islander	1	2	2	1	0	56
American Indian/Alaska Native	0	0	0	0	0	30
Transmission category						
Hemophilia/coagulation disorder	0	0	0	0	0	234
Mother with, or at risk for, HIV infection	185	115	116	103	58	8,749
Injection drug use	44	21	13	8	7	3,326
Sex with injection drug user	26	13	8	4	6	1,541
Sex with bisexual male	6	2	4	3	0	203
Sex with person with hemophilia	2	0	1	0	0	37
Sex with HIV-infected transfusion recipient	0	0	0	0	0	28
Sex with HIV-infected person, risk factor not specified	49	36	35	37	17	1,490
Receipt of blood transfusion, blood components, or tissue	1	2	2	2	0	156
Has HIV infection, risk factor not specified	57	41	53	48	28	1,968
Receipt of blood transfusion, blood components, or tissue	0	1	0	1	0	391
Other/risk factor not reported or identified	3	1	3	2	1	45
Total[b]	187	117	119	105	59	9,419

Note: These numbers do not represent reported case counts. Rather, these numbers are point estimates, which result from adjustments of reported case counts. The reported case counts are adjusted for reporting delays and for redistribution of cases in persons initially reported without an identified risk factor. The estimates do not include adjustment for incomplete reporting.

[a]Includes children with a diagnosis of AIDS, from the beginning of the epidemic through 2003.

[b]Includes children of unknown race or multiple races. Cumulative total includes 24 children of unknown race or multiple races. Because column totals were calculated independently of the values for the subpopulations, the values in each column may not sum to the column total.

SOURCE: "Table 4. Estimated Numbers of AIDS Cases in Children <13 Years of Age, by Year of Diagnosis and Transmission Category, 1999–2003—United States," in *HIV/AIDS Surveillance Report: Cases of HIV Infection and AIDS in the United States, 2003*, Department of Health and Human Services, Centers for Disease Control and Prevention, December 2004, http://www.cdc.gov/hiv/stats/2003SurveillanceReport.pdf (accessed March 31, 2005)

Indian/Alaska Native women had the highest infection rate due to injecting drugs (39% of the racial category) followed by whites (29%). (See Table 9.7.) In the case of infection caused by sex with a drug-injecting male, white women were highest at 12%.

PEDIATRIC CASES. Among the ninety cases (in the twenty-five states with confidential, name-based reporting) of HIV/AIDS in infants born to infected mothers in 2003, seven involved a mother who injected drugs, and another six involved mothers who had sex

FIGURE 9.1

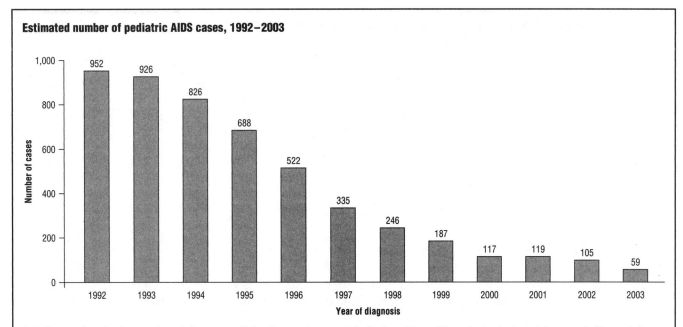

Estimated number of pediatric AIDS cases, 1992–2003

Note. These numbers do not represent reported case counts. Rather, these numbers are point estimates, which result from adjustments of reported case counts. The reported case counts are adjusted for reporting delays. The estimates do not include adjustments for incomplete reporting.

SOURCE: "Figure 1. Estimated Numbers of AIDS Cases in Children <13 Years of Age, by Year of Diagnosis, 1992–2003—United States," in *HIV/AIDS Surveillance Report: Cases of HIV Infection and AIDS in the United States, 2003,* Department of Health and Human Services, Centers for Disease Control and Prevention, December 2004, http://www.cdc.gov/hiv/stats/2003SurveillanceReport.pdf (accessed March 31, 2005)

with injected drug users. In thirty-eight cases, the mother had sex with a person infected by HIV from an unknown source. Sixty-two of the ninety infants in reported cases were non-Hispanic African-Americans, while fifteen were white and eight were Hispanic. (See Table 9.8.)

MORTALITY

In 1993, 12,587 adults and adolescents died as a direct consequence of AIDS acquired by injecting drug use (IDU), according to figures in the CDC's *HIV/AIDS Surveillance Report.* These deaths exclude deaths indirectly due to IDU such as heterosexual or homosexual contact with a drug user. In 1993 these deaths represented 27.8% of all deaths from AIDS, 51.4% of all female deaths from AIDS, and 24% of male deaths from AIDS. Among females with AIDS in 1993, AIDS acquired by injecting drug use caused the greatest number of deaths; among males, sex between males was the leading cause of infection leading to death.

Since 1993 total deaths due to AIDS have decreased, but the percentage of deaths due to needle-sharing have increased from 27.8 to 34.5% in 2003. The number of women who have died of AIDS acquired by injection of drugs has remained fairly constant for several years. While IDU is the leading cause of infection among women who have died of AIDS cumulatively since 1993, it is, as of 2003, second to heterosexual contact (which may also involve contact with a partner who uses

intravenously injected drugs) in the transmission cause of women who die of AIDS. IDU-related deaths among males had increased from 24% in 1993 to 31.6% of all AIDS deaths in 2003, according to the CDC. In the 1999–2003 period, both total AIDS deaths, and IDU AIDS deaths remained fairly constant.

SYRINGE- OR NEEDLE-EXCHANGE PROGRAMS

Drug users share equipment because syringes and needles are difficult to obtain and difficult (as well as time-consuming) to sterilize in domestic environments. This has led to the establishment of syringe-exchange programs (SEPs; more popularly known as needle-exchange programs or NEPs). The logic behind these programs is that some drug users will use injection equipment to administer drugs to themselves. Therefore it could save lives—those of the drug users as well as those of their children and those with whom they have sex—if users could exchange contaminated syringes and needles for sterilized equipment. These programs are controversial. In summary, the scientific consensus appears to be that SEPs work in saving lives, but national policy opposes funding SEPs because such programs appear to encourage drug use.

Historical Background

Although there has been some regulation of hypodermic syringes in the United States since they were invented in the nineteenth century, they were widely

TABLE 9.6

Adult and adolescent male AIDS cases, by race/ethnicity and transmission category, 2003

Transmission category	White, not Hispanic 2003 No.	%	Cumulative through 2003* No.	%	Black, not Hispanic 2003 No.	%	Cumulative through 2003* No.	%	Hispanic 2003 No.	%	Cumulative through 2003* No.	%
Male-to-male sexual contact	7,679	66	244,758	73	4,699	34	93,413	37	3,054	43	57,128	43
Injection drug use	1,051	9	31,164	9	2,454	18	80,282	32	1,290	18	44,277	33
Male-to-male sexual contact and injection drug use	793	7	28,795	9	548	4	19,182	8	311	4	9,313	7
Hemophilia/coagulation disorder	56	0	3,964	1	6	0	599	0	9	0	453	0
Heterosexual contact:	454	4	7,010	2	2,047	15	24,428	10	799	11	9,021	7
Sex with injection drug user	76	1	2,221	1	253	2	6,410	3	141	2	2,195	2
Sex with person with hemophilia	4	0	38	0	2	0	29	0	0	0	11	0
Sex with HIV-infected transfusion recipient	4	0	177	0	11	0	205	0	7	0	109	0
Sex with HIV-infected person, risk factor not specified	370	3	4,574	1	1,781	13	17,784	7	651	9	6,706	5
Receipt of blood transfusion, blood components, or tissue	30	0	3,227	1	49	0	1,205	0	28	0	646	0
Other/risk factor not reported or identified	1,640	14	14,519	4	3,932	29	33,905	13	1,544	22	12,659	9
Total	**11,703**	**100**	**333,437**	**100**	**13,735**	**100**	**253,014**	**100**	**7,035**	**100**	**133,497**	**100**

Transmission category	Asian/Pacific Islander 2003 No.	%	Cumulative through 2003* No.	%	American Indian/Alaska Native 2003 No.	%	Cumulative through 2003* No.	%	Total 2003 No.	%	Cumulative through 2003* No.	%
Male-to-male sexual contact	254	56	4,084	69	93	58	1,299	56	15,859	48	401,392	55
Injection drug use	26	6	292	5	22	14	370	16	4,866	15	156,575	21
Male-to-male sexual contact and injection drug use	19	4	227	4	15	9	392	17	1,695	5	57,998	8
Hemophilia/coagulation disorder	2	0	72	1	1	1	32	1	74	0	5,130	1
Heterosexual contact:	42	9	305	5	11	7	92	4	3,371	10	40,947	6
Sex with injection drug user	3	1	55	1	2	1	28	1	477	1	10,930	1
Sex with person with hemophilia	0	0	1	0	0	0	0	0	7	0	80	0
Sex with HIV-infected transfusion recipient	1	0	8	0	1	1	3	0	24	0	505	0
Sex with HIV-infected person, risk factor not specified	38	8	241	4	8	5	61	3	2,863	9	29,432	4
Receipt of blood transfusion, blood components, or tissue	3	1	118	2	0	0	9	0	111	0	5,219	1
Other/risk factor not reported or identified	110	24	792	13	19	12	130	6	7,274	22	62,217	9
Total	**456**	**100**	**5,890**	**100**	**161**	**100**	**2,324**	**100**	**33,250**	**100**	**729,478**	**100**

*Includes persons with a diagnosis of AIDS, reported from the beginning of the epidemic through 2003. Cumulative total includes 1,316 males of unknown race or multiple races.

SOURCE: "Table 19. Reported AIDS Cases for Male Adults and Adolescents, by Transmission Category and Race/Ethnicity, Cumulative through 2003—United States," in *HIV/AIDS Surveillance Report: Cases of HIV Infection and AIDS in the United States, 2003*, Department of Health and Human Services, Centers for Disease Control and Prevention, 2003, http://www.cdc.gov/hiv/stats/2003SurveillanceReport.htm (accessed March 31, 2005)

available until the 1970s. Needles could be purchased without a prescription and without limits on quantities purchased.

In the 1970s and 1980s most states and the District of Columbia criminalized the possession or sale of syringes without a prescription. Syringes had been sold alongside cocaine kits and marijuana paraphernalia at "head shops" (stores selling materials utilized by drug users) in cities across the country. As part of a larger project to get tough on drug use and eliminate head shops, laws were passed to limit the sale of syringes.

As it became recognized that dirty needles/syringes were causing HIV transmission in the late 1980s, syringe-exchange programs began in some cities. Since then they have provided a publicly visible and measurable means of reducing HIV transmission among intravenous (IV) drug users. However, despite the positive impact of SEPs, these largely voluntary efforts may not meet the need for syringes. Furthermore SEPs are illegal in a number of states. Efforts are underway, supported by advocacy and scientific groups, to decriminalize syringe sales, to legalize SEPs, and to obtain public funding for their operations.

TABLE 9.7

Adult and adolescent female AIDS cases, by race/ethnicity and transmission category, 2003

Transmission category	White, not Hispanic 2003 No.	%	Cumulative through 2003* No.	%	Black, not Hispanic 2003 No.	%	Cumulative through 2003* No.	%	Hispanic 2003 No.	%	Cumulative through 2003* No.	%
Injection drug use	557	29	13,695	41	1,277	17	35,767	37	385	18	11,695	37
Hemophilia/coagulation disorder	3	0	117	0	5	0	128	0	3	0	60	0
Heterosexual contact:	809	42	13,877	41	3,253	44	40,193	42	1,055	50	15,294	48
Sex with injection drug user	220	12	5,293	16	525	7	12,526	13	218	10	6,103	19
Sex with bisexual male	47	2	1,701	5	118	2	1,885	2	54	3	701	2
Sex with person with hemophilia	12	1	314	1	3	0	103	0	1	0	42	0
Sex with HIV-infected transfusion recipient	4	0	334	1	25	0	230	0	7	0	114	0
Sex with HIV-infected person, risk factor not specified	526	28	6,235	19	2,582	35	25,449	26	775	37	8,334	26
Receipt of blood transfusion, blood components, or tissue	18	1	1,868	6	60	1	1,477	2	25	1	604	2
Other/risk factor not reported or identified	522	27	4,127	12	2,734	37	18,796	20	630	30	3,901	12
Total	**1,909**	**100**	**33,684**	**100**	**7,329**	**100**	**96,361**	**100**	**2,098**	**100**	**31,554**	**100**

Transmission category	Asian/Pacific Islander 2003 No.	%	Cumulative through 2003* No.	%	American Indian/Alaska Native 2003 No.	%	Cumulative through 2003* No.	%	Totals 2003 No.	%	Cumulative through 2003* No.	%
Injection drug use	6	6	121	13	23	39	242	43	2,262	20	61,621	38
Hemophilia/coagulation disorder	0	0	8	1	0	0	3	1	11	0	318	0
Heterosexual contact:	56	55	459	51	22	37	228	41	5,234	45	70,200	43
Sex with injection drug user	11	11	104	12	4	7	92	16	985	9	24,148	15
Sex with bisexual male	3	3	78	9	1	2	29	5	223	2	4,402	3
Sex with person with hemophilia	0	0	4	0	0	0	2	0	16	0	465	0
Sex with HIV-infected transfusion recipient	1	1	20	2	0	0	3	1	37	0	705	0
Sex with HIV-infected person, risk factor not specified	41	40	253	28	17	29	102	18	3,973	34	40,480	25
Receipt of blood transfusion, blood components, or tissue	4	4	101	11	1	2	15	3	108	1	4,076	2
Other/risk factor not reported or identified	36	35	212	24	13	22	70	13	3,946	34	27,181	17
Total	**102**	**100**	**901**	**100**	**59**	**100**	**558**	**100**	**11,561**	**100**	**163,396**	**100**

*Includes persons with a diagnosis of AIDS, reported from the beginning of the epidemic through 2003. Cumulative total includes 338 females of unknown race or multiple races.

SOURCE: "Table 21. Reported AIDS Cases for Female Adults and Adolescents, by Transmission Category and Race/Ethnicity, Cumulative through 2003—United States," in *HIV/AIDS Surveillance Report: Cases of HIV Infection and AIDS in the United States, 2003*, Department of Health and Human Services, Centers for Disease Control and Prevention, 2003, http://www.cdc.gov/hiv/stats/2003SurveillanceReport.htm (accessed March 31, 2005)

As of the end of 2002, it was legal for a person to sell syringes to a person known to be a drug user in nineteen states and Puerto Rico, there was a "reasonable claim to legality" (some reason to claim the practice legal) in twenty-two states, and such sales were clearly illegal in nine states, the District of Columbia, and the Virgin Islands ("Preventing Blood-Borne Infections through Pharmacy Syringe Sales and Safe Community Syringe Disposal," *Journal of the American Pharmaceutical Association Supplement*, November/December 2002). States, however, have enabled their health departments to establish SEPs even where sale of syringes is prohibited, according to the CDC. Some cities have permitted SEPs to be established by declaring a local state of health emergency.

SEP Statistics

The first programs in the United States were opened in San Francisco in 1987 and Tacoma, Washington, in 1988. By September 1, 1993, at least thirty-seven SEPs were operating in thirty cities in twelve states. The CDC publishes data on SEPs and updates its tallies from time to time. The most recent survey available from the CDC was published in 2001 with data from 1998 ("Syringe Exchange Programs," *Morbidity and Mortality Weekly Report*, vol. 50, no. 19, Atlanta, GA: CDC, May 18, 2001). In 1998 a total of 131 SEPs were known to be operating in eighty-one cities in thirty-one states, the District of Columbia, and in Puerto Rico. SEPs had nearly doubled in number since the 1994–95 period, when

TABLE 9.8

Pediatric AIDS cases by selected characteristics, 1994–2003

	Year of report									
	1994	1995	1996	1997	1998	1999	2000	2001	2002	2003
Child's race/ethnicity										
White, not Hispanic	80	76	49	28	30	20	14	20	22	15
Black, not Hispanic	226	217	171	144	100	83	90	91	68	62
Hispanic	34	24	20	14	11	14	17	15	18	8
Asian/Pacific Islander	1	1	0	2	2	0	1	1	1	1
American Indian/Alaska Native	4	1	0	1	0	1	0	0	1	1
Perinatal transmission category										
Mother with, or at risk for, HIV infection:										
Injection drug use	131	94	82	59	29	28	32	26	10	7
Sex with injection drug user	70	48	44	31	16	20	12	11	11	6
Sex with bisexual male	8	10	5	4	2	5	2	5	2	5
Sex with person with hemophilia	2	2	0	0	1	1	1	1	0	1
Sex with HIV-infected transfusion recipient	1	0	0	0	0	0	0	0	0	0
Sex with HIV-infected person, risk not specified	81	95	53	57	51	31	44	47	39	38
Receipt of blood transfusion, blood components, or tissue	5	3	3	3	2	1	0	3	1	0
Has HIV infection, risk not specified	48	68	53	38	42	34	31	34	48	33
Child's diagnosis status[a]										
HIV infection	148	158	138	117	103	79	95	91	77	75
AIDS	198	162	102	75	40	41	27	36	34	15
Total[b]	**346**	**320**	**240**	**192**	**143**	**120**	**122**	**127**	**111**	**90**

Note: Since 1994, the following 25 states have had laws and regulations requiring confidential name-based HIV infection reporting: Alabama, Arizona, Arkansas, Colorado, Idaho, Indiana, Louisiana, Michigan, Minnesota, Mississippi, Missouri, Nevada, New Jersey, North Carolina, North Dakota, Ohio, Oklahoma, South Carolina, South Dakota, Tennessee, Utah, Virginia, West Virginia, Wisconsin, and Wyoming.
Data include children with a diagnosis of HIV infection. This includes children with a diagnosis of HIV infection only, a diagnosis of HIV infection and a later AIDS diagnosis, and concurrent diagnoses of HIV infection and AIDS.
[a]Status in the surveillance system as of June 2004.
[b]Includes children of unknown or multiple race.

SOURCE: "Table 23. Reported Cases of HIV/AIDS in Infants Born to HIV-Infected Mothers, by Year of Report and Selected Characteristics, 1994–2003—25 States with Confidential Name-Based HIV Infection Reporting," in *HIV/AIDS Surveillance Report: Cases of HIV Infection and AIDS in the United States, 2003*, Department of Health and Human Services, Centers for Disease Control and Prevention, 2003, http://www.cdc.gov/hiv/stats/2003SurveillanceReport.htm (accessed March 31, 2005)

sixty-eight facilities were known to exist. The number of syringes exchanged had increased from eight million to 19.4 million in the same period. Most SEPs are thought to be members of the North American Syringe Exchange Network (NASEN), based in Tacoma, Washington. NASEN conducted a survey in 2000 in which it obtained responses from 127 programs, of which eighty-nine operated legally, twenty-six illegally, and twelve had uncertain legal status (*National Surveys of Syringe Exchange Programs*, NASEN, http://www.nasen.org/). Because many SEPs operate illegally or have doubts about their status, some of those responding to surveys do not permit disclosure of details of their operations.

CDC-published surveys for 1997 and 1998 show that of 107 SEPs responding in 1998, thirty-nine were large and twelve were very large—as measured by number of syringes exchanged. The twelve largest SEPs in 1998 were responsible for 62.4% of syringe exchanges; the thirty smallest (exchanging fewer than ten thousand syringes each) accounted for less than 1% (0.6%) of syringes exchanged. Exchanges increased 11.2% between 1997 and 1998 overall. Growth was

greatest for the smallest programs (31.3%), least for the large programs (1%); the very largest had a growth of 17.3% and medium-sized exchanges of 10.9% from 1997 to 1998.

In addition to syringes, virtually all SEPs offered information about safer injection methods and referral to substance abuse treatment programs.

Professional/Scientific Support for SEPs

THE PUBLIC HEALTH PERSPECTIVE. The Centers for Disease Control and Prevention, in "Changing Syringe Laws Is Part of Strategy to Help Stem HIV Spread" (*HIV/AIDS Prevention*, December 1997), pointed out that drug users must have access to clean syringes and drug treatment as part of a complete HIV prevention plan. One way to make this happen is to change the drug paraphernalia laws so that clean needles and syringes are available to intravenous drug users.

Public Health Service policy recommends that IV drug users be counseled and encouraged to stop using and injecting drugs, if possible, through substance abuse treatment, including relapse prevention. Failing this, however, drug users should follow various preventive measures, such as:

- Never reusing or sharing syringes, water, or drug preparation equipment
- Using only syringes obtained from a reliable source (e.g., pharmacies)
- Using a new, sterile syringe to prepare and inject drugs
- Safely disposing of syringes after one use

FOREIGN PERSPECTIVES. Susan F. Hurley, Damien J. Jolley, and John M. Kaldor, in "Effectiveness of Needle-Exchange Programmes for Prevention of HIV Infection" (*The Lancet*, June 21, 1997), studied cities around the world with and without NEPs. They found that, on average, HIV increased 5.9% in cities without NEPs and decreased by 5.8% in cities with NEPs.

They also observed that "NEPs led to a reduction in HIV incidence among injecting drug users" and that their findings "strongly support the view that NEPs are effective." The researchers concluded that with their findings "and the interpretation of previous studies by the Panel on Needle Exchange and Bleach Distribution Programs [National Research Council and Institute of Medicine], the view that NEPs are not effective no longer seems tenable."

INSTITUTIONAL SUPPORT. The National Academy of Sciences, American Medical Association, American Public Health Association, National Institutes of Health Consensus Panel, CDC, American Bar Association, and President George Herbert Walker Bush's and President Bill Clinton's AIDS Advisory Commissions—virtually every established medical, scientific, and legal body that has studied the issue of needle exchange programs—agree on the validity of improved access to sterile syringes to reduce the spread of infectious diseases, including HIV/AIDS. In July 1997 the U.S. Conference of Mayors endorsed federal and state policy changes to improve access to sterile syringes.

Fifteen of the top twenty most widely circulated U.S. newspapers have editorialized in favor of SEPs or syringe deregulation. Public opinion has been moderately in favor of SEPs. A 2000 Kaiser Family Foundation poll found 58% of the population favor SEPs and 61% favor allowing users to purchase needles at pharmacies.

The Political Debate

Needle exchange has led to intense political debate in the United States, particularly in some states (California and New York) and cities (Baltimore, Maryland; New York City; Boston, Massachusetts; and Berkeley, California). However, in many cities (Seattle, Washington; Tacoma, Washington; San Francisco, California; Honolulu, Hawaii; and New Haven, Connecticut), large-scale SEPs were set up with substantial community support.

Those who support SEPs stress the importance of the programs as gateways to counseling, education, and other referral services for addicts. This comprehensive approach is known as "harm reduction." Supporters also say that SEPs facilitate proper disposal of injection equipment and serve as outlets to supply addicts with materials that help to curb the spread of HIV.

Those opposing SEPs fear that needle programs will increase drug use by providing the means (needles and syringes) to inject drugs, although no American or foreign study has shown that SEPs increase drug use. Opponents also believe providing SEPs would appear to condone drug use and therefore undermine the message that using drugs is illegal, unhealthy, and morally wrong. In addition, they maintain that SEPs may draw scarce resources away from other, possibly more effective, programs, such as drug treatment.

Some opponents claim that needle exchange programs are not in fact exchanges, but giveaways. They say that participants rarely exchange dirty needles for clean ones, meaning that the dirty needles are still on the streets. However, SEPs typically operate on the principle of a one-for-one exchange.

Banning Federal Funds

In 1988 Congress passed the Health Omnibus Programs Extension Act (PL 100-607), banning the expenditure of federal funds for needle exchange. At the same time, Congress authorized funding for research into needle exchange programs. Under the conditions of the Department of Health and Human Services Appropriations Act of 1997 (PL 105-78), lifting the ban and using federal funds to support SEPs depended on a determination by the Secretary of Health and Human Services (HHS) that such programs reduce transmission of HIV without encouraging the use of illegal drugs.

In a February 1997 report to Congress, then HHS Secretary Donna E. Shalala announced that a review of the scientific literature indicated that needle exchange programs "can be an effective component of a comprehensive strategy to prevent HIV and other blood-borne infectious diseases in communities that choose to include them." For example, *Preventing HIV Transmission: The Role of Sterile Needles and Bleach* (Washington, DC: National Research Council and Institute of Medicine, September 1995) concluded that SEPs have beneficial effects on reducing behaviors such as multiperson reuse of syringes. This report estimated a reduction in risk behaviors of 80% and a reduction in HIV transmission of 30% or greater.

In April 1998 Secretary Shalala reported that a review of research findings indicated that needle exchange programs "do not encourage the use of illegal drugs." In addition, SEPs can reduce drug use through effective referrals to drug treatment and counseling.

RELUCTANCE TO LIFT THE BAN. Both Congress and two presidents (Bill Clinton and George W. Bush) have been very reluctant to lift the ban on federal monies for needle exchange programs. To approve of such programs might appear to give official sanction to a strategy some voters consider equivalent to promoting drug use. Some legislators fear that approving such a policy would be the first step along the road to the legalization of drugs.

President Bill Clinton, who saw drug abuse increase during his term in office, was very reluctant to approve any program that could be perceived as being weak on drugs. George W. Bush opposed needle-exchange programs while running for the presidency in 2000. In response to the AIDS Foundation of Chicago, then Governor Bush stated that "needle exchange programs signal nothing but abdication, that these dangers are here to stay" ("2000 Candidate Questionnaire," AIDS Foundation of Chicago, http://www.aidschicago.org/advocacy/candidate_00.php). The Bush administration has, since taking office, consistently opposed lifting the ban on funding SEPs.

Others fear that approval of syringe exchange programs, while perhaps good policy, is only an inadequate first step toward the comprehensive drug treatment program needed to reduce drug addiction.

THE AMERICAN BAR ASSOCIATION AND STATE LEGISLATION RELATED TO NEEDLE POSSESSION. A report prepared by the AIDS Coordinating Committee of the American Bar Association (ABA) outlined the ABA's stance on the deregulation of syringes (*Deregulation of Hypodermic Needles and Syringes as a Public Health Measure: A Report on Emerging Policy and Law in the United States*, Washington, DC, 2001). The ABA supports the deregulation of needle exchange programs and the relaxation of laws concerning the sale and possession of syringes.

The association advocates an approach that extends beyond SEPs. They advocate laws that allow IV users to obtain needles from any pharmacy whenever they are needed. There are several advantages of this approach. One is that it sidesteps the objection that states should not fund SEPs because it sends the "wrong message." Legalizing possession of syringes would allow users to purchase needles directly from pharmacies like any other purchase, thus not involving the government or government funds.

A second benefit is that such policies would allow much greater access to needles than SEPs allow. Because of the stigma attached to IV drug use, many users do not want to enter SEPs and be identified as addicts. Also, it is often inconvenient for users to get to SEPs, which may be located many miles from where they live. In addition, users may not be able to get as many needles as they need at once, considering that some users inject a dozen or more times a day.

The ABA identifies three types of deregulation that have been passed in state legislatures. In Oregon and Alaska, syringes are "completely deregulated"—that is, they can be bought and sold by anyone, under any circumstances. Next are states that have "unrestricted pharmacy sales," where anyone can buy as many needles as desired without a prescription so long as it is at a pharmacy. Finally, a number of states have passed "10 and under deregulation," which allows the sale and possession of up to ten syringes.

As of spring of 2005, thirteen states allowed users increased access to syringes. Alaska, Hawaii, New Mexico, Oregon, and Washington have completely deregulated the sale of syringes. Ohio, Rhode Island, and Wisconsin allowed unrestricted pharmacy sales. Connecticut, Maine, Minnesota, New Hampshire, and New York have enacted deregulation of the purchase/sale of ten or fewer syringes. The regulatory environment, however, continues to be in flux, with some regulations intended to be temporary, to be renewed only after studies show their effectiveness in controlling HIV/AIDS. Trends are in the direction of deregulation under pressure from medical authorities who clearly see a benefit in drug users having access to clean needles and in other mechanisms, such as SEPs, that minimize infection.

CHAPTER 10
THE NATIONAL DRUG CONTROL STRATEGY

Drug dependence is a chronic, relapsing disorder that exacts an enormous cost on individuals, families, businesses, communities, and nations. Addicted individuals frequently engage in self-destructive and criminal behavior. Treatment can help them end dependence on addictive drugs. Treatment programs also reduce the consequences of addiction on the rest of society. Providing treatment for America's chronic drug users is both compassionate public policy and a sound investment.

—*National Drug Control Strategy, 2001*, Office of National Drug Control Policy

THE COST OF DRUG ABUSE

The Office of National Drug Control Policy (ONDCP), a part of the White House, issued a report in 2004 on the economic costs of drug abuse, *The Economic Costs of Drug Abuse in the United States: 1992–2002* (http://www.whitehousedrugpolicy.gov/publications/economic_costs/economic_costs.pdf). The report included such costs as those to the health care system; the cost of crime associated with drug abuse; and such economic impacts as job loss and decreased productivity. The estimated direct and indirect societal cost for 2002 was $180.9 billion, according to the agency; corresponding costs for 1992 were $102.2 billion and for 1998 were $143.4 billion. Costs increased in the 1992–2002 period at a rate of 5.3% a year. The nation's Gross Domestic Product (GDP) for the entire economy, in comparison, increased in this same period at a rate of 5.1% a year. (See Table 10.1 and Table 10.2.)

The raw number—$180.9 billion—is huge and difficult to grasp without comparisons. The cost is very significant. In 2002, for instance, doctors' offices had total revenues of $236 billion and all dentists earned $69 billion (*Service Annual Survey: 2002*, U.S. Census Bureau). Total expenditures of all colleges and universities in 2001-2002 were $317 billion (*Digest of Educational Statistics*, U.S. National Center for Education Statistics, annual).

Most of the $180.9 billion cited by ONDCP is accounted for by estimates of lost productivity ($128.6 billion or 71%). Elements of this figure are premature death, time lost through illness and incarceration, time spent in criminal careers, and other unproductive time expended by victims of crime and of individuals during hospitalization. Direct health care costs accounted for $15.8 billion in 2002 and other expenses for $36.4 billion. The two largest components of the "other" category were state corrections expenditures (34% of the category) and police protection (28% of the category).

ORIGINS OF THE NATIONAL STRATEGY

The Anti-Drug Abuse Act of 1988 (PL 100-690) established the creation of a drug-free America as a U.S. policy goal. As part of this initiative, Congress established the Office of National Drug Control Policy in order "to set priorities and objectives for national drug control, promulgate *The National Drug Control Strategy* on an annual basis, and oversee the strategy's implementation." To stress the importance of the issue, the director of the ONDCP has been given a cabinet-level position. The person holding the position, John P. Walters as of mid-2003, is usually dubbed the nation's "drug czar" by the media.

The first National Drug Control Strategy (NDCS) was submitted by President George H. W. Bush in 1989. It had been prepared under the reign of the nation's first drug czar, William J. Bennett. Its chief emphasis was on the "principle of user accountability—in law enforcement efforts focused on individual users; in decisions regarding sentencing and parole; in school, college, and university policies regarding the use of drugs by students and employees; in the workplace; and in treatment" (*White House Fact Sheet on the National Drug Control Strategy*, The White House, September 5, 1989, http://bushlibrary.tamu.edu/research/papers/1989/89090503.html). The strategy called for active

TABLE 10.1

Direct societal costs of drug abuse, 1992–2002

[In millions]

Year	Health care costs	Other costs	Total direct costs
1992	13,719	24,909	38,629
1993	14,736	24,662	39,398
1994	14,761	25,892	40,653
1995	14,087	28,091	42,178
1996	13,249	28,325	41,574
1997	13,337	29,905	43,242
1998	13,569	31,334	44,903
1999	13,873	33,572	47,445
2000	13,974	35,280	49,254
2001	14,700	35,118	49,818
2002	15,675	36,363	52,038

SOURCE: "Table 24. Estimated Direct Costs to Society of Drug Abuse, 1992–2002," in *National Drug Control Strategy: Data Supplement*, The White House, March 2004, http://www.whitehousedrugpolicy.gov/publications/policy/ndcs04/data_suppl_2004.pdf (accessed March 31, 2005)

efforts directed at countries where cocaine originated, improved targeting of interdiction, increasing the capacity of treatment providers, and accelerated efforts aimed at prevention and at the education of youth. In its details, the drug strategy laid emphasis on law enforcement activities and the expansion of the criminal justice system.

Since that time, the basic building blocks of the national strategy have remained the same, but the specific emphases taken by different administrations, or the same one in different years, have changed, at times leaning more toward enforcement, at other times more toward fighting drug racketeers, and at yet others more toward treatment and prevention. The Clinton administration, in its 2000 strategy, emphasized 1) empowering young people to reject drugs; 2) treatment for drug offenders within the criminal justice system; 3) increasing treatment resources

for those who need them; 4) interdicting the flow of drugs across the nation's borders; and 5) aid to other democracies to help them fight traffickers (*The President's Message to Congress on the 2000 National Drug Control Strategy*, Washington, DC: U.S. State Department, April 12, 2000, http://www.ncjrs.org/ondcppubs/publications/policy/ndcs00/message.html).

In the 2004 National Drug Control Policy (http://www.whitehousedrugpolicy.gov/publications/policy/ndcs04/2004ndcs.pdf), the ONDCP under George W. Bush established three priorities:

- Stopping Use Before It Starts: Education and Community Action

- Healing America's Drug Users: Getting Treatment Resources Where They Are Needed [and]

- Disrupting the Market: Attacking the Economic Base of the Drug Trade

Table 10.3 presents the administration's stated benchmarks for measuring the success of its strategy.

The Clinton administration adopted the view that the "war on drugs" was the wrong model because wars could be expected to end and the effort to control drugs could not. Drugs, therefore, should be seen as a disease, like cancer, requiring long-term strategies (*NDCS 2001*). The George W. Bush administration adopted the view that drug use was akin to cholera and should be fought on public health principles (*NDCS 2003*). Whatever the model, all strategies to date have had the same components: prevention and treatment (together constituting demand reduction) and law enforcement, interdiction, and international efforts (together constituting supply disruption). The emphasis given to each of these components has been reflected in federal budgets.

TABLE 10.2

Indirect societal costs* of drug abuse, 1992–2002

[In millions]

Year	Premature death	Drug abuse related illness	Institutionalization/ hospitalization	Productivity loss of victims of crime	Incarceration	Crime careers	Total
1992	28,961	18,214	1,894	2,640	22,961	24,617	99,287
1993	27,877	17,138	1,870	3,098	24,110	24,595	97,688
1994	28,034	19,234	2,043	3,100	25,607	23,796	101,815
1995	28,406	20,938	2,210	2,806	27,130	23,812	105,301
1996	23,745	23,241	1,758	2,674	28,473	27,241	107,132
1997	19,901	22,323	1,863	2,570	30,511	29,824	106,993
1998	19,323	25,542	1,971	2,279	33,257	27,180	109,553
1999	22,535	26,995	1,873	2,111	35,399	26,952	115,866
2000	23,045	28,654	1,782	1,930	36,244	26,836	118,492
2001	23,686	30,681	1,870	1,835	36,869	26,957	121,897
2002	24,646	33,452	1,996	1,797	39,095	27,576	128,563

*"Indirect costs" are productivity losses attributable to drug abuse.

SOURCE: "Table 25. Estimated Indirect Costs to Society of Drug Abuse, 1992–2002," in *National Drug Control Strategy: Data Supplement*, The White House, March 2004, http://www.whitehousedrugpolicy.gov/publications/policy/ndcs04/data_suppl_2004.pdf (accessed March 31, 2005)

TABLE 10.3

National drug control strategy goals, 2004

Two-year goals:	A 10 percent reduction in current use of illegal drugs by 8th,10th, and 12th graders.
	A 10 percent reduction in current use of illegal drugs by adults age 18 and older.
Five-year goals:	A 25 percent reduction in current use of illegal drugs by 8th,10th, and 12th graders.
	A 25 percent reduction in current use of illegal drugs by adults age 18 and older.

Note: Progress toward youth goals will be measured from the baseline established by the Monitoring the Future survey for the 2000–2001 school year. Progress toward adult goals will be measured from the baseline of the 2002 National Survey on Drug Use and Health. All strategy goals seek to reduce current use of any illicit drug. (Use of alcohol and tobacco products, although illegal for youths, is not captured under any illegal drug.)

SOURCE: "National Drug Control Strategy Goals," in *National Drug Control Strategy: Update*, The White House, March 2004, http://www.whitehousedrugpolicy.gov/publications/policy/ndcs04/2004ndcs.pdf (accessed March 31, 2005)

TABLE 10.4

Total federal drug control budget, 1996–2005

[In millions]

FY 1996 actual	$6,274.1
FY 1997 actual	7,531.2
FY 1998 actual	7,628.0
FY 1999 actual	9,209.1
FY 2000*	10,151.5
FY 2001*	9,823.8
FY 2002*	10,891.9
FY 2003*	11,397.0
FY 2004 enacted	12,082.3
FY 2005 request	12,648.6

*Final budget authority

SOURCE: "Total Federal Drug Control Budget (in Millions)," in *Drugs and Crime Facts*, U.S. Department of Justice, Bureau of Justice Statistics, 2004, http://www.ojp.usdoj.gov/bjs/dcf/contents.htm (accessed February 14, 2005)

THE FEDERAL DRUG BUDGET

Redoing the Accounts

Table 10.4 presents an overview of drug control spending in the federal budget. In its 2002 National Drug Control Strategy, the ONDCP published budget requests for Fiscal Year (FY) 2003 of $19.2 billion. A year later the FY 2003 budget had shrunk to $11.4 billion. This change was not the consequence of a severe cut in the drug budget but, rather, the consequence of a one-time reorganization of the budget categories that define drug control spending. The missing $8 billion was still in the overall FY 2003 federal budget, but the sum had been taken out of the "drug control" category as newly defined by the office.

In every category of expenditure, changes had taken place because of the reorganization, but the largest change came in the category of domestic law enforcement, where the change between the new and the old way of reckoning the budget had resulted in a decrease of $6.5 billion, accounting for 82% of the downward shift in the total budget. Nearly 70% of domestic law enforcement expenditure was moved out of the new, more narrowly defined "drug control" category. The prevention budget lost 21%, treatment 13.9%, interdiction 14.4%, and international operations 4.3% of funds. At the same time, ONDCP also restated previous years' budgets using the new definitions back to FY 1995.

The principal reason for this budgetary reorganization was to show clearly what funds were being (and had been) expended on the actual control of the drug phenomenon, rather than including in the federal definition funds expended in dealing with the consequences of drug use and trafficking. Thus, for instance, funds that had been allocated to the prosecution and incarceration of drug offenders were removed from the "control" categories. Expenditures on consequences, according to

ONDCP's discussion of this subject in *NDCS 2003*, would henceforth still be reported in the agency's report (cited above) on *The Economic Costs of Drug Abuse in the United States* but would be excluded from the drug control budget definition.

Using the old method, in the 1995–2003 period (fiscal years), $146.5 billion had been expended on drug control; using the new method, $83.7 billion had been expended—suggesting that 42.9% of historical expenditures at the federal level had gone for managing the consequences of drug abuse rather than for trying to control the phenomenon. During the entire period, most of the funding excluded from the new definition was associated with domestic law enforcement activities. Domestic law enforcement has not been eliminated under the new accounting method, but it is no longer the dominant category it has been. Under the new budgetary definition, treatment programs, including associated research, are the leading category of expenditure.

Budget Components

The national drug control budget (using the new accounting method) is shown as Table 7.3 in Chapter 7. Data are from FY 1996 to the budget request for FY 2005. The federal fiscal year extends from October 1 through September 30, so that FY 2005 dollars include funding for the last quarter of calendar year 2004 and the first three quarters of 2005. The budget has grown from $6.3 billion in FY 1996 to well over $12 billion in FY 2005, an annual percentage increase of 5.8%.

The budget is divided into two broad components aimed at reducing the demand for drugs and disrupting their supply. The budgets span five years of the Clinton administration and five years (including one projected based on the 2005 request) of the George W. Bush administration. One administration was Democrat, the other Republican, yet the allocation of funding to the demand and the supply sides have been similar. Both the highest and lowest percentage of funds allocated to the demand side took place in the Clinton administration, the highest in FY 1998 when 50.1% of the budget went to treatment and prevention, the lowest in FY 2000, when only 43.2% of funds went to stem demand. FY 2000, conversely, also saw the highest allocation of funds to disrupting the supply of drugs, 56.7% of the budget. The Bush administration's request for FY2005 divided funding 45% for demand reduction and 55% for disrupting supplies. In every year since FY 1998, funds for law enforcement, interdiction, and international programs have been higher than funds allocated to treatment, prevention, and the research to support these efforts.

CURBING DEMAND. Funding aimed at stopping drug use has been divided (unequally) between drug abuse treatment and programs of prevention. Treatment has received 24.5% of the total budget during the FY 1996–2005 period, prevention 14.4%. In the requested budget for FY 2005, treatment made up 24.4% and prevention 12.4%, both increases over the previous few years, but still below historic averages over the previous decade.

When the research funding to support these two activities is added, treatment got 29.2% of total budget over the period and 29.4% in the 2005 budget request (28.1% enacted in 2004); prevention, with research, averaged 17.6% over the ten-year period and received 15.6% in the 2005 budget request (16.4% enacted by Congress in FY 2004). (See Table 7.1 in Chapter 7.)

On average, over the ten-year period shown, treatment (with research) received 62.5 and prevention (with research) 37.1% of the demand reduction component of the budget. Treatment funds go into actual treatment of individuals, typically through grant programs to states. Prevention budgets support many educational activities, including television ads.

DISRUPTING SUPPLY. During the entire ten-year period shown in Table 7.3 in Chapter 7, supply disruption consumed 53.2% of the total federal drug control budget—slightly less the percentage that it was allocated in the FY 2005 budget request. Within this component, domestic law enforcement was the largest piece (46.6% over the ten-year period). Interdiction came next (36.9%) and international programs were last (16.5%).

Most domestic law enforcement funds are spent by the U.S. Department of Justice (DOJ) (or on its behalf) and underwrite the operations of the Drug Enforcement Administration, the chief domestic drug control agency. Interdiction funds are managed by the U.S. Department of Homeland Security (DHS), which now oversees all border control functions and the U.S. Coast Guard. Inter-

national funds are divided roughly equally between the U.S. State Department and the U.S. Department of Defense. The Department of State's Bureau of International Narcotics and Law Enforcement Affairs is the lead agency managing international programs. The Department of Defense is involved in supporting anti-insurgency programs in the Andean region and elsewhere.

As shown in Table 7.3 in Chapter 7, the most budgetary fluctuation over time has been associated with international programs. Funds ranged from 3.9% of total budget (FY 1996) to 15.9% (FY 2000); in 2001 funding dropped again to 6.3%. Significant portions of this budget are expended on supporting international eradication efforts which, in turn, depend on the cooperation of other countries and on the U.S. drug certification program, which may temporarily deny funding to certain regimes.

Seen as part of the total drug control budget, domestic law enforcement has represented 27.4% of the budget on average in the FY 1996–2005 period, interdiction 17.9%, and international programs 7.9%. In the FY 2005 budget request, the corresponding allocations are 25.3% for law enforcement, 20.6% for interdiction, and 9.1% for international activities.

HIGHLIGHTS OF THE CURRENT STRATEGY

The 2004 National Drug Control Policy, which features the FY 2005 budget request, takes as its main theme performance-based management of the drug problem in America. One element of this is the already-described reorganization of the budget categories so that actual control activities are featured, rather than expenditures forced on the nation by the fact that people use and trade in drugs. The managerial emphasis is further underlined by streamlining and rationalizing authority for programs within the federal departments. The newly created DHS thus takes control of all interdiction activities and funding for the Organized Crime Drug Enforcement Task Forces (OCDETF) Program, which is an interagency effort and is consolidated in the DOJ.

Within the prevention functionality, the strategy includes an investment of $25 million in programs for drug testing of young people. Another highlight is a $145 million national youth antidrug media campaign. It also features funding for one hundred new local community antidrug coalitions working to prevent substance abuse among young people.

A closer look at two of the strategy's initiatives follows.

Drug Testing of Kids

NDCS 2004 calls for and funds expansion of a program introduced the previous year for testing high school students for drugs. Grants are available to schools that implement appropriate programs. Students who test positive will also have access to treatment under the provisions of the program.

The initiative was based on findings cited in the strategy that drug use in some Oregon schools, where athletes were tested, was 25% less than in schools that did not test. Similar but lower declines were also noted in a New Jersey regional high school after a two-year testing program. The national program was launched in part because the legality of testing students was clarified by a Supreme Court decision in 2002.

The legal situation is broadly defined by the Fourth Amendment of the Constitution, which protects "the right of the people to be secure in their persons, houses, papers, and effects, against unreasonable searches and seizures." In 1989, in *Skinner v. Railway Labor Executives' Association*, the Supreme Court held that state-compelled collection and testing of urine constituted a "search." It would thus appear that mandatory drug testing of youths was unconstitutional without a showing of probable cause for a "search"—such as unruly and strange behavior.

In 1995, however, the Court ruled in an Oregon case that drug testing of high school athletes was constitutional, even if individuals were not suspected of drug use. The Court held that special needs governed the school environment and that determining "probable cause" for each individual in the school environment was unnecessary (*Vernonia School District v. Wayne Acton*, 515 U.S. 646, 1995).

Vernonia involved only school athletes and was not seen as unambiguously permitting "suspicion-free" drug testing in the context of other schools activities. In 2002, however, in the case of *Board of Education of Independent School District No. 92 of Pottawatomie County et al. v. Earls et al.* (536 U.S., 2002), the Supreme Court extended its judgment to all activities. The case involved drug testing for all extracurricular activities before students could take part in them, testing at random during their participation, and also testing when suspicions arose. This Oklahoma case provides broad authority for school districts and thus represents the "go ahead" for the strategy first adopted in *NDCS 2003*.

Vouchers for Treatment

According to data from the Substance Abuse and Mental Health Services Administrations (SAMHSA), cited in *NDCS 2004*, there were an estimated 7.7 million individuals in need of drug abuse treatment in 2002—yet more than three quarters of such individuals did not feel that they were in need of treatment. (See Figure 10.1.) These findings underlie the initiative, announced in 2003, to expend $1.6 billion on drug abuse treatment over the next three years. In the FY 2004 budget, the government allocated $600 million as a down payment toward this

FIGURE 10.1

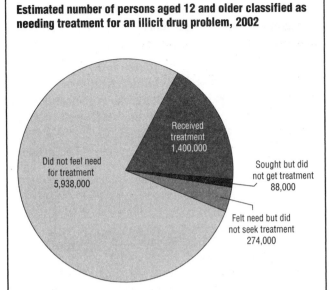

Estimated number of persons aged 12 and older classified as needing treatment for an illicit drug problem, 2002

Received treatment 1,400,000

Did not feel need for treatment 5,938,000

Sought but did not get treatment 88,000

Felt need but did not seek treatment 274,000

SOURCE: "Figure 7. Most of Those in Need of Drug Treatment Do Not Seek It," in *National Drug Control Strategy: Update*, The White House, March 2004, http://www.whitehousedrugpolicy.gov/publications/policy/ndcs04/2004ndcs.pdf (accessed March 31, 2005)

TABLE 10.5

Key elements of Access to Recovery

- *Flexibility.* With a voucher, people in need of treatment or recovery support services will have the freedom to select the programs and providers that will help them most—including programs run by faith-based organizations.
- *Results Oriented.* Grantee institutions will be asked to develop systems to provide an incentive for positive outcomes.
- *Increased Capacity.* Access to Recovery is projected to support treatment or recovery support services for approximately 100,000 people per year.

SOURCE: "Key Elements of Access to Recovery," in *National Drug Control Strategy: Update*, The White House, March 2004, http://www.whitehousedrugpolicy.gov/publications/policy/ndcs04/2004ndcs.pdf (accessed March 31, 2005)

goal, the money to be dispensed to individuals in the form of vouchers that can be exchanged for actual treatment services. The FY 2005 budget request increased funding for this voucher program, known as the Access to Recovery (ATR) initiative, by another $100 million. Table 10.5 outlines the key elements of the program.

Vouchers are made available to health professionals in hospital emergency rooms, in clinics, and in private practice; vouchers are also available from justice system officials and others able to determine an individual's need for treatment. The concept is to use such professionals, in contact with those who require treatment but do not perceive the need themselves, to suggest that treatment is in order while also enabling the professional to give the individual the means of obtaining treatment at whatever facility the individual may choose to use. The program is aimed principally at people who do not have provisions in their health policies (if they have such policies) that pay for drug abuse treatment.

Unique features of this approach to drug abuse treatment include provisions that individuals can "cash in" the vouchers at all kinds of drug treatment facilities, including those operated by religious organizations, and that the redemption value of the vouchers, from the treatment provider's point of vantage, will be on a sliding scale that rewards treatment effectiveness. The incentive for the person counseled to seek treatment is that the treatment is paid for; the incentive for the provider is to help the treatment-seeker to succeed so that a higher reward is paid out. The strategy calls this a "consumer-driven path to treatment."

Vouchers will cover the full range of services—from working with youths who need help detaching from the drug culture, to outpatient services, and finally to intensive residential treatment. Which level of service is required will be determined by the health professionals involved.

CHAPTER 11
LEGALIZATION

Drug abuse existed long before the Nixon administration declared a "war on drugs" in the 1970s. More than thirty years later this "war" continues with no end in sight.

- Drug arrests increased from 580,900 in 1980 to 1.7 million in 2003; in 1984 they represented 6.1% of all arrests, while in 2003 they were 12.3% (*Crime in the United States, 2003*, Washington, DC: FBI).

- In 2003, 20% of state prisoners were held for drug offenses, up from 6.5% in 1980, according to the U.S. Department of Justice's Bureau of Justice Statistics.

- Annual expenditures to fight the war just at the federal level have exceeded $10 billion a year every year since 2000, and now exceed $12 billion, according to the Office of National Drug Control Policy. Judicial dockets have become crowded and prisons are operating above capacity.

- Heroin in the 1970s came primarily from Asia; now it comes from Mexico and Colombia in the western hemisphere. Synthetic drugs have multiplied, and one of the most potent, methamphetamine, is produced in every state.

- The population using drugs has been growing in recent years in every age group rather than declining.

Not surprisingly, the war on drugs, and/or the national policy under which it has been fought by administrations of both major parties, have many critics. One major alternative to the "war" is legalization. The issue, however, is inherently complex and controversial, in part because, as will be shown, a preponderant majority of the public opposes even the mildest form of legalization, the legalization of marijuana.

AN OUTLINE OF THE ISSUES
Marijuana

In the United States legalization of drugs almost invariably refers to the legalization of marijuana rather than, for instance, heroin and cocaine. Use of "hard drugs" like these is relatively limited, and most Americans consider them to be highly addictive and damaging to one's physical and mental health. Marijuana's situation is different. According to the Substance Abuse and Mental Health Services Administration (SAMHSA), in 2003 more than three-quarters of all current drug users (75.2%) were using marijuana, and more than half of all current drug users used only marijuana and no other drugs. "Current drug use" is defined by SAMHSA as drug use in the thirty days before a person participated in SAMHSA's annual Household Survey of Drug Abuse. Some studies have suggested significant harm from marijuana use, including effects on the heart, lungs, brain, and social and learning capabilities. Others have found little or no harm from moderate marijuana use. Regardless of what the research says, marijuana is generally thought of as a relatively mild drug, an opinion supported by government initiatives in Canada, where marijuana possession has been decriminalized in many localities, or in the Netherlands, where marijuana sales are tolerated in "coffee shops."

The Constituency

Based on SAMHSA data from its 2003 National Survey, 14.6 million people (age twelve and older) had used marijuana or hashish within a month of the agency's survey; twenty-five million had used these drugs in the past year; and 96.6 million people had smoked marijuana or hashish at some point in their lives. The increase in lifetime users between 2002 and 2003 alone was 1.67 million people.

Not all of these current and past users can be assumed to favor legalization, but Gallup polling data for selected years from 1969 to 2001 show public opinion increasingly favoring the legalization of marijuana. (See Table 11.1.) In 1969, 84% of the public opposed legalization, and 12% favored it. By 2001 those opposed had shrunk to 62% of the public, while 34% were in favor. In that year, 34% of the adult population (eighteen and older) represented 77.4 million people. Trends, if they continue, suggest that by about 2010 those who favor legalization of marijuana will be in the majority. Gallup surveys of public opinion regarding decriminalization of medical marijuana use when prescribed by a physician were 73% in favor in 1999.

It is with the support of this population that a number of initiatives and referenda attempting to legalize marijuana for medical purposes or to decriminalize possession of modest quantities have appeared on state ballots (to be discussed in more detail below). The pro-legalization constituencies express themselves through activist organizations, e.g., Marijuana Policy Project (MPP), The National Organization for the Reform of Marijuana Laws (NORML), Hemp Evolution, and state-level organizations. Some legal reform organizations, notably the American Civil Liberties Union (ACLU), advocate reforms. A number of groups specialize in advocacy for the medical uses of marijuana. By contrast there are no large organizations that promote the legalization of drugs like cocaine and heroin, showing that "legalization" really refers to marijuana legalization.

A Sliding Scale

Many of those who advocate legalization wish to reform a national policy they see as using the criminal justice system to solve a public health problem. Instead of arresting and incarcerating people for drug possession, authorities should send them to treatment. Instead of eradicating coca crops in Colombia, the government should deal with socioeconomic problems or educational deficits that lead adults and youths to turn to drugs. Another viewpoint comes from those who advocate legalization on libertarian or constitutional grounds: the government has no right telling adults what to consume. These two positions result in a range of approaches on a sliding scale.

DECRIMINALIZATION. A basic first step, advocated by the ACLU, for instance, is decriminalization (Ira Glasser, Executive Director, ACLU, in Testimony before the Criminal Justice, Drug Policy and Human Resources Subcommittee of the House Government Reform Committee, June 16, 1999). The ACLU argued that current drug policy produces harm in various forms—harm to individuals who must get drugs in

TABLE 11.1

Attitudes toward legalization of the use of marijuana, 1969–2001

[QUESTION: "DO YOU THINK THE USE OF MARIJUANA SHOULD BE MADE LEGAL, OR NOT?"]

	Yes, legal	No, illegal	No opinion
1969	12%	84%	4%
1972	15	81	4
1973	16	78	6
1977	28	66	6
1979	25	70	5
1980	25	70	5
1985	23	73	4
1995	25	73	2
2000	31	64	5
2001	34	62	4

Note: Sample sizes vary from year to year; the data for 2001 are based on telephone interviews with a randomly selected national sample of 1,017 adults, 18 years of age and older, conducted Aug. 3–5, 2001.

SOURCE: "Table 2.66. Attitudes toward Legalization of the Use of Marijuana," in *Sourcebook of Criminal Justice Statistics Online*, U.S. Department of Justice, Bureau of Justice Statistics, http://www.albany.edu/sourcebook/pdf/section2.pdf (accessed February 21, 2005)

dangerous circumstances and suffer from abuse without treatment, harm to individuals who cannot use drugs in medical contexts, and harm to society by incarcerating large numbers of people. Criminalization of drug use, according to the ACLU, has curbed neither drug use nor the availability of drugs but has, instead, eroded liberties and imposed unnecessary costs on society.

REGULATORY MANAGEMENT. Pharmaceuticals are strictly regulated by requiring doctors to prescribe them. Legal recreational drugs (tobacco and alcohol) are subject to regulation as well but are not prohibited; their mere possession will not land someone in jail. One expression of drug legalization is the call to substitute regulatory management for prohibition in drug use, providing the public limited access to some drugs. The legalization of syringe exchange programs would be an example of such regulatory approaches—as might be provision of heroin to addicts under controlled conditions. Those who advocate a regulatory system (e.g., the ACLU) stop well short of what an unbridled free-market approach might produce.

COMMERCIALIZATION. Opponents of legalization envision an environment in which brightly packed and machine-rolled joints would be sold in drug stores alongside cigarettes, with the result that lung cancer rates, slowly decreasing as tobacco use declines, would take off again. Almost no one advocates replacing a system in which marijuana is prohibited with one where it is promoted on billboards. But such an outcome is at least possible under some implementations of drug legalization.

Institutionalized Opposition

According to Gallup data cited above, about six out of ten people were against legalization of marijuana in 2001. The majority's views are expressed in a massive institutional system that has been fighting the war on drugs with billions of dollars yearly for many decades at home and abroad.

Somewhat more than half of all federal expenditures on drug control are dedicated to controlling the trade in drugs, and substantially more than half of all drug-related expenditures within the criminal justice system are included. Federal funds on drug control are expended by dozens of agencies; these funds flow to states, then to lower levels of government. The war on drugs has become a well-funded institutional habit, not likely to yield rapidly to a slowly changing public mood.

ARGUMENTS PRO AND CON

For Legalization

Most of those who favor legalization in some form (decriminalization, regulation, for medical use) use two arguments in combination. The first is that an approach to drugs based on prohibition and criminalization does not work, produces excessive rates of incarceration, and costs a lot of money that could be more productively spent on treatment and prevention. The second is that drug use is an activity arbitrarily called a crime. It is imposed by law on some drugs and not on others, and can be seen as criminal at one time but perhaps not at another. Murder, rape, and robbery have always been considered inherently criminal acts, but drug use is just a consumption of substances; its control is arbitrary and follows fashions. Alcohol consumption was once prohibited but is now legal. In the early 1900s opiates were sold in pharmacies and Coca-Cola contained small quantities of cocaine.

While some who advocate legalization of drugs come at the issue from a libertarian perspective—the belief that the government has no business telling people what they may and may not ingest—most proponents do not deny that many drugs can be harmful (though many dispute the degree); they merely point out that tobacco use and alcohol abuse are harmful too—more harmful and/or more addictive in fact than some drugs that are illegal. The policy they recommend is based on educational and public health approaches also used vis-à-vis tobacco and alcohol. A greater harm is imposed on society by prohibiting such substances, as evidenced by the consequence of the Prohibition period of the early twentieth century, during which alcohol was banned and crime, racketeering, and homicide rates soared.

HARM REDUCTION. The general policy as advocated by most mainstream proponents of legalization is sometimes summed up in the phrase "harm reduction."

The ACLU's Ira Glasser outlines the issues, in testimony cited above, concisely in three paragraphs:

> There are two kinds of harms associated with the use of drugs. One set of harms may be caused by the drugs themselves, and varies widely, depending on the particular drug, its potency, its purity, its dosage, and the circumstances and frequency of its use. Distinctions must be made between the harms caused by heavy, compulsive use (e.g., alcoholism) and occasional, controlled use (e.g., a glass of wine each night with dinner). Distinctions must also be made between medical use (e.g., heavy dosages of morphine prescribed by doctors over a two-week period in a hospital setting or methadone prescribed daily on an outpatient basis as maintenance) and uncontrolled use (e.g., by addicts on the street using unregulated heroin and unclean needles). And distinctions must be made as well between relatively benign drugs (e.g., marijuana) and drugs with more extreme short-term effects (e.g., LSD) or more severe long-term effects (e.g., nicotine when delivered by smoking tobacco).

> The second kind of harm associated with the use of drugs is the harm caused not by the drugs themselves but by dysfunctional laws designed to control the availability of the drug. These harms include massive incarceration, much of it racially disparate, and the violation of a wide range of constitutional rights so severe that it has led one Supreme Court justice to speak of a "drug exception" to the Constitution. Dysfunctional laws have also led to reduced availability of treatment by those who desire it (e.g., methadone maintenance), as well as a number of harms created by uncontrolled and unregulated illegal markets (e.g., untaxed and exaggerated subsidies for organized criminals; street crime caused by the settling of commercial disputes with automatic weapons; unregulated dosages and impurities; unclean needles and the spread of disease, etc.)

> All laws that address the issue of drugs ought to be evaluated by assessing whether or not they reduce or enhance such harms.

BENEFITS. Many proponents see the chief benefits of legalization in decreased crime from trafficking, gang wars, and crimes committed to obtain drugs, lower incarceration rates and associated cost savings, and more funds available for treatment from savings and from taxes on legally distributed drugs. Legalization of drugs is also seen as making available marijuana in medical applications, such as relieving the suffering of cancer and AIDS patients.

Against Legalization

The government's case against legalization is summarized in a brochure published by the Drug Enforcement Administration in 2003 entitled *Speaking Out against Drug Legalization*. The ten arguments presented by the Drug Enforcement Administration (DEA) are shown in Table 11.2.

TABLE 11.2

Ten facts cited by the Drug Enforcement Administration on legalization of drugs, 2003

Fact 1: We have made significant progress in fighting drug use and drug trafficking in America. Now is not the time to abandon our efforts.

Fact 2: A balanced approach of prevention, enforcement, and treatment is the key in the fight against drugs.

Fact 3: Illegal drugs are illegal because they are harmful.

Fact 4: Smoked marijuana is not scientifically approved medicine. Marinol, the legal version of medical marijuana, is approved by science.

Fact 5: Drug control spending is a minor portion of the U.S. budget. Compared to the social costs of drug abuse and addiction, government spending on drug control is minimal.

Fact 6: Legalization of drugs will lead to increased use and increased levels of addiction. Legalization has been tried before, and failed miserably.

Fact 7: Crime, violence, and drug use go hand-in-hand.

Fact 8: Alcohol has caused significant health, social, and crime problems in this country, and legalized drugs would only make the situation worse.

Fact 9: Europe's more liberal drug policies are not the right model for America.

Fact 10: Most non-violent drug users get treatment, not jail time.

SOURCE: "Summary of the Top Ten Facts on Legalization," in *Speaking out against Drug Legalization*, U.S. Department of Justice, Drug Enforcement Administration, May 2003

The DEA's case is also organized around the concept of harm. Drugs are illegal because they cause harm. Legalization of drugs—even if only marijuana—will increase the harm already suffered by the drug-using public by spreading use to ever larger numbers of people. The agency cites Alaska's experience. Marijuana was legalized there in the 1970s and the DEA states that the Alaskan teenage consumption of marijuana at more than twice the rate of teenagers elsewhere was a direct consequence of the Alaska Supreme Court ruling. In 1990 there was a voter initiative that criminalized any possession of marijuana.

Yet despite the DEA's opinion, on August 29, 2003, a state appellate court affirmed the right of Alaskans to possess a small amount of marijuana in their homes; anything under four ounces might be deemed "for personal use." Anything over that amount is still illegal, since it is assumed the person is dealing drugs.

The DEA points to National Institute on Drug Abuse (NIDA) studies that show that smoking a marijuana joint introduces four times as much tar into the lungs as a filtered cigarette. The agency makes the point that drugs are much more addictive than alcohol and invites the public to contemplate a situation in which commercial interests might be enabled to promote the sale of presently illegal substances.

The DEA counters the "criminalization" charge by pointing out that only 5% of drug offenders in federal prisons and 27% of drug offenders in state prisons are held for possession, the rest for trafficking. The agency points out that even these numbers are deceptive because those imprisoned for possession are usually imprisoned after repeated offenses, and many of those serving a sentence for possession were arrested for trafficking but reached plea bargains permitting them to plead guilty to the lesser offense of possession.

Would legalization reduce crime? The DEA does not believe it would. Under a regulated drug-use system, age restrictions would apply. A criminal enterprise would continue to supply those under age. If marijuana were legalized, trade in heroin and cocaine would continue. If all three of the major drugs were permitted to be sold legally, other substances, like PCP and methamphetamine, would still support a criminal trade. The DEA does not envision that a black market in drugs could be eliminated entirely, because health authorities would never permit very potent drugs to be sold freely on the open market.

For all of these reasons, the DEA advocates the continuation of a balanced approach to the control of drugs including prevention, enforcement, and treatment.

Contradictions and Inconsistencies

Both proponents and opponents of legalization produce good arguments for their cases, but contradictions and inconsistencies are present in both presentations, suggesting that the ultimate evolution of this issue will turn on political, i.e., pragmatic, issues.

Proponents of legalization sometimes find the question of where to draw the legal line problematic. How harmful must a drug be before it should be made illegal? In an environment where public pressures are mounting against the use of tobacco, legalization of marijuana has a contradictory aspect. Funds expended now on incarcerating drug offenders may have to be expended in some future time on public health programs to treat ills caused by newly legalized drugs, though whether or how much the use of such drugs as marijuana would increase if it were legal remains entirely unknown.

Opponents of legalization fail to coherently address the question of alcohol and tobacco. One must engage in serious logical contortions to justify their legality when consumptions of comparably harmful substances can yield lengthy prison sentences.

Arguments claiming that the war on drugs is succeeding because drug use is down as measured against some point in the past ignore the fact that drug use is a cyclical phenomenon with ebbs and flows. In *Speaking Out*, for instance, the DEA presents a chart comparing overall drug use between 1979 and 2001, showing a decline in current users from 25.4 to 15.9 million people. In that period, however, current drug use first declined to twelve million persons in 1992 and then rose again to 15.9 million by 2001 while the same policies were being pursued. If the DEA had used 1992 as its base year, it would have had to argue that its programs were not working.

MEDICAL MARIJUANA

Before the passage of the Marijuana Tax Act of 1937, which effectively prohibited the sale of marijuana, more than twenty pharmaceuticals were on the market with marijuana as an ingredient (*Medical Marijuana Briefing Paper—2005*, Washington, DC: Marijuana Policy Project, http://www.mpp.org/pdf/mmjbrief.pdf). In the 1970s marijuana's medicinal properties were rediscovered by recreational users. In the November 1996 elections, California and Arizona voters approved referenda legalizing the possession of marijuana and other drugs for medical purposes. California Proposition 215, enacted as The Compassionate Use Act of 1996, permitted patients and primary caregivers to possess and/or cultivate marijuana without fear of prosecution under state laws. The act permitted physicians to recommend (not to prescribe) the use of marijuana as a treatment for cancer, AIDS, anorexia, chronic pain, glaucoma, arthritis, migraine headaches, "or any other illness for which marijuana provides relief." More than half (56%) of California voters supported Proposition 215.

In neighboring Arizona, 65% of the voters supported Proposition 200, enacted as the Drug Medicalization, Prevention, and Control Act. It provided that, in the case of medical necessity, marijuana and other drugs (including heroin and LSD) could be used in medical treatment. Two doctors would have to prescribe the use of these drugs. The law also called for probation and treatment rather than incarceration for first- and second-time nonviolent drug offenders. The Arizona legislature amended the measure, saying that voters had committed a grave error, and sent it back to the voters. In 1998 Proposition 200 again passed, this time with a 57% majority.

The Justice Department brought suit in 1998 against the Oakland Cannabis Buyers' Club, which supplied marijuana for medical purposes. The government argued that the club's activities, even if legal under California law, violated federal law, specifically the Controlled Substances Act. The case reached the Supreme Court in 2001. The Court ruled in favor of the federal government and struck down state laws legalizing the use of marijuana for purposes of medical necessity, arguing that the intention of Congress in classifying marijuana as a Schedule I substance was unambiguously clear. Schedule I drugs have, by definition, "no currently accepted medical use in treatment in the United States," have "a high potential for abuse," and have "a lack of accepted safety for use under medical supervision." (*United States v. Oakland Cannabis Buyers' Cooperative et al.*, 532 U.S. 483, decided May 14, 2001.)

The high court's actions are not the final word on medical uses of marijuana, especially because the Court's ruling was narrowly cast around the classification of marijuana as a Schedule I drug. Future amendments of the Controlled Substances Act could well remove marijuana from Schedule I and place it on Schedule II with morphine, cocaine, and methamphetamine. Schedule II states that "the drug or other substance [on the schedule] has a currently accepted medical use in treatment in the United States or a currently accepted medical use with severe restrictions."

The U.S. Supreme Court issued another relevant ruling in June of 2005, overturning a 2003 federal appeals court decision that shielded California's Compassionate Use Act, the medical marijuana initiative adopted by California voters nine years earlier. The Supreme Court's ruling in this case reaffirmed the ability of Congress to prohibit and prosecute for the possession and use of marijuana even in states (eleven as of the decision) that allow it under state law. As with the earlier Supreme Court decisions, this ruling was not the final word on medical marijuana. Other challenges to the application of federal drug laws may still be issued.

Medical Opinion

The medicinal value of THC (tetrahydrocannibinol), the active ingredient in marijuana, has long been known to the medical community. The drug has been shown to alleviate the nausea and vomiting caused by chemotherapy used to treat many forms of cancer. Marijuana has also been found useful in alleviating pressure on the eye in glaucoma patients. The drug has also been found effective in helping to fight the physical wasting that usually accompanies AIDS. AIDS patients lose their appetites and can slowly waste away because they do not eat. Marijuana has been found effective in restoring the appetites of some AIDS patients. Many of the newer AIDS remedies must be taken on a full stomach. Other studies, in contrast, have found that marijuana suppresses the immune system and contains a number of lung-damaging chemicals.

NIDA GREW IT. During the 1970s and 1980s the National Institute of Drug Abuse grew marijuana in Mississippi to supply the drug to experimental research programs in six states. Such action is expressly permitted under the Controlled Substances Act. In 1986 the Reagan administration, feeling increasingly uncomfortable with this program and concerned that the growing AIDS epidemic might lead to increased demand for the medical legalization of marijuana, accelerated the approval of Marinol, a drug containing a synthetic form of THC. The state experimental programs were closed.

MARINOL. Opponents of the medical legalization of marijuana often point to Marinol as a superior alternative.

However, many patients do not respond to Marinol; the determination of the right dose is variable from patient to patient. Nonresponding patients claim that smoking marijuana allows them to control the dosage they get. Marijuana has been used, illegally, of course, by an unknown number of cancer and AIDS patients on the recommendation of doctors.

NEW ENGLAND JOURNAL OF MEDICINE. In 1997 the highly respected *New England Journal of Medicine* came out in favor of legalizing marijuana for medical use. Jerome P. Kassirer, the journal's editor, published an editorial entitled "Federal Foolishness and Marijuana" in which he wrote: "I believe that a federal policy that prohibits physicians from alleviating suffering by prescribing marijuana is misguided, heavy-handed and inhumane" (vol. 336, January 30, 1997). Dr. Kassirer acknowledged that marijuana use could cause long-term adverse effects and could even lead to serious addiction, but he felt that these risks were irrelevant when the drug was used to combat uncontrollable nausea and pain in patients critically ill with cancer, AIDS, and other serious diseases.

The editorial mentioned that dronabinol (the generic name of Marinol) contains THC, but this legal drug is not widely prescribed because its therapeutic dosing is difficult to determine. "By contrast," wrote Kassirer, "smoking marijuana produces a rapid increase in the blood level of the active ingredients and is thus more likely to be therapeutic." He makes the point that doctors can prescribe morphine and other very strong drugs that can cause death, but with marijuana there is no immediate risk of death.

THE INSTITUTE OF MEDICINE STUDY. With the California and Arizona medical legalization propositions as background, General Barry McCaffrey, the Clinton administration's drug czar, asked the Institute of Medicine (IOM), a private organization that advises the government on medical matters, to review the scientific evidence on marijuana in order to assess the potential health benefits and risks of marijuana and its constituent cannabinoids. The review began in August 1997 and culminated in March 1999 with a report entitled *Marijuana and Medicine: Assessing the Science Base* (Janet E. Joy, Stanley J. Watson, Jr., and John A. Benson, Jr., eds., Washington, DC: National Academy Press, 1999).

Cannabinoids, a group of compounds found in marijuana, contain THC, the primary psychoactive ingredient in marijuana. The IOM report drew the following general conclusions regarding cannabinoids:

- Cannabinoids likely have a natural role in pain modulation, control of movement, and memory.

- The natural role of cannabinoids in immune systems is likely multifaceted and remains unclear.

- The brain develops tolerance to cannabinoids.

- Animal research demonstrates the potential for dependence, but this potential is observed under a narrower range of conditions than with benzodiazepines, opiates, cocaine, or nicotine.

- Withdrawal symptoms can be observed in animals but appear mild compared with those of opiates or benzodiazepines such as diazepam (Valium).

The IOM report concluded that "the future of cannabinoid drugs lies not in smoked marijuana, but in chemically defined drugs that act on the cannabinoid systems that are a natural component of human physiology. Until such drugs can be developed and made available for medical use, the report recommends interim solutions."

John Benson and Stanley Watson, the report's principal investigators, determined that marijuana's effects are limited to symptom relief and that, for most symptoms, more effective drugs already exist. However, for patients who do not respond well to standard medications, cannabinoids seem to hold potential for treating pain, chemotherapy-induced nausea and vomiting, and the poor appetite and wasting caused by AIDS and advanced cancer.

The report noted that medical use of marijuana is not without risk. The primary negative effect is diminished control over movement (psychomotor performance). In some cases users may experience unpleasant emotional states or feelings. In addition, the usefulness of medical marijuana is limited by the harmful effects of smoking, which can increase a person's risk of cancer, lung damage, and problems (such as low birth weight) with pregnancies. Therefore, the report concluded, smoking marijuana should be recommended only for terminally ill patients or those with debilitating symptoms who do not respond to approved medications.

The report recommended that patients with no alternative to smoking marijuana be allowed to use it on a short-term, experimental basis. Both physical and psychological effects should be closely monitored and documented under medical supervision. Clinical trials of marijuana should be carried out parallel with the development of new delivery systems, such as inhalers, that are safe, fast-acting, and reliable but that do not involve inhaling harmful smoke. Cannabinoid compounds that are produced under controlled laboratory conditions are preferable to plant products because they deliver a consistent dose.

Data collected in the review did not support the contention that marijuana should be used to treat glaucoma. Though smoked marijuana can reduce some of the eye pressure related to glaucoma, it provides only short-term relief that does not outweigh the hazards associated with long-term use of the drug. Also, with the exception of painful muscle spasms in multiple sclerosis, there is little evidence of marijuana's potential for treating migraines or movement disorders like Parkinson's disease or Huntington's disease.

INDUSTRIAL HEMP

Industrial hemp and marijuana both come from the *Cannabis sativa* plant, but while marijuana can contain THC levels of 3 to 15%, cannabis plants grown for industrial hemp contain less than 1% of THC. Industrial hemp can be used to make many products, including rope, textiles, plastics, paper products, and oil.

U.S. law bans the cultivation of hemp but permits the sale of hemp products. From only a few million dollars in the early 1990s, global hemp sales reached $75 million in 1997. According to the Hemp Industries Association, sales of hemp products were about $250 million in 2004 and were expected to reach $350 million in 2005, largely on the strength of increased demand for hemp-based food products. Many agree with David Monson, a farmer and state legislator in North Dakota, who said, "We in North Dakota believe this [hemp] is a legitimate crop that can make us some money, help the environment, and maybe save some family farms" (*U.S. News & World Report*, March 8, 1999). Growing hemp is legal in Germany, France, Spain, and Britain. Romania is the largest commercial hemp producer in Europe.

The changing economic fortunes of many of the nation's farmers have forced them to look to new alternatives. An acre of hemp can earn more than an acre of wheat, soybeans, or barley in some states—but cannot compete with tomatoes, potatoes, or tobacco. In 1999 the Virginia legislature approved the "controlled, experimental" cultivation of hemp. By 2001 Arkansas, California, Hawaii, Illinois, Maryland, Minnesota, Montana, North Dakota, Vermont, and Virginia had all passed legislation supporting either research into or cultivation of hemp, and several others had considered but rejected such proposals.

The DEA opposes the cultivation of hemp and has indicated that it will not register or permit it. The DEA indicates that it is hard to distinguish between a field of legitimate hemp and one of illegal cannabis. Since laboratory testing is needed to absolutely determine the difference, this would certainly slow down the process of fighting drugs. Finally, the DEA fears that legalizing hemp may be the first step on the way to legalizing marijuana.

IMPORTANT NAMES AND ADDRESSES

AAA Foundation for Traffic Safety
607 14th St. NW, Ste. 201
Washington, DC 20005
(202) 638-5944
FAX: (202) 638-5943
E-mail: info@aaafoundation.org
URL: www.aaafoundation.org/home

Adult Children of Alcoholics
P.O. Box 3216
Torrance, CA 90510
(310) 534-1815
E-mail: info@AdultChildren.org
URL: www.adultchildren.org

Al-Anon/Alateen
Family Group Headquarters, Inc.
1600 Corporate Landing Pkwy.
Virginia Beach, VA 23454-5617
(757) 563-1600
1-888 425-2666
FAX: (757) 563-1655
E-mail: wso@al-anon.org
URL: www.al-anon.alateen.org

Alcoholics Anonymous
Grand Central Station
P.O. Box 459
New York, NY 10163
(212) 870-3400
URL: www.alcoholics-anonymous.org

American Association for World Health
1825 K St. NW, Ste. 1208
Washington, DC 20006
(202) 466-5883
FAX: (202) 466-5896
URL: www.thebody.com/aawh/
aawhpage.html

**Bureau for International Narcotics
and Law Enforcement Affairs**
U.S. Department of State
2201 C St. NW
Washington, DC 20520
(202) 647-4000
URL: www.state.gov/g/inl

Center for Women Policy Studies
National Resource Center on Women
and AIDS Policy
1211 Connecticut Ave. NW, Ste. 312
Washington, DC 20036
(202) 872-1770
FAX: (202) 296-8962
E-mail: cwps@centerwomenpolicy.org
URL: www.centerwomenpolicy.org

**Centers for Disease Control and
Prevention**
National Prevention Information Network
P.O. Box 6003
Rockville, MD 20849-6003
1-800 458-5231
FAX: (888) 282-7681
E-mail: info@cdcnpin.org
URL: www.cdcnpin.org

Cocaine Anonymous World Services
3740 Overland Ave., Ste. C
Los Angeles, CA 90034
(310) 559-5833
FAX: (310) 559-2554
E-mail: cawso@ca.org
URL: www.ca.org

Drug Enforcement Administration
2401 Jefferson Davis Hwy.
Alexandria, VA 22301
(202) 307-1000
URL: www.usdoj.gov/dea

Drug Policy Alliance
925 15th St. NW, 2nd Fl.
Washington, DC 20005
(202) 216-0035
FAX: (202) 216-0803
E-mail: dc@drugpolicy.org
URL: www.dpf.org

Nar-Anon Family Groups
22527 Crenshaw Blvd., #200B
Torrance, CA 90505
(310) 534-8188
1-800 477-6291
FAX: (310) 534-8688

E-mail: naranonWSO@hotmail.com
URL: http://nar-anon.org/index.html

Narcotics Anonymous World Services
P.O. Box 9999
Van Nuys, CA 91409
(818) 773-9999
FAX: (818) 700-0700
E-mail: fsmail@na.org
URL: www.na.org

**National Council on Alcoholism and Drug
Dependence**
22 Cortlandt St., Ste. 801
New York, NY 10007-3128
(212) 269-7797
1-800 622-2255
FAX: (212) 269-7510
E-mail: national@ncadd.org
URL: www.ncadd.org

National Institute on Drug Abuse
National Institutes of Health
6001 Executive Blvd., Rm. 5213
Bethesda, MD 20892-9561
(301) 443-1124
1-800 662-HELP
E-mail: Information@lists.nida.nih.gov
URL: www.nida.nih.gov

**National Organization for the Reform of
Marijuana Laws (NORML)**
1600 K St. NW, Ste. 501
Washington, DC 20006-2832
(202) 483-5500
FAX: (202) 483-0057
E-mail: norml@norml.org
URL: www.norml.org

National Women's Health Network
514 10th St. NW, Ste. 400
Washington, DC 20004
(202) 347-1140
FAX: (202) 347-1168
E-mail: nwhn@nwhn.org
URL: www.womenshealthnetwork.org

Office of National Drug Control Policy
Drug Policy Information Clearinghouse
P.O. Box 6000
Rockville, MD 20849-6000
1-800 666-3332
FAX: (301) 519-5212
URL: www.whitehousedrugpolicy.gov

Office of Safe & Drug-Free Schools
U.S. Department of Education
400 Maryland Ave. SW, Rm. 3E300
Washington, DC 20202-6450
202 260-3954
FAX: (202) 260-7767
URL: http://www.ed.gov/about/offices/list/osdfs

Substance Abuse and Mental Health Services Administration
Center for Substance Abuse Prevention
One Choke Cherry Rd., Rm. 8-1054
Rockville, MD 20857
(240) 276-2420
FAX: (240) 276-2430
E-mail: info@samhsa.gov
URL: www.samhsa.gov

RESOURCES

One of the seldom noted but most valuable services provided by the government is statistical information on subjects of national interest and concern. Substantial resources are expended by the federal government in tracking trends in drug use in the United States, both from a health policy and an enforcement policy perspective, both nationally and internationally.

The national policy on combating drug abuse is centered in the White House Office of National Drug Control Policy (ONDCP). The office prepares a drug control policy each year for the President's signature, coordinates efforts across the federal bureaucracy, and is an excellent source for statistics, collected from many other agencies, and displayed on ONDCP's Web site at http://www.whitehousedrugpolicy.gov/. Publications consulted for this volume include *International Narcotics Control Strategy Report* (2005), *The President's National Drug Control Strategy* (2004), the *National Drug Control Strategy, FY 2005 Budget Summary*, and national drug control strategy documents published in earlier years.

Several elements of the U.S. Department of Health and Human Services (DHHS) are involved in monitoring the prevalence of drug use across the population, health consequences of drug use, and interventions to provide treatment. Valuable data are available from the Substance Abuse and Mental Health Services Administration (SAMHSA), reachable at http://www.samhsa.gov/. Detailed current and historical data sets on drug use incidence and prevalence are provided in an annual series titled the National Survey on Drug Use and Health (formerly called the National Household Survey on Drug Abuse). SAMHSA also tracks treatment services. The most recent survey was the *National Survey of Substance Abuse Treatment Services (N-SSATS), 2003*, the new implementation of an earlier survey called the *Uniform Facility Data Set (UFDS)*, last published for 1998. SAMHSA also tracks reported episodes of drug abuse; the most recent published results were issued

as the *Treatment Episode Data Set (TEDS), 1992–2002*. The agency also operates the Drug Abuse Warning Network, which collects data from emergency rooms. The last report in the series from the network was *Drug Abuse Warning Network, 2003: Interim National Estimates of Drug-Related Emergency Department Visits* (2004).

The National Institute on Drug Abuse (NIDA) provides information on all drugs for both users and professionals. The Institute is reachable at http://www.nida.nih.gov/. The Institute published *Principles of Drug Addiction Treatment: A Research-Based Guide* (1999) and is the funding agency for Monitoring the Future, a study program conducted by the University of Michigan. The study tracks high school students and their patterns of drug use. The results of this study are published in the annual report *Monitoring the Future: National Results on Adolescent Drug Use* .

The Centers for Disease Control and Prevention (CDC), another agency under the DHHS, publishes a wealth of information on health-related topics, including drugs and their abuse. A good point of entry to CDC on the Internet is through the National Center for Health Statistics at http://www.cdc.gov/nchs/default.htm. Data on HIV/AIDS in this edition came from CDC's *HIV/AIDS Surveillance Report*. Another valuable resource is CDC's journal *Morbidity and Mortality Weekly Report*, accessible at http://www.cdc.gov/mmwr/mmwrsrch.htm.

Domestic law enforcement and interdiction activities fall under the U.S. Department of Justice (DOJ). The U.S. Drug Enforcement Administration (DEA) has charge over all domestic drug control activities. DEA's Web site is at http://www.usdoj.gov/dea/. In support of its own activities, DEA collects information on street-level activities using knowledgeable informants. A source for pricing is DEA's *Illegal Drug Price and Purity Report* (2003). The DEA also publishes *Drugs of Abuse*, a resource tool that educates the public about drug facts and the inherent dangers of illegal drugs. The agency issues periodic reports, such as *Drug Intelligence Brief: Changing Dynamics of Cocaine Production in the Andean Region* (2002), *Drug Intelligence Brief: Heroin Signature Program: 1999*, and *Meth in America: Not In Our Town* (2002). DEA also uses its publication arm to advance the administration's position on the issue of legalizing drugs, in such publications as *Speaking Out against Drug Legalization* (2003).

An excellent source for data on what happens to drug users when caught is DOJ's Bureau of Justice Statistics (BJS), reachable at http://www.ojp.usdoj.gov/bjs/. BJS focuses on criminal prosecutions, prisons, sentencing, and related subjects. Its annual publications, *Compendium of Federal Justice Statistics* and *Sourcebook of Criminal Justice Statistics*, are good starting points. A segment of the BJS Web site entitled *Drug & Crime Facts* provides a good overview of statistics on drug-related crimes and legal consequences in the United States. Details are available in such publications as *Felony Sentences in State Courts, 2000, Trends in State Parole, 1990–2000*, and *Prison and Jail Inmates at Midyear 2003*.

Data on federal prisons are available from the Federal Bureau of Prisons at http://www.bop.gov/. The Federal Bureau of Investigation is a rich source on arrests of people for drug offenses. The data appear in annual editions of *Crime in the United States*.

The effort to control drugs beyond the nation's borders is largely under the supervision of the U.S. Department of State, although certain activities, such as the control of money laundering, also involve the U.S. Treasury. The agency within the State Department in charge of the drug control effort is the Bureau for International Narcotics and Law Enforcement Affairs (http://www.state.gov/g/inl/). An excellent source of information are the Bureau's strategy reports published as the annual publication *International Narcotics Control Strategy Report*.

The U.S. Department of Defense conducts periodic surveys of drug use among service people. The most recent one, used in this edition, was the *2002 DoD Survey of Health Related Behaviors among Military Personnel*.

Congress employs the U.S. General Accountability Office (GAO), one of its staff agencies, to monitor how well federal agencies are carrying out mandates Congress has framed into law. GAO's Web site is at http://www.gao.gov/. GAO serves as a source of sometimes critical assessments of executive branch activities. GAO conducts reports at the request of Congressional committees. Reports consulted for this edition that provide a look at the scope of these investigations include: *Drug Control: U.S.-Mexican Counternarcotics Efforts Face Difficult Challenges* (1998), *Drug Control: Counternarcotics Efforts in Columbia Face Continuing Challenges* (1998), *Drug Control: U.S. Assistance to Colombia Will Take Years to Produce Results* (2000), and *U.S. Nonmilitary Assistance to Colombia Is Beginning to Show Intended Results, but Programs Are Not Readily Sustainable* (2004).

Many private organizations use statistics in support of their positions; these are largely drawn from the federal sources cited above. Two private sources used in this edition were based on original data collection. One is polling data developed by The Gallup Organization, used with Gallup's permission. Gallup is at http://www.gallup.com/. Another source has been Quest Diagnostics Incorporated, (http://www.questdiagnostics.com/), the nation's leading drug testing firm, which assembles and publishes data on private drug testing results for general use by the public.

To all sources, public and private, Information Plus expresses its appreciation and thanks for invaluable assistance.

INDEX

Wellstone, Paul, 128
Workplace issues. *See* Employment and
    workplace issues
World Drug Report 2004 (United Nations),
    78
Wright, C. R., 2

Y

Young, Francis, 21

Youth
    anabolic steroid use, 22
    availability perception, 48–49, 55*f*–56*f*
    cocaine use, 49(*f*4.9)
    disapproval of drug use, 42–43,
        52*t*, 53*f*
    drug testing, 146–147
    Ecstasy use, 50*f*
    heroin use, 49(*f*4.10)

    illicit drug use, 40, 40(*f*4.2), 40(*f*5.3),
        41*f*, 42*f*–43*f*, 44*t*–47*t*, 51*f*
    inhalant use, 48(*f*4.8)
    marijuana use, 48(*f*4.7)
    risk perception, 43, 48, 54*f*
    See also Children

Z

Zinberg, Norman, 113